T0328940

"Chen and Nonaka have assembled a stellar group of contributors who shed new light on this important and interesting topic, this volume will advance an understanding of knowledge management, business models, and innovation. It is provocative, integrative, and compelling."

− David J. Teece, Director of Tusher Initiative for the Management of Intellectual Capital, Institute for Business Innovation, University of California, Berkeley, CA, USA

"This is an essential reading for scholars and managers interested in knowledge management and the complex dynamics of knowledge creation, which over the years has become a central element in the theory and evolution of the firm. In its broad structure, this beautiful book is a must-read for an understanding of the pervasive role of knowledge in innovation and competition in the age of globalization, new information and communication technologies and artificial intelligence."

− Franco Malerba, Professor of Applied Economics, Bocconi University, Milan, Italy; Previous President of the Schumpeter Society

"Congratulations for the completion of this timely and comprehensive Handbook on Knowledge Management, which I shall highly recommend to all scholars/teachers and practitioners of technology and innovation management. In the modern age of knowledge economy, this handbook will help us fill any gap in our learning in the theories and applications in the important field of Knowledge Management, to benefit from the views from both western and eastern perspectives, and to appreciate the role of 'learning by doing' in the education and development of future public and private sector leaders."

− Hang Chang Chieh, Executive Director of Institute for Engineering Leadership, National University of Singapore, Singapore

THE ROUTLEDGE COMPANION TO KNOWLEDGE MANAGEMENT

Knowledge when properly leveraged and harnessed contributes to effective organizational performance. How much an organization benefits from knowledge would depend on how well knowledge has been managed. There have been challenges to implementing knowledge management in today's dramatically different world from before. This comprehensive reference work is a timely guide to understanding knowledge management.

The book covers key themes of knowledge management which includes the basic framework of knowledge management and helps readers to understand the state of art of knowledge management both from the aspects of theory and practice, from the perspectives of strategy, organization, resources, as well as institution and organizational culture. This reference work reflects the increasingly important role of both philosophy and digital technologies in knowledge management research and practice.

This handbook will be an essential resource for knowledge management scholars, researchers and graduate students.

Jin Chen is Professor at the Department of Innovation, Entrepreneurship and Strategy, School of Economics and Management, Tsinghua University, China.

Ikujiro Nonaka is a Japanese organizational theorist and Professor Emeritus at the Graduate School of International Corporate Strategy of Hitotsubashi University, Japan.

ROUTLEDGE COMPANIONS IN BUSINESS, MANAGEMENT AND MARKETING

Routledge Companions are prestige volumes which provide an overview of a research field or topic. Surveying the business disciplines, the books in this series incorporate both established and emerging research themes. Compiled and edited by an array of highly regarded scholars, these volumes also benefit from global teams of contributors reflecting disciplinary diversity.

Individually, *Routledge Companions in Business, Management and Marketing* provide impactful one-stop-shop publications. Collectively, they represent a comprehensive learning and research resource for researchers, postgraduate students and practitioners.

For more information about this series, please visit: www.routledge.com/Routledge-Companions-in-Business-Management-and-Marketing/book-series/RCBUS

THE ROUTLEDGE COMPANION TO KNOWLEDGE MANAGEMENT

Edited by
Jin Chen and Ikujiro Nonaka

LONDON AND NEW YORK

Cover image: © Getty Images

First published 2022
by Routledge
4 Park Square, Milton Park, Abingdon, Oxon OX14 4RN

and by Routledge
605 Third Avenue, New York, NY 10158

Routledge is an imprint of the Taylor & Francis Group, an informa business

British Library Cataloguing-in-Publication Data
A catalogue record for this book is available from the British Library

Library of Congress Cataloging-in-Publication Data
Names: Chen, Jin (Economist) editor. | Nonaka, Ikujiro, 1935- editor.
Title: The Routledge companion to knowledge management / edited by Jin Chen and Ikujiro Nonaka.
Description: 1 Edition. | New York, NY : Routledge, 2022. | Series: Routledge companions in business, management & marketing | Includes bibliographical references and index.
Identifiers: LCCN 2021057005 (print) | LCCN 2021057006 (ebook) | ISBN 9780367631055 (hardback) | ISBN 9780367631048 (paperback) | ISBN 9781003112150 (ebook)
Subjects: LCSH: Knowledge management. | Information technology—Management. | Organizational behavior.
Classification: LCC HD30.2 .R678 2022 (print) | LCC HD30.2 (ebook) | DDC 658.4/038—dc23/eng/20220114
LC record available at https://lccn.loc.gov/2021057005
LC ebook record available at https://lccn.loc.gov/2021057006

ISBN: 9780367631055 (hbk)
ISBN: 9780367631048 (pbk)
ISBN: 9781003112150 (ebk)

DOI: 10.4324/9781003112150

Typeset in Bembo
by codeMantra

CONTENTS

FIGURES

TABLES

CONTRIBUTORS

Véronique Ambrosini is a Professor of Management (Strategic Management) at Monash University, Australia. Her research interests include dynamic capabilities, business ecological sustainability, tacit knowledge, causal ambiguity, value creation and management education.

Rachelle Bosua is an Assistant Professor at the Open University of the Netherlands. Her current research includes the use of social media by adults with chronic illness, the GDPR and privacy, knowledge sharing in the context of work and mobility, knowledge leakage and loss.

Luca Cacciolatti is a Reader in Marketing and Innovation at University of Westminster. He is the Director of the MSc Entrepreneurship, Innovation, and Enterprise Development and Head of the Entrepreneurship and Social Innovation Research Group at Westminster Business School. His research interests are in the areas of marketing strategy, entrepreneurship and innovation with a particular focus on innovation systems and social innovation.

Jin Chen is a Professor of Innovation Management and Policy, at the School of Economics and Management, Tsinghua University, China. He serves as the Director of Research Center of Technological Innovation at Tsinghua University. His research interests include management of technological innovation and knowledge management. He serves as Editor in Chief of *International Journal of Innovation Studies*.

Kai Chen is a master's candidate at the College of Management and Economics, Tianjin University, China. His research interests are data mining and machine learning.

Yihang Cheng is a PhD candidate at the College of Management and Economics, Tianjin University, China. His research interests include knowledge management in the digital environment and data mining.

Valentina Cillo is an Assistant Professor at "Roma Tre University" (Italy). She is qualified as an Associate Professor in Business Enterprise and Management. She also serves as a scientific advisor for several businesses and institutions involved in Research & Development and Technology transfer. Her main research interests include, among others, innovation management, knowledge management and sustainable innovation management.

Naerelle Dekker is a project manager with a leading healthcare retailer. She has formulated strategies that have significantly increased the sales of multiple brands in challenging economic climates in a highly competitive sector. Her expertise encompasses project management, marketing, brand strategies, product management, supply chain development, stakeholder management and ethical compliance.

Xiaoying Dong is an Associate Professor at the Guanghua School of Management, Peking University, China. Her research interests include knowledge and innovation management, digital strategy and transformation, data-driven organizational change.

Nikolina Dragičević is a postdoctoral researcher at the Faculty of Economics and Business in University of Zagreb. Her research centres on design-based and human-centred approach to innovation, knowledge dynamics and (digital)work in business and educational contexts.

Xirong Gao is a Professor at the School of Economics & Management, Chongqing University of Posts and Telecommunications, China. His research interests focus on the areas of information technology innovation and digital economic development.

Manlio Del Giudice is a Full Professor of Management at the University of Rome "Link Campus" (Italy), where he also serves as Coordinator of the PhD Programme "Tech for Good". He serves as Editor in Chief of *Journal of Knowledge Management* (Emerald). His scientific interests focus on the themes of innovation management, technology management, marketing and knowledge management.

Norbert Gronau holds the Chair of Business Informatics, especially Processes and Systems and is the Director of the Centre Industry 4.0 at the University of Potsdam, Germany. His main research activities concentrate on the areas of Knowledge Management, Business Process Management and Industry 4.0.

Bach Q. Ho is an Assistant Professor of Management at the Tokyo Institute of Technology, Japan. He is a co-founder of the Japan Transformative Service Research Community.

Kazuo Ichijo is the Dean and a Professor at the School of International Corporate Strategy, Hitotsubashi University Business School, Japan. His research interests are concentrated on innovation through organizational knowledge creation.

Aino Kianto is a Professor of Knowledge Management in School of Business and Management at the Lappeenranta-Lahti University of Technology, Finland. Her research interests include knowledge management, intellectual capital, organizational renewal and creativity.

Sanjay Kumar is Director (Personnel) with Western Coalfields Ltd, a subsidiary of Coal India Ltd, world's largest coal producing company. He possesses over three and half decades of experience with leading state-owned enterprises.

Rongbin WB Lee is the Emeritus Professor in the Department of Industrial and Systems Engineering at The Hong Kong Polytechnic University, Hong Kong, China. He is the former Director of the Knowledge Management and Innovation Research Centre. His teaching and research interests include advanced manufacturing technology and knowledge management. Currently, he is the editor-in-chief of the *Journal of Information and Knowledge Management Systems*.

Soo Hee Lee is a Professor in Organization Studies at Kent Business School, University of Kent, UK. His research focuses on institutional and behavioural underpinnings of strategy and innovation and organizational dynamics of knowledge, trust and power.

Regina Lenart-Gansiniec is an Associate Professor of the Faculty of Management and Communication, Jagiellonian University in Krakow, Poland. Her research revolves around crowdsourcing and organizational learning.

Gang Liu is a PhD graduate from The Hong Kong Polytechnic University. Now he is an Associate Professor from Business School, Shenzhen Technology University, China. His research interests cover knowledge management and performance, innovation and entrepreneurship, and knowledge management in cross-cultural contexts.

Patricia Ordóñez de Pablos is a Professor in the Department of Business Administration and Accountability in the Faculty of Economics at The University of Oviedo, Spain. Her teaching and research interests focus on the areas of strategic management, knowledge management, intellectual capital and China.

Guannan Qu is an Assistant Professor in School of Public Policy and Management, University of Chinese Academy of Sciences, China.

Dai Senoo is a Professor of Management at the Tokyo Institute of Technology, Japan. He serves as the president of the Japan Society for Management Information.

Vivien WY Shek is the Project Manager in the Knowledge Management and Innovation Research Centre at The Hong Kong Polytechnic University, Hong Kong, China.

Fangqing Tian is a master's candidate at the College of Management and Economics, Tianjin University, China. Her research interest is talent management in digital environments.

Eric Tsui is Associate Director of the Knowledge Management and Innovation Research Centre and a Senior Educational Development Officer at The Hong Kong Polytechnic University.

André Ullrich is working as a postdoctoral researcher at the University of Potsdam, Germany, as part of the junior research group ProMUT. He is interested in sustainability of organizations, the role of humans in change processes and knowledge dynamics in digital environments.

Krishna Venkitachalam is a Professor of Strategy at Estonian Business School, Estonia. His research interests include strategic knowledge management (SKM), organizational knowledge strategies, tacit knowledge and knowledge processes in organizations.

Luyao Wang is a postdoctoral research assistant at the School of Economics and Management, Tsinghua University, China.

Xuyan Wang is a PhD candidate at the College of Management and Economics, Tianjin University, China. Her research interests include knowledge management and talent management in digital environments.

Qinghai Wu is Founder & Chief Expert of Pioneers Alliance Technology Co. Ltd. He is also a member of China national standardization technical committee of knowledge management. He has been engaged in research, counselling, training and field work in the areas of enterprise knowledge management and innovation for more than 20 years.

Yang Yang is a master's candidate in public administration at the School of Public Administration, Jilin University, China. Her research interests include the management of knowledge, business model innovation strategy and innovation policy.

Zhen Yang is a PhD candidate at the School of Economics and Management, Tsinghua University, China.

Yan Yu is an Associate Professor at the School of Information, Renmin University of China. Her research interests include digital innovation, knowledge management and social intelligence.

Xi Zhang is a Professor and the Head of Department of Information Management & Management Science (IMMS), at the College of Management and Economics, Tianjin University, China. His research interests include knowledge management, digital transformation and AI behaviour.

Yue-Yao Zhang is a PhD candidate at the School of Economics and Management, Tsinghua University, China.

Juxiang Zhou is the chief accountant of Hangzhou Children's Hospital, China. She received her PhD in Management Science and Engineering at Zhejiang University in China. Her research interests focus on the management of innovation, management of clinician knowledge and health economy.

PART I

Theoretical Perspectives in Knowledge Management

1

OUTLOOK ON KNOWLEDGE MANAGEMENT

The Origin and Basic Framework of Knowledge Management

Jin Chen

History of Knowledge Management

Athens derived its name from the goddess of wisdom—Athena. In the 5th century BC, Athens became an important center for political, economic, and cultural exchanges in the Eastern Mediterranean, eclipsing Sparta and other Greek city-states. Due to its emphasis on the use of dispersed knowledge, people often refer to Athens in the 5th century BC as "the miracle of Greece". Pericles, the Archon of Athens in ancient Greece, said proudly in his speech: "Athens is the school of all of Greece". The Use of Knowledge in Society by Friedrich A. Hayek (1945) clearly describes that knowledge about change has never existed in a concentrated form. Whenever there is a change, some individual minds always feel the change, but merely partially.

Moreover, no one can possess this knowledge about change. However, Ancient Athens broke through the dilemma described by Hayek and succeeded in effectively using dispersed knowledge to form knowledge aggregation, knowledge alignment, and knowledge codification. Therefore, knowledge management has played a critical role in the city-state construction of ancient Athens. Table 1.1 shows ancient Athens and its use of dispersed knowledge.

Table 1.1 Ancient Athens and Use of Dispersed Knowledge

Process	Problem	Solution
Aggregation of knowledge	How to apply scattered and valuable knowledge to the needed problem	Promoting information communication through strong and weak ties in social network
Alignment of knowledge	How do people with knowledge align their actions to achieve common goals?	Encouraging the public to master common sense and participate in public activities regularly
Codification of knowledge	How to reduce the opportunity cost of acquiring and sharing knowledge	Reducing inequality in knowledge sharing through the establishment of formal and informal systems

DOI: 10.4324/9781003112150-2

Management Master's View on Knowledge

Robert M. Grant (1996), the famous strategic management master, once said that knowledge serves as the foundation of all critical advances since the origin of human civilization. Nowadays, the amount of knowledge stock relates directly to productivity and economic growth. The real challenge is not to discuss the knowledge economy and the concept of knowledge workers in general but to explore the essence of knowledge in depth and the use of knowledge which is quite different at other times.

The Origin of Knowledge Management

Peter F. Drucker (1999) believes that "the most valuable asset of an organization in the 21st century is the knowledge workers within the organization and their productivity". Therefore, the organization must encourage enterprise knowledge sharing through knowledge management and improve its adaptability and innovation capabilities through collective wisdom. Knowledge flow within and across organizational boundaries enables enterprises to respond to external demands quickly and predict the market environment changes using the knowledge resources obtained. In the age of the knowledge economy, the cultivation of corporate competitiveness is inseparable from knowledge management.

The development of knowledge management is closely related to the concept of "intellectual capital". In 1969, in the letter to a Polish economist, John Kenneth Galbraith pointed out that intellectual capital is not only pure knowledge in the form of knowledge but also includes intellectual activities; that is, intellectual capital is not only fixed capital but also a process of effective use of knowledge and a means to achieve goals. The best model of intellectual capital is the Skandia model, which was created in 1991 by Leif Edvinsson (1996), Intellectual Capital Manager of Skandia, drawing on the ideas of an "intangible balance sheet" and "balanced scorecard" in combination with Skandia's practice.

The Practical Background of Knowledge Management

Since the 1980s, due to intensified competition, downsizing has become a common strategy for companies to increase profits. However, the downsizing strategy has led to the loss of necessary knowledge, and companies have begun to adopt a "knowledge management" strategy, trying to store and maintain employee knowledge that is in line with the company's future interests. Scholars created theoretical frameworks of knowledge management that preceded related standards. APQC (American Productivity and Quality Center) defines knowledge management as a conscious strategy adopted by an organization to ensure members can promptly acquire the knowledge they need. Effective knowledge management can help people share information and then put it into practice in different ways to improve organizational performance ultimately. According to China's National Standard for Knowledge Management (GB/T 23703.2-2010), knowledge management is an activity of planning and managing knowledge itself, the process of knowledge creation, and the application of knowledge.

Two Typical Models of Knowledge Management

The first one is the Thomas H. Davenport (1996, 1998) model, in which knowledge is a dynamic mixture of factors, including structured experience, values, relative information, and expert opinions. It provides the framework for measuring and absorbing new information.

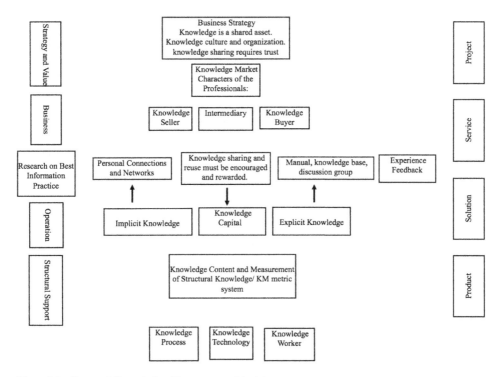

Figure 1.1   Siemens' Knowledge Management Model

Such an explicit model is well illustrated by the knowledge management model at Siemens (Figure 1.1).

The other one is the Ikujiro Nonaka (1994) model. In the mid- to late 1990s, Japanese professor Ikujiro Nonaka further developed a management system for intellectuals and practitioners. Through innovative case studies of Japanese companies, such as Sony, Panasonic, Honda, Canon, NEC, and Fuji Copiers, he attributed their success to the knowledge creation capabilities of the organization, which can fully mobilize the individual knowledge hidden deep in their minds in an "organized way" (Figure 1.2).

Based on the knowledge dichotomy by Polanyi (2009), Ikujiro Nonaka (1994) subdivided knowledge into "explicit knowledge" and "tacit knowledge", starting from the relationship between these two concepts. He believes that the creation of new knowledge depends on the accumulation of tacit knowledge, which means that organizations have to explore implicit beliefs, intuitions, and inspirations in employees' minds to produce new knowledge. In Ikujiro Nonaka's perspective, knowledge is embedded in subjective experience, abstract concepts, standard operating procedures, systematic documents, or specific techniques. His knowledge management concepts are mostly new theories and new insights obtained from philosophy and sociology, which have great significance for reference.

Ikujiro Nonaka drew on the wisdom of Eastern and Western philosophies to construct the knowledge creation theory based on the successful practical experience of Japanese companies. With the socialization, externalization, combination, and internalization (SECI) model as the core, he organically combined subjective and objective, tacit and explicit knowledge, direct experience, and logical analysis to form a series of classics in knowledge management.

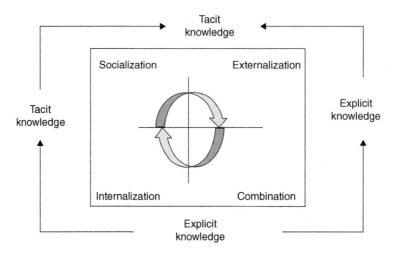

Figure 1.2 Ikujiro Nonaka's SECI Model

Based on the concept proposed originally by Kitaro Nishida (1992), the Japanese philosopher Ikujiro Nonaka (1998, 2000) defined "Ba" as a shared context in motion, which is for the continuous creation of practical meanings toward a certain objective. In "Ba", knowledge is shared, created, and practiced. "Ba" also provides knowledge with energy, quality, and place to complete the transformation of individual knowledge into shared knowledge, and it rises along the knowledge creation spiral. "Ba" is the site of creative interaction. The space, time, and scene in "Ba" may be real or virtual; it may only exist on the cognitive level or a mixture of the above. "Ba" will appear and disappear along the real timeline. "Ba" is not limited to a single organization but can be created across organizational boundaries. "Ba" can be created as a joint meeting with suppliers, as an alliance with competitors, or as an interactive event with customers, universities, local communities, or government. Organization members transcend the boundary by participating in "Ba", and when "Ba" connects with other "fields", they further transcend the boundaries.

In the Ikujiro Nonaka model, tacit and explicit knowledge interact to constitute a series of knowledge creation processes. Knowledge creation enriches tacit knowledge while making it explicit, then combines with explicit knowledge and forms a new tacit knowledge again based on practice. This dynamic spiral movement process consists of four parts: socialization, externalization, combination, and internalization. Professor Ikujiro Nonaka took the initials of the four English words and named this process the SECI Model (Ikujiro Nonaka, 1994). This model is applied to individuals, groups, and organizations and needs to adapt to the social context.

Then, the Hitotsubashi Paradigm, introduced by Professor Nonaka (2015), is a widely accepted knowledge management model in the academic and practical worlds. This model has potential valuable extensions: adding technology factors, emphasizing value realization, focusing on breakthrough innovation, and invoking general wisdom. Therefore, we have to continue to pursue improvement.

The Latest Developments in Knowledge Management

First, the Carnegie Mellon paradigm is worthy of reference. Chinese firms' knowledge management system derives primarily from information management infrastructures. The second is to apply further and improve the Hitotsubashi Paradigm, emphasizing the knowledge creation spiral and practical wisdom. Finally, we hope knowledge management forms a Chinese Paradigm, emphasizing meaning pursuit and technological innovation and integrating innovation and knowledge management. The above three aspects underlie what the traditional Carnegie Mellon Paradigm and Hitotsubashi Paradigm lack and need further exploration.

Therefore, the development of knowledge management should emphasize the breadth of social interaction and the depths of information technology drive and philosophical guidance.

Extending the Breadth of Social Interaction

It has been 25 years since the introduction of knowledge creation theory. The world has undergone profound and drastic changes in these two-and-a-half decades. For those who need to apply the knowledge creation theory, how significant are the challenges and difficulties they face? Along with the drastic changes in the world, the knowledge scene has also undergone profound changes. The organization is unable to complete the continuous horizontal movement from "socialization" to "externalization", "combination", and "internalization". Otherwise, it cannot complete the vertical transition from a SECI transformation to the next SECI transformation.

Based on this, Ikujiro Nonaka (2011) proposed the importance of practical wisdom or phronesis as six abilities to deepen the knowledge creation spiral. First is the ability to understand what is beneficial to the society in advance and make judgments and decisions for organization. Second is, regardless of the situation or problem faced, the ability to quickly grasp the essence of the problem and use intuition to understand the nature and meaning of people, things, and matters. Third is the ability to continue to create formal and informal shared contexts, "Ba", to construct new meanings through interactions between people. Fourth is the ability to use analogies and stories to understand various situations, master different experiences, and intuitively understand the essence of things. Fifth is the ability to, when necessary, take all possible means, including Machiavellian methods, to unite people with different goals and inspire them to act. Sixth is the ability to spread the practical idea of "learning by doing" to others, especially front-line employees.

In this process, we should pay attention to the further use of the knowledge creation spiral and the further improvement of globalization. Globalization makes it easier for companies to go beyond their boundaries, and its direct result is the globalization of all knowledge. Open innovation also makes it easier for companies to cross their boundaries so that the creation of knowledge benefits both the organization itself and the ecosystem at the same time.

The current social interaction has taken on the following characteristics:

Technologies such as big data, cloud computing, and artificial intelligence (AI) have brought endless treasures of data and information. Knowledge, information, and data have become increasingly difficult to distinguish. At the same time, the problem of information overload has begun to emerge. The combination of the Internet, social media, and mobile technology has brought about a "Hyper-linked" world, in which everybody participates in others' lives.

Knowledge sharing has become more pervasive. The Internet of Things has brought a new generation of products, and each new product is also a new service. Knowledge becomes free, unbounded, and personalized. Over-reliance on explicit knowledge makes companies unable to handle change. The scientific, deductive, and theory-advanced approach assumes that the world exists independently of context. It searches for a universal answer. However, social phenomena, including those of commerce and enterprise, exist precisely depending on context. If humans' personal goals, values, and interests and the interpersonal dependence between people are ignored, all analyses would be futile. However, many managers have not recognized this.

Based on the practical phenomena and characteristics mentioned above, Japanese managers emphasized that the concept of "wisdom" should be established and made into a new focus in knowledge management in terms of theory. For example, it seems that we have passed through the ocean of knowledge management and dived into a deeper ocean of wisdom, which is full of vitality and mystery. We must draw on the concept of Aristotle's practical wisdom, namely "practical wisdom" (Phronesis). He emphasized the critical role of Phronesis in management and organizational activities. In terms of practice, knowledge creation should be a lifestyle for everyone. It is an arduous task to achieve without strict self-discipline, unremitting efforts, empathy, and love. It is also inseparable from "Ba", the concept brought forward by the Japanese philosopher Kitaro Nishida (1992).

Depth of Information Technology-Driven

It is necessary to deepen further the information knowledge generated through interaction, that is, to drive innovation based on information technology. For example, Wiki allows different users to create content and modify and update content, conducive to knowledge innovation. Great companies, such as IBM, Cisco, and Oracle, have spared no effort to launch enterprise-level WEB2.0 products and services, covering the companies' collaborative management, customer relationship management, and portal systems.

Case: Pfizer: Enterprise Web2.0 Initiative

> In response to the constantly updated and changing competitive environment with new products outside, Pfizer's strategy was to establish innovation and continuous product improvement culture. The application of Wikis in Pfizer began in 2006 when a team leader at the Research Technology Center (RTC) installed Mediawiki. His goal was to launch a scientific encyclopedia to facilitate external users' collaborative knowledge creation efforts with Pfizer's internal R&D team. History has proved that Pfizer's wiki (Pfizerpedia) is extremely popular, recording 12,000 hits among 13,000 employees worldwide in the first year. Pfizerpedia has become an integral part of Pfizer's IT field, and it has strengthened collaboration and information sharing among employees worldwide. Pfizerpedia makes connections between researchers closer, which helps to stimulate innovation, accelerate the pharmaceutical development process, and maximize Pfizer's R&D return.
>
> Pfizer has used the information platform, including the Wiki innovation platform, to form a collaborative work network with knowledge management, including knowledge creation, knowledge sharing, and knowledge storage, thereby supporting the innovation and strategic management of the enterprise.

The next step involves the application of AI. China's AI industry is developing rapidly, with the emergence of many AI service companies. AI companies can conduct intelligent searches, intelligent creation, intelligent push, and intelligent decision-making. AI and knowledge management are the next areas of focus for knowledge management service organizations (Figure 1.3).

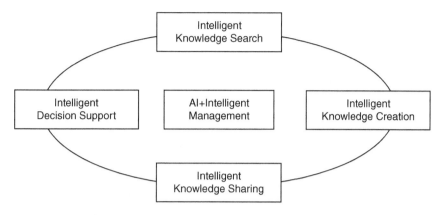

Figure 1.3 Artificial Intelligence and Knowledge Management

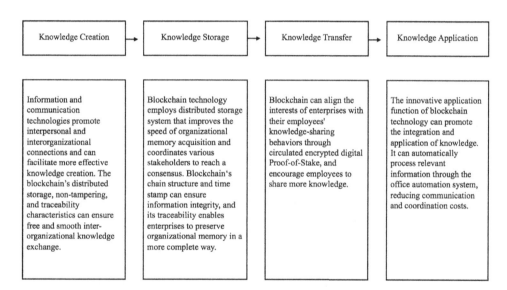

Figure 1.4 Blockchain and Knowledge Management

Moreover, a promising area is the utilization of blockchain; blockchain is a distributed shared ledger and database that can serve as a helpful tool for knowledge management with its characteristics of decentralization, openness, and transparency (Figure 1.4).

Case: Dual-screen Innovation of COMAC

Commercial Aircraft Corporation of China, Ltd. (COMAC) focuses on the construction of core capabilities. It takes the promotion of knowledge accumulated learning and knowledge management as the start to carry out the "Second Screen" construction activity (including the three steps of "establishing an electronic library, creating a scene-based knowledge application platform, and promoting intelligent knowledge services"). The company pays attention to capacity building while training its model team and values management innovation while strengthening technology innovation.

The "second screen" refers to employees add a new computer screen to their daily work computer as an information reference, data support, and knowledge reference medium for routine work to improve efficiency and speed up learning.

The essence of "Dual-screen Innovation" is a mechanism innovation that enterprises pay attention to knowledge management and optimize their learning capabilities. At the micro-level, every employee can benefit from the "second screen", allowing employees to have a sense of participation in the construction of the knowledge system and then enjoy the sense of gaining innovation and performance improvement. On the macro level, it optimizes the learning atmosphere and organizational learning mechanism of the enterprise, improves the core capability of the enterprise as an innovation subject, and lays a good foundation for COMAC to create a learning-oriented organization.

The "Dual-screen Innovation" of knowledge established an electronic library to realize the "systematization" of knowledge. With a problem-solving mind, it accomplishes the situational application of knowledge in the production of service products. For example, the design of tooling at Shanghai Aircraft Manufacturing Center has been shortened from 22 working days on average to 14, and the efficiency has increased by 36%. At the same time, the improvement of the knowledge management system has made problem-oriented scene-based knowledge identification and integration work a routine at work. Finally, it comprehensively enhances the enterprise's core competence and achieves the intelligent knowledge service.

The "Dual-screen Innovation" strategy is implemented consistently from top to bottom, stimulating all departments and employees to participate, and can be implemented continuously for a long time. The participation of all employees will produce unexpected ideas and thoughts. As an example, COMAC contributes more than 37,000 knowledge points each year, and the average contribution is 12 knowledge points per person. This kind of participation of all employees with the support of senior leaders guarantees the vigorous promotion and effective implementation of "Dual-screen Innovation". Meanwhile, "Dual-screen Innovation" guides the integration of internal and external knowledge of the enterprise.

Height of Philosophy Steering

Western philosophy has an extended, deep, and rich epistemology. Generally, Western epistemology focuses on abstract theories and assumptions and regards them as an iron-clad norm. It has driven the development of science, and the background of this tendency is the long tradition of advocating accurate conceptual knowledge and systematic science in the West, which traces back to the Descartes era.

Kitaro Nishida (1992), the 20th-century philosopher, mainly represents Japanese epistemology, which is derived from the fact of pure experience, advocating to express the individual's direct experience. This tendency corresponds to the Japanese corporate managers' emphasis on the "real-time" experience. In the perspectives of Japanese managers, reality exists in a state of constant and eternal change, and it is composed of tangible and concrete materials, which is opposed to the mainstream view of reality in the West. That is, in the West, managers believe that reality is an eternal and intangible abstract entity. Japanese managers discover the truth through physical and spiritual interactions between themselves and nature and between themselves and others. This thought originates from the long intellectual tradition of Japan, which emphasizes "the unity of nature and man", "the unity of mind and body", and "the unity of self and others".

Practical wisdom beyond the "economic goals" of organizational development and quantitative management will cultivate beliefs with high ethical values and form organizations with a sense of mission. The joys of "buying, selling, and producing" put forward by Soichiro Honda and Kazuo Inamori's motto of "Revere God and Love People" are classic examples of leadership with practical wisdom, which is very inspiring for us.

The concept of "wisdom" can be traced back to ancient Greek philosophy, but philosophers pay more attention to theoretical research rather than theoretical practice. The founder of phenomenology, the study of subjective experience, Husserl (1999) further realized the importance of human subjectivity and empathy at the end of the 19th century. Therefore, from Husserl and Heidegger to Merleau-Ponty in France, they all emphasized that knowledge is always based on subjective vision and subjective experience. Subjective experience can come from the interaction between man and nature, which is physical interaction. Husserl's research was about creating meaning and value, which lays the foundation for phenomenology. In order to link knowledge with the application of knowledge, Husserl mainly devoted himself to the research of subjective human experience. Husserl proposed that to reveal how human knowledge functions, the human experience must be described and analyzed thoroughly. Husserl believed that to make wise judgments about our actions, we need subjective experience instead of objective experience. In the latter part of his academic career, he thoroughly analyzed the concept of intersubjectivity, how multiple individuals share their subjectivities. Husserl pointed out that the state of intersubjectivity comes from people's empathy, that is, to discover and understand the intentional behavior of others by "putting oneself in others' place". He called this mechanism of empathy "pairing". Once the two individuals are "paired", the narrow egoism that initially separated the two would disappear and be replaced by the sense of a shared subjectivity. In order to create the state of intersubjectivity to form the sense of "us" rather than "me", the organization must help each member breakthrough narrow egoism and take care of each other sincerely.

China's view of knowledge ranges from Pre-Qin Confucianism and Yangming's theory of "unity of knowledge and doing" in the Middle Ages to Mao Zedong's materialistic view of knowledge and practice in modern times. This chapter holds that the logical starting point of China's view of knowledge lies in people's virtue ethics, and has always been discussed around the basic relationship between "knowledge" and "doing" in the process of evolution, resulting in basic problems such as where knowledge comes from, how to obtain knowledge, the basic process of knowledge innovation, and the value and efficacy of knowledge. China's view of knowledge directly points to people and human society (inward knowledge system) in terms of the object of knowledge, the ways and means of acquiring knowledge, and the value of knowledge. And it can promote human beings to deal with the relationship between good people and adjust the conflict of interest between good people. However, it ignores the full use of human relations in nature. Therefore, it has seriously affected the development of material society and productivity.

When we fully understand the critical enlightenment of philosophy to knowledge management, then knowledge management should develop in three directions next: the first is to emphasize group interaction further; the second is to value the knowledge management model driven by information; the third is to develop philosophical concepts, especially the practical wisdom proposed by Husserl's philosophy as the leading phenomenology and Mao-zedong's materialistic view.

The Rise of Knowledge Management and Management Changes

In the era of increasingly fierce global economic competition, it is critical to design the philosophy, operating system, and management model of organizational development from a "knowledge management" perspective. In the past century, management has experienced two critical development stages: the first is the stage of scientific management which regards employees as "economic man" represented by Frederick Winslow Taylor et al.; the second is the stage of the knowledge economy and knowledge management that regards employees as "intellectual man" represented by Drucker - (2017, 2020).

Taylor was the first to regard management as a science. He pointed out that establishing various clear rules, regulations, and standards to make everything scientific and institutional is the key to improve management efficiency. Henri Fayol (1999, 2016) from France and Max Weber (2013) from Germany supplemented and improved Taylor's management theory. They focused on the rationalization of organizational structure and management principles and the rationalization of the function division of managers, which laid the foundation for classical organization theory. Based on scientific management literature, a mature management model of quality and project management was formed, emphasizing a data-based management system.

As early as the early 1960s, Peter F. Drucker (1993) put forward knowledge workers and knowledge management concepts. In a knowledge society, the most basic economic resource is knowledge. Knowledge workers will play an increasingly important role, and every knowledge worker is a manager. Knowledge workers have higher quality and good self-management abilities. In the industrialized world, experts define working methods and procedures, and once they are defined, they cannot be changed. No matter how creative the employees are, the opportunities to show their talents decreased. In the 1980s, Drucker proposed that "The typical enterprise in the future is based on knowledge and consists of various experts who make decisions and manage themselves based on a large amount of information from colleagues, customers, and superiors".

From the "intellectual man" perspective, corporate management's philosophy, style, and the system should undergo more significant changes. First of all, the model of "support and care" must be vigorously advocated. Nowadays, managers should consider caring for and motivating employees and creating favorable environments and conditions. They should develop and use the potential and creativity of employees to realize their dignity and value and then help and guide employees to achieve self-management. This management model also contains another vital concept: whether it succeeds or not, courage is instilled in the face of challenges. In short, this should be the focus of business management in the new era.

Ikujiro Nonaka's theory of knowledge creation emphasizes that "people are the most important asset, and knowledge is the strategic asset of an enterprise", and modern organizational management theories should be "human-centered". *The Wise Company: How Companies Create Continuous Innovation* by Ikujiro Nonaka and Hirotaka Takeuchi expounded and proved that wisdom is essential to cope with the rapidly changing world. Moreover, wisdom is a kind of high-level tacit knowledge.

There are three aspects in Dr Debra's law of knowledge dynamics: the first is to replace information with knowledge since knowledge is the most valuable asset; the second is to replace change with innovation, which means the source of innovative knowledge must be transferred to where it is most needed, and the third is to replace competition with cooperation.

Therefore, knowledge management ideas should be deepened in three aspects: the first is to emphasize emotional interaction, that is, to further develop the knowledge creation spiral model; the second is to emphasize a digital drive, and use advanced digital technology, including network technology, to drive the effectiveness and benefits of knowledge management; and the third is to sublimate the pursuit of philosophy from objective pursuit to subjective pursuit, the pursuit of meaning, the pursuit of value, and the pursuit of happiness.

Emotional interaction broadens knowledge; data-driven increases the depth of knowledge management, and the pursuit of meaning raises the height of knowledge management. Entrepreneurs and managers are expected to optimize knowledge management from the height, breadth, and depth of knowledge and be the guides in a knowledge-needed new era. They need to resist the temptation of short-termism and maintain the company's sustainable development and dynamic capabilities. We should create a future beyond the reach of our competitors, a future that brings comparatively excellent value to customers. In that future, people can live harmoniously in society with moral aspirations and pursue public interests as a way of life.

Finally, let us come back to the Budapest tradition of knowledge management. Michael Polanyi (2009) creatively proposed "tacit knowledge", which can be used as a reference for human development. We emphasize knowledge based on Michael Polanyi's thoughts. However, in the new era, only through the extension of information, emotionalization, and philosophy can one achieve the transformation proposed by his brother Karl Polanyi (2001). The transformation is with particular reference to a society's transformation into a healthy and sustainable organization based on knowledge. Such a society values public interests and morals, strengthens trust and dependence between people, and uses advanced information technology in depth.

References

Davenport, T. H. (1996). Some principles of knowledge management. *Strategy & Business, 1*(2), 34–40.

Davenport, T. H., De Long, D. W., & Beers, M. C. (1998). Successful knowledge management projects. *MIT Sloan Management Review, 39*(2), 43.

Davenport, T. H., & Prusak, L. (1998). *Working knowledge: How organizations manage what they know.* Brighton, MA: Harvard Business Press.

Drucker, P. F. (1993). The rise of the knowledge society. *The Wilson Quarterly, 17*(2), 52–72.

Drucker, P. F. (1999). Knowledge-worker productivity: The biggest challenge. *California Management Review, 41*(2), 79–94.

Drucker, P. F. (2017). *The end of economic man: The origins of totalitarianism.* Oxfordshire: Routledge.

Drucker, P. F. (2020). *The essential drucker.* Oxfordshire: Routledge.

Edvinsson, L., & Sullivan, P. (1996). Developing a model for managing intellectual capital. *European Management Journal, 14*(4), 356–364.

Fayol, H. (1999). *Administration industrielle et générale.* Malakoff Cedex: Dunod.

Fayol, H. (2016). *General and industrial management.* Ravenio Books (online).

Grant, R. M. (1996). Toward a knowledge-based theory of the firm. *Strategic Management Journal, 17*(S2), 109–122.

Hayek, F. A. (1945). The use of knowledge in society. *The American Economic Review, 35*(4), 519–530.

Husserl, E. (1999). *The essential Husserl: Basic writings in transcendental phenomenology.* Bloomington, IN: Indiana University Press.

Nishida, K. (1992). *An inquiry into the good.* London: Yale University Press.

Nonaka, I. (1994). A dynamic theory of organizational knowledge creation. *Organization Science, 5*(1), 14–37.

Nonaka, I., & Konno, N. (1998). The concept of "Ba": Building a foundation for knowledge creation. *California Management Review, 40*(3), 40–54.

Nonaka, I., & Takeuchi, H. (2011). The wise leader. *Harvard Business Review, 89*(5), 58–67.

Nonaka, I., & Toyama, R. (2015). The knowledge-creating theory revisited: Knowledge creation as a synthesizing process. In *The essentials of knowledge management* (pp. 95–110). London: Palgrave Macmillan.

Nonaka, I., Toyama, R., & Konno, N. (2000). SECI, Ba and leadership: A unified model of dynamic knowledge creation. *Long Range Planning, 33*(1), 5–34.

Polanyi, K. (2001). *The great transformation the political and economic origins of our time* (2nd Beacon Paperback ed.). Boston, MA: Beacon Press.

Polanyi, M., & Sen, A. (2009). *The tacit dimension*. Chicago, IL: University of Chicago Press.

Weber, M. (2013). *From Max Weber: Essays in sociology*. Oxford: Routledge.

2

THE SPIRAL OF KNOWLEDGE CREATION IN A DYNAMIC AND EVOLVING BUSINESS ENVIRONMENT

Manlio Del Giudice and Valentina Cillo

A Glance at Knowledge-based Economy: Knowledge, Innovation and Competitiveness

In recent years, there has been a growing interest among companies, institutions and scholars in the knowledge-based economy, which has led to studies, research and institutional debates.

Knowledge-based economy has been identified as one of the pillars of the 21st century.

Since the Lisbon European Council in 2000 fixed the goal for Europe to "become the most competitive and dynamic knowledge-based economy in the world", the theory of knowledge management (KM) has attracted the attention of multiple stakeholders and policy makers interested in promoting smart, sustainable and socially inclusive growth.

One of the main features of knowledge-based economy is that it is rooted in intellectual capital, skills, dynamic capabilities and the ability of organisations to enable them. The basic factors include "a greater reliance on intellectual capabilities than on physical inputs or natural resources, combined with efforts to integrate improvements in every stage of the production process, from the R&D lab to the factory floor to the interface with customers" (Powell and Snellman, 2004, p. 201).

As the French philosopher Jean Francois Lyotard already theorised in the late 1970s in his seminal work *The Postmodern Condition: A Report on Knowledge*, knowledge acquisition is not the final aim but is functional to the achievement of economic objectives (Olson and Lyotard, 1995).

With this in mind, the importance of "knowledge" grew on the wake of Nelson and Winter's evolutionary theories of economic change (1985), becoming the main driving force of the development and growth process and supplanting the central role played by "material" resources in Ford's *weltanshauung*.

Over the years, there has been a growing awareness that the "fast development of technologies and the rapidly changing markets, combined with increased global competition and changing customer demands, imply that a company focused just on production capacity and cost reduction can only generate a temporary competitive advantage" (Cillo et al., 2019, p. 532).

In particular, the spread of technology innovation enabled by the "Knowledge Society" have triggered a disruptive development that has transformed the characteristics of work

DOI: 10.4324/9781003112150-3

as well as the organisation of production, leading tangible and intangible assets to play a different role in businesses (Castelfranchi, 2007). This confirms that the basic neoclassical assumptions about profit maximisation and market equilibrium are not adequate to capture the dynamics of technological innovation and competition between companies.

These transformations are closely linked to the rising role of "intangible" capital in gross domestic product (Abramovitz and David, 1996). As a matter of fact, interest of companies in intangible assets and knowledge has grown significantly in many OECD countries, leading intangible investment to exceed tangible investment (Laghi et al., 2020).

In this context, KM has been identified as a strategic managerial process for gaining a competitive advantage. In particular, it is based on the assumption that tangible resources lead to a competitive advantage only if they are managed with specific knowledge (Grant, 1996). The advantage lies in differentiation and, in particular, in the complexity of imitating knowledge (Nonaka, 1994; Nonaka and Takeuchi, 1995; Meroño-Cerdán, Soto-Acosta and López-Nicolás, 2008).

Following these basic factors, over the past 20 years, KM theory has evolved in its capacity to interpret institutional, social and economic phenomena, providing conceptual and operational tools to manage ongoing change.

A first issue arose, with regard to the types of knowledge and their interaction.

Scholars have recognised three main forms of knowledge: explicit, implicit and tacit knowledge. These different types of knowledge work together: explicit knowledge resides in documented information; implicit knowledge is based on applied information; tacit knowledge, which plays a strategic role for the competitive advantage of businesses, is linked to the so-called "understood information".

Within the multitude of theories, constructs and tools developed in the scientific literature to explain the contribution of knowledge to the development and growth of organisations, the knowledge creation model developed by Nonaka and Takeuchi is widely recognised as a theoretical milestone. In particular, it emphasises on the role of tacit and explicit knowledge in organisations.

The model was first presented in 1991 by Nonaka, although it was later extended and deepened in the popular book *The Knowledge Creating Company* by Nonaka and Takeuchi (1995).

It is based on four main dimensions of knowledge and is generally referred to as SECI model (the acronym refers to the processes of Socialisation, Externalisation, Combination, and Internalisation).

The SECI model has achieved widespread success, particularly among managers and entrepreneurs, thanks to its practical nature and clear description of knowledge types, starting from the difference between tacit and explicit knowledge already promoted in management theory by Polanyi (1958).

The model stands out because it defines knowledge creation as a dynamic process based on the continuous interaction between tacit and explicit knowledge and across different levels (individual, organisational, inter-organisational) (Nonaka, 1994; Nonaka and Takeuchi, 1995; von Krogh et al., 2001; Ngai, Jin and Liang, 2008; Terhorst et al., 2018).

The central theoretical and practical implication of the model is that in order to improve both tacit and explicit knowledge stocks, companies must continuously promote knowledge sharing between individuals and groups.

A second issue arose in the scientific debate concerning the balance between *internal* and *external resources* of organisations, to deal with *continuous innovation*.

To survive and to compete in a dynamic environment, companies should develop high capabilities and sufficient knowledge capital to innovate continuously and to gain a competitive advantage (Lianto, Dachyar and Soemardi, 2018). On the other hand, to innovate continuously, companies need to focus on a long-term perspective and also acquire the wisdom to ensure that their interests are aligned with those of society (Nonaka and Tekeuchi, 2009).

Innovation is the consequence of new knowledge acquired through cumulative processes of various exchanges of internal and external knowledge (Menon and Pfeffer, 2003). For this reason, internal and external knowledge are seen as complementary in the innovation strategy.

Since innovation is the result of the ability to share, combine and create new knowledge, a balanced mix of internal and external knowledge sources can also enable better exploitation of business opportunities (Vrontis et al., 2017).

This phenomenon is consistent with the open innovation paradigm, according to which much of the knowledge needed to create new products and services comes from outside and explains why companies increasingly need to collaborate with other players to strengthen their innovative capacity (Vrontis et al., 2017).

According to Nonaka and Toyama (2007), "as knowledge is created in dynamic interactions with the environment, managing the knowledge creating process requires the ability to foster and manage those interactions according to the situation" (p. 377).

In line with this perspective, Zhang and Huang (2020) explored the knowledge creation and conversion model by studying knowledge flows within and between organisations on the basis of open innovation principles.

A third relevant issue regarding the KM theory is the emerging risks and opportunities concerning information and communication technologies (ICTs) that is attracting attention from several research perspectives. Among the many contributions made in this direction, several studies have explored the role of KM (Caputo et al., 2019).

In the paper *From information processing to knowledge creation: A paradigm shift in business* management, Nonaka, Umemoto and Senoo (1996) have shown how information technology (IT) can enable the process of "the knowledge-creating company". The authors present the theory of organisational knowledge creation as a management paradigm for the emerging "knowledge society" and provide several practical examples and applications.

The emerging challenges and opportunities derived from ICTs for KM are attracting interest and efforts from multidisciplinary scientists, promoting the integration and cross-fertilisation of research domains.

In particular, the spread of the Industry 4.0 paradigm has opened a new era, described as "The Fourth Industrial Revolution", which has been leading to the digitisation of all industrial processes, as well as the integration of different aspects of production and the interconnection between different departments and functions. In this scenario, companies are adopting technology to develop process and product innovations and to achieve greater value. To successfully manage these processes, companies need to develop knowledge, processes and infrastructure (Caputo et al., 2019). Knowledge management in the context of Industry 4.0 (KM 4.0) has a strategic and operational function which includes both exploration and exploitation processes. KM 4.0 enables value generation through improved knowledge generation and utilisation capabilities and facilitates the development of collective human-machine intelligence (Ansari, 2019).

In this context, the model of knowledge creation introduced by Nonaka is a useful tool for interpreting and addressing economic and social challenges, calling for new studies on the antecedents of knowledge creation, the mediating factors and the main impacts at individual, organisational and inter-organisational levels.

Towards a Theory of Knowledge Acquisition and Creation

According to knowledge-based theory, knowledge is the main source of competitive advantage (Foss, 1996; Grant, 1996). In particular, the development of efficient processes for the extraction and creation of value through KM becomes a strategic factor in improving performance (Hsu and Sabherwal, 2011)

To this end, the SECI model described an interaction process through which knowledge is transmitted in a spiral dynamic, where the value of knowledge increases through interactions between individuals and groups. The model highlights that the simple existence of knowledge is not sufficient to achieve a sustainable competitive advantage: knowledge only leads to added value when organisations manage it in an appropriate way.

In this scenario, the transition to knowledge-based economy requires a semantic change in the conceptualisation of knowledge and information and indicates an alternative perspective in the scientific literature.

As Wallace (2007) points out,

> the presentation of the relationships among data, information, knowledge, and sometimes wisdom in a hierarchical arrangement has been part of the language of information science for many years. [...] The ubiquity of the notion of a hierarchy is embedded in the use of the acronym DIKW as a shorthand representation for the data-to-information-to-knowledge-to-wisdom transformation.

The popular data-to-information-to-knowledge-to-wisdom (DIKW) paradigm emphasises that the integration of data leads to information, and the integration of information, in turn, leads to the creation of knowledge (Hicks, Dattero and Galup, 2007).

Therefore, KM has more elements of complexity than data or information (Al-Alawi, Al-Marzooqi and Mohammed, 2007), becoming a source of competitive advantage only when it is spread to create new organisational knowledge or innovation (Kinnear and Sutherland, 2000).

The development of both theory and practice in this emerging field is being driven by two main strategic issues: on one hand, since knowledge generally is embedded in peoples' heads (Lee and Yang, 2000), managers and scholars have extensively analysed how to facilitate the conversion of tacit knowledge into explicit knowledge; on the other hand, since internal knowledge is not enough to create innovation, a plethora of research in recent years has questioned how to integrate and balance internal knowledge with knowledge acquired outside the company. In particular, some studies have focused their attention on how to explore and exploit external knowledge in order to achieve a competitive advantage.

Tacit and Explicit Knowledge

Reciprocal influence between tacit and explicit knowledge constitutes the foundation of knowledge creation. According to Nonaka and Takeuchi (1995), this process is characterised by holistic dynamics, which, through the transformation of knowledge from tacit to explicit, bring to life a new type of knowledge.

As the SECI model underlines, knowledge creates value through the interaction between individuals and groups at different organisational levels.

Following Penrose (1959) and Polanyi's (1958) insights, management studies generally make a difference between explicit and tacit forms of knowledge.

Polanyi (1967) stated that the relationship between tacit and explicit knowledge can be symbolised through the metaphorical image of an iceberg.

Explicit knowledge represents the visible part of the iceberg above the surface of the water: it is knowledge which we consciously manage, encode and transfer through formal language. To cite some practical examples, we can refer to the various forms of institutional communication, training and brainstorming initiatives, such as conferences and training courses, as well as tools to codify, share or protect knowledge, such as websites, social media, databases, manuals and patents.

Explicit knowledge, however, relies on a deeper system of tacit knowledge and is therefore associated with the submerged part of the iceberg. It is linked to the know-how of individuals, embedded in the specific work context and based on routines and habits of which individuals are often unaware (Warnier, 1999).

The concept of tacit knowledge indicates the different forms of knowledge that cannot be explicitly expressed and codified through documents. The complexity of this form of knowledge is also due to its cognitive and technical nature: the cognitive nature relates to the mental models, beliefs and scripts that underlie individuals' perceptions; on the other hand, the technical component of knowledge concerns the know-how and professional skills.

Although this knowledge is managed at an unconscious level, it can be used by individuals in problem-solving and decision-making processes (Reber, 1989).

Although tacit knowledge has been neglected in the KM literature, in recent years, it has been recognised as a key factor in managing globalisation, complexity and turbulence associated with the exponential progress of IT (Howells, 1996; Johannessen, Olaisen and Olsen, 2001).

In particular, the consolidation of the resource-based view of companies has led the managerial literature to consider tacit knowledge as central to the acquisition of a sustainable competitive advantage. As a matter of fact, tacit knowledge is rare and difficult to imitate and transfer (Ambrosini and Bowman, 2001). Since it can be transferred only through personal interaction, it plays a critical role in differentiation and innovation strategies (Senker, 2005).

Explicit knowledge, on the other hand, is rational, sequential and theoretical in nature.

According to Nonaka and Takeuchi (1995), while tacit knowledge is individual, context-specific and difficult to transmit, explicit knowledge is codified and as such can be disseminated through formal language such as documents, operating procedures and manuals.

In this context, information systems can play a strategic role in accelerating the dissemination of explicit knowledge resources within organisations, e.g. through intranets, or at the inter-company level through the internet, based on a structured, managed and scientific learning process.

External and Internal Knowledge Sources

One of the most strategic decisions that companies have to make when faced with the challenges of knowledge creation and innovation concerns sourcing strategy. In particular, companies have to decide whether to create valuable knowledge internally or through external sourcing.

Consistent with the early studies conducted to explore the effects of boundary spanning in innovative environments, several researches related to R&D management have shown that in a dynamic high-tech research environment, the ability to cross organisational boundaries is extremely important (Ebadi and Utterback, 1984)

To this aim, KM strategy should be conceptually differentiated into two sub-dimensions: internally and externally oriented strategy (Choi, Poon and Davis, 2008).

The internally oriented strategy stresses the role of knowledge creation and sharing within the organisation; on the other hand, the externally oriented strategy highlights the function of learning, imitation and knowledge transfer at an inter-organisational level (Choi, Poon and Davis, 2008).

Internal knowledge creation occurs within the boundaries of the company, for example, through internal R&D activities. In these cases, as several studies point out, a companies' ability to innovate depends largely on its internal capabilities and resources (Becheikh, Landry and Amara, 2006).

However, many companies increasingly rely on knowledge acquired from external sources to enable the development of internal capabilities (Kim, 1997).

In recent years, many management studies have shown that the use of external knowledge sources are crucial to increase the innovation capacity of a company (Caloghirou, Kastelli and Tsakanikas, 2004; Cassiman and Veugelers, 2006). For example, research on strategic alliances (Grant and Baden-Fuller, 2004; Khamseh and Jolly, 2014) and joint ventures (Inkpen and Dinur, 1998; Dhanaraj et al., 2004) stress the importance of acquiring knowledge from external sources. In particular, it has been shown that heterogeneous knowledge enhances innovation success: on one hand, by providing multiple learning opportunities and, on the other hand, by diversifying risk (Rodan, 2002; Ye, Hao and Patel, 2016).

In this context, Nonaka and Takeuchi (1995) emphasise the crucial role of the interaction between individuals and their organisations in the creation and acquisition of knowledge and also highlight the importance of external knowledge in the innovation process.

Knowledge creation based on external sources takes place when boundary spanners bring in new knowledge through acquisition or imitation. This knowledge is then shared with the whole organisation. A practical example of this is the learning that takes place through conference attendance or through training activities provided by suppliers of new technological services and products.

Both types of sourcing are important for the company and are generally seen as mutually interdependent and complementary (Bierly and Chakrabarti, 1996).

Therefore, several studies have argued that in order to improve innovative performance and achieve a competitive advantage, companies should integrate internal and external knowledge (Iansiti and Clark, 1994).

Although numerous studies have shown that both learning from external and internal sources are important sources for knowledge creation, another key element needs to be considered: the ability to explore, absorb and exploit knowledge.

Since it is not possible to create new knowledge without considering already existing knowledge, several studies pay specific attention to *absorptive capacity* as the capacity to explore and exploit technological opportunities developed outside the company (Cohen and Levinthal, 1990; Lane and Lubatkin, 1998; Zahra and George, 2002).

The concept of *absorptive capacity* was introduced by Kedia and Bhagat (1988). However, it was the conceptualisation proposed in the seminal studies of Cohen and Levinthal (1989) that made this construct so influential in the management and organisational literature.

Cohen and Levinthal (1990) defined absorptive capacity as "[…] an ability to recognise the value of new information, assimilate it, and apply it for business purposes" (p. 128).

Based on the Cohen and Levinthal (1989, 1990) studies, Zahra and George (2002) added that absorptive capacity is "a dynamic capability that influences the creation of other organisational competencies and provides the company with multiple sources of competitive advantage (p. 186)". In particular, absorptive capacity implies the ability to manage the tacit nature of the absorbed knowledge (Mowery and Oxley, 1995) and requires particular attention on the ability to solve problems and to learn (Kim, 1997). In light of these observations, absorptive capacity can be defined as "a set of organisational routines and processes through which companies acquire, assimilate, transform, and exploit knowledge to produce a dynamic organisational capability" (Zahra and George, 2002; p. 187).

In this context, *organisational ambidexterity* has catalysed growing attention (Adler et al., 1999; Gibson and Birkinshaw, 2004).

When a company is ambidextrous, it is able to both exploit existing expertise and explore new opportunities, thereby improving its performance (Carayannis and Rakhmatullin, 2014) and achieving competitive advantage (Del Giudice, Della Peruta and Maggioni, 2013). In particular, companies access different ideas and knowledge through collaboration with customers, suppliers, competitors, consultants, universities and research centres (Vrontis et al., 2017) and subsequently exploit this knowledge to create new innovative products and services (Del Giudice and Straub, 2011; Del Giudice and Maggioni, 2014).

As a result, many studies have analysed the spiral of knowledge creation process within the "open innovation" paradigm (Martin and Allen, 2013; Wu and Hu, 2018; Bereznoy, Meissner and Scuotto, 2021).

Coherently with the "open innovation" paradigm postulated by Chesbrough (2003, 2006), the effectiveness of innovation is closely linked to openness and co-operation mechanisms with external parties. In this vein, these studies explore the impact of stakeholder relations on a company's ability to "absorb" external knowledge (Cohen, Levinthal, 1989, 1990).

Open innovation is generally described as a distributed innovation process in which knowledge flows across company boundaries (Chesbrough and Bogers, 2014).

Based on Vygotskian theory, this paradigm requires decentralisation of research and development activities and a lean configuration of the organisation.

Coherent with what Hewitt and Scardamalia (1998) point out about "Distributed Knowledge Building Processes", the open innovation approach highlights that "knowledge exists in the way that social groups communicate, make use of symbols and tools, and organise their belief systems" (p. 77).

Since "the theory of the knowledge-creating company explains the differences among companies not as a result of market failure, but as a result of the company's visions of the future and strategy" (Nonaka and Toyama, 2005, p. 419), companies should improve their orientation towards openness and collaboration in order to access knowledge of the external environment (Scuotto et al., 2020) and to actively participate in the process of value co-creation with the innovation ecosystem according to the quadruple helix approach (Carayannis and Campbell, 2010; Carayannis and Rakhmatullin, 2014; Del Giudice, Carayannis and Maggioni, 2017; Abdulkader et al., 2020).

As Krogh, Nonaka and Aben argue (2001),

> companies can leverage their knowledge throughout the organisation, expand their knowledge based on existing expertise, appropriate knowledge from partners and other

organisations, and develop completely new expertise by probing new technologies or markets. The two core processes of knowledge creation and transfer are central to the execution of these strategies, as are the company's domains of knowledge (p. 421).

However, collaboration processes between individuals within and across organisations have several factors that inhibit knowledge sharing. These factors are syntactic (lack of knowledge sharing), semantic (lack of knowledge translation) and pragmatic (lack of interest in sharing knowledge) in nature (Bartel and Garud, 2009).

However, tacit knowledge can be difficult to transfer and share. It is embedded in the actions, values, emotions, professional experience and know-how of individuals.

While explicit knowledge is easy to codify and transfer, tacit knowledge has several limitations that may inhibit sharing processes at an organisational and inter-organisational level (Nonaka and Takeuchi, 1995). Several scholars confirm that individuals possess both tacit and explicit knowledge. Only explicit knowledge is available, codified and sharable. Tacit knowledge, on the other hand, resides in people, is not codified and therefore its socialisation is problematic (Song and Chermack, 2008). This explains why organisational behaviour and knowledge management literature has dedicated a lot of attention to informal knowledge and learning processes (Hoe, 2006).

Despite numerous interdisciplinary studies, many challenges remain.

The Spiral of Knowledge Creation

Knowledge Creation as a Dynamic and Dialectic Process

As authors Ichijo and Nonaka (2007) highlight in their book *Knowledge Creation and Management: New Challenges for Managers*, rapid changes in the competitive environment and pressing stakeholder expectations related to environmental, social and economic issues have created new challenges for practitioners and scholars.

In this framework, knowledge generation is crucial to ensure the adaptation of companies to the external environment. As theorised by Nonaka (1994), it can be described as a systemic, dynamic and continuous process that emerges and recurs over time.

As previously mentioned, the codification and conversion of tacit knowledge is a strategic factor for creating new knowledge and presents enormous challenges (Nonaka, 2004).

Reviewing the main managerial and organisational studies, Hicks, Dattero and Galup (2007) developed a metaphor for knowledge management (KM) defining it as "explicit islands in a tacit sea". The authors specified that explicit knowledge is comparable to an island sustained by the tacit knowledge sea. Moreover, they stated that tacit knowledge is crucial for creating, executing and maintaining explicit knowledge.

Tacit and explicit knowledge have a complementary nature. Through a dynamic process, the conversion from one state to the other is facilitated by social interaction. In addition, the conversion of tacit knowledge into explicit knowledge develops the conditions to enable the process of knowledge generalisation from the individual level to the organisational and inter-organisational level (Herschel, Nemati and Steiger, 2001; Choo, 2006).

While individuals have a strategic role in developing new knowledge, organisations articulate and amplify this knowledge (Nonaka, 1994).

Starting from the premise that knowledge creation is based on the interaction between tacit and explicit knowledge, Nonaka and Takeuchi (1995) develop a matrix model where four different modes of knowledge conversion operate.

Individual knowledge is socialised and becomes, "part of the knowledge network of an organisation" (Nonaka, 1994, pp. 17–18). More specifically, knowledge creation amplifies individual knowledge and crystallises it as part of an organisation's knowledge system (Nonaka, Takeuchi and Umemoto, 2014).

This process is labelled as a "spiral" and involves an interplay between socialisation (from tacit to tacit knowledge), externalisation (from tacit to explicit knowledge), combination (from explicit to explicit knowledge) and internalisation (from explicit to tacit/implicit knowledge).

The SECI model, unlike previous KM models, is not based on a sequential evolution of knowledge, but develops a holistic dynamic in which the conversion of knowledge from one type to another leads to a new quality of knowledge (Bandera et al., 2017).

The dynamic interaction between knowledge dimensions generates a spiral conversion process that fosters a quantitative and qualitative expansion of knowledge. In this sense, one of the main practical implications of the model is that organisations should combine and co-ordinate all modes of conversion through different policies and practices (Nonaka, 1994).

While the volume *Knowledge-Creating Company: How Japanese Companies Create the Dynamics of Innovation* (Nonaka and Tekeuchi, 1995) emphasised the difference between "explicit knowledge" and "tacit knowledge", *The Wise Company: How Companies Create Continuous Innovation* (Nonaka and Tekeuchi, 2019) addresses the gap between knowledge creation and knowledge practice and, in particular, the overcoming of the "SECI block". As a matter of fact, the process of knowledge creation in the SECI model can be blocked if an organisation is not able to implement the sequential, horizontal movement from socialisation to externalisation, combination and internationalisation, or if organisations are not able to make a vertical leap from one cycle of SECI to the next. Referring to several business cases, the authors highlight some leadership practices that characterise the wise company. The study, in particular, focuses on the need for organisations to create new common meanings through human interactions and recalls the Japanese concept of "ba" already introduced in 1998 by Nonaka and Konno in order to better understand the fundamental conditions for nurturing knowledge creation.

"Ba" can roughly be translated to the English word "place" and can be described as a platform at the basis of individual and organisational knowledge development. This shared space can be physical, such as the workplace, or virtual, such as teleconferences. It can also be mental, such as shared experiences.

Drawing on internal knowledge resources, organisations develop new knowledge through the SECI dynamic that resides in "ba". This process is continuous. In fact, new knowledge forms the foundation for a new spiral of knowledge creation (Nonaka, Toyama and Konno, 2000; Nonaka, Konno and Toyama, 2001; Nonaka, Toyama and Byosière, 2001).

Nonaka and Toyama (2003) further extended the knowledge creation model and the concept of "ba" by integrating the perspective of dialectical thinking. In particular, the authors highlight how the dynamic relations at individual, intra-organisational and inter-organisational level could generate various idiosyncratic effects in the knowledge creation process. In order to manage such effects, companies should improve "synthesis capabilities" starting from the knowledge vision and "ba", considering also human resource management policies and organisational structures, incentive systems and leadership models (Nonaka and Toyama, 2002, 2003). In this context, Nonaka et al. (2006) point out that "[…] knowledge originates in ba, and therefore the concept of ba assumes a particular importance in organisational knowledge creation theory".

Thus, the concept of "ba" occupies a strategic role in Nonaka's studies. Despite numerous research findings in this area, further studies are needed (Nonaka, Von Krogh and Voelpel, 2006; Nonaka and Von Krogh, 2009), also in light of recent social, organisational and economic changes imposed by technological advancement and, in particular, by COVID-19, which has induced emerging KM strategies, new organisational models and different ways of working.

The Four Dimensions

To depict the knowledge conversion process, the SECI model introduces four main dimensions: Socialisation; Externalisation; Combination; Internalisation (Nonaka, 1994).

The first stage of the spiral is *Socialisation*, which occurs when individuals exchange tacit knowledge. More specifically, Socialisation has been described as the conversion of tacit knowledge into more complex tacit knowledge throughout shared experiences, observation and imitation.

Since this process occurs even in the absence of formal language, tacit knowledge formalisation is problematic. The main difficulty lies in enucleating tacit knowledge from the context and time in which it occurred. Hence, its sharing and acquisition can only occur when individuals directly share work experiences. Working side by side, for example, promotes learning and the acquisition of tacit knowledge. A practical example of this is apprenticeship programmes in which new recruits acquire tacit knowledge by observing the work of senior colleagues (Nonaka and Toyama, 2003). Socialisation can also take place through informal social interactions, where tacit knowledge, values and mental models can be shared. A practical example is lunchtime chats or tea breaks with colleagues (Yoshimichi, 2011).

Basically, this first stage concerns the interpersonal level and, in particular, the sharing of values, beliefs, models and working practices. Therefore, the main factor for enabling socialisation is experience.

Assuming that according to Nonaka and Konno (2005) the simple transfer of information is meaningless if it is unrelated to specific context, we can state that shared experiences and mental models promote socialisation through the creation of a common "field" of interactions.

The next mode of knowledge conversion is *Externalisation* through which tacit knowledge is converted into new explicit knowledge through formal documents or explicit activities. Individuals encode tacit knowledge and use dialogue, metaphors and group comparisons to externalise knowledge.

Externalisation is based on the conversion of tacit knowledge into explicit knowledge (Nonaka and Takeuchi, 1995).

Since "members come and go, and leadership changes, but the memories of organisations retain certain behaviours, mind maps, norms and values over time" (Hedberg, 1981, p. 6), it is necessary that this knowledge becomes an organisational resource and not only of the individuals directly involved.

Therefore, an important issue is the generation of crystallised knowledge through metaphors, concepts and models, which represents the "organisational memory" and leads to new knowledge that can be used by other members of the organisation (Hedberg, 1981). Hence, as a result of this dynamic, knowledge can be shared between individuals and becomes the basis of new knowledge.

As pointed out by Nonaka, von Krogh and Voelpel (2006), this process is at the basis of "synthesising", where new models or mind maps are created and linked to the organisation's knowledge system.

The next mode that characterises the spiral of knowledge is *Combination*, in which explicit knowledge is combined with other explicit knowledge at an intra- or inter-organisational level to form new, more complex explicit knowledge (Nonaka et al., 1996). For this reason, Wickes et al. (2003) describe combination as the conversion of explicit knowledge into more complex explicit knowledge.

The source of explicit knowledge may be internal or external to the company. Through formal interactions, such as meetings or working groups, various types of explicit knowledge are combined and modified to generate new explicit knowledge, which is then shared with members of the organisation (Alavi and Leidner, 2001).

Because of the explicit nature of knowledge, which enhances coded information sharing, IT can have a crucial role in the conversion process.

In particular, the adoption of digital communication networks and business intelligence systems can accelerate this mode of knowledge conversion. For this reason, an increasing number of studies in recent years have analysed the role of groupware, online databases, intranets and virtual communities in combining various types of explicit knowledge (Koh and Kim, 2004).

From these knowledge-sharing processes, higher-order knowledge is created through templates, best practices, manuals and information systems (Van den Hooff and Van Weenen, 2004). The high rate of formalisation of this knowledge guarantees its dissemination even in the absence of interpersonal relations.

The last mode of the SECI spiral is *Internalisation*. According to Nonaka and Takeuchi (2019), "explicit knowledge created and shared throughout an organisation is then converted into tacit knowledge by individuals. This stage can be understood as praxis, where knowledge is applied and used in practical situations and becomes the base for new routines" (p. XIII).

The acquisition of new explicit knowledge by individuals amplifies their tacit knowledge and becomes the basis for a new process of transfer and application in practical situations.

Internalisation is the process of transforming explicit knowledge into tacit knowledge. In order for the individual to internalise new knowledge, practical actions are required. In particular, individual learning can be facilitated by practical experiences, observation, direct social interactions and training programmes. Through training activities, individuals can acquire new knowledge by enriching their mental models and professional know-how.

This new internalised knowledge is re-socialised in the knowledge spiral, triggering further conversion processes.

The internalisation process can be fostered by various textual forms, such as written, video or audio modes. According to Nonaka and Takeuchi (1995), particularly, to foster the internalisation process, it is necessary to adopt documentation and manuals through which individuals can learn from the experience of other members of the organisation. Therefore, Nonaka (1994) calls the knowledge created by an internalisation process "operational knowledge".

The interaction between the described modes of conversion originates the spiral of knowledge generation (Nonaka, 1994).

The SECI model has been successfully applied in various disciplines, for instance, in engineering, and in other fields of research, such as general manufacturing (Li et al., 2018), automotive manufacturing (Erichsen et al., 2016) and software engineering (Chikh, 2011). Furthermore, the model has been applied in cross-cultural studies set in Japan (Bratianu, 2010), United Kingdom (Scully et al., 2013) and Africa (Ngulube, 2005).

Conclusions and Future Streams of Research

Following the growing debate about the knowledge society and the knowledge creation process, in this chapter, we have explained how during the past decade we have observed an increase of studies about organisational knowledge from various perspectives.

In this scenario, the main aim of the contribution was to try to systematise these considerations and provide an overview of the scholarly literature in the social sciences on creation, reshaping, accumulation and crystallisation of knowledge within and across company boundaries.

According to the knowledge-based view (KBV), we highlighted that knowledge is the primary source of having a competitive advantage (Grant, 1996). Thus, the dynamics by which organisations explore and exploit knowledge become a strategic factor for value creation.

Although previous studies have already analysed knowledge creation from multiple perspectives, there is still a lack of knowledge about how emerging social and economic challenges can affect the concept of "the knowledge-creating company" (Nonaka, Umemoto and Senoo, 1996).

Research on knowledge creation has clearly highlighted that new knowledge is created by exploiting prior knowledge. Hence, the role of existing knowledge is strategic and deserves specific attention. As a matter of fact, it is difficult for companies to create new knowledge if they do not have a strong existing knowledge base.

As a preview to Nonaka and Takeuchi's (1995) knowledge creation theory, we have also stressed how the reciprocal influence between tacit and explicit knowledge constitutes the source of knowledge creation.

The codification of tacit knowledge and the internalisation of explicit knowledge lead to new and superior knowledge. In particular, labelling knowledge as "new" highlights that organisations are not just processing information, unlike a computer system, but are using their resources to create a superior level of knowledge (Nonaka, 1994).

Explicit knowledge is codified and as such can be disseminated through formal language such as documents, operating procedures and manuals. In this context, an open research question is to what extent information systems can play a strategic role in accelerating the dissemination of explicit knowledge resources.

On the other hand, tacit knowledge is central to the acquisition of a sustainable competitive advantage. As a matter of fact, tacit knowledge is rare and difficult to imitate and transfer.

Even if tacit knowledge has been neglected in the KM literature, in recent years, it has been recognised as a key factor in managing social, environmental and economic challenges. However, a lack of knowledge still exists regarding the transmission of tacit knowledge. More specifically, new studies are needed on the role of informal learning programmes (Enos, Kehrhahn and Bell, 2003) and lean organisational structures (Dombrowski, Mielke and Engel, 2012).

Through our analyses, we have highlighted that one of the most strategic decisions which companies have to make when faced with the challenges of knowledge creation and innovation concerns sourcing strategy. Specifically, companies have to decide whether to develop knowledge from internal or external sources. The main challenge then, is how to share, absorb and retain external knowledge internally. In this context, based on Nonaka and Takeuchi's knowledge creation theory, several studies have analysed knowledge creation dynamics in an open innovation paradigm context (Žemaitis, 2014).

As Chesbrough (2012, p. 701) argues

[...] to transfer knowledge effectively so that companies can really make use of it, you need a certain amount of creative abrasion and a certain amount of time together, working on the problem. Open innovation works best when people are collaborating side by side.

Despite several advancements in this domain, a specific research gap in the literature concerns the practical approaches that companies should adopt to improve the absorption of knowledge from open environments. Studies conducted on KM, however, focus mainly on the typology and transfer of knowledge (Nonaka and Konno, 1998). What is missing and deserves further investigation is the definition of new managerial and organisational tools to improve knowledge acquisition and learning for innovation development activities. Moreover, fresh studies are needed to investigate to what extent openness orientation leads to better performance. As a matter of fact, the openness-performance connection is not always positive (Huang, Chen and Liang, 2018).

Also, the interaction between tacit and explicit KM across company boundaries suggests future research stream in an open innovation context.

To fill these gaps, a new strand of studies is needed to investigate how opportunities and barriers posed by socio-economic context can facilitate, boost and humanise the knowledge creation process.

In line with the words of Nonaka and Tekeuchi (2011), in order to go beyond economic breakdowns of the past two decades caused by an overemphasis on explicit knowledge, which inhibits companies from dealing with emerging challenges, a new generation of wise leaders is needed.

In this framework, the contribution which managerial and organisational scientific literature can provide is to identify a clear theoretical framework to conceptualise and transfer the ancient Greek concept of *phronesis* into practice.

Only by investing in experiential knowledge, businesses can enable "people to make prudent judgments in a timely fashion, and to take actions guided by values, principles, and morals" (Nonaka and Tekeuchi, 2019, p. 25).

References

Abdulkader, B., Magni, D., Cillo, V., Papa, A., & Micera, R. (2020). Aligning firm's value system and open innovation: A new framework of business process management beyond the business model innovation. *Business Process Management Journal, 26*, 999–1020.

Abramovitz, M., & David, P. (1994). Convergence and deferred catch-up. Productivity leadership and the waning of American exceptionalism. In Landau, R., Taylor, T. & Wright, G. (Eds.). *The Mosaic of Economic Growth*. Stanford: Stanford University Press (pp. 21–62).

Adler, P. S., Goldoftas, B., & Levine, D. I. (1999). Flexibility versus efficiency? A case study of model changeovers in the Toyota production system. *Organization Science, 10*(1), 43–68

Al-Alawi, A. I., Al-Marzooqi, N. Y., & Mohammed, Y. F. (2007). Organizational culture and knowledge sharing: Critical success factors. *Journal of Knowledge Management, 11*(2), 22–42

Alavi, M., & Leidner, D. (2001). Review: Knowledge management and knowledge management systems: Conceptual foundations and research issues. *MIS Quarterly, 25*, 107–136.

Ambrosini, V., & Bowman, C. (2001). Tacit knowledge: Some suggestions for operationalization. *Journal of Management Studies, 38*, 811–829.

Ansari, F. (2019). Knowledge management 4.0: Theoretical and practical considerations in cyber physical production systems. *IFAC-PapersOnLine, 52*, 1597–1602.

Bandera, C., Keshtkar, F., Bartolacci, M. R., Neerudu, S., & Passerini, K. (2017). Knowledge management and the entrepreneur: Insights from Ikujiro Nonaka's Dynamic Knowledge Creation model (SECI). *International Journal of Innovation Studies, 1*, 163–174.

Bartel, C. A., & Garud, R. (2009). The role of narratives in sustaining organizational innovation. *Organization Science, 20*(1), 107–117.

Becheikh, N., Landry, R., & Amara, N. (2006). Lessons from innovation empirical studies in the manufacturing sector: A systematic review of the literature from 1993–2003. *Technovation, 26*, 644–664.

Bereznoy, A., Meissner, D., & Scuotto, V. (2021). The intertwining of knowledge sharing and creation in the digital platform based ecosystem. A conceptual study on the lens of the open innovation approach. *Journal of Knowledge Management, 25*(8), 2022–2042.

Bierly, P., & Chakrabarti, A. (1996). Generic knowledge strategies in the U.S. pharmaceutical industry. *Southern Medical Journal, 17*, 123–135.

Bratianu, C. (2010). A critical analysis of the Nonaka's model of knowledge dynamics. In *Proceedings of the 2nd European Conference on Intellectual Capital*, ISCTE Lisbon University Institute, Lisbon, Portugal, 29–30 March 2010, pp. 115–120.

Caloghirou, Y., Kastelli, I., & Tsakanikas, A. (2004). Internal capabilities and external knowledge sources: Complements or substitutes for innovative performance? *Technovation, 24*, 29–39.

Caputo, F., Papa, A., Cillo, V., & Giudice, M. (2019). Technology readiness for education 4.0: Barriers and opportunities in the digital world. In Ordóñez de Pablos, P., Lytras, M.D., Zhang, X. & Tai Chui, K. (Eds), *Opening up education for inclusivity across digital economies and societies*, Pennsylvania (USA): IGI Global.

Carayannis, E., & Campbell, D. J. (2010). Triple helix, quadruple helix and quintuple helix and how do knowledge, innovation and the environment relate to each other? A proposed framework for a trans-disciplinary analysis of sustainable development and social ecology. *International Journal of Social Ecology and Sustainable Development, 1*, 41–69.

Carayannis, E.G., & Rakhmatullin, R. (2014). The quadruple/quintuple innovation helixes and smart specialisation strategies for sustainable and inclusive growth in Europe and beyond. *Journal of the Knowledge Economy, 5*(2), 212–239.

Cassiman, B., & Veugelers, R. (2006). In search of complementarity in innovation strategy: Internal R&D and external knowledge acquisition. *Management Science, 52*, 68–82.

Castelfranchi, C. (2007). Six critical remarks on science and the construction of the knowledge society. *Journal of Science Communication, 6*(4), 1–3.

Chesbrough, H. (2003). Open innovation: The new imperative for creating and profiting from technology. Boston, Mass: Harvard Business School Press.

Chesbrough, H. (2006). Open business models: How to thrive in the new innovation landscape. Boston, Mass: Harvard Business School Press.

Chesbrough, H., & Bogers, M. (2014). Explicating open innovation: Clarifying an emerging paradigm for understanding innovation. In H. Chesbrough, W. Vanhaverbeke, & J. West (Eds.), *New frontiers in open innovation*. Oxford: University Press (pp. 3–28).

Chikh, A. (2011). A knowledge management framework in software requirements engineering based on the SECI model. *Journal of Software Engineering and Applications, 4*, 718–728.

Choi, B., Poon, S., & Davis, J. G. (2008). Effects of knowledge management strategy on organizational performance: A complementarity theory-based approach. *Omega-international Journal of Management Science, 36*, 235–251.

Choo, C.W. (2006). *The knowing organization*. New York: Oxford University Press.

Cillo, V., Garcia-Perez, A., Giudice, M., & Vicentini, F. (2019). Blue-collar workers, career success and innovation in manufacturing. *Career Development International, 24*, 529–544.

Cohen, W. M., & Levinthal, D. A. (1989). Innovation and learning: The two faces of R&D. *The Economic Journal, 99*, 569–596.

Cohen, W. M., & Levinthal, D. A. (1990). Absorptive capacity: A new perspective on learning and innovation. *Administrative Science Quarterly, 35*, 128–152

Dhanaraj, C., Lyles, M. A., Steensma, H., & Tihanyi, L. (2004). Managing tacit and explicit knowledge transfer in IJVS: The role of relational embeddedness and the impact on performance. *Journal of International Business Studies, 35*, 428–442.

Del Giudice, M., Carayannis, E., & Maggioni, V. (2017). Global knowledge intensive enterprises and international technology transfer: Emerging perspectives from a quadruple helix environment. *The Journal of Technology Transfer, 42*, 229–235.

Del Giudice, M., Della Peruta, M. R., & Maggioni, V. (2013). Collective knowledge and organizational routines within academic communities of practice: An empirical research on science–entrepreneurs. *Journal of the Knowledge Economy, 4*(3), 260–278.

Del Giudice, M., & Maggioni, V. (2014). Managerial practices and operative directions of knowledge management within inter-firm networks: A global view. *Journal of Knowledge Management, 18*(5), 841–846.

Del Giudice, M., & Straub, D. (2011). Editor's comments: IT and entrepreneurism: An on-again, off-again love affair or a marriage? *MIS Quarterly, 35*(4), iii–viii.

Dombrowski, U., Mielke, T., & Engel, C. (2012). Knowledge management in lean production systems. *Procedia CIRP, 3*, 436–441.

Ebadi, Y. M., & Utterback, J. (1984). The effects of communication on technological innovation. *Management Science, 30*, 572–585.

Enos, M., Kehrhahn, M., & Bell, A. (2003). Informal learning and the transfer of learning: How managers develop proficiency. *Human Resource Development Quarterly, 14*, 369–387.

Erichsen, J. A., Pedersen, A. L., Steinert, M., & Welo, T. (2016). Using prototypes to leverage knowledge in product development: Examples from the automotive industry. *2016 Annual IEEE Systems Conference (SysCon)*, 1–6.

Foss, N. (1996). More critical comments on knowledge-based theories of the firm. *Organization Science, 7*, 519–523.

Gassmann, O., Enkel, E., & Chesbrough, H. (2010). The future of open innovation. *R&D Management, 40*(3), 213–221.

Gibson, C. B., & Birkinshaw, J. (2004). The antecedents, consequences, and mediating role of organizational ambidexterity. *Academy of Management Journal, 47*(2), 209–226.

Grant, R. (1996). Toward a knowledge-based theory of the firm. *Strategic Management Journal, 17*(Suppl 2), 109–122.

Grant, R., & Baden-Fuller, C. (2004). A knowledge accessing theory of strategic alliances. *Journal of Management Studies, 41*, 61–84.

Hedberg, B. (1981). How organizations learn and unlearn. In P. Nystrom & W. H. Starbuck (Eds.), *Handbook of organizational design* (Vol. 1). London: Cambridge University Press.

Herschel, R. T., Nemati, H., & Steiger, D. (2001). Tacit to explicit knowledge conversion: Knowledge exchange protocols. *Journal of Knowledge Management, 5*(1), 107–116.

Hewitt, J., & Scardamalia, M. (1998). Design principles for distributed knowledge building processes. *Educational Psychology Review, 10*, 75–96.

Hicks, R. C., Dattero, R., & Galup, S. D. (2007). A metaphor for knowledge management: Explicit islands in a tacit sea. *Journal of Knowledge Management, 11*(1), 5–16.

Hoe, S. (2006). Tacit knowledge, Nonaka and Takeuchi SECI model and informal knowledge processes. *International Journal of Organization Theory and Behavior, 9*, 490–502.

Howells, J. (1996). *Technology analysis & strategic management*. London: Taylor & Francis.

Hsu, I., & Sabherwal, R. (2011). From intellectual capital to firm performance: The mediating role of knowledge management capabilities. *IEEE Transactions on Engineering Management, 58*, 626–642.

Huang, S., Chen, J., & Liang, L. (2018). How open innovation performance responds to partner heterogeneity in China. *Management Decision, 56*, 26–46.

Iansiti, M., & Clark, K. (1994). Integration and dynamic capability: Evidence from product development in automobiles and mainframe computers. *Industrial and Corporate Change, 3*, 557–605.

Ichijo, K., & Nonaka, I. (2007). *Knowledge creation and management: New challenges for managers*. New York: Oxford University Press.

Inkpen, A. C., & Dinur, A. (1998). Knowledge management processes and international joint ventures. *Organization Science, 9*, 454–468.

Johannessen, J., Olaisen, J., & Olsen, B. (2001). Mismanagement of tacit knowledge: The importance of tacit knowledge, the danger of information technology, and what to do about it. *International Journal of Information Management, 21*, 3–20.

Kedia, B., & Bhagat, R. (1988). Cultural constraints on transfer of technology across nations: Implications for research in international and comparative management. *Academy of Management Review, 13*, 559–571.

Khamseh, H.M., & Jolly, D. (2014). Knowledge transfer in alliances: the moderating role of the alliance type. *Knowledge Management Research & Practice, 12*(4), 409–420.

Kim, L. (1997). *From imitation to innovation: The dynamics of Korea's technological learning*. Cambridge, MA: Harvard Business School Press.

Kinnear, L., & Sutherland, M. (2000). Determinants of organisational commitment amongst knowledge workers. *South African Journal of Business Management, 31*(3), 106–112.

Koh, J., & Kim, Y. (2004). Knowledge sharing in virtual communities: An e-business perspective. *Expert Systems with Applications, 26*, 155–166.

Krogh, G., Nonaka, I., & Aben, M. (2001). Making the most of your company's knowledge: A strategic framework. *Long Range Planning, 34*, 421–439.

Laghi, E., Marcantonio, M. D., Cillo, V., & Paoloni, N. (2020). The relational side of intellectual capital: An empirical study on brand value evaluation and financial performance. *Journal of Intellectual Capital*. https://www.emerald.com/insight/content/doi/10.1108/JIC-05-2020-0167/full/html.

Lane, P. J., & Lubatkin, M. (1998). Relative absorptive capacity and interorganizational learning. *Strategic Management Journal, 19*, 461–477.

Lee, C. C., & Yang, J. (2000). Knowledge value chain. *Journal of Management Development, 19*, 783–794.

Li, Z., Wang, W. M., Liu, G., Liu, L., He, J., & Huang, G. Q. (2018). Toward open manufacturing: A cross-enterprises knowledge and services exchange framework based on blockchain and edge computing. *Industrial Management & Data Systems, 118*, 303–320.

Lianto, B., Dachyar, M., & Soemardi, T. (2018). Continuous innovation: A literature review and future perspective. *International Journal on Advanced Science, Engineering and Information Technology, 8*, 771–779.

March, J. G. (1991). Exploration and exploitation in organizational learning. *Organization Science, 2*(1), 71–87.

Mårtensson, M. (2000). A critical review of knowledge management as a management tool. *Journal of Knowledge Management, 4*(3), 204–216.

Martin, D., & Allen, A. (2013). Intermediaries for open innovation: A competence-based comparison of knowledge transfer offices practices. *Technological Forecasting and Social Change, 80*(1), 38–49.

Menon, T., & Pfeffer, J. (2003). Valuing internal vs. external knowledge: Explaining the preference for outsiders. *Management Science, 49*, 497–513.

Meroño-Cerdán, Á. L., Soto-Acosta, P., & López-Nicolás, C. (2008). How do collaborative technologies affect innovation in SMEs? *International Journal of e-Collaboration, 4*, 33–50.

Mowery, D., & Oxley, J. (1995). Inward technology transfer and competitiveness: The role of national innovation systems. *Cambridge Journal of Economics, 19*, 67–93.

Ngai, E., Jin, C., & Liang, T. (2008). A qualitative study of inter-organizational knowledge management in complex products and systems development. *Wiley-Blackwell: R&D Management, 38*(4), 421–440.

Ngulube, P. (2005). Using the SECI knowledge management model and other tools to communicate and manage tacit indigenous knowledge. *Innovation-the European Journal of Social Science Research, 27*, 21–30.

Nonaka, I. (1991) The knowledge creating company. *Harvard Business Review, 69*, 96–104.

Nonaka, I. (1994). A dynamic theory of organizational knowledge creation. *Organization Science, 5*, 14–37.

Nonaka, I. (2004). The knowledge-creating company. In H. Takeuchi & I. Nonaka (Eds.), *Hitotsubashi on Knowledge Management*. Singapore: Wiley.

Nonaka, I., & Konno, N. (1998). The concept of "Ba": Building a foundation for knowledge creation. *California Management Review, 40*, 40–54.

Nonaka, I., & Konno, N. (2005). The concept of Ba: Building a foundation for knowledge creation. *Knowledge Management: Critical Perspectives on Business and Management, 2*, 53.

Nonaka, I., Konno, N., & Toyama, R. (2001). Emergence of "Ba". A conceptual framework for the continuous and self-transcending process of knowledge creation. In I. Nonaka & T. Nishigushi (Eds.), *Knowledge emergence. Social, technical and evolutionary dimensions of knowledge creation*. Oxford and New York: Oxford University Press, pp. 3–29.

Nonaka, I., & Takeuchi, H. (1995). *The knowledge-creating Company: How Japanese companies create the dynamics of innovation*. Oxford: Oxford University Press.

Nonaka, I., & Takeuchi, H. (2011). The wise leader. *Harvard Business Review, 89*(5), 58–67, 146.

Nonaka, I., & Takeuchi, H. (2019). *The wise company: How companies create continuous innovation*. New York: Oxford University Press

Nonaka, I., Takeuchi, H., & Umemoto, K. (2014). A theory of organizational knowledge creation. *International Journal of Technology Management, 11*, 833–845.

Nonaka, I., Toyama, R., & Konno, N. (2000). SECI, Ba and leadership: A unified model of dynamic knowledge creation. *Long Range Planning, 33*, 5–34.

Nonaka, I., & Toyama, R. (2002). A firm as a dialectical being: Towards a dynamic theory of a firm. *Industrial and Corporate Change, 11*, 995–1009.

Nonaka, I., & Toyama, R. (2003). The knowledge-creating theory revisited: Knowledge creation as a synthesizing process. *Knowledge Management Research & Practice, 1*, 2–10.

Nonaka, I., & Toyama, R. (2005). The theory of the knowledge-creating firm: Subjectivity, objectivity and synthesis. *Industrial and Corporate Change, 14*, 419–436.

Nonaka, I., & Toyama, R. (2007). Strategic management as distributed practical wisdom (phronesis). *Industrial and Corporate Change, 16*, 371–394.

Nonaka, I., Toyama, R., & Byosière, P. (2001). A theory of organizational knowledge creation: Understanding the dynamic process of creating knowledge. In M. Dierkes, A. B. Antel, J. Child, & I. Nonaka (Eds.), *Handbook of organizational learning and knowledge*. Oxford: Oxford University Press, pp. 491–517.

Nonaka, I., Umemoto, K., & Senoo, D. (1996). From information processing to knowledge creation: A Paradigm shift in business management. *Technology in Society, 18*, 203–218.

Nonaka, I., von Krogh, G., & Voelpel, S. (2006) Organizational knowledge creation theory: Evolutionary paths and future advances. *Organization Studies, 27*, 1179–1208.

Nonaka, I., & von Krogh, G. (2009) Tacit knowledge and knowledge conversion: Controversy and advancement in organizational knowledge creation theory. *Organization Science, 20*(3), May–June, 635–652.

Olson, G., & Lyotard, J. (1995). Resisting a discourse of mastery: A conversation with Jean-François Lyotard. *JAC, 15*(3), 391–410.

Penrose, E. (1959). *The theory of growth of the firm*. Oxford: Basil Blackwell.

Polanyi, M. (1958). Personal knowledge: Towards a post-critical philosophy. Chicago: University of Chicago Press.

Polanyi, M. (1967). *The tacit knowledge dimension*. London: Routledge & Kegan Paul.

Powell, W., & Snellman, K. (2004). The knowledge economy. *Review of Sociology, 30*, 199–220.

Reber, A. S. (1989). Implicit learning and tacit knowledge. *Journal of Experimental Psychology: General, 118*(3), 219–235.

Rodan, S. (2002). Innovation and heterogeneous knowledge in managerial contact networks. *Journal of Knowledge Management, 6*, 152–163.

Scully, J., Buttigieg, S., Fullard, A., Shaw, D., & Gregson, M. (2013). The role of SHRM in turning tacit knowledge into explicit knowledge: A cross-national study of the UK and Malta. *The International Journal of Human Resource Management, 24*, 2299–2320.

Scuotto, V., Beatrice, O., Valentina, C., Nicotra, M., Gioia, L., & Briamonte, M. F. (2020). Uncovering the micro-foundations of knowledge sharing in open innovation partnerships: An intention-based perspective of technology transfer. *Technological Forecasting and Social Change, 152*, 119906.

Senker, J. (2005). The contribution of tacit knowledge to innovation. *AI & Society, 7*, 208–224.

Song, J. H., & Chermack, T. J. (2008). A theoretical approach to the organizational knowledge formation process: Integrating the concepts of individual learning and learning organisation culture. *Human Resource Development Review, 7*(4), 424–442.

Terhorst, A., Lusher, D., Bolton, D., Elsum, I., & Wang, P. (2018). Tacit knowledge sharing in open innovation projects. *Project Management Journal, 49*, 19–25.

van den Hooff, B., & de Leeuw van Weenen, F. (2004). Committed to share: Commitment and CMC use as antecedents of knowledge sharing. *Knowledge and Process Management, 11*, 13–24.

von Krogh, G., Nonaka, I., & Aben, M. (2001). Making the most of your company's knowledge: A strategic framework. *Long Range Planning: International Journal of Strategic Management, 34*(4), 421–439.

Vrontis, D., Thrassou, A., Santoro, G., & Papa, A. (2017). Ambidexterity, external knowledge and performance in knowledge-intensive firms. *The Journal of Technology Transfer, 42*, 374–388.

Ye, J., Hao, B., & Patel, P. (2016). Orchestrating heterogeneous knowledge: The effects of internal and external knowledge heterogeneity on innovation performance. *IEEE Transactions on Engineering Management, 63*, 165–176.

Yoshimichi, A. (2011). An examination of the SECI model in Nonaka's theory in terms of the TEAM linguistic framework. *Yamanashi Glocal Studies; Bulletin of Faculty of Glocal Policy Management and Communications, 6*, 21–33.

Zhang, Z., & Huang, F. (2020). An extended SECI model to incorporate inter-organisational knowledge flows and open innovation. *International Journal of Knowledge Management Studies, 11,* 408.

Zahra, S., & George, G. (2002). Absorptive capacity: A review, reconceptualization, and extension. *Academy of Management Review, 27,* 185–203.

Žemaitis, E. (2014). Knowledge management in open innovation paradigm context: High tech sector perspective. *Procedia – Social and Behavioral Sciences, 110,* 164–173.

Wallace, D. P. (2007). *Knowledge management: Historical and cross-disciplinary themes.* Westport, Conn: Libraries Unlimited, pp. 1–14.

Warnier, J.-P. (1999). *Construire la culture matérielle – L'homme qui pensait avec ses doigts,* Parigi: PUF.

Wickes, M., Leslie, A., Lettice, F., Feeney, A. & Everson, P. (2003). *A Perspective of Nonaka's SECI Model From Programme Management: Combining Management Information, Performance Measurement and Information Design.* 4th Organisational Knowledge, Learning and Capabilities Conference, Barcelona.

Wu, I., & Hu, Y. (2018). Open innovation based knowledge management implementation: A mediating role of knowledge management design. *Journal of Knowledge Management, 22,* 1736–1756.

3

RETAINING KNOWLEDGE
Human and Intellectual Capital

Rongbin WB Lee and Vivien WY Shek

Background

According to Andriessen (2007), the first appearance of the term "Intellectual Capital" (IC) in press appeared in Thomas Stewart's article called "Brainpower" in 1991. Four years later, the first meeting in IC management took place to boost the thinking on IC management and knowledge management (KM). Leif Edvinsson, who is a leading expert on IC, was the world's first corporate director of IC at Skandia AFS. Edvinsson (1997) first coined the term "intellectual capital management" and explains IC as "knowledge convertible into value", highlighting that the main objective of IC management is to create and leverage intellectual assets (IA) and to improve the value-creating capabilities of an organization from a strategic perspective.

Since then, there is a worldwide interest in the adoption of IC management. In 2004, the European Commission (EC) had set up a high-level expert group to stimulate the reporting of IC in research-intensive small and medium-sized enterprises (SMEs), government subsidized R& D organizations and universities. In Germany, companies are recommended to include IC in their management report. In Denmark, IC is a requirement to be included in the management reports of all companies. In Austria, IC Reporting has become mandatory for all universities. In Australia, following a mandate from the government, a guiding principle is being developed by the Society of Knowledge Economics aimed at the development and reporting and management of IC. The Ministry of Economy, Trade and Industry of Japan is actively pursuing the voluntary participation of SMEs in intellectual asset-based management.

According to the study of Ocean Tomo (2020) between 1995 and 2015, the share of market value of intangible assets increased from 68% to 84%. COVID-19 has increased this trend by over 90% in companies listed in the Standard & Poor's 500 (S&P 500).

Definition of Intellectual Capital

A new perspective on knowledge assets in value creation emerged in the mid-nineties, namely IC, which is recognized as the foundation of individual, organizational and national competitiveness in the 21st century (Stewart, 1991; Edvinsson and Sullivan, 1996; Edvinsson, 1997; Edvinsson and Malone, 1997a, Wiig, 1997; Ehin, 2000; Nemec Rudež, 2004; Bounfour and Edvinsson, 2005).

DOI: 10.4324/9781003112150-4

Table 3.1 A Summary of Intellectual Capital Definition

Scholar	Definition of Intellectual Capital (IC)
Klein and Prusak (1994)	Intellectual material that has been formalized, captured and leveraged to produce a higher-valued asset.
Bontis (1996)	Intellectual capital that has been defined as the difference between a firm's market value and cost of replacing its assets.
OECD (1996)	Intellectual capital as a value-creation process.
Stewart (1997)	Intellectual capital referred to as the combination of enterprise, comparative advantage and individual knowledge; those, which can be used to create wealth, such as IC and experience, are referred to as intellectual material.
Edvinsson and Malone (1997a)	Intellectual capital can control knowledge, practical experience, organizing technology, customer relationship and professional skill. These can give an enterprise competitive advantage in the market.
Bell (1997)	Intellectual capital is knowledge resource to an organization. It encompasses the model, strategies, unique approaches and mental methodologies organizations use to create, compete, understand, problem-solve and replicate.
Bassi (1997)	A firm's IC, employees' brainpower, know-how, knowledge and processes, are always a source of competitive advantage.
Roos et al. (1997)	An enterprise's IC is the sum of staff knowledge, which can be transformed into an object, such as a trade mark, a registry or a process. All the resources within the organization that can create value but cannot be seen are called IC.
German Federal Ministry of Economics and Labour (2004)	Intellectual capital is the existing knowledge of an organization that is critical to success.

According to Chatzkel (1998), IC is the non-financial resource of an organization. It has been identified as a set of intangibles, including both human and non-human resources or capabilities, that drive organizational performance and value creation (Edvinsson, 1997; Roos and Roos, 1997, Bontis, 1998; Bontis et al., 2000; Ehin, 2000). IC is not only about the people, their knowledge and skills, but also about organizational processes, competences and relationships with customers. Table 3.1 summarizes some of the definitions of IC by different scholars.

Although there is no widely accepted definition of IC, the literature revision shows that IC is essentially related to the knowledge that can be converted into value (Edvinsson and Sullivan, 1996). One widely accepted notion is that IA and intellectual property (IP) are regarded as the subsets of IC. Figure 3.1 shows the relationships between IC, IA and IP.

Sullivan (1998) suggests that IA are created whenever the human capital commits to media any bit of knowledge, know-how or learning. Once "written", the knowledge is codified and defined. IA refers to the codified knowledge that can be used to create value. Examples of IA include plans, procedure, memos, sketches, drawings, blueprints and computer programs. Any items in this list that are legally protected are called IP. IP covers several types of legally recognized rights to intangible things such as ideas (copyrights) or practical implementation (patents). In today's legal systems, IP typically includes at least copyrights, trademarks, patents and trade secrets (Miller and Davis, 1990; Hildreth, 1998).

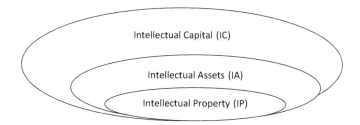

Figure 3.1   Relationships between IC, IA and IP

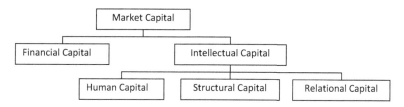

Figure 3.2   A Classification Scheme for IC (Edvinsson and Malone, 1997a)

On the other hand, from other scholars' points of view, IC can be classified into several essential elements, namely, human capital, structural capital and relational capital (Saint-Onge, 1996; Sveiby, 1997; Bontis, 1998; German Federal Ministry of Economics and Labour, 2004). These elements combine and interact with each other and with financial capital (physical things and monetary elements) in ways unique to individual companies to create value which becomes the market capital. Figure 3.2 shows the classification schemes of these three capital elements.

Human Capital

Human interaction is regarded as the critical source of intangible value (O'Donnell et al., 2003). As a result, human capital becomes the primary component of IC (Bontis, 1998; Choo and Bontis, 2002; Edvinsson and Malone, 1997a; Stewart, 1997). According to Hudson (1993), human capital is defined as a combination of four elements, which are genetic inheritances, education, experience and attitudes about life and business. On the organizational level, human capital refers to the source of innovation and strategic renewal (Bontis, 1998). Bontis et al. (2002) further define human capital as simply representing the individual knowledge stock of an organization.

Structural Capital

Roos et al. (1997) indicate that structural capital is what remains in the company when employees go home for the night. According to Cabrita and Vaz (2006), structural capital represents the organization's capabilities to meet its internal and external challenges. It includes infrastructures, information systems, procedures and organizational culture. In other words, structural capital includes all the non-human stockpiles of knowledge and ability in organizations, which include the databases, organizational charts, process manuals, strategies, routines and anything that has a value higher than its material value.

Relational Capital

Relational capital is the knowledge embedded in the relationships with any stakeholder that influences the organization's life (Cabrita and Vaz, 2006). It refers to the external relations with customers, suppliers, partners, networks, regulators and the public. This capital of relationships with stakeholders allows the organization to access critical and complementary resources for building, maintaining and renewing its resources, structures and processes.

The most popularized classification scheme of IC is probably due to the Swedish assurance group Skandia, and its former Director of Intellectual Capital, Leif Edvinsson. Intellectual capital is defined as the possession of knowledge, applied experience, organizational technology, customer relationships and professional skills that provide the company with a competitive edge in the market (Skandia, 1994). Figure 3.3 shows the Skandia classification scheme with two dimensions of knowledge, which are human capital and structural capital (Edvinsson and Malone, 1997b).

Skandia's Intellectual Capital scheme presents a distinction between human capital (implicit) and structural capital (explicit). Human capital refers to the combined knowledge, skill, innovativeness, attitude and ability of the company's individual employees to meet tasks at hand. However, such capital cannot be owned by the company.

On the other hand, structural capital is mainly related to the organization, including the hardware, software, databases, information channels, organizational structure, patents, trademarks, culture, company's values and philosophy as well as everything else of organizational capability that supports those employees' productivity. Structural capital is usually owned or directly controlled by the company, and thus continues working after the employees are gone. Structural capital also includes customer capital, the knowledge embedded in the marketing channels and customer relationships. Saint-Onge (1996) defines customer capital as the value of its franchise, its ongoing relationships with the people or organizations to which it sells. It is obviously valuable, and relatively easy to track its indicators such as market share and customer retention. Prahalad and Ramaswamy (2000) suggest that customers become a new source of competence for the organization. According to Kaplan and Norton (1996, 2004), there is evidence of how employees' satisfaction, motivation and commitment have a positive influence on customer satisfaction, loyalty and retention, leading to a firm's higher productivity. Such a relationship with customers helps reduce costs and increase assurance of supply for the company. Another subset of structural capital is organizational capital, which

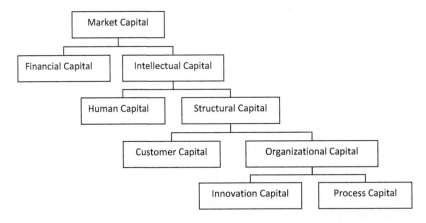

Figure 3.3   Skandia Classification Scheme of Intellectual Capital (Skandia, 1994)

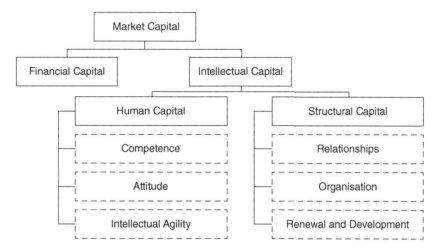

Figure 3.4 The Intellectual Capital Distinction Tree (Roos et al., 1997)

again is divided into innovation capital and process capital. Unlike human capital, structural capital can be owned and therefore traded.

Human capital is the source of innovation and renewal, but smart people alone are not sufficient. In order to make human capital productive structural assets are needed that facilitate the development and exchange of knowledge. From a management perspective, structural capital is more important than human capital because it is the management's responsibility to build organizational assets.

Roos et al. (1997) have different ideas about the classification into human and structural capital, initially suggested by Skandia (1994). They suggest a further division of these two groups into three subcategories as shown in Figure 3.4. Human capital is composed of competence, which is based on knowledge and skills, attitude which is based on motivation, behavior and conduct as well as intellectual agility, which is based on innovation, imitation, adaptation and packaging. Structural capital, in turn, consists of relationships including customers, suppliers, alliance partners, shareholders and other stakeholders, organizations including infrastructure, processes and culture as well as renewal and development.

Compared with the various focuses and content of what is to be found out in a knowledge audit (KA), the IC framework is more comprehensive and covers basically all the elements of the intellectual resources from the soft and invisible (such as culture) to the more visible and codified parts such as IP and know-how database.

Assessment and Measurement of Intellectual Capital

The traditional accounting approach aims to quantify intangible assets of a company in financial terms by using the cost, market or income approach. This monetary approach lacks the ability to identify the strengths and weaknesses of intellectual resources as well as pathways to the creation of future value crucial to managing a firm's IC. Concerning this limitation, different models for IC assessment have been developed.

A taxonomy of existing methods for IC assessment from the European Commission (2005) to reporting IC to augment research, development and innovation in SMEs is shown in Figure 3.5. This chart classifies methods along the *x*-axis ranging from the "classical" valuation of "intellectual assets", such as IP items, toward "modern" value determinations that

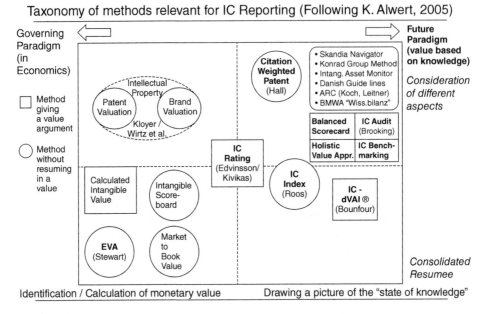

Figure 3.5 A Taxonomy of Existing Methods for IC Assessment (European Commission, 2005).

include financial and non-financial values. The right end of the *x*-dimension represents future knowledge economics concepts. Along the *y*-axis, the methods are positioned using the criterion of whether a method provides calculated summary values or whether it produces a group of IC statement indicators, leaving the end result open for interpretation.

It is noted that that most of the methods are positioned in the upper right quarter. These methods are intended to disclose which factors and elements make an organization use its knowledge to achieve competitive advantage. In contrast, methods positioned at the left side conform to the traditional understanding of knowledge economics, mainly in terms of IP that can be traded or dealt with as economic objects.

Skandia Navigator, Intangible Asset Monitor, IC Rating™ and Balanced Scorecard are the most commonly used methods for IC assessment. Their characteristics are introduced below.

Edvinsson and Sveiby, who are the leading practitioners in the field of IC, developed two different models for IC assessment, which are "Skandia Navigator" (Edvinsson and Malone, 1997a) and "Intangible Asset Monitor" (Sveiby, 1997), respectively aiming to measure the components of IC by using qualitative and quantitative indicators. The Skandia Navigator is established as a widely spread structure model. It facilitates a holistic understanding of the organization and its value creation along five focus areas including, financial, customer, process, human as well as renewal and development (Edvinsson and Malone, 1997a). The Intangible Asset Monitor is a method for measuring intangible assets. It indicates the change and knowledge flows measuring four areas (i.e. growth, renewal/innovation, efficiency and risk/ stability). The indicators correlate with the growth of the asset, its renewal rate, the efficiency at utilizing it and the risk of losing it (Sveiby, 1997).

Another way of measuring IC is IC Rating™ which is a proprietary tool of the company Intellectual Capital Sweden AB (Hofman-Bang and Martin, 2005). IC Rating™ measures and describes the non-financial assets from three different perspectives, namely effectiveness, risk and renewal. It looks at the current effectiveness of the organization, the efforts and abilities to renew and develop itself as well as the risk as the current effectiveness declines. It also tries to benchmark companies as well as units within a company.

Kaplan and Norton (1996) propose the "Balanced Scorecard" as a strategic approach for performance measurement by the use of both financial and non-financial indicators. It considers four perspectives including financial, customer, business process as well as learning and growth. It tries to identify gaps between strategy/high-level financial performance indicators and operational measures for local activities.

Management of Knowledge Assets

The rise of the knowledge-driven economy highlights the fact that the growth and value created in an organization depend on its knowledge rather than on its physical assets. The term "assets" means something that is valuable and in economic terms carries an opportunity cost to acquire and/or to sell. According to Baldrige Glossary HD, the terms knowledge assets, intangibles and intellectual asset or IC are used interchangeably by some researchers as virtual synonyms depending on the disciplines of the authors using them. Knowledge assets are usually used by economists. Intangibles are used predominantly in the accounting field, whereas IC is used by many disciplines in the management literature. While intangibles denote that part of the organizational assets that are recognized by the accounting profession such as IP rights, franchises, licenses and users rights, which are legally protected, IC embraces now a much broader sphere. The term knowledge assets has both a pragmatic meaning, such as when it is used to denote the part of intellectual or intangible assets that can be captured and codified in some form, or has a broader meaning as discussed below.

Definition of Knowledge Assets

According to Baldrige Glossary HD, knowledge assets refer to the accumulated intellectual resources possessed by an organization and its employees in the form of information, policies, ideas, learning, understanding, memory, insights, cognitive and technical skills and capabilities. Building and managing these knowledge assets can help an organization create value for its stakeholders and sustain competitive advantage. Nonaka et al. (2000) define knowledge assets as the inputs, outputs and moderators of the knowledge-creating process, which are the "firm-specific" resources creating values for the firm.

Schiuma and Marr (2001) proposed a Knowledge Asset Map for the structure of a firm's knowledge assets, as shown in Figure 3.6. This map is based on an interpretation of a firm's knowledge assets as being the sum of two organizational resources, namely stakeholder resources and structural resources. Stakeholder resources refer to both internal and external

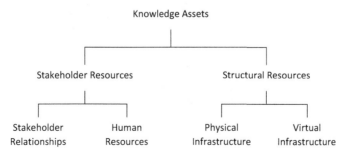

Figure 3.6 Knowledge Asset Map (Schiuma and Marr, 2001)

factors in the organization, including stakeholder relationships and human resources. On the other hand, structural resources are regarded as the constituent elements forming the basis of the organization's processes, including its physical and virtual infrastructure such as culture, routine and practices, as well as IP.

Mapping of Knowledge Assets

Boisot (1987) proposed a classification of knowledge assets by the degree of codification and diffusion, namely the C-D Theory (Figure 3.7). Codification and diffusion define a two-dimensional Culture Space (C-Space) in which the existing social distribution of knowledge and individual communication strategies interact in specifiable ways. Under the two dimensions, codified knowledge refers to that which can easily be set out on paper for transmission while diffused knowledge refers to that which is readily shared.

Under the dichotomized version of codification and diffusion, a 2×2 matrix for typology of knowledge can be produced as shown in Figure 3.8. These are public knowledge, proprietary knowledge, personal knowledge and common sense.

Public knowledge is codified and diffused. It is generally available and subject to checking from many sources giving it a self-correcting character. Textbooks and newspapers, publications and financial records are some examples of public knowledge. Proprietary knowledge is codified, but not yet diffused. It has scarcity value over and above its reproduction costs for which people will pay. Examples are monthly financial reports, mathematical formulae and patentable technical knowledge.

Personal knowledge is an individual's perceptions, insights or intuitions that have not been given a structure. It is neither codified nor diffused. It cannot be stored, examined or evaluated either by its possessor or those around him to whom it is made manifest. Others

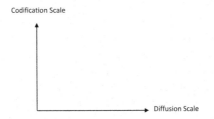

Figure 3.7   Boisot's C-Space

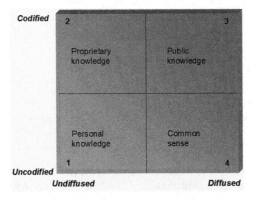

Figure 3.8   Typology of Knowledge in the C-Space (After Boisot, 1998)

can be invited to share the experiences that give rise to personal knowledge, but different intuitions and perceptions will then result. The ability to recognize somebody who has not been seen for many years is one typical example of personal knowledge. Last but not the least, codified and diffused knowledge is common sense. It is built up very slowly through a process of socialization and diffused by osmosis. For instance, we shake hands to express our goodwill when we first see a new friend.

Boisot's I-Space Model

Based on the C-D Theory, Boisot (1998) further proposed the I-Space model which illustrates that knowledge assets can be located within a three-dimensional space representing three different aspects of information (Figure 3.9)

Figure 3.10 shows the representation of three different spaces in the I-Space model. First, the epistemological dimension (the E-space) maps the extent to which information is coded or uncoded and concrete or abstract. Second, the utility dimension (the U-Space) links

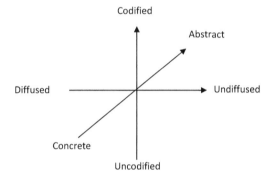

Figure 3.9 Boisot's I-Space Model

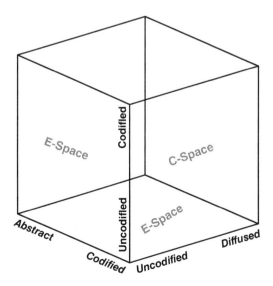

Figure 3.10 Three Spaces in the I-Space Model (After Boisot, 1998)

the diffusibility of a message to its degree of abstraction. Third, the culture dimension (or C-space), which is discussed in the previous section, represents different kinds of knowledge through linking the degree of codification and diffusion of a message.

The dynamic evolution of knowledge in the I-Space is illustrated in Figure 3.11. That in region A of the space is highly personal knowledge of particular events, which, with successive efforts at structuring it, comes to gain in generality. It then becomes sharable and usable by others. If it is controlled in the case of patents or copyright, it then becomes proprietary and can be traded for a position in region B. Over time, proprietary knowledge falling into the public domain becomes diffusible. It moves into region C as public or textbook knowledge. When knowledge is used and applied in a variety of different circumstances, it gets internalized in region D and integrated into people's common sense view of world. After that, individuals possess and convert the shared common-sense world back into personal and cognitive experiences and thus the evolution cycle continues.

The creation and diffusion of new knowledge effectively activate all three dimensions of the I-Space model. Boisot (1998) suggests that they do so in a particular sequence in a "Social Learning Cycle" (SLC) through the six phases of knowledge flow as shown in Figure 3.12:

1   Scanning: insights are gained from generally available (diffused) data.
2   Problem-solving: problems are solved giving structure and coherence to these insights. Knowledge becomes "codified".
3   Abstraction: newly codified insights are generalized to a wide range of situations. Knowledge becomes more "abstract".
4   Diffusion: new insights are shared with a target population in a codified and abstract form. Knowledge becomes "diffused".
5   Absorption: newly codified insights are applied to a variety of situations producing new learning experiences. Knowledge is absorbed and produces learnt behavior and so becomes "uncodified".
6   Impacting: abstract knowledge becomes embedded in concrete practices, rules or behavior patterns. Knowledge becomes "concrete".

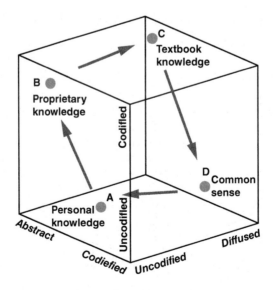

Figure 3.11   The Movement of Knowledge in the I-Space (After Boisot, 1998)

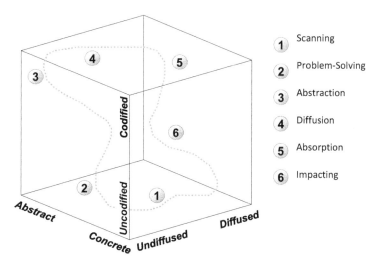

Figure 3.12 Social Learning Cycle of I-Space (After Boisot, 1998)

The dynamics of the SLC reflect the dynamic nature of knowledge. Data is filtered and processed in order to produce meaningful information and this information is then abstracted and codified to produce useful knowledge. The knowledge is then applied in diverse situations creating new experiences in an uncodified form that produces the data for a new cycle of knowledge creation. This is the continual lifecycle of knowledge innovation and application. In other words, knowledge moves through the organizational learning cycle to a new phase at different times in the changing business environment. This results in a change in KM strategies in organizations.

Relationship between Intellectual Capital and Knowledge Management

What is the difference between KM and IC management? Knowledge management should be the first competency that the organization develops for IC management. Meanwhile, IC management and KM not only differ from each other, but also complement one another. Due to the similarities and complementariness, Zhou and Fink (2003) claimed IC management and KM should be linked to achieve added value and must be integrated by combining KM activities with IC elements to maximize the effectiveness.

Wiig (1997) identified that IC management should focus at the strategic and top management levels. Moreover, Edvinsson (1997) and Wiig (1997) also mentioned that ICM focuses on value creation and extraction. However, KM focuses on tactical and operational implementation of knowledge-related activities. In general, KM is concerned with knowledge creation, capture, transformation and use with an ultimate goal of an effectively performing intelligent organization by creating and maximizing IC.

Zhou and Fink (2003) provided an example which explains the relationship between KM and IC as shown in Figure 3.13. In order to maximize relational capital, an organization might decide to develop an outstanding relationship with its customers, which is achieved by superior products and services. Therefore, the organization needs to keep ahead in the market by maintaining a program of continued discovery and innovation. Hence, the organization might focus on developing a knowledge-friendly culture to enable effective

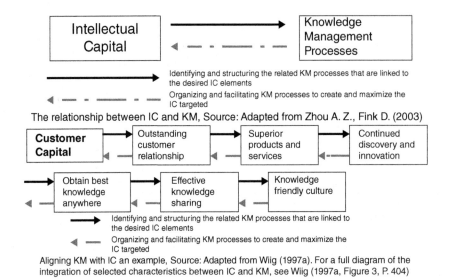

Figure 3.13 Relationship between KM and IC: an Example (Zhou and Fink, 2003)

knowledge sharing as well as develop the best knowledge. By developing the linkages, KM can be applied to contribute to the IC of organizations.

By linking value creation to KM, the objective of maximizing IC can be achieved if knowledge activities are managed systematically and intensely to create value in effective ways. Roos et al. (1997) mentioned that the systematic approach requires management and measurement, so that organizations should be measured as what they want to manage as a part of the management agenda. Hence, Iazzolino and Pietrantonio (2005) recommended the knowledge audit (KA), which can be effectively supporting organizations in managing their own knowledge, consequently achieving targeted objectives, as well as favoring the value creation of an organization in terms of IC valuing. The KA should focus on both the stock nature of knowledge, as it relates to the KM activities within the business processes.

The relation between IC and KM has been further elaborated in a three-dimensional model by Lee et al. (2007a). Such a model relates KM and IC in three main value-added activities in KM, namely (a) to preserve knowledge by accumulating its structural capital through IT and computing systems, (b) to create and acquire new knowledge by nourishing and digging into its human capital and (c) to share its knowledge by building its relational capital through knowledge flow among its employees, partners and customers to get understanding, loyalty, trust and so on. Figure 3.14 shows the intrinsic relationship between KM and IC as well as the value-added process through knowledge conversion, information technology and systems and organizational networks. Despite a lot of research in IC and KM, there have been few research attempts in relating them. An important thrust is to link up IC assessment with the KA in the key quality management processes.

A KA with the integration of both KA and KM Audit (KMA) approaches, which would provide a systematic investigation and evaluation of the 'knowledge health' of an organization, is the first important phase of any KM initiative. Hence, KM would help facilitate and manage knowledge-related activities, to create a knowledge-friendly environment for the aim of IC growth.

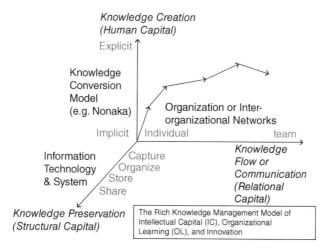

Figure 3.14   The mapping of IC into KM (Lee et al., 2007a)

Knowledge Audit vs. Knowledge Management Audit

According to Hylton (2002b, 2002c), a KA is a systematic and scientific examination and evaluation of the explicit and implicit knowledge resources, including what knowledge exists and where it is, where and how it is being created and who owns it in the company. It is different from a KMA. Mertins et al. (2003) defines the KMA as an investigation on how an organization applies KM within its business processes. The term "KM audit" is used to achieve the following objectives:

i   Uncovering strengths and weaknesses within the actual management of corporate knowledge. It permits an objective assessment of whether KM activities are integrated successfully in the business processes.

ii   Analyzing circumstances, barriers and enablers for KM in various areas, including corporate culture, leadership, collaboration in team work, human resource management, information technology, process technology, process organization and control.

iii   Increasing awareness of KM within the company through the involvement of employees and the internal communication of a detailed audit report.

iv   Designing a roadmap for future KM measures as it clarifies which measures should be taken and where the starting points should be.

v   Collecting measurable data for the control of KM and measurement of the benefits achieved through KM initiatives.

Based on the definitions, KA is not aiming at the complete range of objectives mentioned above, but focusing on the relevant contents of knowledge assets. In other words, KA refers to the process of identifying and naming the existing, as well as missing, organizational knowledge and its flow in an organization. A KMA, however, refers to how knowledge is managed in an organization in the KM process (i.e. knowledge creation, acquisition, retention, distribution, transfer, sharing and re-usage). Organizational strategy, leadership, collaborative and learning culture as well as technology infrastructure should also be taken into consideration.

Reasons for Conducting a Knowledge Audit

There is no doubt about the benefits of KM to an organization. Hylton (2002a, 2002b, 2002c) suggests that most of the KM programs failed because of their failure to identify what knowledge is needed and how it can be managed. Therefore, the importance of KA is seen as the first and critical step prior to the launching of any KM program in organizations (Liebowitz, 1999; Liebowitz et al., 2000; Henczel, 2001; Hylton, 2002a, 2002b, 2002c, 2004; Tiwana, 2002). The reasons for having a KA before implementing any KM strategies are that:

- companies themselves lack knowledge about KM
- they do not know what knowledge they possess and its "health status" in the organization
- they do not know everything that their staff know or how their staff work with each other

Large amounts of valuable explicit and implicit knowledge are embedded in a company. If it does not know what knowledge it already has and what knowledge is important, resources will be wasted on developing tools or policies in unimportant areas. Therefore, KM strategies formulated are not suited to the real situation and resources are spent, but no return is realized. It is a risk for the company to implement KM strategies before conducting any KA. Besides, many cases show that many companies do not know what knowledge their staff have and how their staff work. It is impossible for them to formulate appropriate strategy if they do not really understand the working behavior of their staff.

Knowledge audit and analysis approaches and tools are mostly used by companies to plan where their new KM efforts should be focused. This guides companies toward an informed view of KM. The two reasons that a KA is essential before KM implementation are:

- We need to know what we know and what we do not know
- We need to know what benefits KM can confer

As a result, KAs are indispensable to the success of KM.

Capturing of Critical Knowledge in Workplaces

The effective management of an organization's knowledge assets has been recognized as being a critical success factor in business performance. A systematic, contextual and action-oriented KA and KMA integrated audit methodology called "STOCKS" (Strategic Tool to Capture Critical Knowledge and Skills) has been hence developed by the Knowledge Management Research Centre of the Hong Kong Polytechnic University. Based on input from both structured questionnaires and interactive workshops, STOCKS (Lee et al., 2007b) can map out the organization's knowledge assets in an open and participative manner.

Various questionnaires were compiled for respondents to fill in the explicit and tacit knowledge items, the flow and the ratings according to several criteria by staff inside the specific business processes. Workshops were also held for the participants who come from different levels and clustered into one group for consolidating different knowledge items. The follow-up elements used SWOT analysis after KA results to evaluate the KM strategy in terms of the KMA approach.

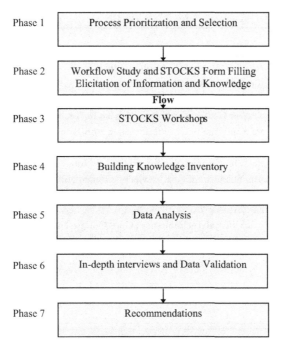

Figure 3.15   The Seven Phases of STOCKS Knowledge Audit Approach (Shek et al., 2007b)

Phases for STOCKS Knowledge Audit

STOCKS, which is a new systematic knowledge audit methodology (with integration of both KA and KMA approaches), can address the shortcomings of the traditional approach of KAs. Lee et al. (2007b) describe STOCKS composing of seven phases as shown in Figure 3.15.

The first phase involves the selection and prioritization of critical business processes, then a study of the workflow of selected processes and collection of the data through the STOCKS form filling. After holding a STOCKS workshop and building the knowledge inventory, data analysis can be conducted and reported. In-depth interviews and data validation are followed by recommendations of KM strategies. STOCKS is a structured and contextual knowledge-inquiring tool, and the data and information of each task of the completed process is collected through the filling in of eight different designed forms as shown in Table 3.2.

Comparison of STOCKS to Other Knowledge Audit Methods

Lee et al. (2007b) emphasized that the objective of a workshop is for the internal staff of a business process "to consolidate and validate the data collected from the completed STOCKS forms". A STOCKS schema should be prepared before conducting the workshop. As shown in Figure 3.16, the schema contains the fields which include a selected business process, the tasks inside the process, industrial technology, documents and tacit knowledge. All workshop participants have to agree on the terminology of the knowledge items and staff names,

Table 3.2 Eight Various Designed STOCKS (Shek, 2007a)

Form No.	Form Name
Form 1	Information Technology Tools and Platforms
Form 2	Document Received/Retrieved
Form 3	Document Sent/Submitted/Forwarded/Uploaded/Produced
Form 4a	People You Usually Consult for Advice on Technical Implicit Knowledge
Form 4b	People You Usually Consult for Advice on Non-Technical Implicit Knowledge
Form 5a	People Who Contact You for Advice on Technical Implicit Knowledge
Form 5b	People Who Contact You for Advice on Non-Technical Implicit Knowledge
Form 6	Document and Implicit Knowledge Owned and Used by You Only
Form 7	Extra Knowledge Possessed by You Related to Your Industry but Not Used in Your Present Post
Form 8	List of Industrial Technologies /Core Competences
Practical Hints for Describing Implicit Knowledge	

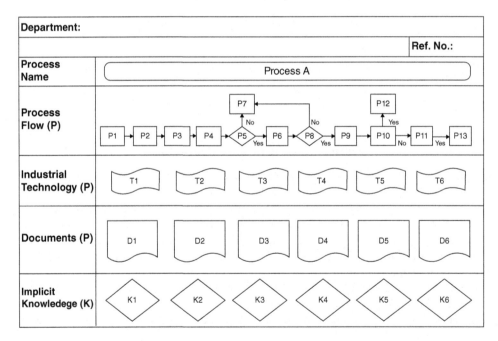

Figure 3.16 Template of STOCKS Workshop Schema (Lee et al., 2007b)

as well as the relationship and hierarchy of such items, in order to control the vocabulary, thesaurus and taxonomy.

After the workshop, explicit and tacit knowledge inventories, stakeholders analysis, identification of critical documents and knowledge workers, distribution of explicit and tacit knowledge in each task and even the mapping of knowledge flows and document flows can be also included in the output from the STOCKS KA methodology.

According to the findings, an in-depth interview with selected staff is conducted for detailed data validation. The analysis and results should be also based on the interview, with

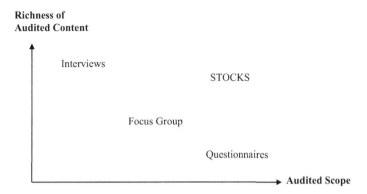

Figure 3.17   Comparison of STOCKS with Traditional Knowledge Audit Methods (Shek, 2007a)

the aim of getting pertinent information and gaining more understanding of the underlying story before giving any recommendations to the organization for implementing KM strategies. Therefore, STOCKS can help management to visualize and externalize the existing knowledge environment in the organization. By adopting the STOCKS KA methodology, information is collected though questionnaire surveys, interviews and a small group workshop. Shek (2007a, 2007b) showed a comparison of STOCKS with traditional KA methods in terms of audited scope and richness of the information collected, which means the breadth and depth of issues that can be explored. Figure 3.17 shows the comparison of STOCKS with traditional KA methods.

Shek (2007b) also stated that STOCKS is an effective way to collect a large amount of information from participants at different levels of the organization. It enables a larger scale of study when compared with interviews, which only cover a limited sample size of participants. Moreover, STOCKS workshops provide a chance to a group of participants to communicate systematically with their peers, so as to share their knowledge of the business process in an interactive manner. It helps to promote team learning and generate innovative ideas among team members. Last but not least, STOCKS's interactive nature enables participants to play different roles. Since STOCKS involves parties from different levels, it enhances the KM awareness in the organization as a whole.

References

Andriessen, D. (2007). Combining Design-Based Research and Action Research to Test Management Solutions. Paper presented at the 7th World Congress Action Learning, Action Research and Process Management, Groningen, 22–24 August, 2007.

Bassi, L.J. (1997). Harnessing the Power of Intellectual Capital. *Training and Development*, 51(12), 25–30.

Bell, C.R. (1997). Intellectual Capital. *Executive Excellence*, 14(1), 15–26.

Boisot, M.H. (1987). *Information and Organizations: The Manager as Anthropologist*. Fontana, London.

Boisot, M.H. (1998). *Knowledge Assets: Securing Competitive Advantage in the Information Economy*. Oxford University Press, Oxford.

Bontis, N. (1996). There is Price on your Head: Managing Intellectual Capital Strategically. *Ivey Business Quarterly*, Summer.

Bontis, N. (1998). Intellectual capital: An Exploratory Study that Develops Measures and Models. *Management Decision*, 36(2), 63–76.

Bontis, N., Crossan, M. M. and Hulland, J. (2002). Managing an organizational learning system by aligning stocks and flows. *Journal of Management Studies*, 39(4), 437–467.

Bontis, N., Keow, W.C. and Richardson, S. (2000). Intellectual Capital and Business Performance in Malaysian Industries. *Journal of Intellectual Capital*, 1(1), 85–100.

Bounfour, A. and Edvinsson, L. (2005). *Intellectual Capital for Communities – Nations, Regions, and Cities.* Butterworth-Heinemann, Oxford.

Cabrita, M. and Vaz, J. (2006). Intellectual Capital and Value Creation: Evidence from the Portuguese Banking Industry. *The Electronic Journal of Knowledge Management*, 4(1), 11–20.

Chatzkel, J. (1998). Measuring and Valuing Intellectual Capital: From Knowledge Management to Knowledge Measurement. http://www.free-press.com/journals/knowledge

Choo, C.W. and Bontis, N. (2002). *The Strategic Management of Intellectual Capital and Organizational Knowledge.* Oxford University Press, Inc, New York.

Edvinsson, L. (1997). Developing Intellectual Capital at Skandia. *Long Range Planning*, 30(3), 366–373.

Edvinsson, L. and Malone, M. (1997a). *Intellectual Capital: Realising Your Company's True Value by Finding Its Hidden Brainpower.* Harper Collins, New York.

Edvinsson, L. and Malone, M. (1997b). *Intellectual Capital: The Proven Way to Establish Your Company's Real Value by Measuring its Hidden Brainpower.* Piatkus Books, London.

Edvinsson, L. and Sullivan, P. (1996). Developing a Model for Managing Intellectual Capital. European. *Management Journal*, 14(4), 356–364.

Ehin, C. (2000). *Unleashing Intellectual Capital.* Butterworth-Heinemann, Boston.

European Commission (2005) RICARDIS: *Reporting Intellectual Capital to Augment Research, Development and Innovation in SMEs.* http://ec.europa.eu/invest-in-research/pdf/download_en/2006-2977_web1.pdf

German Federal Ministry of Economics and Labour (2004.) *Intellectual Capital Statement – Made in Germany: Guideline.* German Federal Ministry of Economics and Labour, Berlin.

Henczel, S. (2001). *The Information Audit: A Practical Guide.* K.G. Saur, München.

Hildreth, R.B. (1998). *Patent Law: A Practitioner's Guide.* Practising Law Institute, New York.

Hofman-Bang, P. and Martin, H. (2005) IC Rating. E-mentor, Warsaw School of Economics. No. 4(11). Available at http://www.e-mentor.edu.pl/eng

Hudson, W.J. (1993). *Intellectual Capital: How to Build It, Enhance It., Use It.* Wiley, Louisville, KY, USA.

Hylton, A. (2002a). *A KM Initiative is Unlikely to Succeed Without a Knowledge Audit.* http://www.knowledgeboard.com/library/the_need_for_knowledge_audits.pdf

Hylton, A. (2002b). *Knowledge Audit Must Be People-Centered and People Focused.* http://www.knowledgeboard.com/library/people_centered_knowledge_audit.pdf

Hylton, A. (2002c). *Measuring & Assessing Knowledge-Value & the Pivotal Role of the Knowledge Audit.* http://www.knowledgeboard.com/cgi-bin/item.cgi?id=1172

Hylton, A. (2004). *The Knowledge Audit is First and Foremost an Audit.* http://www.annhylton.com/siteContents/writings/writings-home.htm

Iazzolino, G. and Pietrantonio, R. (2005). An Innovative Knowledge Audit Methodology: Some First Results from an Ongoing Research in Southern Italy, Proceedings of International Conference on Knowledge Management, University of New Zealand.

Kaplan, R.S. and Norton, D.P. (1996). Strategic learning & the Balanced Scorecard. *Strategy & Leadership*, 24(5), 18–24.

Kaplan, R.S. and Norton, D.P. (2004). Measuring the Strategic Readiness of Intangible Assets. *Harvard Business Review*, 82(10), 52–63.

Klein, D.A. and Prusak, L. (1994). *Characterizing Intellectual Capital.* Center for Business Innovation, Ernst & Young LLP Working Paper, Cambridge, MA.Lee, W.B., Cheung, C.F., Tsui, E. and Kwok, S.K., (2007a). Collaborative Environment and Technologies for Building Knowledge Work Teams in Network Enterprises. *International Journal of Information Technology and Management*, 6(1), 5–22.

Lee, W.B., Shek, W.Y. and Cheung, C.F. (2007b). Auditing and Mapping the Knowledge Assets of Business Processes – An Empirical Study. *Proceedings of Second International Conference on Knowledge Science, Engineering and Management (KSEM'2007)*, November 28–30, Melbourne, Australia, pp. 11–16

Liebowitz, J. (Ed.) (1999). *The Knowledge Management Handbook.* CRC Press, Boca Raton, FL.

Liebowitz, J., Rubenstein-Montano, B., McCaw, D., Buchwalter, J. and Browning, C. (2000). The Knowledge Audit. *Knowledge and Process Management*, 7(1), 3–10.

Mertins, K., Heisig, P. and Jens, V. (2003). *Knowledge Management Concepts and Best Practices*, Springer, New York.

Miller, A.R. and Davis, M.H. (1990*). Intellectual Property: Patents, Trademarks, and Copyrights in a Nutshell*. 2nd ed. West Publishing, St. Paul, MN.

Nemec Rudež, H. (2004). Intellectual Capital - A Fundamental Change in Economy: A Case Based on Service Industries. Intellectual Capital and Knowledge Management. *Proceedings of the 5th International Conference of the Faculty of Management Koper*, University of Primorska, Portorož, Slovenia. http://www.fm-kp.si/zalozba/ISBN/961-6486-71-3.htm

Nonaka, I., Toyama, R. and Konno, N. (2000). SECI, Ba and Leadership: A Unified Model of Dynamic Knowledge Creation. *Long Range Planning*, 33(1), 5–34.

Ocean Tomo (2020). Available at: https://www.oceantomo.com/intangible-asset-market-value-study/ (accessed on 30 January 2022).O'Donnell, D. (2003). Human Interaction: The Critical Source of Intangible Value. *Journal of Intellectual Capital*, 4(1), 82–99.

O'Donnell, D., O'Regan, P., Coates, B., Kennedy, T., Keary, B. and Berkery, G. (2003). Human interaction: The Critical Source of Intangible Value. *Journal of Intellectual Capital*, 4(1), 82–99.

OECD (1996). *Measuring What People Know*. Paris.

Prahalad, C.K. and Ramaswamy, V. (2000). Co-opting Customer Competence. *Harvard Business Review*, Jan–Feb, pp. 79–87.

Roos, G. and Roos, J. (1997). Measuring Your Company's Intellectual Performance. *Long Range Planning*, 30(3), 413–426.

Roos, J., Roos, G., Dragonetti, N.C. and Edvinsson, L. (1997). *Intellectual Capital: Navigating in the New Business Landscape*. Macmillan Press, London.

Saint-Onge, H. (1996). Tacit Knowledge the Key to the Strategic Alignment of Intellectual Capital. *Planning Review*, 24(2), 10–16

Schiuma, G. and Marr, B. (2001). *Managing Knowledge in e-Businesses: The Knowledge Audit Cycle. Profit with People*, Russell Publishing, London, in Deloitte & Touche.

Shek, W.Y. (2007a). Auditing Organizational Knowledge Assets: Case Study in a Power Company of Hong Kong, Department of Industrial and Systems Engineering, The Hong Kong Polytechnic University.

Shek, W.Y. (2007b). Mapping and Auditing Organizational Knowledge through an Interactive STOCKS Methodology. *International Journal of Learning and Intellectual Capital*, 6(1/2), 71–102.

Skandia (1994). *Visualizing Intellectual Capital in Skandia*. Supplement to Skandia's 1994 Annual Report, Skandia, Stockholm.

Stewart, T.A. (1991). *Brainpower: How Intellectual Capital is Becoming America's Most Valuable Asset*. Fortune, No. 3, 44–60.

Sullivan, P.H. (1998). *Profiting from Intellectual Capital: Extracting Value from Innovation*. John Wiley and Sons, New York.

Sveiby, K.E. (1997). *The New Organizational Wealth: Managing and Measuring Knowledge-Based Assets*. Berrett-Koehler, San Francisco.

Tiwana, A. (2002). *The Knowledge Management Toolkit: Orchestrating IT, Strategy, and Knowledge Platforms*, 2nd Ed, Prentice Hall, Upper Saddle River, New Jersey.

Wiig, K.M. (1997). Integrating Intellectual Capital and Knowledge Management. *Long Range Planning*, 30(3), 99–405.

Zhou, A.Z. and Fink, D. (2003). The Intellectual Capital Web: A Systematic Linking of Intellectual Capital and Knowledge Management. *Journal of Intellectual Capital*, 4(1), 34–48.

4

TOWARDS A BETTER UNDERSTANDING OF STRATEGIC KNOWLEDGE DYNAMICS

A Dynamic Capability Exploratory Study

*Véronique Ambrosini, Naerelle Dekker and
Krishna Venkitachalam*

Introduction

Teece, Pisano and Shuen (1997) introduced the dynamic capability (DC) perspective to explain why firms in rapidly changing environments experience performance differences. It addresses how firms can utilise their DCs to transform their resource base so that they sustain or enhance their competitive advantage (Teece, 2007; Ambrosini & Bowman, 2009; Wilden, Devinney, & Dowling, 2016; Schilke, Hu, & Helfat, 2018). One of these resources is knowledge (Grant, 1996). The argument that knowledge is a fundamental resource, as it is a source of competitive advantage is solidly established (Spender, 1996; Oh & Han, 2020). Following Venkitachalam and Willmott (2015) and Barley, Treem and Kuhn (2018)'s argument, we consider knowledge strategy dynamics by adopting a DC approach, and we expand our appreciation of knowledge creation processes. This is an important endeavour as "knowledge management scholarship has paid little attention to mechanisms by which organisations create new knowledge" (Barley et al., 2018, p. 286). Hence, it is critical to understand how firms can continually refresh their knowledge base so that they can innovate by continuously creating knowledge and remain competitive in the marketplace.

We need to understand better the knowledge strategy dynamics of firms, i.e. how they acquire and utilise their knowledge and align it with the changing environment (Venkitachalam & Willmott, 2015). To advance the literature, there is a need for a better appreciation of the practice of strategic knowledge management (SKM) (Venkitachalam & Willmott, 2015; Barley et al., 2018). We address this shortcoming by reporting here on a fine-grained qualitative analysis of a case study: 'Snack-Co'. It is a firm that has been able to sustain over time its competitive advantage in the highly competitive Australian Snack Food-Manufacturing industry. Constant change and uncertainty, which can drastically alter the competitive position of food-manufacturing firms, characterise this industry. Yet despite the context, the company has remained successful. Based on our findings, we contribute to the knowledge

DOI: 10.4324/9781003112150-5

management scholarship by addressing the critical question of *how do firms facilitate knowledge creation in an Australian Snack food-manufacturing firm?* We bring some insights into how DCs underpin knowledge creation. Second, we show that an adaptive learning culture is one of the dynamics that influences effective SKM of a firm.

Theoretical Background

Strategic Knowledge Management

The strategic value of knowledge is well established. It is arguably the most strategically significant resource of the firm (Grant, 1996; Martelo-Landroguez, Cegarra Navarro, & Cepeda-Carrión, 2019). While knowledge management, generally speaking, is about accumulating, creating, applying knowledge and capturing value from knowledge (Liebowitz, 1999; Mirzaie, Javanmard, & Hasankhani, 2019), SKM is concerned with how firms harness their knowledge to both influence and respond to their environment (Venkitachalam & Willmott, 2015, 2017). This means that SKM is critical to a firm's prosperity and long-term survival.

Coming to the knowledge management literature, two fundamental processes are identified: knowledge creation and knowledge transfer (von Krogh, Nonaka, & Aben, 2001). Knowledge creation is a dynamic process, and signals that organisational knowledge is linked intrinsically to a firm's macro and micro-environment (Nonaka, Toyama, & Hirata, 2008). It is also the essence of innovation (Nonaka, 1994; Cho & Pucik, 2005) as innovation is often part of a firm's strategic agenda. Without innovation, firms can hardly cope with the changing dynamics and external pressure in the environment, be it heightened competition or new demands from customers or clients. This is why knowledge creation is critical to the success of SKM.

The literature has addressed knowledge creation in several ways. Nonaka and Takeuchi's (1995) conceptual SECI model (socialisation; externalisation; combination; internalisation) is arguably at the cornerstone of this literature. It concentrates on the processes of knowledge transfer and conversion from tacit to explicit knowledge in organisations (a focus that is not without its criticisms; see Tsoukas & Vladimirou, 2001). For more on the knowledge creation process, studies (such as Nonaka & Toyama, 2003; Nonaka & Toyama, 2005; Nonaka & Hirose, 2015) have provided a deeper perspective and understanding. For example, Nonaka and Toyama (2003, p. 1) illuminate that "knowledge creation is conceptualized as a dialectical process, in which various contradictions are synthesized through dynamic interactions among individuals, the organisation, and the environment". Moreover, knowledge creation can be linked to "mutual learning based on individual experiences" that is reminiscent of the personalisation approach to SKM (Venkitachalam & Willmott, 2015, p. 346).

Scholarly work has also included the role of organisational design, social network, team composition, technology and tools to mention a few (see Argote & Miron-Spektor, 2011). However, there is still little attention to the mechanisms underpinning new knowledge creation (Argote & Miron-Spektor, 2011; Barley et al., 2018), notably given the ongoing environmental dynamism firms face. So, firms cannot remain fixated on a certain knowledge, as without creating knowledge, they may become irrelevant to their changing environment and their competitive advantage will be eroded. To avoid doing so, firms must focus on the dynamics of their SKM.

Dynamic Capability View

There is a range of theoretical foundations of knowledge management (Baskerville & Dulipovici, 2006). Amongst them is strategic management, and specifically the DC view. The DC perspective is an extension of the resource-based view of the firm (Barney, 1991). In the early 1990s, the resource-based view came under scrutiny for its lack of emphasis on market dynamism (Wang & Ahmed, 2007; Schilke et al., 2018). The DC perspective (Teece et al., 1997; Ambrosini, Bowman, & Collier, 2009) explains why over time and despite significant challenges in the external environment firms thrive and outrival their competitors. DCs are "the capacity of an organisation to purposefully create, extend, or modify its resource base" (Helfat et al., 2007, p. 1).

In environments characterised by constant change and uncertainty, resources are more homogeneous and are likely to be easily replicated by competitors. So, the value generated by a resource is not expected to last a long time (Teece, 2000). To overcome the constraints imposed by the external environment, a firm has to create, extend and modify its existing resource base to generate a new set of valuable resources, which then can be used to retain or improve its competitive position. We also need to note that managerial perceptions of environment dynamism are determining factors in the choice of whether or not to deploy DCs (Adner & Helfat, 2003). The literature also emphasises the role of managerial agency in the creation and deployment of DC (Helfat & Martin, 2015). Managers must orientate the business in the direction seen fit for the external environment (Augier & Teece, 2009). Without an appropriate managerial vision, a firm cannot effectively align its DCs with the organisation's intended strategic objectives (Zahra, Sapienza, & Davidsson, 2006).

Teece's (2007) framework pinpoints that a DC has three dimensions: sensing opportunities, seizing opportunities and transforming the resource base. Sensing is akin to opportunity recognition thanks to scanning and interpreting the environment, hence knowledge and information acquisition is core to sensing. Seizing is about decision making and choosing the opportunities to follow and delivering value. Transforming is about integrating resources and transforming the resource base, hence knowledge management is critical to the resource modification process. This means that DCs and SKM are interrelated in their focus on the dynamics of knowledge, developing knowledge, seizing opportunities and addressing the environmental landscape. This suggests that the study of DCs should afford us to understand better the underdeveloped area of the dynamics of knowledge creation.

Research Design

We adopted a constructivist perspective in this study. It focuses on the full complexities of human interpretations, by assuming that people develop subjective understandings of their experiences, through language and shared ideas (Creswell, 2002; Eriksson & Kovalainen, 2008). Since knowledge about DCs is driven by managerial perceptions of the internal and external environment, this is an appropriate stance, and so is the use of a qualitative approach as they provide "detailed descriptions of what processes are involved, the role of management, the reconfiguration of the DCs, and the interaction with the environment" (Easterby-Smith et al., 2009, p. S6). It is also so because Edmondson and McManus (2007) maintain that when the understanding of a phenomenon is nascent, as our understanding of knowledge creation is (Barley et al., 2018), with many open-ended questions needing to be answered, qualitative research methods are most appropriate.

Regarding the case study background, Snack-Co operates in the highly competitive Australian Snack Food-Manufacturing Industry. It has over time, been able to sustain a competitive advantage. Hence it was considered to be a suitable case to study DCs. The Australian Snack Food-Manufacturing Industry is responsible for the production of snack food products, such as potato chips, corn chips, nuts, pretzels, health bars or chocolate bars, to service wholesalers and retailers (IBISWorld, 2011). At present, the Industry consists of several players; however, Frito-Lay Australia Holdings Pty Limited and Snack Foods Limited enjoy significant market share. Frito-Lay Australia is the industry leader with a market share of 35.8%. Its industry brand names include Doritos, Lays and Cheetos. Snack Foods Limited accounts for 14.6% of the total market. Its industry brand names include Kettle Chips, Thins, Cheezels, Tasty Jacks, French Fries, CC's and Samboy. The remaining 49.6% of the industry comprises other smaller players. This includes Nestle Australia Ltd (3.5%), Australian Health & Nutrition Association Ltd (2.3%) and Kellogg Australia Holdings Pty Ltd (2.0%) (IBISWorld, 2011). The Industry is also an important aspect of the Australian economy. Revenue in 2011 generated $2.9 billion and profit amounted to $151.9 million.

In recent years, this industry has undergone significant changes. This is primarily the result of the increasing power of the two supermarket giants Woolworths and Coles, shifts in globalisation and changing societal attitudes of consumers towards snack food products. Woolworths and Coles are the largest suppliers of supermarket groceries in Australia, with a combined market share of 71.0%. As a consequence, the two supermarket giants contribute to a large proportion of this Industry's revenue (IBISWorld, 2011). According to Wells (2012, p. 1), "More than half of all the money Australian households spent on food each year – including groceries, restaurant and takeaway meals – goes into the coffers of supermarket giants Coles and Woolworths" (p. 1).

We interviewed eight Snack-Co top-level managers, with a wealth of experience, could be drawn on and who belonged to separate divisions within the company. The selected interviewees represented the company's marketing (three managers, labelled manager D/E/G in the findings), operations (two managers, labelled manager A/H in the findings), finance (one manager, labelled manager B in the findings) and business development (two managers, labelled manager C/F in the findings) divisions. The interviews were conducted face-to-face at the company's headquarters. Each lasted between 20 and 45 minutes. We collected data using semi-structured interviews. The questions asked were open-ended in nature and were presented to respondents in a fluid, conversational like manner (Tharenou et al., 2007) (see Table 4.1). This method was chosen as it provides an opportunity for participants to clarify and discuss in depth the issues that are pertinent to the research that otherwise may be difficult to obtain in a questionnaire format (Eriksson & Kovalainen, 2008). This allows participants to provide insight into the complexity of the research problem presented in the study (Yin, 2003).

The interviews were transcribed in full. To analyse the data, the editing approach to content analysis was chosen because of its strong interpretative and inductive focus, which is best suited for exegesis and generating new insight (Tharenou et al., 2007). A preliminary analysis of the data was first undertaken, which involved reading each interview transcript at least twice in its entirety. This is important in the initial phase of analysis, as it allows the researcher to get an overture in understanding of the key ideas expressed by the participants (Creswell, 2002). Once reviewed, all the interview transcripts were coded for analysis. Codes are labels that give meaning to segments of the text. They are often generated through the isolation of key themes within the text. This allows the researcher to organise and easily retrieve data applicable to research questions (Creswell, 2002).

Table 4.1 Examples of interview questions

The Australian snack food industry has undergone significant changes in recent years, which has made it more difficult to compete for the long term. What do you believe are some of the major issues confronting Australian snack food manufacturers?

Why do you think this is the case?

What do you think makes your company unique? Why?
What do you perceive as the cause of your success?
Why do you regard this as a cause of your success?
In what ways does this help you maintain an advantage over your competitors?
What aspects of your business are most important to achieving this?
Do you proactively try to change the way you do things in your company because of the changing environment?
How? Can you give examples?
When did you last do so? Did you use the same response as before?
Is there a source of advantage that you used to have but do not have anymore?
Why was this advantage lost?

Table 4.2 Example of the coding process

First-order code:

Managerial perceptions of the external environment

Second-order code:

Fluctuating world commodity prices:
I think one of the other things is we are becoming much more global as a business and when you look at the range of products that are becoming more and more accessible from lower-cost countries are sourcing becoming more and more prevalent in the marketplace so that is one of our pressures
– Top Level Manager KR
The power of Woolworths and Coles:
The other external factor I would say is the retailer competition within the Australian environment, obviously Woolworths and Coles are a significant per cent of the market and they have a lot of marketing power
– Top Level Manager MS

Coding of the data began by generating first-order codes for the major themes that stood out from the text. This was necessary to categorise the major themes and key ideas expressed by the participants. The data corresponding to each first-order code was then explored further to derive the underlying meanings behind the text. This subsequently led the researcher to generate second-order codes (see Table 4.2 for an example of the coding process).

Findings and Analysis

Managerial Perceptions of a Changing Environment

To explore DCs, we had to first ascertain managers' perceptions of the external environment and whether they identified a need for change, since no DCs would be deployed to change the resource base if no change would have been observed (Barreto, 2010; Schilke et al. 2018). The changes were multi-fold. They related, for instance, to the influx of cheaper foreign products into the market or the marketing power of the giant retailers Woolworths and Coles and their control and influence over Snack-Co's strategic objectives. The two retailers have become stridently sophisticated in the way they operate, with each having the resolve to exploit and expunge the market share of its competitors through increased offerings of its own brands.

We are being influenced by what we would call cheaper imports… that is one thing that is very high on our agenda.

(top manager F/ business development)

The other external factor I would say is the retailer competition within the Australian environment. Obviously Woolworths and Coles are a significant per cent of the market, and they have a lot of marketing power.

(top manager B/ finance)

Other environmental pressures included the difficulty of staying relevant to today's consumers, given the shifts in their lifestyle, well-being and attitudes or the volatile world commodity prices. Due to price fluctuations, it becomes increasingly difficult for the company to set the price of their products for the end-consumer. In the absence of an alternative and viable choice, they are compelled to bear the costs of these changes, which thereby pose a detriment to their short- and long-term profitability.

The consumer's becoming more picky with healthy snacks, they want more convenience, and they want to be able to eat on the go.

(top manager H/ operations)

Today's consumer I think is quite different to the type of consumer that existed 10 to 20 years ago. There's much greater emphasis on better for you or healthier options

(top manager A/ operations)

Then more recently in the last five years you've also got commodity volatility, which in a lot of categories [of product] has – you know the ability to impact your profitability short and long term quite significantly.

(top manager E/ marketing).

From this, it can be seen that the managers perceive the need for change so that they address their rapidly changing external environment. Next, we explore how in practice they did so and deploy DCs enabling the creation of knowledge to compete successfully for the future.

The Dynamic Capability Process

Our findings reveal that Snack-Co managers perceive that the organisation's comprehension of what is happening in its business environment (e.g. changes in consumers' taste) and its ability to grasp the opportunities this affords in return as the company's major strengths. This drives innovation and change. This reflects that the organisation is using a DC to renew its resource base. It senses what is happening in the environment, thanks to its surveillance of the market, seizes the opportunity and transforms its current capabilities. These are as seen earlier in the three stages of DCs (Teece, 2007). It also reflects that DCs are innovation based (Pavlou & Sawy, 2011).

Developing innovative offerings that capture people's imaginations and encourages new and different products to be purchased and tried form a vital part of what they do.

> *I think the thing that's most unique around us is we have a very strong drive to innovate it is something that we see as critical for our success and our survival.*
>
> (top manager A/operations).

> *We've always been as a business very innovative when you think about some of the brands that have launched this year – Fantastic Wonders [pseudonym for the brand] would be amongst the most successful launches that certainly the ANZ business has delivered in the last 10 years and Melvida [pseudonym] earlier this year so I think it's about being innovative and being on the front foot*
>
> (top manager D/ marketing)

Once an opportunity is sensed, to bring repeatedly new products into the marketplace, the company relies on its innovative capability (Intan-Soraya & Chew, 2010). This means it must engage in learning to find new solutions and create new knowledge (Pavlou & Sawy, 2011). This innovative capability allows the firm to swiftly respond to changing market conditions, compete successfully in local and international markets, re-align its strategies to shifts in customer demands, generate value and growth and achieve superior performance.

Learning underpins knowledge creation and innovation. It encourages experimentation and innovation; it encourages reflecting on success and failure (Teece et al., 1997; Pavlou & El Sawy, 2011). It utilises various skills, knowledge and expertise that exist throughout the organisation to harness and develop new ideas and transform them into new products, processes or systems. Learning is not just harnessed in the seizing and transforming process i.e. the innovation process *per se*, but it also comes to the fore prior to it. Snack-Co top-level managers spend time sensing the market. They work collaboratively with a team of experts, to try and understand the way the market is operating and where potential opportunities for growth might lie. This matters because, without such knowledge, they cannot seize the opportunity and transform their resource base:

> *We have a strong consumer insight team, and so we would try to understand sort of what the consumer trends are, for example, whether it would be health and wellness or convenience and we would try to identify innovation that aligns with those consumer trends.*
>
> (top manager B/ finance).

> *So there's a lot of consumer insights – there's a large group of people within our organisation that looks at that so what are the trends.*
>
> (top manager F/ business development).

This confirms Pavlou and Sawy's (2011) emphasis that sensing and learning are distinct but interrelated as sensing is about gaining knowledge about the new environment and learning is about using this market intelligence to create new knowledge.

Snack-Co top-level managers create, extend and modify their resource base by creatively assimilating the diverse skills, knowledge and expertise of various functional groups throughout the organisation. Once Snack-Co top-level managers realise a prospective opening in the market for a new product, they call upon different parts of the organisation to help create and deliver it to the market. Different people with different functional backgrounds bring to the table a diverse range of ideas, solutions and experiences. The integration of this knowledge is central to create products that are distinctive and unique to other competitors in the marketplace.

In this knowledge integration endeavour, the company can rely on its worldwide network to draw on the capacity to bring in ideas and expertise from different parts of the globe. People are encouraged to see what has worked successfully in other countries and what has not otherwise worked so entirely well. This allows the company to learn from the experiences of other people and avert making costly mistakes. It also lets them share best practices around the world and increasingly leverage on that global capacity.

Ensuring that the integration process is coordinated and managed successfully is critical to the development and execution of the final end-product.

> *So we would get R&D involved to I guess create the products that sell and whether that involves a specific technology, we would have a marketing program to be able to market the particular product and then manufacturing solution, whether that be internal or external.*
>
> *(top manager B/ finance).*

> *So we would get the R&D guys and the marketing guys you know they look at marketing trends, flavours and you can do that in a number of different ways by surfing the Internet, what gets served in restaurants, what things they're doing overseas and then also working in conjunction with the R&D with you know Coles to develop the flavours.*
>
> *(top manager C/ business development).*

> *I think that Snack-Co is unique because… it is a very large company so there is scale there, there's a worldwide network to draw on as well, as you know potentially being able to import products you also can learn how to make products effectively better. I suppose it helps with innovation as well because you can see a lot of cases of what has worked overseas and then you can adapt those learnings to the local market and hopefully makes less mistakes and so less costly mistakes.* (top manager C/ business development).

This exemplifies the 'differentiated to integrated' knowledge trajectory (moving from specialised/divisional knowledge to producing common knowledge) (Barley et al., 2018), viewing the recombination of knowledge as core to organisational innovation and success (Gertler, 2003). However, the mechanism allowing the process of this trajectory is not permanent. The web of collaboration is established and disestablished as needed.

Snack-Co's innovative capabilities are well-thought-out, carefully orchestrated and constantly evaluated to ensure that they are aligned to the company's vision and strategy for the future. This proves they are indeed a DC. They are not deployed on an ad-hoc basis; they are recursively deployed.

> *I think success brings success, so we call it our innovation our pipeline we refer to it internally as the 4-2-1 – so we look at all our innovation for all our [product] categories – 4 being the first four quarters 2 being the next two halves and 1 being a year so it's a three year progression. So at anytime we review our innovation agenda on what we call a 4-2-1 we make sure the 4-2-1 is linked to strategy and we, like a lot of organisations are continually challenging ourselves to do fewer, bigger, better so a small projects sucks almost the same resources as a big project so it just makes sense if you're going*

to back a project makes sure their focussed so don't too many make sure you're backing the biggest projects and execute with excellence.

(top manager D/ marketing)

As suggested in the literature (e.g. Lavie, 2006; Pablo et al., 2007), DCs are also costly to deploy. To be a strong innovator, the company needs to invest substantially in their innovative capabilities. This is ultimately to spend time creating and developing unique products that people want to buy.

The amount of resources we dedicate to innovation relative type of business is really high.

(top manager D/ marketing)

You know we're fortunate to have the resources to spend time thinking deeply about the market and the way the market operates and understanding where growth might evolve from so what are the macro trends and what's a differentiated way of viewing the market and the opportunities.

(top manager E/ marketing)

Aside from being costly to deploy, DCs also take considerable time to deploy. Some products can be in a developmental pipeline for up to four years before their launch. This shows that the resource base is not easy to change and that it takes a significant degree of time and effort for DCs to take effect.

I'll give you an example, Novel Sensations [pseudonym] launched a soft-centred jelly called Delight [pseudonym] which has been really successful and highly incremental that took sort of four years from the concept to launch and it was about two years longer than it was originally thought – a product like Fantastic Wonders [pseudonym] has been a phenomenal success story was around the same – three and half years to four.

(top manager D/ marketing)

An Adaptive Learning Culture as a Dynamic Capability Enabler

According to several Snack-Co top-level managers, the company's growth and success can be attributed to their adaptive learning culture (Verdu-Jover, Alos-Simo, & Gomez-Gras, 2018). Within the company, there is a strong emphasis on embedding a culture that encourages people to learn, grow and realise their full potential. The company devotes considerable time and effort into fostering a collective ethos whereby people can share in the company's desire for challenging the status quo and exceeding consumers' expectations. Having everyone within the organisation empowered, engaged and aligned to the company's vision and values is believed to be extremely important for the development of new and original products.

This company, in particular, has a culture, I think they've got a really good culture of can do.

(top manager G/ marketing)

There is a culture of empowerment and ownership in this business that is well articulated and engrained in organisational philosophy in a way of working and a key set of values.

(top manager E/ marketing)

Within every organisation lies a system of underlying shared beliefs, ideas, guidelines and certain expectations that influence the way individuals and groups interact with each other and with various stakeholders outside the organisation. Jung and Takeuchi (2010) highlight that culture helps organisations cope with external adaptation or internal integration. This suggests that it also helps support the learning DC as it is about responding to external pressure and recombining, integrating and creating new knowledge, thanks to 'webs of collaboration' (Eisenhardt & Martin, 2000). Culture is a vital contextual component for effective learning, in that culture supports values, beliefs, work systems and specific kinds of behaviours that encourage and endorse learning (Janz & Prasarnphanich, 2003; Kandemir & Hult, 2005).

When organisations create a culture that facilitates the acquisition of knowledge and information as well as the distribution and sharing of learning, they are more likely to withstand the forces of a changing environment (Phipps, Prieto, & Verma, 2012). This is because a learning culture encourages the free open exchange of information and ideas in ways that facilitate inquiry, risk-taking, experimentation and creativity (Bates & Khasawneh, 2005; Jung & Takeuchi, 2010). Organisations with strong learning cultures are therefore generally good at creating, acquiring and transferring knowledge, as well as altering their behaviour to reveal new knowledge and insight (Skerlavaj, Stemberger, Skrinjar, & Dimovski, 2007).

This leads us to conclude that the company's adaptive learning culture is a learning DC enabler because it supports its deployment. Their strong set of core values coupled with their will to find new insights primarily feeds into their capability to inspire synergetic creativity, collaboration and effective teamwork. One top-level manager explained how the company's adaptive learning culture allowed her to turn around a part of her portfolio that had been in decline for several years. She was able to use this culture to encourage her team to work diligently, towards deadlines they had never worked to before.

> *I have a large portfolio, and it's an area that has been in decline... I spent a lot of time setting up saying ... what does success look like where can we go wrong let's have those discussions early so going down that path – so it was quite a small thing, but if we not had that culture in place, we couldn't have fast tracked that the way we did ....and in this particularly area we might put out two products per year, we're putting out thirty-six and I think it's been exciting.*
>
> *(top manager G/ marketing)*

To foster their adaptive learning culture, the company hosts several events to bring people together to celebrate the successes of the company. There is also a cross-functional group called the 'Culture Club' whereby each month they organise a variety of fun activities for people to take part in. This is akin to trying to create communities of practice (Brown & Duguid, 1991). These dynamic knowledge management activities are key ingredients in building the culture (Liebowitz, 1999; Choi, Ahn, Jung & Kim, 2020). They promote an appreciation of people's work and capabilities and encourage informal exchanges and dialogues. Culture is in this respect a mechanism that facilitates effective knowledge management. It helps to bring down silos and dampen ambiguity or friction.

> *They spend a lot of time on embedding strategy and embedding culture so relative in other businesses that I've worked in there's actually a lot of things that sound like fun. They do a lot of dinners, newsletters, we all get together and celebrate success and I think it's very powerful. Whereas other companies get into that cycle: "it's getting hard-things are tough-we're going to cut back on all those nice to have". [this] is one way to go but then you lose all of those long-term benefits.*
>
> *(top manager G/ marketing)*

The CEO is also believed to play a key part in shaping the company's adaptive learning culture. According to one manager, the CEO has a distinctive leadership style. She emphasises the importance of learning to facilitate growth and success. This echoes the literature regarding the role of leaders: their ability to create a firm where people trust each other and an organisational culture that embraces change are key DC enablers (Pablo et al., 2007; Rosenbloom, 2000). It also supports that one of the critical factors for knowledge management success is the commitment of top managers (Liebowitz, 1999).

> *Our CEO will always talk about finding the insight, she doesn't – she's not all about blame. I've never met anyone like her, and that flows through directly. She's Buddhist as well so she talks about her values all the time, she's interested in the what, so what, what's next and what do we learn, so that's that adaptive learning culture which comes from the top.*

> *(top manager G/ marketing)*

Conclusions

Building on Venkitachalam and Willmott (2015) and Barley et al. (2018), we have expanded our understanding of knowledge strategy dynamics. SKM is an important consideration (or basis) for firms to build new DCs and renew existing ones. They are both concerned with aligning firm's know-how (its critical resource base) with a changing environment. We have argued DCs are one of these dynamics. This has allowed us to bring the much needed empirical evidence regarding the link between knowledge management and DCs (Easterby-Smith & Prieto, 2008). They allow firms to create and refresh their knowledge and harnessing innovation so that they address the changes in the competitive landscape. We also further confirm that DCs are costly to deploy and take effect over time. This highlights that although DCs can lead to the successful renewal of a firm's knowledge base, it does require considerable investment on the part of the organisation to do so.

Specifically, we have empirically advanced the knowledge management scholarship in two main ways. By evidencing the process of DC in a firm context, we have contributed to the literature by showing how DCs foster knowledge creation and innovation and future value in practice (Venkitachalam & Willmott, 2015) and also that SKM is not without time and financial cost for the organisation. We have also empirically revealed how an *adaptive learning* culture can act as a DC enabler. This brings empirical support to the nascent and essentially conceptual argument of the importance of culture for DCs (Wilden et al., 2016). This culture is one of the dynamics of the processes by which knowledge management is enacted. It enables knowledge creation that is more associated with the personalisation strategy contributing to effective knowledge management. In so doing, we have brought some further empirical evidence that 'cultural aspects' (Van Wijk, Jansen & Lyles, 2008) and especially an adaptive learning culture underpin SKM. It also supports Walczak's (2005, pp. 330–331) assertion that knowledge management is concerned with "managing and creating a corporate culture that facilitates and encourages the sharing, appropriate utilization, and creation of knowledge that enables a corporate strategic competitive advantage".

Bringing together the concepts of DC and SKM offers a deeper understanding of the different considerations connected to knowledge creation as a dynamic process within the broad field of knowledge management. Considering adaptive learning culture as an important DC enabler in Snack-Co's knowledge creation process, it can be suggested as more context sticky and not easily replicable by competitors. This means that a context-specific

DC enabler can alleviate an open and better knowledge creation process aligning with an effective personalisation approach to SKM.

To illuminate further, it brings some theoretical, through the DC lens, and empirical support of how SKM can be a factor of continuous change, facilitating adaptation and alignment with the changing environment through a DC perspective in this study. In short, it brings to the fore the dynamic dimension of strategic knowledge and knowledge management (Venkitachalam & Willmott, 2015). We have made progress towards addressing the call for action from Barley et al. (2018, p. 299): "we believe an important step forward for knowledge management research will involve broadening our analytic scope to include a more dynamic vantage of managing knowledge in organisational contexts".

One main managerial implication can be derived from this study. The findings show that DCs underpinned by an adaptive learning culture can help firms become innovative and ultimately improve their competitive advantage. Since there is a platform for environmental adaptation and growth despite the drawbacks in terms of time and money, managers should realise that these negative factors are far outweighed by the benefits and hence they should work towards creating and deploying DC enablers and supporting organisational culture.

The main limitations of this study are the focus of only a single large firm and the food industry. For this reason, the findings of this study cannot be generalised.

Another limitation is the use of only interviews to substantiate the findings of the study. While we attended to trustworthiness by asking the participants to check the interview transcripts and read studies in a similar sector, multiple sources and more participants might have given us richer data.

This study can be seen to lay a foundation for future research. A potential area for future research could be to investigate and identify whether learning DCs are present in many sectors, regardless of their level of turbulence. Similarly, studies could ascertain what other factors, beyond an adaptive learning culture shape SKM. Another possible area for future research could be the use of a longitudinal case study design to fully explore the way DCs take effect over time and affect knowledge dynamics other than creation, e.g. transfer.

References

Adner, R., & Helfat, C. E. (2003). Corporate effects and dynamic managerial capabilities. *Strategic Management Journal, 24*(10), 1011–1025.

Ambrosini, V., & Bowman, C. (2009). What are dynamic capabilities and are they a useful construct in strategic management? *International Journal of Management Reviews, 11*(1), 29–49.

Ambrosini, V., Bowman, C., & Collier, N. (2009). Dynamic capabilities: An exploration of how firms renew their resource base. *British Journal of Management, 20*, S9–S24.

Argote, L., & Miron-Spektor, E. (2011). Organizational learning: From experience to knowledge. *Organization Science, 22*(5), 1123–1137.

Augier, M., & Teece, D. J. (2009). Dynamic capabilities and the role of managers in business strategy and economic performance. *Organization Science, 20*(2), 410–421.

Barley, W. C., Treem, T. W. and Kuhn, T. (2018). Valuing multiple trajectories of knowledge: A critical review and agenda for knowledge management research. *Academy of Management Annals, 12*(1), 278–317.

Barney, J. (1991). Firm resources and sustained competitive advantage. *Journal of Management, 17*(1), 99–120.

Barreto, I. (2010). Dynamic capabilities: A review of past research and an agenda for the future. *Journal of Management, 36*(1), 256–280

Baskerville, R., & Dulipovici, A. (2006). The theoretical foundations of knowledge management. *Knowledge Management Research & Practice, 4*(2), 83–105.

Bates, R., & Khasawneh, S. (2005). Organizational learning culture, learning transfer climate and perceived innovation in Jordanian organizations. *International Journal of Training and Development, 9*(2), 96–109.

Brown, J. S., & Duguid, P. (1991). Organizational learning and communities-of-practice: Toward a unified view of working, learning and innovation. *Organization Science, 2*(1), 40–57.

Cho, H. J., & Pucik, V. (2005) Relationship between innovativeness, quality, growth, profitability and market value. *Strategic Management Journal, 26*(6), 555–575.

Choi, H. J., Ahn, J. C., Jung, S. H., & Kim, J. H. (2020). Communities of practice and knowledge management systems: Effects on knowledge management activities and innovation performance. *Knowledge Management Research & Practice, 18*(1), 53–68.

Creswell, J. W. (2002). *Research design: Qualitative, quantitative and mixed methods approaches (2nd ed.).* California: Sage Publications.

Easterby-Smith, M., Lyles, M. A., & Peteraf, M. A. (2009). Dynamic capabilities: Current debates and future directions. *British Journal of Management, 20*, S1–S8.

Easterby-Smith, M., & Prieto, I. M. (2008). Dynamic capabilities and knowledge management: An integrative role for learning? *British Journal of Management, 19*(3), 235–249.

Edmondson, A. C., & McManus, S. E. (2007). Methodological fit in management field research. *Academy of Management Review, 32*(4), 1246–1264.

Eisenhardt, K. M., & Martin, J. A. (2000). Dynamic capabilities: What are they? *Strategic Management Journal, 21*(10/11), 1105–1121.

Eriksson, P., & Kovalainen, A. (2008). *Qualitative methods in business research.* Los Angeles: Sage Publications.

Gertler, M. S. (2003). Tacit knowledge and the economic geography of context, or the undefinable tacitness of being (there). *Journal of Economic Geography, 3*(1), 75–99.

Grant, R. M. (1996). Toward a knowledge-based theory of the firm. *Strategic Management Journal, 17*(S2), 109–122.

Helfat, C. E., Finkelstein, S., Mitchell, W., Peteraf, M. A., Singh, H., Teece, D. J., & Winter, S. G. (2007). *Dynamic capabilities: Understanding strategic change in organizations.* Oxford: Blackwell Publishing.

Helfat, C. E., & Peteraf, M. A. (2015). Managerial cognitive capabilities and the microfoundations of dynamic capabilities. *Strategic Management Journal, 36*(6), 831–850.

IBISWorld. (2011, July). *Snack food manufacturing in Australia (C2175).* Retrieved from IBISWorld database.

Intan-Soraya, R., & Chew, K. (2010). A framework for human resource management in the knowledge economy: Building intellectual capital and innovative capability. *International Journal of Business and Management Science, 3*(2), 251–273.

Janz, B. D., & Prasarnphanich, P. (2003). Understanding the antecedents of effective knowledge management: The importance of a knowledge-centered culture. *Decision Sciences, 34*(2), 351–384.

Jung, Y., & Takeuchi, N. (2010). Performance implications for the relationships among top management leadership, organizational culture and appraisal practice: Testing two theory-based models of organizational learning theory in Japan. *The International Journal of Human Resource Management, 21*(11), 1931–1950.

Kandemir, D., & Hult, G. T. M. (2005). A conceptualisation of an organizational learning culture in international joint ventures. *Industrial Management Marketing, 34*, 430–439.

Lavie, D. (2006). The competitive advantage of interconnected firms: An extension of the resource-based view. *Academy of Management Review, 31*(3), 638–658.

Liebowitz, J. (1999). Key ingredients to the success of an organization's knowledge management strategy. *Knowledge and Process Management, 6*(1), 37–40.

Martelo-Landroguez, S., Cegarra Navarro, J. G., & Cepeda-Carrión, G. (2019) Uncontrolled counter-knowledge: Its effects on knowledge management corridors. *Knowledge Management Research & Practice, 17*(2), 203–212.

Mirzaie, M., Javanmard, H. A., & Hasankhani, M. R. (2019) Impact of knowledge management process on human capital improvement in Islamic Consultative Assembly. *Knowledge Management Research & Practice, 17*(3), 316–327.

Nonaka, I. (1994). A dynamic theory of organizational knowledge creation. *Organization Science, 5*(1), 14–37.

Nonaka, I., & Hirose, A. (2015). Practical strategy as co-creating collective narrative: A perspective of organizational knowledge creating theory. *Kindai Management Review*, 3, 9–24.

Nonaka I, Takeuchi H (1995). The Knowledge Creating Company: How Japanese Companies Create the Dynamics Innovation. Oxford Univ. Press, Oxford, UK.

Nonaka, I., & Toyama, R. (2003). The knowledge-creating theory revisited: Knowledge creation as a synthesizing process. *Knowledge Management Research & Practice*, 1(1), 2–10.

Nonaka, I., & Toyama, R. (2005). The theory of the knowledge-creating firm: Subjectivity, objectivity and synthesis. *Industrial and Corporate Change*, 14(3), 419–436.

Nonaka, I., Toyama, R., & Hirata, T. (2008). *Managing flow: A process theory of the knowledge-based firm.* Basingstoke: Springer.

Oh, S., & Han, H. (2020). Facilitating organisational learning activities: Types of organisational culture and their influence on organisational learning and performance. *Knowledge Management Research & Practice*, 18(1), 1–15

Pablo, A. L., Reay, T., Dewald, J. R., & Casebeer, A. L. (2007). Identifying, enabling and managing dynamic capabilities in the public sector. *Journal of Management Studies*, 44(5), 687–708.

Pavlou, P. A., & El Sawy, O. A. (2011). Understanding the elusive black box of dynamic capabilities. *Decision Sciences*, 42(1), 239–273.

Phipps, S. T. A., Prieto, L. C., & Verma, S. (2012). Holding the helm: Exploring the influence of transformational leadership on group creativity and the moderating role of organizational learning culture. *Journal of Organizational Culture, Communications and Conflict*, 16(2), 145–156.

Rosenbloom, R. S. (2000). Leadership, capabilities and technological change: The transformation of NCR in the electronic era. *Strategic Management Journal*, 21, 1083–1103.

Schilke, O., Hu, S., & Helfat, C. E. (2018). Quo Vadis, dynamic capabilities? A content-analytic review of the current state of knowledge and recommendations for future research. *Academy of Management Annals*, 12(1), 390–439.

Skerlavaj, M., Stemberger, M. I., Skrinjar, R., & Dimovski, V. (2007). Organizational learning culture – the missing link between business process change and organizational performance. *International Journal of Production Economics*, 106, 346–367.

Spender, J. C. (1996). Making knowledge the basis of a dynamic theory of the firm. *Strategic Management Journal*, 17(S2), 45–62.

Teece, D. J. (2000). Strategies for managing knowledge assets: The role of firm structure and industrial context. *Long Range Planning*, 33(1), 35–54.

Teece, D. J (2007). Explicating dynamic capabilities: The nature and microfoundations of (sustainable) enterprise performance. *Strategic Management Journal*, 28, 1319–1350.

Teece, D. J., Pisano, G., & Shuen, A. (1997). Dynamic capabilities and strategic management. *Strategic Management Journal*, 18(7), 509–533.

Tharenou, P., Donohue, R., & Cooper, B. (2007). *Management research methods.* Port Melbourne: Cambridge University Press.

Tsoukas, H., & Vladimirou, E. (2001). What is organizational knowledge? *Journal of Management Studies*, 38(7), 973–993.

Van Wijk, R., Jansen, J. J., & Lyles, M. A. (2008). Inter- and intra-organizational knowledge transfer: A meta-analytic review and assessment of its antecedents and consequences. *Journal of Management Studies*, 45(4), 830–853.

Venkitachalam, K., & Willmott, H. (2015). Factors shaping organizational dynamics in strategic knowledge management. *Knowledge Management Research & Practice*, 13(3), 344–359.

Venkitachalam, K., & Willmott, H. (2017). Strategic knowledge management—Insights and pitfalls. *International Journal of Information Management*, 37(4), 313–316.

Verdu-Jover, A. J., Alos-Simo, L., & Gomez-Gras, J. M. (2018). Adaptive culture and product/service innovation outcomes. *European Management Journal*, 36(3), 330–340.

Von Krogh, G., Nonaka, I., & Aben, M. (2001). Making the most of your company's knowledge: A strategic framework. *Long Range Planning*, 34(4), 421–439.

Walczak, S. (2005). Organizational knowledge management structure. *The Learning Organization*, 12(4), 330–339.

Wang, C. L., & Ahmed, P. K. (2007). Dynamic capabilities: A review and research agenda. *International Journal of Management Reviews*, 9(1), 31–51.

Wells, R. (2012, February 24). Call to rein in Coles, Woolies, *The Age*. Retrieved from Factiva database.

Wilden, R., Devinney, T. M., & Dowling, G. R. (2016). The Architecture of dynamic capability research identifying the building blocks of a configurational approach. *The Academy of Management Annals, 10*(1), 997–1076.

Yin, R. K. (2003). *Case study research: Design and methods* (3rd ed.). Newbury Park, CA, USA: Sage Publications.

Zahra, S. A., Sapienza, H. J., & Davidsson, P. (2006). Entrepreneurship and dynamic capabilities: A review, model and research agenda. *Journal of Management Studies, 43*(4), 917–955.

5

KNOWLEDGE MANAGEMENT AND THE LEARNING ORGANIZATION

Rongbin WB Lee

Background

In the post-industrial or post-capital society, knowledge has become the most valuable resource and an asset of individuals, organizations, society, and nations at large. How can knowledge be nurtured and developed? What is the driving force behind the differences in the evolutionary paths of different species of life on earth? The answer lies simply in learning. According to Charles Darwin, it is not the strongest who are supposed to survive but those who have learnt to adapt themselves to the changing environment. Charles Darwin has been often misquoted for his avocation of the law of the jungle that the strongest will dominate over the weakest. Survival is nonrandom. Learning is the very process that enables an organism to change its behavioral pattern, and cope with the external changes imposed upon it. In order to survive, the speed of learning should be greater than or at least equal to the speed of change. And to be effective, learning by its very nature should be a spontaneous, dynamic, and continuous process, in response to often complex and unpredictable environmental changes.

Living organisms are dynamic and evolving, and embody the accumulation of millions of years of adaptive learning. Life is engaged in a continuous re-programming of its genetic codes. These processes are self-organizing, the outcome of self-directed choices that create a living organism. In a biological community (such as a group of plants), although the individual parts have their own autonomous behavior, the function of the whole depends on the cooperation and integration of the parts. They self-organize through complex systems of information feedback, and there is no central control or hierarchy of authority. Such an evolutionary concept of self-adaptation and self- organization has shaken our traditional view of the Newtonian science model, and has re-shaped our understanding of how our economy (as an ecology), enterprises, organizations, and society as an organism work.

What Is an Organization?

Whereas cells are the building blocks of an organism, organization is the building fabric of modern society. An understanding of its formation and operation has been the focus of study

DOI: 10.4324/9781003112150-6

in sociology, anthropology, organization theory, and management science. The issues that need to be addressed include:

- What is an organization?
- How should it be run?
- What is the best structure for an organization?
- How is the performance of an organization measured?
- What is an excellent organization and how should it be modeled?

Organization and management are closely related. Organization is a tool formed by a group of people to help them achieve their goals, something they desire or value. What then is management? In simple words, management is working with people and through other people to achieve the goals of an organization. The organization should be the object that is managed (not its people). An organization can only achieve its goals through effective management. An organization exists for the simple reason that people working together to produce more goods and service can be more effective and create more value than people working separately. An organization can be in many forms. Some we know about are: governments, hospitals, charity bodies, clubs, churches and temples, schools, and firms.

A firm is a special form of organization which engages in production activities and provides a kind of cooperative resource mechanism. As an organization consists of people having diverse and even sometimes conflicting interests, it was pointed out by Barnard as early as 1938 that there is a gap between the organizational perspectives pursued by the executives and individual members, so that successful organizational performance would require effective coordination of activities and the satisfaction of individual members (Barnard 1938).

In Weber's classical work, *Theory of Social and Economic Organization*, published in 1924, the "bureaucratic system" is described as the ultimate form of organization in the then newly industrialized world of the early 21st century, in which "The organization of officers follows the principle of hierarchy: that is, each lower officer is under the control and supervision of a higher one". The organization operates as a machine, and nowadays, the advances in technology are helping to make the machine run smarter and faster. Up to now, the bureaucratic model has remained alive and well in many organizations (such as in many governments and even learning institutions) which are characterized by needless hierarchies, increased specialization, and exhaustive rules and regulations.

There are two metaphors for organizations: organization as a machine or a living organism; organization (as a machine or clockwork mechanism) is composed of static and discrete elements. To understand and optimize the performance of the whole, we need to understand the parts and how they function. The study of these can be isolated from their environments without the machine itself being changed. Such a reductionist view perceives the system as deterministic and hierarchical, and is designed according to a blue print. In the organization metaphor, a system consists of interacting elements and units that cooperatively give rise to the properties and functions of the whole. The sum is greater than its parts. In contrast to classical mechanics, parts can only be understood by their relationship to the larger whole. All living systems exhibit the capability of self-organization.

Since the industrial revolution, the bureaucratic type of administrative organization (which is capable of achieving the highest degree of efficiency) has become the norm for organizing human activities. Ironically, it is from the industrial firm that many features of the bureaucratic system have been derived and tested upon after experimenting with many other forms of transformation from its top-down decision-making rule. Nevertheless, the bureaucratic system, as described by Weber together with the scientific management model of Frederick Taylor (1913), is still deeply reflected and embedded in the management practice of many of today's organizations and firms.

Among many other objectives, companies and firms are set up to maximize their revenue and to strive for the benefits of their stakeholders. The pressure for competition in the business world has forced many firms to look for determinants of successful and profitable strategies. These give rise to the popularity of strategic studies in business schools. Michael Porter in his influential book *Competitive Strategy* has laid down a conceptual foundation for competitiveness based on the differentiation of either value added to customers or cost leadership. The strategic issues were later further expanded in an ambitious attempt to examine retrospectively what makes a nation's firms and industries competitive in the global market, which make up the theme of his next book *The Competitive Advantage of Nations* (Porter 1990). The main focus of the book was on environmental and external factors, and productivity, as key concerns to improve a firm's economic performance. However, few of the concerns regarding the internal working of the firms, such as corporate culture or human issues, were addressed.

Frederick Taylor, the father of scientific management and industrial engineering, was the first one to study how to improve work efficiency systematically by decomposing each task into individual components to determine the optimum time to complete the whole task. Taylor puts the following paragraph in his book *The Principles of Scientific Management*.

> The determination of the best method of performing all of our daily acts will, in future, be the work of experts who first analyze and then accurately time while they watch the various ways of doing each piece of work and who finally know from exact knowledge – not from anyone's opinion – which method will accomplish the results with the leads effort and in the quickest time.

The development of mass production techniques taken up by Henry Ford in the production of automobiles is the triumph of the Taylor approach in American management thinking, and has widespread effect on industrialization in the West. While the methodology was revolutionary in his times, his obsession with efficiency and measurement neglected individual initiative and the human aspects. The popular reengineering movement in the nineties is in essence simply a late 20th-century replica of Taylorism with the focus to simplify, remove unnecessary effort and to do more with less.

Most of these thoughts are still prevalent in most organizations as well as in the thoughts of policy makers we know today. The challenge to the rationality is echoed more deeply in Charles Handy's *The Age of Unreason* in which he pointed out that people who have thought "unconventionally" and "unreasonably" will have more a profound impact on our living, and education will have to alter radically as the way people think can only be changed by revolutionizing the way they learn (Handy 1998). These ideas challenged the rationalist ideologies of a universe with immutable laws within which all human problems could be reduced to a single answer through the application of logic and rationality, with the answer being delivered in almost exclusively financial terms.

A study carried out by de Gues (1997), a retired Royal Dutch/Shell Group Executive (who is also one of the originators of the concept of the learning organization), identifies characteristics of corporate longevity. One-third of 1970's Fortune 500 companies were found to have disappeared by 1983, and the average life span of a Fortune 500 company is less than half a century. Many such companies do not survive more than a few years. Why?

Geus challenges most of the conventional management wisdom of today and treats an organization like a living being in his book *The Living Company*. In this book, a commitment to values, people, learning, and innovation defines the living work community. He writes "Companies die because their managers focus on the economic activity of producing goods and services, and they forget that their organization's true nature is that of a community of humans". A successful company is one that can learn effectively. Learning is tomorrow's capital and learning means accepting continuous change.

What Is Learning?

What is learning? This is a big question in many disciplines ranging from brain science, neuroscience, computer science, biology, and anthropology. Intelligence and learning are closely related. This is equivalent to the acquisition of environmental associations (such as an association between a sound and a predator or between food and location).

The word learning can be both a verb and a noun. As a verb, it refers to the process (i.e., learning accountancy or learning Japanese). As a noun, it refers to what the learner has learnt such as the outcome, the result, or the product of the learning process. Säljö (1979) interviewed a group of 90 people with different backgrounds, asked about their understanding of word learning, and concluded with five different perceptions. These perceptions were:

i   Learning as acquiring information or "knowing a lot". It is a quantitative increase in knowledge.
ii   Learning as memorizing. It is storing information that can be reproduced.
iii   Learning as acquiring skills, methods, and know-how that can be retained and re-used when necessary.
iv   Learning as making sense or abstracting meaning. It involves relating parts of subject matter to each other and to the real world.
v   Learning as interpreting and understanding reality from a different perspective. It involves comprehending the world by reinterpreting knowledge.

The simple view of learning implies that knowledge is an object that can be transferred from one person to another. Learning is something external to the learner and we learn best by listening and watching. The last two conceptions (iv) and (v) are different from the first three, and look to the "internal" or personal aspect of learning, which is seen as something to increase a person's capacity for life, looking for new meaning in the real world, or enabling us to see our life as a learning experience.

Learning theories describe ideas about how learning occurs and what factors influence learning. There are many learning theories. Among these, behaviorism, cognitivism, and constructivism are the most influential. An awareness of the fundamentals of these theories will give us a better insight into the design and practice of organizational learning. In learning, we organize our experience and sort our memories according to our hopes and desires. Psychologists learn a great deal about human motivation that goes beyond traditional intrinsic factors (personal reasons for doing things) and extrinsic factors (such as the fear of punishment). Learning can never be deep if it is based on reward and punishment as suggested in classical behaviorism. Why do human beings devote so much time and effort to the acquisition of knowledge? Two aspects of motivation for learning are important, namely, curiosity and interest as the driving force.

The meaning of learning and how to make sense of it is found to be different for different people. The word learning becomes even more complex as we try to understand how it occurs, its governing factors, as well as how and why we should learn. The unfolding of various learning theories from behaviorist, cognitivist, and constructivist is a good example in itself to demonstrate how our interpretation of the world depends much on prior knowledge, belief, culture, values, and intention of the interpreter. Your interests in reading through all the pages of this lesson are guided by various motives, depending on how you make sense of the information that is presented to you and those that you read between the lines.

All the above theoretical background is needed to fill the gap of understanding the difference between individual learning and organizational learning. No universally accepted theory of organizational learning yet exists (due to its very multi-disciplinary nature or there is really no need for one anyway). Most research work in organizational learning tends to clarify or propose new underlying frameworks to support the implementation of the learning organization concept and to highlight the processes involved and the learning methods deployed. Interestingly, the development of various learning theories from the behavioral to the constructivist school compares well with the opening up of nature's black box in the study of atoms from the days of the Greeks to the discovery of quantum mechanics. As we learn more and more about reality (be it about human behavior or an atom), it seems to be less and less "tangible". This would give us a new context to understand how a complex organization works and learns. Based on the cognitive information processing psychology, an organization consists of cognitive structures (sensory register, memory, attention, forgetting, etc.) that we use to find the equivalence in an organization that we can model accordingly, in order to study how it works. On the other hand, based on the more sophisticated model of constructivism, an organization could be viewed as a culture (no more visible than the electrons in quantum mechanics), which includes myths, stories, rituals, roles, language, and symbols associated with it. This opens up another perspective to explore organizational learning.

What Is a Learning Organization?

In the late seventies, action learning ideas evolved and the "Learning Organization" movement began to pick up speed. With the increase in social awareness of the importance of learning, attached both to society and to the economy (look up the terms learning society and learning economy), the ability of an organization to learn has become an urgent issue among business professionals and academics from various disciplines. The learning organization is an important attempt to define a new paradigm of management and represents about a decade of research within that framework (you can find the "Timeline of Learning organization Concepts" at the Dance of Change website http://www.fieldbook.com/DoC/DOCtimeline.html, choose the link of "Timeline of Learning organization Concepts"), building on more than a decade of earlier work by many other scholars, such as Argyris and Schon (1978) who first published their book using the name "Organizational Learning". However, it is not until the publication of the internationally influential book of Peter Senge, *The Fifth Discipline: The art and practice of the learning organization*, in 1990 that the concept of the learning organization became massively popularized outside academic circles (Senge 1990). We will examine what a learning organization is and note its characteristics.

Various disciplines and schools of thought have an interest in learning organization (see Section 1.4), and this gives rise to diversity in thinking and to difficulties in defining the concept of the learning organization. So it is hard to find a definition that is universally agreed

Table 5.1 Definitions of Learning Organization (Adapted from Otala 1995)

Type of Definition	Example	References
Philosophical	"where people continually expand their capacity to create results they truly desire, where new and expansive patterns of thinking are nurtured, where collective aspirations is set free, and where people are continually learning how to learn together"	Senge (1990)
Mechanistic	"A learning organization is an organization skilled at creating, acquiring and transferring knowledge, and modifying its behav-ior to reflect new knowledge and insights"	Garwin (1993)
Educational	"It is an organization that has woven a continuous and enhanced capacity to learn, adapt, and change its culture. Its values, poli-cies, practices, systems and structures support and accelerated learning for all employees"	Bennet and O'Brien (1994)
Adaptive	"...... is the intentional action of an organization to continuously transform itself through adaptive and innovative thinking"	Dixon (1994)
Organic	"A Learning organization is like a living organism, consisting of empowered, motivated employees, living in a clearly perceived symbiosis, sharing the feeling of a common destiny and profit, striving towards jointly defined goals, anxious to use every op-portunity to learn from situations, processes and competition in order to adapt harmoniously to the changes in their environment and to improve continuously their own and their company's competitive performance"	Otala (1994)

upon. There is neither a precise definition of learning nor agreement on how an organization can be classified as a learning organization. Otala (1995) classified the definitions into five types, namely, philosophical, mechanistic, educational, adaptive, and organic definitions. These definitions are listed in Table 5.1 with quoted references.

There are other researchers who doubt that a definition of the learning organization can serve any purpose at all. Smith and Tosey (1999) call the learning organization concept more rhetorical than actual, more a concept to focus aspiration than some objective state. According to Solomon (1994), there is no such thing as a learning organization, but a vision that sees the world as interdependent and changing. A learning organization is always evolving. Senge recently remarked that "No one understands what a learning organization is, at least of all me ...... anyone's description of a learning organization is, at best, a limitation" (Abernathy 1999). Is a learning organization a myth or reality? Hammond and Wille (1994) opined that "You never arrive ...... You can never say *we are a learning organization*".

Apart from the difficulty in defining a learning organization, there are other concerns that challenge the validity and usefulness of the learning organization concept. These include:

i   The doubt of whether a learning organization can lead to any fruitful and measurable results.
ii There are many people talking about the learning organization but few people know how to apply it.

iii   The performance that is expected of a learning organization is over-exaggerated.

iv   Kuchinke (1995) thinks that the concept is being oversold as a near-universal remedy for a wide variety of organizational problems, as the primary purpose of most organizations is not to acquire knowledge/learning but to produce goods and services.

v   The over-emphasis on learning on an organizational basis can be exploited by organizational authority to induce obedience and loyalty from their subordinates (Kunda 1992; Van Maanen 1998).

vi   Most of the learning taking place within an organizational setting is conducted under a stable environment (such as continuous improvement and Kaizen) and not under rapid change. The reinforcement of such an organizational culture may cause barriers to organizational changes (Fiol and Lyles 1985).

vii   The potential side effect of "superstitious learning" when individuals are forced to be in accord with the organizational objectives (Levitt and March 1988).

viii   The wrong application of past experience to plans for the future.

Despite these challenges to the learning organization concept, the number of scholars who still hold that the concept is fallacious is much fewer than those that existed 20 years ago. However, the difficulty of arriving at a precise meaning of a learning organization does not hinder the practicalities of looking for ways that can translate the concept into business practice. Typical issues include:

- The development of processes in order to obtain outcomes claimed by the achievement of a learning organization
- How the learning of individuals becomes organizational
- How to measure the performance of a learning organization

The above list can be endless. Besides those mentioned above, learning organizations can also be characterized by various attributes that can be a combination of the following:

- An attitude to support continuous learning that supports the working environment
- Communication and openness
- Inquiry and emphasis on feedback
- Self-reflection on situations
- Fostering community building
- Enhancing employees' capacity to create
- Mutual trust and support instead of blame
- Dialogue rather than discussion
- Link individual performance with organizational performance
- Less use of defensive mechanisms and rationalization of negative events

Watkins and Marsick (1993) summarize the characteristics of a learning organization with seven Cs which include *Continuous* learning, *Collaborative* relationships, *Connectedness* among staff and between the organization and the community, *Collective* ideas to share, *Creative* spirit, *Capturing* and *Codification* of information and knowledge in a systematic manner, and *Capacity building* for lifelong learning.

According to some practitioners, learning organizations are best characterized by carrying out the five disciplines introduced by Senge (1990). These five disciplines are *personal mastery, mental models, shared vision, team building,* and *systems thinking.* Although Senge's framework is the most influential and the most widely quoted in the literature, it should be remembered that there are also many other perspectives of what a learning organization should be.

How does one identify a learning organization and that organizational learning has occurred? It would be just futile to look for comprehensive guidelines. From a more pragmatic point of view, it is more important to see if a better understanding of the following issues can give us a better insight into the concept of organizational learning and into the characteristics of learning organizations:

- What learning organization characteristics are most correlated with the high performance of an organization?
- How much do these characteristics vary across business settings?

Organizational Learning vs. Learning Organization

As with a learning organization, there is no consensus on the definition of organizational learning. "Organizational learning" is a subtle concept, as it touches upon a variety of disciplines and topics from sociology, psychology (both cognitive and behavioral), organizational development, management science, anthropology, epistemology, education theory, etc. Figure 5.1 illustrates the frequency (the top 20 results) with which the word "organizational learning" is associated with various topics and disciplines in the World Wide Web based on a Google (http://www.google.com) search. You can try to do this yourself. Use Google (http://www.google.com) or other search engines to search for the word "learning organization", plus other keywords, for example, "learning organization" and "Fifth Discipline". Compare with the results as shown in Figure 5.1.

The concept of organizational learning dates back to at least 40 years. Table 5.2 gives some typical definitions proposed by various researchers active in the field (listed in chronological order).

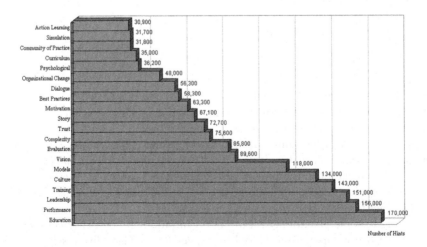

Figure 5.1 Google Search Result on "organizational learning"

Table 5.2 Definitions of organizational learning

	Year	Definition
Cyert and March	1963	The adaptation of organizational goals, attention rules, and search rules as a function of its experience.
Cangelosi and Dil	1965	A series of interactions between adaptation at the individual/subgroup and organizational levels stimulated through stress.
March and Olson	1975	Individual beliefs lead to individual action, which in turn may lead to an organizational action and a response from the environment, which may induce improved individual beliefs and the cycle then repeats over and over. Learning occurs as better beliefs produce better actions.
Argyris, C.	1977	Organizational learning is a process of detecting and correcting error.
Argyris *et al*	1978	The ability to detect and correct error, the mismatch of outcome to expectation.
Duncan and Weiss	1979	The process by which knowledge about action–outcome relationships and the effects of the environment on these relationships is developed.
Fiol and Lyles	1985	Organizational learning means the process of improving actions through better knowledge and understanding. The process by which organizations change a focal learning content, via behaviors, cognitions, or both.
De Geus	1988	The process whereby management teams change their shared mental models of their company, their markets, and their competitors.
Levitt and March	1988	The encoding of inferences from history into routines that guide behavior.
Senge	1990	The continual expansion of the organization's capacity to create its future.
Huber	1991	The acquisition of knowledge by any of its units that it recognizes as potentially useful.
Garvi	1993	The skill of creating, acquiring, and transferring knowledge, and of modifying its behavior to reflect new knowledge and insights.
Probst and Büchel	1997	The ability of the institution as a whole to discover errors and correct them, and to change the organization's knowledge base and values so as to generate new problem-solving skills and new capacity for action.
DiBella and Nevis	1998	The capacity or process within an organization to maintain or improve performance based on experience.
Huysman	2000	Organizational learning is the process through which an organization constructs knowledge or reconstructs existing knowledge.
García and Vaňó	2002	Organizational learning can be understood as a collective phenomenon in which new knowledge is acquired by the members of an organization with the aim of settling, as well as developing, the core competences in the firm, taking individual learning as the basic starting point.

The What and How

The terms organizational learning and learning organization are often used interchangeably. For example, McGill and Slocum (1992) regard learning as a process to improve behavior through the accumulation of knowledge, insights, and experience, but do not think there is a need to differentiate much between organizational learning and the learning organization, nor pay attention to whether the learning is conducted by individuals or by the organization (Fiol and Lyles 1985; Huber 1991).

Organizational learning and learning organization are closely related, but the focus is different. Ang and Joseph (1996) looked into the difference between organizational learning and learning organization. Organizational learning focuses on the process, whereas learning organization focuses on the structure of the organization to acquire the learning and realize its objectives. Structure refers to the task and authority relationship within which the communication, decision-making, and social interaction occur. According to Marquardt and Reynold (1994), a learning organization focuses on the "what" of an organization (i.e., its systems, characteristics, and structure to support learning), whereas organizational learning focuses on the "how" (i.e., the learning methods and processes used by an organization). Organizational learning is a concept to describe the quality of activities that take place in an organization and is concerned with organizational behavior. The learning organization is the outcome of organizational learning when it has reached a certain level.

Organizational learning is built on individual learning, but is not the sum of individual learning. It is not rare to find out that during the transfer, sharing, and accumulation of knowledge, the effect and outcome of organizational learning is often far less than the sum of the outcome of individual learning. Senge gives an impressive account of such a phenomenon in his book that whereas each individual member in a team may have an intelligence quotient of 120, the team as a whole may behave as if it has a quotient of only 62 (Senge 1990). The whole can be less than the sum of its parts.

Recalling the questions raised previously, we asked what organizational learning means. What should be the learning content? Can organizations themselves learn? If the answer is yes, then how can organizations learn? Or is it the individuals in the organizations who learn? What is the difference? Before attempting to answer these questions, the following issues need to be clarified: What is organizational knowledge?

There are two kinds of organizational knowledge, which are embedded in the organizational routines (established ways, procedures, and know-how for handling situations) or embodied in the form of an intangible organizational culture. The organizational routines usually lend themselves to codification and are often explicit in nature. They could be stored in the organizational or corporate memory. Examples of such organizational routines include technological artifacts (technical know-how, design specifications, quality standards, etc.) and those related to the implementation of organizational systems and processes, such as total quality management (TQM), performance measurement system (PMS), and continuous improvement (CI).

On the other hand, organizational culture is related to ways of thinking, presumptions, governing principles, values of the organization, etc. Such knowledge is often tacit in nature, but permeates our decisions and actions. It is at least as important, if not more important, than the explicit knowledge that can be easily codified in the organizational memory.

Summary

Learning is concerned with the behavior of living systems, humans, and organizations toward external changes. The self-adaptation and self-organization concept embedded in the complexity of science (as distinguished from our Newtonian worldview and the industrial Taylor model of the machine metaphor) has exerted a profound effect on our understanding of the learning process and the evolution of organizations. It can be seen that learning is fundamental to the evolution of all living systems, to which an organization is no exception as it is *the most complex form of a social unit.*

The ability of an organization to learn by acquiring new knowledge, correcting its mistakes, anticipating changes, and modifying its environment is considered to be its *only sustainable competitive ad*vantage. How an organization can learn is of both academic and practical interest. The study of organizational learning deals with the portfolio of theories, approaches, processes, and practices that an organization can **learn about learning** in order to enhance our capacity to innovate. The outcome of this may be called an adaptive organization, intelligent organization, excellent organization, or just a learning organization. These are the focuses of this subject.

Organizational learning is multi-disciplinary in nature as seen from the diversity of professionals (business professionals, educational psychologists, consultants in human resource management, public policy makers, economists, etc.) and academics (sociologists, behavioral psychologists, anthropologists, organization strategists, systems thinkers, communication scientists, etc.) who are interested in this subject. Learning is a continuous process, and the content of a learning organization constantly evolves over a period of time.

References

Abernathy, D. "Leading-edge learning", *Training and Development*, Vol. 53, No. 3, p. 40–42 (March 1999)

Argyris, C., "Double loop learning in organizations", *Harvard Business Review*, p. 115–126 (September–October 1977)

Argyris, C., and Schon, D., *Organizational learning: A theory of action perspective*, Reading, MA: Addison Wesley (1978)

Barnard, C.I., *The functions of the executive*, Cambridge, MA: Harvard University Press (1938)

Bennet, J.B., and O'Brien, M.J. "The building blocks of the learning organization", *Training*, Vol. 31, No. 6, p. 41–49 (June 1994)

Cangelosi, V. E., and Dill, W. R., "Organizational learning: Observations towards a theory", *Administrative Science Quarterly*, Vol. 10, No. 2, p. 175–203 (1965)

Cyert, R.M., and March, J.G., *A behavioral theory of the firm*, Englewood Cliffs, NJ: Prentice-Hall (1963)

De Geus, A. " The living company", *Harvard Business Review*, Vol. 75, No. 2, p. 51–9, (1997)

De Geus, A.P., "Planning as learning", *Harvard Business Review*, Vol. 66, No. 2, p. 70–74 (1988)

DiBella, A. J., and Nevis, E. C., *How organizations learn: An integrated strategy for building learning capability*, San Francisco: Jossey-Bass Publishers (1998)

Dixon, N., *The organizational learning cycle*. Maidenhead: McGraw-Hill (1994)

Duncan, R., and Weiss, A., "Organizational learning: Implications for organizational design", *Research in Organizational Behavior*, Vol. 1, p. 75–123 (1979)

Fiol, C.M., and Lyles, M.A., "Organizational learning", *Academy of Management Review,* Vol. 10, No. 4, p. 03–813 (1985)

García, M. Ú., and Vañó, F. L., "Organizational learning in a global market", *Human Systems Management*, Vol. 21, No. 3, p. 169–181 (2002)

Garwin, D.A., "Building a learning organization", *Harvard Business Review*, Vol. 71, No. 4, p. 78–91 (July–August 1993)

Hammond, V., and Wille, E., "The learning organization", *Gower Handbook of Training and Development*, 2nd ed., Toronto, ON: Brookfield (1994)

Handy, C., *The Age of unreason*, Brighton, MA: Harvard Business School Press (1998).

Huber, G. P., "Organizational learning: The contributing processes and the literatures", *Organization Science*, Vol. 2, No. 1, p. 88–115 (1991)

Huysman, M., "An organizational learning approach to the learning organization", *European Journal of Work and Organizational Psychology*, Vol. 9, No. 2, p. 133–145 (2000)

Kuchinke, K.P., "Managing learning for performance", *Human Resource Development Quarterly*, Vol. 6, No. 3, p. 307–317 (1995)

Kunda, G., *Engineering culture: Control and commitment in a high-tech corporation*, Philadelphia, PA: Temple University Press (1992)

Levitt, B., and March, J.G., "Organizational learning", *Annual Review of Sociology*, Vol. 14, p. 319–340 (1988)

March, J.G., and Olson, J.P., "The uncertainty of the past; organizational ambiguous learning", *European Journal of Political Research*, Vol. 3, p. 147–171 (1975)

Marquardt, M., and Reynolds, A., *The global learning organization: Gaining competitive advantage through continuous learning*, New York: Irwin-Burr Ridge (1994)

McGill, M., and Slocum, J., "Management practice in learning organizations", *Organizational Dynamics*, Vol. 21, No. 1, p. 5–14 (1992)

Otala, M., "Die Lemende organization", *Office Management*, p. 14–22 (December 1994)

Otala, M., "The learning organization: Theory into practice", *Industry & Higher Education*, Vol. 9, No. 3, p. 157–164 (1995)

Porter, M.E., *The competitive advantage of nations*, Washington, D.C.: Free Press (1990)

Probst, G., and Büchel, B., *Organizational learning: The competitive advantage of the future*, Prentice Hall, Europe (1997)

Senge, P.M., *The fifth discipline: The art & practice of the learning organization*, Doubleday/Currency, New York (1990)

Smith, P.A.C., and Tosey, P. "Assessing the learning organization: Part 1-theoretical foundations", *The Learning Organization*, Vol. 6, No. 2, p. 70–75 (1999)

Solomon, C. M., "HR facilitates the learning organization concept", *Personnel Journal*, Vol. 73, No. 11, p. 56–66 (1994)

Taylor, W.F., *The principles of scientific management*, Glasgow: Harper (1973)

Van Maanen, J., "Identity work: Notes on the personal identity of police officers", *The Annual Meeting of the Academy of Management*, San Diego (1998)

Watkins, K. E., and Marsick, V. J., *Sculpting the Learning Organization*, San Francisco: Jossey-Bass (1993)

References of learning organization definitions

Ang, S., and Joseph, D., "Organizational learning and learning organizations: Triggering events, processes and structures", *Proceedings of the Academy of Management Meeting*, Cincinnati, Ohio (Aug 9–12, 1996)

Argyris, C., "Double loop learning in organizations", *Harvard Business Review*, Vol. 55, No. 5, p. 115–126 (September–October 1977)

Argyris, C., and Schön, D.A., *Organizational learning: A theory of action perspective*, Reading, MA: Addison-Wesley (1978)

Cangelosi, V. E., and Dill, W. R., "Organizational learning: Observations towards a theory", *Administrative Science Quarterly*, Vol. 10, No. 2, p. 175–203 (1965)

Cyert, R.M., and March, J.G., *A behavioral theory of the firm*, Englewood Cliffs, NJ: Prentice-Hall (1963)

De Geus, A.P., "Planning as learning", *Harvard Business Review*, Vol. 66, No. 2, p. 70–74 (1988)

DiBella, A. J., and Nevis, E. C., *How organizations learn: An integrated strategy for building learning capability*, San Fransisco: Jossey-Bass Publishers (1998)

Duncan, R., and Weiss, A., "Organizational learning: Implications for organizational design", *Research in Organizational Behavior*, Vol. 1, p. 75–123 (1979)

Fiol, C.M., and Lyles, M.A., "Organizational learning", *Academy of Management Review,* Vol. 10, No. 4, p. 803–813 (1985)

García, M. Ú., and Vañó, F. L., "Organizational learning in a global market", *Human Systems Management*, Vol. 21, No. 3, p. 169–181 (2002)

Huber, G. P., "Organizational learning: The contributing processes and the literatures", *Organization Science*, Vol. 2, No. 1, p. 88–115 (1991)

Huysman, M., "An organizational learning approach to the learning organization", *European Journal of Work and Organizational Psychology*, Vol. 9, No. 2, p. 133–145 (2000)

Levitt, B., and March, J.G., "Organizational learning", *Annual Review of Sociology*, Vol. 14, p. 319–340 (1988)

March, J.G., and Olson, J.P., "The uncertainty of the past: Organizational ambiguous learning", *European Journal of Political Research*, Vol. 3, p. 147–171 (1975)

Marquardt, M., and Reynolds, A., *The global learning organization: Gaining competitive advantage through continuous learning*, New York: Irwin-Burr Ridge (1994)

Probst, G., and Büchel, B., *Organizational learning: The competitive advantage of the future*, Europe: Prentice Hall (1997)

Schiefele, U., "Interest and learning from text", *Scientific Studies of Reading*, Vol. 3, No. 3, p. 257–279 (1999)

Säljö, R. "Learning about learning", *Higher Education*, Vol. 14, p. 443–451 (1979)

Senge, P.M., *The fifth discipline: The art & practice of the learning organization*, New York: Doubleday/Currency (1990)

Watkins, K., and Marsick, V. (Eds.), *Sculpting the learning organization: Lessons in the art and science of systematic change*, San Francisco: Jossey-Bass (1993)

6

EVOLUTION LOGIC AND MODERN VALUE OF CHINESE KNOWLEDGE-BASED VIEW

From Confucian View of Knowing and Doing to Mao Zedong's Theory on Practice

Jin Chen, Zhen Yang and Yue-Yao Zhang

Foreword

From the standpoint of the history of scientific development, the modern notion of natural science stems from the formation and developments of Western theories on mathematics, physics and astronomy, particularly because undeniably the Western world has been the center of global science and technology in the modern age. As a matter of fact, in ancient China, there had been a series of important scientific and technological developments that were brilliantly outstanding achievements of the ancient time, and embodied in the famous Four Great Inventions known to the entire world. From the perspective of knowledge production of scientific and technological development and innovation, this series of technological achievement and innovation are essentially discovery, production and innovation of knowledge. Knowledge is an integration of basic cognition, viewpoints, experiences and patterns obtained through a series of practice processes where humans transform the objective world, and knowledge includes both the natural and empirical knowledge acquired through an understanding of the real world, as well as regular and social knowledge through objective connection to human society. Considering the category of world philosophy, the beginning of the pursuit of knowledge in the Western world dates back to as early as the time of ancient Greece, with a long-standing ideological tradition on understanding knowledge and the formation and evolution of the Knowledge-based View. The earliest proposal and discussion of Knowledge-based View can be traced back to ancient Greek philosophy, during an age when a large number of knowledge methodology-seeking philosophers emerged, including Socrates, Plato and Aristotle. Look at how Socrates pursued an understanding of the world, as declared in his statement that "all virtue is knowledge," he believed that the premise of knowing the world was to first understand oneself, developing from a self-intellect progressing to and exploring the objective-world intellect. The logic of knowledge-based view is that only those who are intellectual, wise and reasonable and those who possess virtue can understand the good and evil of the world. This has set a clear distinction of the subjectivity of knowledge production and the process of knowledge production, together with the

DOI: 10.4324/9781003112150-7

convergence and crossover of epistemology and moral philosophy, has exerted a profound impact on the subsequent development of rationalism-dominated moral philosophy, and philosophical epistemology. Subsequently, based on Socrates' Knowledge-based View, Plato further expanded the philosophical idea of Subjectification Theory of knowledge production, stating that knowledge is an external production independent of human subjectivity, a rational or sensual experience surpassing the cognitive subject, an experience truly reflecting the subject matter. In *Theaetetus*, Plato used the words of Socrates and pointed out that knowledge must meet the three conditions of "truth," "belief" and "judgment," in other words, a suggestion of the definition of knowledge that knowledge is justified true belief. Subsequently, there have been substantial debates and studies revolving around the relationship between knowledge and ethics, subjectivity and objectivity of knowledge. Finally, Aristotle, a student of Plato, offered again a clarification of the subjectivity of knowledge, stating that science is a general knowledge about causes.

On entering the near-modern society of the Middle Ages, the Renaissance movement once again sparked widespread discussions and studies on the relationship between humankind and nature, and knowledge and science respectively, with epistemology gradually rising to an important position in Western philosophy and history of natural sciences. The need to explain the different epistemological questions such as the origin, fundamentals, definitiveness and scope of knowledge gave birth to the two schools of thoughts of rationalism and empiricism. Rationalism, represented by Rene Descartes, Baruch Spinoza and Gottfried Leibniz, advocates rational deduction and holds that source and acquisition of knowledge is a deduction with the talent of reason. Empiricism, represented by Francis Bacon, Thomas Hobbes, John Locke, George Berkeley and David Hume, states that rational deduction is an incorrect concept, and believes that sources and content of knowledge come primarily from human sensory experience. The conflict between rational mentality and perceptual mentality is a subject of constant discussions and disputes among Western philosophers. Subsequently, in a stroke of brilliance, Immanuel Kant neutralized the conflict between reason and sensibility, pointing out that only through "reconciliation" can true knowledge emerge, which means only through an integration of human intuition and innate cognition of the objective world can knowledge be produced. Correspondingly, the scientific and empirical natures of knowledge have been clarified. Overall, in the true explorative sense of contemporary series of Western discussions on the origin and subject of knowledge, this marks a watershed of the study of the internal logical relationship between science and knowledge, as well as scientific knowledge research. However, Western epistemology based on rationalism has been met with doubts and debates, because the "above reason" acquisition and formation of scientific knowledge focus solely on the pursuit of pure objectivity and truth, while ignoring the more colorful and dynamic meaning of the existence of humankind. This resulted in the absence of the crucial characteristics of "scientific knowledge," and the lack of attention given to the rich meaning of the existence of "knowledge subjectivity." The "tacit knowledge" (implicit knowledge), proposed by Michael Polanyi, is exactly the most powerful rebuttal of such kind of "propositional" style knowledge based on the principle of rationalism. He opined that

> there are two kinds of human knowledge. There is one type of knowledge that can be expressed through written words, graphs and mathematical formulas. In contrast, there is the other knowledge that cannot be adequately articulated by verbal means, for instance, the knowledge we possess in acting.

There are considerable differences between explicit and implicit knowledge regarding the formation, acquisition and origin. On the same note, the "non-propositional knowledge" that surpasses "propositional knowledge" also warrants rationality and justification.

As a matter of fact, the origin, fundamental, definitiveness, scope as well as definition of knowledge have always been the subject of epistemological study by both ancient and modern philosophers. In China, there are numerous studies on Knowledge-based View in Confucian philosophy dating back to Spring and Autumn Period and Warring states (Cheng, 2017). The study of epistemology by pre-Qin Confucian philosophy differs from its Western counterpart in that it appears as a "Knowing How to Do" type of Knowledge-based View, that is, a form of knowledge about the "Study of Nature and Proper Path." The study of nature and proper-path-knowledge of pre-Qin Confucianism is a general form of human understanding of the world and oneself. It not only embodies an external formal system and an internal content substance but also relates to the cognitive realm (Ge, 2001). Unlike Western philosophy's focused pursuit of "truth," which is the characteristics of knowledge itself and the basic law that can truthfully reflect the objective world and things, pre-Qin Confucianism placed more importance on issues in the knowledge formation process such as the subjectivity of human mind as well as moral practice. However, in contrast with the Knowledge-based View of Western philosophy, ancient Chinese philosophy always advocated that "Knowing" precedes "Doing," and "Knowing" enjoys higher regards than "Doing." Moreover, the Confucian Knowledge-based View displays an obvious sense of morality, whether it is the human-oriented epistemology of Confucius and Mencius, or Neo-Confucianism school of thoughts, or Wang Yangming's "Innate Knowing" doctrine, the status of "mind" in the culture of the Chinese philosophy has been given primacy over the status of "thinking" as held by Western philosophy and culture. In other words, in the general Chinese philosophy school of thoughts, there is a higher requirement placed on moral philosophy than on the value of knowledge itself, since the "mind" embodies ethical knowledge, i.e. "conscientiousness," but not neutral "thinking" or "wisdom."

From the perspective of evolution, the commonality of Confucian Knowledge-based View and modern day's Materialism-based View is the relationship between "Knowing" and "Doing," with the focal points being the four questions of "which is more important," "which comes first," "which is more difficult" and "whether it is separated or unified." This chapter, from an evolutionary point of view, mainly stresses on reviewing and analyzing the development of Knowledge-based View from ancient Chinese pre-Qin Confucianism, Wang Yangming's school of thoughts in the Middle Ages, to the modern day's Materialism-based View advocated by Mao Zedong. On systematically reviewing and combing through the basic category of knowledge, the basic way of acquiring knowledge and the fundamental relationship between "Knowing" and "Doing," it has been observed that the Knowledge-based View under the Chinese philosophical system has undergone a spiral iterative process, from a separation of "Knowing" and "Doing," to a unification of "Knowing" and "Doing," to the final step of "Practice—Knowledge—Practice—Knowledge." Finally, under the fundamental relationship between "Knowing" and "Doing," this chapter proposes a strategic revelation on China's goal of building a world power in science and technology by the mid-21st century. This includes maintaining perseverance in problem-oriented attitude, formulating a scientific and technological innovation strategy in order to tackle outstanding issues arising from building a world power, strengthening the dominant position of enterprises in knowledge innovation and keep pushing the systematization of enterprise knowledge management, and basing on all kinds of people-oriented demands to build human-oriented and meaning-oriented knowledge innovations, so as to ultimately achieve an inner unity of knowledge, ethics and value.

The Epistemology of Pre-Qin Confucianism

Confucius' Human-centered Epistemology

The Western system of philosophy primarily answers two fundamental questions of what can be known and what one can know, while pre-Qin Confucianism essentially addresses the latter. As Confucius emphasized, "To know what you know and what you do not know, that is true knowledge." In Confucius' epistemology, the quest for knowledge is to explore the boundaries of one's knowledge and to know what one doesn't know, that is, to find the boundaries of one's intellectual quest (Cheng, 2001). In the "Essentials for Keeping a Good Health" of the book *Zhuangzi*, the philosopher states that our life has a limit, but knowledge has none. The total amount of knowledge and its distribution in the world are unknown to man, but one thing is certain that the span of exploration for knowledge in one's life. In other words, the human knowledge of the subjects in the objective reality is necessarily limited, which is the basic premise of the overall epistemology. The fundamental domain underlying the epistemology that Confucius champions is still the world where humans exist, which is mentioned in the "Shu Er" that the master never discussed strange phenomena, physical exploits, disorder or ghost stories. In other words, Confucius respected the ghosts and gods invisible to humanity and holds a cautious view of them, which also means that the world in Confucius' eyes is one of knowledge and vital to the survival and development of humankind. Although in "Wei Zheng," a chapter of *The Analects of Confucius*, Confucius said that he "knew the mandate of heaven at the age of fifty"; the "mandate of heaven" is neither a ghost nor a god, but rather the non-empirical knowledge of the world in which humans live—the specific empirical knowledge that is difficult to be abstracted from the conclusions of humanity. In this sense, Confucius defined the boundaries of knowledge acquisition and believed that they are determined by the boundaries of human connection with objective reality. From the standpoint of the philosophy of values, the epistemology espoused by Confucius is essentially one "centered on humans."

In terms of how knowledge is acquired, Confucius believed that learning is the only way to acquire both empirical and non-empirical knowledge. According to Confucius, the key to being able to know is not whether the subject of knowledge is an empirical one, but whether it has an appropriate way to be associated with humans. That is, the acquisition of empirical and non-empirical knowledge of things objectively connected with humans is primarily accomplished through learning, which is what Confucius considered to be the principal tool for humans to interact with cognized subjects and to acquire relevant knowledge. More importantly, learning is not only about engaging with objective subjects, but also includes a multitude of approaches, such as reflecting on objective phenomena and subjects, perceiving them and tapping into past experiences. In terms of the sources of knowledge, Confucius said,

> Those who are born with the possession of knowledge are the highest class of men. Those who learn, and so, readily, get possession of knowledge, are the next. Those who are dull and stupid, and yet compass the learning, are another class next to these. As to those who are dull and stupid and yet do not learn—they are the lowest of the people.

In doing so, Confucius divided the sources of knowledge into four classes. The first class, that is, the highest one, refers to being born with all knowledge innately, without having to acquire it through any means later in life. The second class is being born without knowledge, but acquiring it mostly through learning later in life, namely, "learning and readily getting possession of knowledge." The third class is having the consciousness to learn after encountering difficulties, which cannot be solved by the existing knowledge and experience, namely, passive learning. The last class is not learning even when encountering difficulties, which is self-abandonment or laziness. Those of this class have abandoned the basic way of seeking knowledge, and it is impossible for them to acquire knowledge and generate new knowledge. They are defined as "the stupidest," in contrast to the first class of "the wisest," who are gifted with knowledge. Confucius further suggested, "There are only the wise of the highest class, and the stupid of the lowest class, who cannot be changed." (Yang Huo) That is, only the "saints" who are gifted with exceptional talent and the "fools" who are self-loathing later in life are impossible to change or even unchangeable. What can be changed are the two intermediate classes of people who learn actively or learn passively.

In terms of the basic way of acquiring knowledge, Confucius considered both types to be "learning and readily getting possession of knowledge," regardless of whether it is passive or active learning. In this sense, Confucius believed that there were principally two sources of knowledge: being born with the possession of knowledge and learning and readily getting possession of knowledge. Confucius himself, however, didn't greatly esteem the former. Although there are many historical figures exalted in Confucius' commentaries, including Yao, Shun and Yu (all legendary kings in ancient China) and the Duke Wen of Zhou (a member of the royal family of the early Zhou Dynasty), Confucius still considered them to fall into the category of those who "learn and readily get possession of knowledge," namely, learning through a lifetime of strenuous endeavor. Confucius' attitude toward the sages who are "born with the possession of knowledge" was unclear. He once, when talking about the men and state of the society of his time, remarked, "I have never witnessed a sage, but I would be content if I could encounter an esquire."

If the way to seek knowledge is learning, then Confucius believed that the goal of seeking knowledge is "benevolence." Thus, a connection is made between knowledge and morality. Throughout his life, Confucius pursued a path that transcends "utensils," "things" and "arts," which is "benevolence." According to Confucius, truth is the ultimate goal in the pursuit of seeking knowledge and learning. Confucius spent his life in the pursuit of truth, emphasizing "setting your heart upon righteousness, supporting yourself by virtue, leaning upon benevolence, seeking enjoyment and relaxation in the six arts." (Shu Er) Confucius' statement makes it clear that "the Way" is the goal for which he strives to learn and pursue knowledge throughout his life, and that the ultimate goal of virtue, benevolence and art is to realize "the Way." So, what is "the Way" that Confucius championed? In "Li Ren," the Master said, 'Dear Zeng Shen, you should know that I cherish a basic principle which goes through all my teachings.' Zeng Zi answered, 'Yes, I do.' When Confucius went out, his disciples enquired Zeng Zi about the principle, and Zeng answered, 'The basic principle or the Way our Master advocates and holds is kind-heartedness, with focus on faithfulness and forgiveness.' (Li Ren) Therefore, Confucius' emphasis on the Way is consistent and unbreakable truth, namely, to know the essence of things, and the doctrine of "faithfulness and forgiveness" is essentially "benevolence." Although Confucius did not directly mention the meaning of "the Way," he believed that "benevolence" is the inner essence of rites—music culture and the transcendent principle of rites and music, and that rites and music depend on benevolence in order to have real meaning. And from the point of view of Confucius' personal aspirations, Confucius said: "If a man in the morning hears the right way, he may die in the evening without regret." The "right way" is "the doctrine of benevolence." What is "benevolence"? "Fan Chi asked about benevolence. Confucius said: 'Love others.'" (Yan Yuan) Zizhang asked Confucius about benevolence. Confucius said, "One who can practice five things everywhere under heaven is benevolent." When Zizhang begged to ask what they were, he said,

> Respectfulness, leniency, trustworthiness, quickness in action, and beneficence. If you are respectful, you will not be insulted. If you are lenient, you will win the multitude. If you are trustworthy, people will put trust in you. If you are quick in action, you will accomplish things. If you are beneficent, you will be able to employ others.
>
> *Yang Huo*

As we can see, Confucius didn't have a standard answer to "benevolence," and his answer varied in emphasis depending on whom he was talking to.

However, Confucius provided an answer to the highest realm of "benevolence." He explained the realm of cultivation and job search in life, saying,

> At fifteen I set my heart upon learning. At thirty, I planted my feet upon the ground. At forty, I no longer suffered from perplexities. At fifty, I knew what the biddings of heaven were. At sixty, I heard them with docile ear. At seventy, I could follow the dictates of my own heart; for what I desired no longer overstepped the boundaries of accepted behavior.

He believed that "the way of benevolence" is a kind of self-awareness of human nature, arriving at the point of "following the dictates of one's own heart without overstepping the boundaries of accepted behavior." Therefore, the highest dimension of Confucius' epistemology is the pursuit of "benevolence," which transcends experience and general knowledge and is the truth that allows one to grow, accomplish and attain the ultimate goodness of human beings. Finally, Confucius defined the practitioner of epistemology by arguing, "When the virtuous learns the Way, they love others; when the unvirtuous learns the Way, they are easily ruled." (Yang Huo) In other words, those who pursue "benevolence" are the virtuous. Zigong said, "The way of Wen and Wu has not fallen to the ground. It is still there among the people. The worthy remember its major tenets, and the unworthy remember the minor ones." (Zi Zhang) Therefore, the "Way of Benevolence" can only be studied by the virtuous to its greatest extent.

In conclusion, Confucius' epistemology defines the basic sources of knowledge, the basic channels and paths of acquiring knowledge, the basic stages of acquiring knowledge and those who possess knowledge. It provides basic answers to the questions of "what can men know" and "what should men know." Additionally, the text fully affirms the limited nature of human cognitive capacity, as well as the notion that "benevolence" is the ultimate and highest objective human beings can achieve while pursuing knowledge and innovation (Feng, 2015).

Mencius' Theory of "Intuitive Knowledge and Intuitive Ability"

Mencius' epistemology inherited Confucius' human-centered Knowledge-based View, that is, the boundary of knowledge that humans can cognize, explore, learn and pursue is the objective world with which humans are connected. If there is no connection between external things and one's existence and development, then they cannot be described as knowledge to be cognized and explored, and through learning and thinking, one is connected to the objective things and space with which humans associate. In Mencius' epistemology, he also believed in the existence of an omniscient "sage," saying:

> What can be desired is called goodness, and having it within oneself is called trustworthiness. What is full and *shi* (brought to fruition) is called beauty. What is full, *shi*, and brightly displayed is called greatness. One whose greatness transforms others is called a sage. A sage who is unfathomable is called an immortal.
>
> *(Jin Xin: Part II)*

Therefore, one who has mastered the highest level of knowledge is a sage who can also be called "immortal." However, unlike Confucius, Mencius believed that one can approach "immortality" infinitely, and that one can attain it through wisdom and virtue, and finally, one can alter "immortality" according to one's own mind and will. Mencius said, "When the sacrificial animals are prime, and the sacrificial grain is purified, and the sacrifice is carried out in a timely fashion, but yet there are droughts and floods, then the national altars are replaced." (Jin Xin: Part II) This fully illustrates the "human-centered" idea and human-centered scope of knowledge. The infinite knowledge of the universe can be accessed through the finite time of one's life. Mencius affirmed the creativity of human beings, that is, through their subjective initiative and wisdom, they can create knowledge and understand truth, and the infinite truth is eventually transformed into something finite.

Regarding the way of exploring knowledge and creating knowledge, Mencius also systematically elaborated and answered the basic question of "how can men know." In contrast to Confucius' ideas of "being born with the possession of knowledge" and "learning and getting the possession of knowledge," Mencius proposed "intuitive knowledge and intuitive ability." He believed that "intuitive knowledge and intuitive ability" are inherent in human beings and are the bedrock of intellectual inquiry. However, unlike Confucius' argument of "being born with the possession of knowledge," Mencius believed that "intuitive knowledge and intuitive ability" need to be expanded and tapped through the process of learning, and that they need to be solidified and stabilized through systematic learning. This is essentially a clarification of the way knowledge is explored, namely, "learning and getting the possession of knowledge" is the only way to acquire knowledge. According to what Mencius stated in "Jin Xin: Part I,"

> When people who have not studied have abilities, these are intuitive abilities. When people who have not deliberated have knowledge, this is intuitive knowledge. An infant carried in the arms has no lack of knowledge of how to love its parents, and when it gets older, it knows automatically how to respect its older brothers. Loving one's parents is humaneness, respecting one's older brothers is rightness. This is because these principles penetrate all people.

Confucian understanding of ethics has always been based on intuition. It does not derive ethics from the cognitive knowledge of ethics. In Confucian philosophy of ethics, virtue is not acquired through the use of pure knowledge or the function of cognition. At the same time, when arguing for the theory of innate goodness, Mencius not only put forward the theory of intuitive knowledge and intuitive ability, but also proposed "the development of the four basic senses." In "Gongsun Chou: Part I," he said,

> The sense of concern for others is the starting point of humaneness. The feeling of shame and disgust is the starting point of rightness. The sense of humility and deference is the starting point of propriety and the sense of right and wrong is the starting point of wisdom.

Finally, in terms of the purpose of knowledge acquisition, Mencius also inherited the "Way" pursued by Confucius. But the "Way" is the pursuit of ruling the country and pacifying the world, that is, knowledge ultimately serves the revitalization of a country and its people and social development. The "Way" advocated by Mencius is the pursuit of active engagement with the world, which essentially provides the subject and legitimacy for the service scope of knowledge. In other words, the ultimate purpose of human inquiry into knowledge is to serve society and the state, and only then is knowledge worth exploration and innovation. He appealed to emperors, "From the commencement of the Zhou Dynasty till now, more than seven hundred years have elapsed. Judging numerically, the date is past. Examining the character of the present time, we might expect the rise of such individuals in it." Regarding himself, he said, "But Heaven does not yet wish that the kingdom should enjoy tranquility and good order. If it wished this, who is there besides me to bring it about? How should I be otherwise than dissatisfied?" (Gongsun Chou: Part II) Such expectations reflect the fact that knowledge serves to "seek the Way," which is also the greatest truth.

Wang Yangming's Epistemology in the Middle Ages

Wang Yangming lived in the middle of the Ming Dynasty, a period when the Ming regime faced the political impact of external uprisings, and the intensifying internal struggles of the rulers, resulting in the dictatorship of eunuchs. Such a chaotic era saw inter-bureaucratic rivalry, ostracism and deception. Moreover, regional feudal kings rebelled one after the other, such as King Zhu Di of Yan, King Zhu Gaoxu of Han and King Zhu Chenhao of Ning, who turned against the central government for all kinds of reasons, and the feudal rule of the Ming Dynasty was in jeopardy. From the viewpoint of the orthodoxy of the time, it was mainly the Cheng–Zhu school (one of the major philosophical schools of Neo-Confucianism). At that time, the imperial examination was mainly based on the Four Books and Five Classics as explained by Zhu Xi. Scholars read no books other than those of Confucius and Mencius, and schools of thought taught nothing other than the theory of *li* (principles). The doctrine of the Cheng–Zhu school became the only criterion for rulers of the time to recruit scholars. The main ideological content of the Cheng–Zhu school is the theory of obtaining knowledge by investigation of things. That is, the practice of human behavior comes from the guidance of established knowledge and truth and is based on established knowledge and experience (Lu, 2016a). In other words, knowledge is a prerequisite for action, knowledge comes before action, and knowledge is more important than action. Zhu Xi inherited Cheng Yi's view that knowledge comes first and action follows. But Zhu thought that action is more important than knowledge, and knowledge and practice are separate but interdependent (Lu, 2016b).

From the perspective of the process of intellectual exploration, Zhu Xi emphasized that the extension of knowledge lies in the investigation of things. In other words, the deepening of human cognition and knowledge is to be able to grasp the ultimate ontological truth through the investigation of things. Zhu Xi applied the way of logical deduction instead of empirical evidence, pointing out that the reason why things are the way they are at present is that there are "innate" rules within things.

> It has been said that the Heavenly Way creates all things. Anything that has sound, color, appearance, and exists between heaven and earth can be considered a thing. Since everything is made up of something else, each having its own innate rules, they are all natural, and thus cannot be a result of human design.

All things exist on the basis of their natural principles and rationale. All things are subject to the constraints of principles, which is what gives them their existence. According to Cheng Yi, action depends on knowledge, and knowledge is always connected to action. His philosophy stated that knowledge is the foundation, followed by action, and he disapproved of discussing action without knowledge. Until knowledge is in place, it will naturally be practiced. "To know but not to do is to know superficially." If one knows but cannot act, then such "knowledge" is not true knowledge, but only rough information. Therefore, the Cheng–Zhu school embraced the objective determinism of knowledge. Its discourse on the objectivity and universality of "principle" is devoted to the interpretation of "certainty" and "reason." As the orthodoxy of Confucianism in the feudal society at that time, the Cheng–Zhu school caused the separation of "knowledge" and "action." The separation and severance of knowledge and action led to the phenomenon of "disconnection between knowledge and action" and "knowing but not acting" in society.

Recognizing the shortcomings of the epistemology advocated by the Cheng–Zhu school, Wang Yangming proposed the "unity of knowledge and action" when he was 38 years old. The proposition of the unity of knowledge and action holds immense connotations and can be used as a method of teaching. From the day it was proposed, it has been constantly questioned and criticized, not only by Cheng–Zhu scholars, but also by Wang Yangming's senior disciples and lifelong friends. Therefore, Wang Yangming advocated the use of meditation to compensate for the shortcomings of the "unity of knowledge and action." However, he found that many scholars were unable to control their thoughts when meditating. Thus, in 1521 A.D., while living in Ganzhou at the age of 50, Wang Yangming proposed "consulting one's own conscience" to address the problem in the unity of knowledge and action. In Wang Yangming's view, knowledge and action are unified and cannot be separated from each other from the source. Knowing but not acting is fundamentally not knowing. He opposed Cheng–Zhu school's view of seeing "knowing and acting as two separate things," arguing that "they have been separated by personal desires and therefore no longer the essence of knowing and acting." Wang Yangming rejected the subjective severance of knowledge and action in Cheng–Zhu school's philosophy by referring to the unity of knowledge and action, not from the perspective of epistemological evolution or intellectual inquiry, but from the perspective of moral practice. It is because he believed that the knowledge of virtue and the action of virtue must manifest simultaneously in the process of concrete social practice and cannot be isolated from each other, nor are they in a relationship of priority and posteriority.

Moreover, Wang Yangming placed knowledge and action in a field or a process of behavior, and abandoned the static view of knowledge of the Cheng–Zhu school, emphasizing the dynamic nature of knowledge itself and the need for a dynamic view of the relationship between knowledge and action. (Wang, 2013) Knowledge or truth is the beginning of the process, and action is the end of the process or the ultimate goal. Both of them are part of the same process and cannot be separated in any way. Specifically, from the perspective of the behavioral process of intellectual exploration, whether knowledge can guide practice or not needs to be tested and verified through action, while action is the main form of acquiring new knowledge, i.e., the creation and exploration of new knowledge. Action is the final practice and the ultimate completion of knowledge. Thus, from a dynamic perspective, the two represent different aspects of the same process.

Wang Yangming still put his emphasis on action, i.e. the practice of knowledge. His purpose in advocating the unity of knowledge and action was to change the unhealthy style of learning and common practice of society, which resulted from the separation of knowledge and action as two opposing things in Cheng–Zhu school's philosophy, and the disconnect between knowledge and action. Wang Yangming advocated the unity of knowledge and action, placing action at least on an equal footing with knowledge, and even making it more important than knowledge. He said, "There is no such thing as knowing but not acting. It's simply not knowing." (Wang, 2013) However, for people to put into action what they know and to put their knowledge into practice, the actual process is more about the practice of knowledge, which is the basis of their behavior. From the perspective of the mutually conducive relationship between knowledge and doing, knowledge can be used as the summary of objective laws or experience, but knowledge itself is not static and unchanged and needs to evolve and develop in dynamic practice; knowledge guides the development of practice, and practice is the way to realize the deepening of knowledge.

Therefore, practice is the main process of strengthening knowledge and the main way to test knowledge, and finally, in turn, it promotes the innovation and development of knowledge. In terms of the relevance of Wang Yangming's Epistemology, he advocated the theory of applying what one has learned, which is the prototype of the early theory of practice. Wang Yangming's emphasis on the unity of knowledge and action reveals that people today should combine academic knowledge and theory with their ability to practice, especially putting theory to practice in the process of academic research and intellectual exploration. We must guide our practice with knowledge, overthrow outdated knowledge or pseudo-propositions in practice, acquire new knowledge, sublimate the original knowledge and finally form a dynamic spiral iterative evolutionary process of "knowing-acting-knowing" to realize the organic unity of the two. In this way, knowledge and action can facilitate each other and be dynamically integrated.

Wang Fuzhi's Epistemology at Turn of The Ming and Qing Dynasties

Wang Fuzhi was born 150 years after Wang Yangming as a philosopher at the turn of the Ming and Qing Dynasties. He criticized and developed the objective idealism of Zhu Xi and Wang Shouren's epistemology, and integrated the Buddhist argument of "eliminating passiveness and incorporating activeness." He emphasized that action is the basis of knowledge, and established the simple materialistic epistemology.

Regarding the source of knowledge, Wang Fuzhi believed that "shape, spirit, and matter" are the three main causes of perception, i.e., "shape, spirit, and matter meet, and perception is developed." (Wang, 1988) By virtue of one's own tangible sense organs, one forms knowledge of objects through contact with them, which is the process of "intake of things." In the understanding of "shape," Wang Fuzhi inherited the idea of Zhang Zai's theory of qi, believing that the human body, the visible and observable objects and images are all real and physical objects produced by and based on qi. As the second cause of perception, "spirit," like "shape," has multiple meanings, encompassing not only the laws of movement and change, but also the thinking ability and spiritual consciousness of human beings. In Wang Fuzhi's view, spirit is the form of qi itself, which is not untraceable, but is rational, inevitable and credible. The term "matter" refers to physical objects, which do not depend on human will and are not affected by the human mind. Therefore, Wang Fuzhi also rejected the idea of the world as nothingness, believing that the world is objective and real.

Regarding the understanding of the relationship between knowledge and action, Wang Fuzhi believed that

> knowledge and action are complementary to each other, but each of them has its own function, and each of them has its own effect, so they are complementary to each other. One must know that they are separate from each other.
>
> *(Wang, 1988)*

That is, "knowledge and action are different," each has its own function and cannot replace each other. In the processes of interaction and transformation between knowledge and action, the relationship between the two is neither Zhu Xi's view that "knowledge comes before action," which separates knowledge from action, nor Wang Yangming's insufficient understanding of the firstness of action in "the unity of knowledge and action." Wang Fuzhi's view of knowledge and action is dialectical, emphasizing action can be combined with knowledge, that knowledge and action are complementary to each other, and that attention to both of them leads to success. He resolutely denounced Wang Yang's "unity of knowledge and action," which confuses knowledge with action and "knowledge separated from action," as a kind of idealism. At the same time, he did not deny the role of "knowledge" in "action."

Wang Fuzhi's view of knowledge is the dialectical unity of knowledge and action, emphasizing that action is the purpose of knowledge and has a decisive role in knowledge, while knowledge can act on action, and its purpose is "practice."(Zhu, 2008) "When knowledge is complete, then practice is all there is to it. If you practice, you will know what your heart knows, and you will be able to do what you want, so you will be happy." (Wang, 1988) He emphasized the subjectivity of human beings in this process. He believed that this subjectivity is not only possessed by a few sages, but also exists in every ordinary person. He opposed the idea of "letting the nature take its course" and believed that "if one lets the nature take its course without doing anything, one cannot be considered a human being. (Wang, 1988) The correct attitude should be to give full play to the subjective initiative of human beings in the world of knowledge and practice. Whether it is the perceptual and intellectual knowledge of "exhausting the tools" or the rational and theoretical knowledge of "exhausting the way," the ultimate goal is the realization of "virtue." (Wu, 2015) This is also the benevolent nature that Wang Fuzhi emphasized, that is, the "essence of the heart."

Modern Knowledge-based View Based on Mao Zedong's Theory of Practice

Mao Zedong grew up in old China, when the predominant form of society was a semi-colonial and semi-feudal state. During that period of time, China was under the invasion of Western imperialistic countries and had almost slipped into a semi-colonial society. Compounded by the prevailing influence of feudalistic culture, socio-economic development in China at that time fell far behind that in Western countries. Judging from the educational conditions during that period, education in old China still relied on a system of old-style private school education coupled with a relatively more advanced classroom teaching, where students were still learning from the outdated eight-legged essay. The majority of students hailed from landowning families and the upper class, and the social condition at the time made it difficult for peasants and workers from relatively lower classes to obtain education. Westernization Movement at the end of the Qing Dynasty had initiated the drive for learning advanced Western technology, which to a certain extent had changed the adverse condition caused by a complete isolation policy; nevertheless, this only stayed at the technical but not the knowledge level; hence, the learning of science and culture did not engender any transformation in the backward ways and conditions of the semi-colonial and semi-feudal society. After the Revolution of 1911, the bourgeois were catapulted to the forefront. In the domain of knowledge and culture, the New Culture Movement had taken bold steps to eradicate the original cultural system, which provided grounds for the Knowledge-based View of Mao Zedong to germinate.

During the young Mao Zedong era, his Knowledge-based View still exhibited some traits of Subjectivism. During his early school year, the young Mao wrote a marginal commentary on reading Friedrich Paulsen's *A System of Ethics*. He remarked that "knowing is premise of belief. There is a kind of knowledge that establishes belief and stimulates action. Knowing, believing and action are the three stages of our mental activities." In the young Mao Zedong's Knowledge-based View, "Knowing" (knowledge, truth) comes first while "Doing" (learning and practice) follows. "Knowing," as a constant knowledge in the human mind, is used to construct a belief and then to initiate certain behavior. In other words, "Knowing" determines "Doing," and "Doing" is a consequence of "Knowing." After the May Fourth Movement, Mao Zedong witnessed an excessive exaggeration of the status and function bestowed on knowledge. During the practice of democratic revolution, the Knowledge-based View theory that knowing before action had become the source for the germination and spread of Subjectivism, Dogmatism and Experientialism, which had in fact been hugely detrimental to the Chinese revolution. In 1919, he joined the vigorous May Fourth Movement, and while carrying out revolution activities, the young Mao realized that his own Knowledge-based View was embedded with non-rational elements, and, therefore, began the exploration of materialism, and gradually eliminated the negative influence of idealism. On September 1, 1919, in his draft of *Problem Research Council Constitution*, Mao Zedong pointed out that "to study a problem, it is necessary to conduct on-site investigation. If an on-site investigation is not needed or can't be conducted for the time being, research should be focused on books, magazines and newspapers." Here, Mao Zedong gave an interpretation of the source of the problem, the method for problem-solving and the channel for knowledge acquisition, expressing the understanding that investigation, research and practice are the fundamental paths for locating a problem and solving it. From then on, the Knowledge-based View of Mao Zedong gradually advanced toward maturity. In May 1930, Mao Zedong wrote the *Oppose Book Worship*, in which he brought forward the famous saying "he who makes no investigation and study has no right to speak" and "all verdicts come at the end of the investigation, not the beginning," scientifically explaining the dialectical relationship between the "right to speak," "verdict" and investigation, raising investigation and practice to the top position.

In July 1937, Mao Zedong wrote the famous philosophy works *On Practice*, in which he pointed out three areas based on the scientific analysis of human cognitive development process and the characteristics of the knowledge movement. (Mao, 1991a) First, "all true knowledge originates from direct experience." Second, "in terms of knowledge as a whole, no matter what kind of knowledge, it is inseparable from direct experience." Third, practice is the basis of knowledge generation, and it has a decisive effect on the formation and development of knowledge because "if you want to obtain knowledge, you have to participate in the practice in transforming the reality." Practice is the motivation for knowledge development, and since the social practice of people constantly develops from the bottom up, knowledge follows the progression of practice to advance upward since it is a product of knowing, advancing from superficial levels to deeper levels, from fragmentary to complete, and from partial to whole, including both knowledge of nature and knowledge of human society. Eventually, practice is the only standard to verify if knowledge is truth. For any kind of knowledge, only when it has undergone the test of practice, proven to be scientifically reflecting the pertinent objective matters, can such knowledge be regarded accurate and trustworthy. Once knowledge is generated and systematically evolves into theory, as in one that can "solve the essence of problem," then this kind of knowledge can in turn affect social practice of people, and exert immense effect on guiding future practice. In this sense, knowledge is embedded with the characteristic of dynamic growth, knowledge originates from practice, and new knowledge is generated through practice, shaping the innovation and iteration of knowledge. Ultimately, this repetitive cycle of knowledge and practice surpasses the limit of human knowledge and the boundary of cognitive realm.

Therefore, the Knowledge-based View of Mao Zedong has expounded systematically the scope and source of knowledge, as well as the process and purpose of knowledge innovation. With regard to the scope of knowledge, to the idealist, the concept of "Knowing" refers to the rational principle of a priori, or a certain inherent experience in people's mind. But to Mao Zedong, with his materialistic belief, knowing was interpreted as the dialectical unity of perceptual knowledge and rational knowledge, and in actuality demonstrated the dialectical unity of explicit knowledge and tacit knowledge. Regarding the source of knowledge, in May 1963, Mao Zedong clearly pointed out in *Where do correct ideas come from*, "where do correct ideas come from? Do they drop from sky? No. Are they innate in mind? No. They come from social practice, and from it alone." Here Mao Zedong specifically defined that knowledge does not belong to the authority of any individuals or organizations, instead it comes from social practice. Looking at the process of attaining knowledge and realizing innovation of knowledge, the processes of knowledge acquisition and knowledge innovation are really processes of complex movements, a sublimation process that elevates perceptual knowledge to experiential knowledge, and finally to rational cognition. (Mao, 1991b)

However, this is also a process restricted by various conditions, namely science and technology on the one hand, and objective process development and degree of presentation on the other (nature of the cognition target not yet exposed). Therefore, the scope of knowledge that Mao Zedong emphasized is transformable knowledge founded upon scientific experiments, while the nature of knowledge and the process of attaining knowledge are dynamic. Judging from the ultimate goal of knowledge acquisition and knowledge innovation, at the end of the day, knowledge has to be put into practice and to serve the ongoing practice to achieve the dialectical unity of knowledge and action. Finally, the authenticity of knowledge has to be tested and manifested in objective realization. Mao Zedong differentiated knowledge and truth, underlining that truth can only exist in knowledge that has undergone a practical test to establish correctness, totality and science. Hence, the validity of truth depends on whether it can withstand the test of practice, before it can be applied to guide practice during the pragmatic process. Finally, true knowledge can be elevated to a level of directive guidance that enables the transformation of the objective reality of human society and promotion of the development of human history.

Revelations from the Relationship between "Knowing" and "Doing" for Technological Innovation

A Renewed Understanding of Relationship between "Knowing" and "Doing"

Judging from how the relationship between "Knowing" and "Doing" is being identified in traditional Chinese culture and philosophy, it would not be an understatement to say that the evolution process and law of the traditional Confucianism View of Knowing and Doing have provided a basic positioning for the theoretical outlook of Wang Yangming's "unity of knowledge and action." The evolution history of traditional Chinese Confucian View of Knowing and Doing can roughly be divided into six significant stages. The first stage is the epistemological stage as represented by Zi Chan of the Spring and Autumn Period. Zi Chan remarked "to think is easy. To act is hard" as "it is easier said than done, it is hard to put into practice what is known." The second stage is a period when Confucius' Moral Cultivation Theory and epistemology co-existed. Confucius stated in *The Analects: Ji Shi*

> those who are born with the possession of knowledge are the highest class of men. Those who learn, and so, readily, get possession of knowledge, are the next. Those who are dull and stupid, and yet compass the learning, are another class next to these. As to those who are dull and stupid and yet do not learn—they are the lowest of the people,

suggesting the two types of knowledge acquisition, namely "being born with the possession of knowledge" and "learning and readily getting possession of knowledge." Sages can be "born with the possession of knowledge," with the kind of knowledge here referring not only to what could be acquired through daily hearing and seeing, but more importantly ethical knowledge. Since "born with the possession of knowledge" constitutes a priori, an innate cognition, whereas "learning and readily getting possession of knowledge" and "being dull and stupid yet compassing the learning" are the second-ranked paths to obtain knowledge, to a certain extent this upholds the notion that truth remains in the hands of a few (the sages).

The third stage occurred during the Cao Wei and Jin dynastic period, when the Theory of Knowing and Doing was being denied. Under the Wei and Jin metaphysical mindset, which is characterized by "employing Taoism for external matters and Confucianism for internal matters," the Theory of Knowing and Doing at this stage was an atypical presentation in a specific thought context. The fourth stage, symbolized by Wang Tong, was a turning point when epistemology completely turned into the Moral Cultivation Theory. Wang Tong believed that acquiring knowledge should not only remain in a format lifelong recitals of word-of-mouth knowledge passed down generations after generations, but instead should combine with action to serve as practice. The unity of Knowing and Doing also has to come under the command of virtue, which equates a self-conscientious state when knowledge and action are in unity and the practice of knowledge is kept within the bounds of virtue, resulting in a peaceful, restful state of being "self-satisfied." The fifth stage is characterized by the principle-oriented Cheng–Zhu school of the Northern Song Dynasty. Priority was placed on knowing, in particular, ethical knowing, and making a priori a prerequisite to suggest the "knowledge comes before action" theory. Following this is the "unity of knowledge and action" theory of Wang Yangming, an important element in the development of the traditional Chinese Confucian View of Knowing and Doing. The last stage is the period when the Western Knowledge-based View was incorporated into the Qing Dynasty principal theory, and in this stage, attempts were made to transform the Theory of Knowing and Doing into pure epistemology.

Generally speaking, the Knowledge-based View dominated by traditional Chinese Confucianism gradually migrated from a state of knowledge and action separated from each other, to a state of knowledge-comes-first type of theory, and finally to a state of unity between knowledge and action. Mao Zedong's *On Practice* pointed out even more clearly the modern meaning of unity of knowledge and action. The Knowledge-based View of Mao Zedong displays a strong sense of materialistic dialectics. From the dimension of epistemology, Mao Zedong focused his solution for knowledge and practice on the basis of "material first, conscientiousness second," leading to the mindset that practice is the source of knowledge. From knowing to practice, and then back from practice to knowing, knowing and practice exercise mutual restraint and interaction, repeating cyclically to proceed forward, advancing after every cycle. Ultimately, solid historical unity of Knowing and Doing is realized, and knowledge and practice reach the finale of a dynamic evolution to advance knowledge, resulting in the basic thesis that knowledge innovation is ultimately beneficial to the practice and development of humankind.

Strategic Value of Relationship between "Knowing" and "Doing" for Building a Technologically Innovative Country

1. Maintain perseverance in problem-oriented attitude to formulate a scientific and technological innovation strategy in order to tackle outstanding issues arising from building a world power.

Since the 18th CPC National Congress, building a world power in science and technology innovation has become the main theme and purpose of China's science and technology innovation strategy. China has put forward the ultimate goal of moving to the forefront of innovation-oriented countries in 2035 and achieving the construction of a science and technology innovation powerhouse in 2050. From the perspective of epistemology, science and technology innovation is essentially a process of systematic and integrated innovation based on knowledge, technology, system and culture. The research process of science and technology is essentially the process of acquiring, absorbing, sharing and innovating existing knowledge based on scientific problems, practical needs and future forecasts. Whether it is Wang Yangming's "unity of knowledge and practice" or Mao Zedong's "theory of practice," the idea of mutual unity of knowledge and practice is implied. That is to say, knowledge is to solve the major problems of reality and potential problems that may be encountered. For China to build a world science and technology innovation powerhouse, whether it is scientific innovation or technological breakthrough, it is essentially the innovation and iteration of knowledge. This process requires changing the phenomenon that scientific research and technological breakthroughs have long been detached from real needs, national strategic planning and enterprise management practices. The institutional mechanism and supporting elements of science and technology innovation need to shift from theory-oriented approach to "practice-oriented" approach, and be based on knowledge. Science and technology innovation consists of basic knowledge in three aspects. They are tacit and explicit, systematic and autonomous, simple and complex, respectively. The goal of scientific research is not theoretical in the first place, but to solve the series of major problems encountered in the development of enterprises, industries and countries that are currently associated with the development of disciplines. Most of these problems come from the objective needs of research and industrial development, and the objective practical problems faced in the process of scientific practice and technological development depend on systematic scientific intellectual exploration and technological innovation.

Therefore, the systematic construction of a world science and technology innovation powerhouse undoubtedly requires the unswerving implementation of a comprehensive independent innovation strategy, and the key to this process is the construction of a problem-oriented strategic promotion system. From the perspective of the major realistic problems that hinder the construction of a science and technology innovation powerhouse, the main problems are the co-existence of "market failure" and "administrative failure" in the science and technology institutional mechanism, the "bottleneck" problem of key core technologies in industries, and the systematic lack of innovation motivation and capability of most enterprises in China, which have led to the unbalanced emphasis on scale and market and the neglect of technological innovation, basic research and other real problems. (Chen and Yang, 2021) Therefore, from the viewpoint of "unity of knowledge and action," we need to continue to address the huge obstacles and outstanding problems that restrict our key enterprises and key industries from exceeding the middle and low end of the global value chain in the future. We need to use the new "comprehensive independent innovation strategy" of science and technology strategy to lead the national innovation system, regional innovation system, industrial innovation system and corporate innovation system. The strategic footing of this approach is to systematically enhance the technological innovation capability for industries and enterprises, and to build a comprehensively independent innovation capability as the prominent orientation for building a world science and technology innovation powerhouse.

2. Strengthen the dominant position of enterprises in knowledge innovation and keep pushing the systematization of enterprise knowledge management.

Enterprise is not only the core of market, but also the key entity in creating knowledge for accomplishing knowledge transfer, knowledge share and knowledge innovation. Since the start of reform and opening-up of China over four decades ago, there has been an obvious advancement in the innovation capability of Chinese enterprises, both in state-owned and private-owned businesses. Corporate investment in research and development accounted for 70% of all R&D investment in, and more than 40% of above-industry-designated-scale enterprises have launched technological innovation projects. However, compared with developed Western countries, the status of Chinese enterprises as the principal entity in knowledge innovation is still not prominent enough, and the pivotal effect of enterprises in innovation has not yet been fully unleashed particularly with regard to integrated-knowledge and complex-knowledge necessary in the breakthrough of key and core technologies. These situations can be seen in, first, inadequate enterprise investment in innovation research and development, and there is much room for improvement for enterprises, in particular in terms of investment allocated to basic research. According to statistics, corporate investment in basic research amounts to less than 3%, far less than the 20% seen in developed countries such as the United States and Japan. Furthermore, the weak corporate role in innovation is also explicitly reflected in the small, scattered and insignificant status of Chinese tech companies. Although there are a considerable number of technology enterprises, the general innovation quality on the whole is not high; breakthrough and disruptive technological innovations are still largely insufficient. The scale, technological foundation and capability of some enterprises are comparatively weak, and they are not able to sustain and launch large-scale, long-term, original innovations marked by technological difficulties and high market risks. Therefore, on the challenging path to develop a world power in science and technology, it is necessary to adhere steadfastly to the goal of improving the status of enterprises as the principal entity in knowledge and technological innovation.

In terms of technological innovation, there is the need to strengthen synergy in the construction of platforms for enterprise-oriented basic research and platforms for the application of technological innovations. Efforts should include enhancing support for corporate market applied research, technological innovation, cutting-edge scientific technology and strategic emerging industries, and encouraging enterprises to plan their development toward the establishment of basic research platforms that target key industry core technology breakthrough, so as to achieve a comprehensive elevation of the status of enterprises in technological innovation. On the other hand, it is necessary to refine the supporting dynamics for corporate innovation policy, strengthen the strategic status of tech entrepreneurs and social policy support, as well as magnifying the sense of social accomplishment among tech entrepreneurs. Moreover, during the allocation process of science and technology innovation factors, it is necessary to allocate more innovation factors toward tech entrepreneurs, and strengthen their ability to obtain scientific and technological innovation resources including policy resource and social resources, so that more companies can bolster their innovation capacity through increased research and development. This will facilitate the strengthening of financial integration and sharing of all kinds of innovation factors among large, medium-sized and small companies, and state-owned and private-owned enterprises, thereby realizing a fully integrated and connected development in its true sense.

3. Building and strengthening people-oriented and significance-oriented knowledge innovation based on various kinds of people-oriented demands

The acquisition of knowledge and knowledge innovation are always people-oriented, regardless of the Knowledge-based View of the pre-Qin Confucian philosophy, or the "unity of knowledge and action" theory of Wang Yangming, or Mao Zedong's "theory of practice." The boundaries of knowledge acquisition and innovation advocated by Confucius and Mencius revolve around the world of life, the subject matter of knowledge is chiefly a revelation of the relationship between the self and the world of life, whereas the general world unrelated to the self can be kept at a distance. Confucius' Knowledge-based View is essentially an insight into and comprehension of the meaning of existence of humankind. The same goes with the idea of "unity of knowledge and action" of Wang Yangming, as humans are the subjects of unity, and he denied the belief that knowledge comes before action, because the only key is the "unmasking" during practice to discover "conscientiousness," from which ethical knowledge and ethical behavior such as filial piety subsequently derived. In this sense, the people-oriented value of knowledge is revealed, a return to humankind's inner "conscientiousness," order of society and morality. The "theory of practice" of Mao Zedong also insists on the basic viewpoint that the people are the pioneers, stating that knowledge must be put through the test of practice to establish the correctness, totality and science to be considered truth. Truth is able to give effective guidance to humankind in their practical activities, transform objective practice, and improve the development of human history. In this regard, the value goal for knowledge is to be ultimately elevated to become truth, and this goal is also one that serves human-oriented development and a meaningful return to humankind at the core. Therefore, unlike the economic-and-market-logic-oriented Innovation Theory of Western scholar Schumpeter, the traditional Chinese Knowledge-based View and the "theory of practice" of Mao Zedong both uphold the social value and human value of knowledge innovation.

As a matter of fact, the value of knowledge and the ultimate value goal of knowledge innovation, when reflected in a target not directed toward any private gains or solely toward economic gains, then people's self-interest-focused, practicality-focused lifestyle and habits, social mentality, thoughts and values can be corrected. In a knowledge-based society, profit-gaining orientation is not the mainstream, but rather a materialistic and spiritually balanced orientation, or better still, a spiritual value-dominated orientation should be the mainstream value. To achieve this, along the path of establishing a scientifically and technologically innovative country, it is necessary to build a new mode of people-oriented and significance-oriented knowledge innovation. In the dimension of significance, the significance of knowledge innovation lies in the ability of the innovating entity to recognize and transform economic significance, social significance, strategic significance and future significance. In this sense, under the new mode of people-oriented and significance-oriented knowledge innovation, progress and development of a scientifically and technologically innovative nation needs to endeavor in the following three areas: First, strengthen the ability in enterprises to develop economic significance-oriented technological innovation, and further enhance the market power of enterprises based on technological innovation. Second, push for responsibility-oriented social innovation and mutual benefit innovation, so that corporate innovation can gain public value by transcending beyond the boundaries of financial value. Third, intensify forward-looking human development, and the technology portfolio and layout of knowledge innovation for future development, take effective measures to respond to possible significant social risks and pitfalls in the process of human development.

References

Chen, J., Yang, Z. Industrial Technology Policy in the New Development Pattern: Theoretical Logic, Outstanding Problems and Optimization. *Economist (Chinese Journal)*, 2021(2):33–42.

Cheng, S. *Collected Interpretations of the Analects – Part II.* Beijing, China: Zhonghua Book Company, 2017.

Cheng, Z. Y. *Combining the External and Internal Ways – Confucian Philosophical Theories.* Beijing, China: China Social Science Press, 2001.

Feng, Y. L. *A Short History of Chinese Philosophy.* Beijing, China: SDX Joint Publishing Company, 2015.

Ge, Y. G. *An Intellectual History of China, Volume Two.* Shanghai, China: Fudan University Press, 2001.

Lu, Y.S. *Mind – Academia – Governance: Research on the Thoughts of Wang Yangming in Central Guizhou during Ming Dynasty.* Shanghai, China: Zhonghua Book Company, 2016a.

Lu, Y.S. *Theoretical Effects and Practical Capacity of Wang Yangming's Unity of Knowledge and Action.* Shanghai, China: Zhonghua Book Company, 2016b.

Mao, Z.D. *Early Manuscripts of Mao Zedong.* Changsha, China: Hunan Publishing House, 1991a.

Mao, Z.D. *Selected Works of Mao Zedong (Vol. 1).* Beijing, China: People's Publishing House, 1991b.

Mao, Z.D. *Selected Works of Mao Zedong (Vol. 3).* Beijing, China: People's Publishing House, 1991c.

Wang, F.Z. *The Complete Works of Chuanshan.* Changsha, China: Yuelu Book Society, 1988.

Wang, Y.M. *The Complete Works of Wang Yangming.* Kunming, China: Yunnan People's Publishing House, 2013, p. 143, p. 175.

Wu, G Y. Re-discussing Wang Fuzhi's View of "knowledge and doing". *Academic Monthly (Chinese journal)*, 2015, 47(3):44–54.

Zhu, X. *Collective Annotations for the Four Books.* Changsha, China: Yuelu Publishing House, 2008.

7

JAPANESE PHILOSOPHY AND KNOWLEDGE

Insights into Ikigai and Wabi-Sabi

Sanjay Kumar

Part I

Introduction

Of late, there is a growing interest in the concepts associated with Japanese philosophy, cutting across multiple realms—both individual and organizational. On a more personal level, Japanese philosophy is being utilized to help change perspectives and attitudes toward life, and at the organizational level, a tendency to move toward minimalism is emerging more and more across a variety of sectors. While such philosophies may not completely revolutionize everyday life, they can certainly help equip people with the required insights that can help provide a sense of stability, and help find the light, even in seemingly endless darkness. Like most philosophical tools, however, the impact depends greatly on interpretation, and how we utilize our own power of thought.

Japanese philosophy, rather than being limited to itself, has assimilated learning and influences from a number of other cultures, Asian and otherwise. As such, the perspectives emanating from such philosophy are incredibly nuanced, and cognizant of the complications associated with cultural relations, similarities, and contrasts. Historically, due to the absence of overtly foreign influences on their sovereignty of thought, Japanese thinkers had the luxury of alternatives outside the binary of simple wholehearted acceptance or utter rejection (Kasulis, 2019). New theories from abroad could be tried and, if need be, experimentally modified before making a final decision about endorsement. As such, as the philosophies have evolved with time, their application across a variety of contexts has evolved alongside, owing to the same being more relatable than a number of other, more localized strands of philosophy.

The purpose of this chapter is not to state that specific elements of Japanese philosophy can be deemed as the necessary solution to problems and challenges plaguing most of us on a personal, professional, or organizational level. Instead, the purpose here is to help provide some context, some alternative perspectives to help recalibrate priorities that may help us contextualize the said challenges in a way which makes them more palatable, and presents them as opportunities to grow instead of a prima facie source of suffering. This is a tricky pursuit, however, as it is difficult to remedy the source of stress and suffering without the ability to clearly identify the same. Stress can often emanate from seemingly desirable

DOI: 10.4324/9781003112150-8

propositions and attributes, which may not strike us as being inherently harmful and thus, may continue to lurk undetected, for instance, our pursuit of perfection.

Perfectionism is lauded as a desirable personal trait by organizations and individuals alike. The desire to produce the perfect output at all times, while seemingly positive, has slowly but surely evolved into a disdain for making mistakes, and consequently, an inability to deal with the consequences. The paradox here is that as we pursue perfection in the quest for a peaceful existence—whether as an individual or an organization—we pay massive, intangible costs in the form of physical, economic, and psycho-social well-being. Perfectionism can therefore be incredibly counterproductive, by inculcating a blinkered focus on the failures, and therefore not allowing for achievements to be celebrated.

This mindset also has a potentially damaging effect on our mental health and well-being—with available evidence and literature suggesting that it can lead to depression and anxiety starting from a fairly young age, tiredness, low mood, increased tendency to self-harm, and a variety of linked and proximate disorders, including eating disorders, PTSD, and OCD (Accordino et al., 2000). Data also suggest a strong correlation between mental health disorders emanating from increased exposure to stress, and an increase in the rates of self-harm including suicides. Grimly enough, this correlation cuts across age groups and includes young people (Flett and Hewitt, 2014).

With mental health issues touted as the next worldwide pandemic (Heale, 2020), there are extremely capable forces, institutions, and individuals working to identify a variety of remedies to help deal with the issue. However, a problem with such deep-rooted causal factors cutting across multiple realms of personal, professional, and organizational structures in society is sure to require a multi-faceted approach in order to deal with it adequately, and this is where key learnings from philosophy can play a crucial role. Japanese philosophy is beautifully balanced in this regard—having developed a nation and more importantly, a culture associated with perfection, it not only encourages, but celebrates imperfections by viewing them as beauty in visible signs of repair (Buetow and Wallis, 2017), which is the basis behind the art of *kintsugi*—the art of repairing broken pottery with lacquer, dusted or mixed with powdered precious metals.

In this way, Japan celebrates imperfections by looking at it as an art form, and by forcing the onlooker to look at imperfections for what they truly are—the opportunity to learn and to elevate the final product into something absolutely unique, while acknowledging the realities of a journey not devoid of hardships, and highlighting perseverance, adaptability, and a healthy respect for factors outside of our control. The beauty of Japanese philosophy therefore lies in its tendency to poke at the obvious to seek out the meaningful, and in this way, it seeks to make even the most abstract of concepts relatable and applicable to daily scenarios. *Kintsugi* could be applied to lives and organizations struggling to deal with the pressure which accompanies the pursuit of excellence, and to help inculcate a culture where mistakes—while still avoidable if possible—are not viewed as sin, and are in fact treated as opportunities for improvement.

To develop such a perspective on life requires a level of consciousness and mindfulness which is not easy to hone, but once achieved, is likely to be sustainable owing to its simplicity of thought. Here, it is fitting to focus on the concept of *Wabi-Sabi*, a very existential, primal philosophy emanating from Japan. It refers to a refreshing attitude toward aesthetics, which focuses on the natural, the impermanent, and the imperfect, originating from philosophies in China, and then settling as a useful way of life in Japan, where it is still difficult to identify one concrete definition for the concept, most framing it instead as a mere state of mind (Juniper, 2003).

For people who incorporate the concept of Wabi-Sabi within their lives, you'll find that they agree on one thing, which is appreciating the cycle of every life—birth and death. All things on earth will eventually move on to a state of decay and humans are not exempt from it. In between birth and death, Wabi-Sabi compels us to age gracefully and enjoy life's journeys and to embrace the idea of coming to terms with the process of getting older while realizing that life is inherently transitory and imperfect.

There is only one thing in this world that's perpetual and that is change. This is something that several people are fearful and anxious about. Humans fear change because we lose control over a situation, we feel powerless, and eventually this deters our self-determination. The principles of Wabi-Sabi make us more accepting of change, especially in dealing with things that are beyond our control, and in this way, we learn to embrace this perpetual phenomenon, allowing us to anticipate the same on a personal and organizational level in a more productive manner.

While Wabi-Sabi could therefore be seen as a state of elevated mindfulness, *Ikigai* helps provide the very reason for our being. This principle simply means a deep and personal pursuit of finding one's purpose for being, i.e. having something or someone to motivate you to carry on and continue living. Your Ikigai is the very reason why you get up in the morning, get dressed, and get out to the world. Ikigai compels us on a journey to find our one true purpose—our calling. Consequently, this brings us happiness and satisfaction.

Most people believe that a purpose-driven life equates to a long life and there are multiple studies that associate longevity to Ikigai. In particular, the Okinawa islands in Japan are among the few places that have an above-average longevity rate, especially for females. The secret? A combination of the Okinawa diet, their regional genome, social support, and of course, Ikigai (Yildirim, 2020).

In the following portions, we will explore these concepts in more depth.

Part II

Ikigai

Time is perhaps the most expensive currency in the world. Ikigai teaches us to spend it wisely by avoiding three common mistakes. First, as humans, we have the tendency to dwell on one thing, wasting our valuable time that can be spent elsewhere. Second, we waste our time on several other things that are unnecessary and superficial. Lastly, we don't spend our time well enough, doing too little (Yildirim, 2020).

What does this imply then? We have the freedom to choose the things in life we want to focus on. It doesn't need to be just a single thing and we definitely don't need to spread ourselves too thin either. With Ikigai, it urges us to engage in activities that interest us and make us truly happy, creative, and fulfilled (Yildirim, 2020).

Ikigai encourages us to leverage our strengths to find our purpose in life. While talent is inherent, skills can be learned. So we can all start from learning to build our strengths. Once we have established our strengths, we'll have more options on how to live our lives and discover our purpose, our Ikigai (Yildirim, 2020).

Devoting our time investing in the skills that we are good at will ultimately lead us to something we enjoy doing, providing us with financial security and letting us contribute to society. These are all fundamental aspects of Ikigai.

Ikigai is finding the convergence or the center of the things you are passionate about, your chosen mission in life, your vocation, and your profession. In other words, it is finding the overlaps between the things you love doing, things you are good at, what you can be paid for doing, and what the world needs from you.

The truth is not all of us can work our way toward the center; nonetheless, there is fulfillment in making headway toward our Ikigai. This is where we should be optimists. It is all about finding healthy approaches in achieving our purpose and in the process of doing so, stay grounded to reality.

Life presents us with plenty of opportunities and it is up to us how we choose to live it. There will always be obstacles but there are also several ways around it. Wabi-Sabi and Ikigai are only examples of life philosophies that provide guidance and balance.

We are not perfect and we can get easily overwhelmed with life but that's perfectly fine. A life coach is always there to provide you with the necessary tools to develop yourself, help you unlock your potential, and live a life that's fulfilling. In all the beauty, madness, and complexities of life, the question now remains—How do you choose to live?

Ikigai therefore revolves around the art of defining your own meaning in life. Usually, this inward journey requires a lot of patience and time before you find this sense of 'purpose' within yourself. It is about establishing a balance between the things you are passionate about, something the world needs (no matter how small or big), the things you are good at, as well as the feasibility of financial scenarios. Of course, there are innumerable ways to interpret *ikigai*; although countless thinkers have come forward with their ideas on how to find the most fulfillment in life, the word remained largely open to interpretation.

Héctor García and Francesc Miralles published a book titled *Ikigai: The Japanese Secret to a Long and Happy Life*. The book explores how the lifestyles of people in Okinawa are directly correlated to their longevity—and this in turn elevated *ikigai* from a concept to a lifestyle. The book attributes the long life of Okinawans to the following (García and Miralles, 2018):

1 Eating only until you're 80 percent full
2 Stay active and don't retire
3 Surround yourself with good friends
4 Get in shape
5 Reconnect with nature
6 Live in the moment
7 Give thanks
8 Take it slow
9 Smile and acknowledge the people around you
10 Follow your *ikigai*

You've probably heard most of these tips before, but García and Miralles ignited further interest on the Japanese philosophy of ikigai, which inspired several TED talks on the topic of 'finding your ikigai.' For Japanese workers in big cities, a typical work day begins with a state called *sushi-zume*, a term which likens commuters squeezed into a crowded train car to tightly packed grains of rice in sushi.

However, the stress doesn't stop there. The country's obsession with a relentless work culture ensures most people put in long hours at the office, governed by strict hierarchical rules. Overwork is not uncommon and the last trains home on weekdays around midnight are filled with people in suits. However, it has become a deep-seated aspect of the culture which begs the question why the people choose to do it, day after day, regardless of the stress that ensues? And this is where Ikigai helps explain this process, by being the very reason why we get up in the morning.

To those in the West who are more familiar with the concept of ikigai, it's often associated with four overlapping qualities: what you love, what you are good at, what the world needs, and what you can be paid for (Mitsuhashi, 2017).

For the Japanese however, the idea is slightly different. One's ikigai may have nothing to do with income. In fact, in a survey of 2,000 Japanese men and women conducted by Central Research Services in 2010, just 31% of recipients considered work as their ikigai (Central Research Services, 2010). Someone's value in life can be work—but it is certainly not limited to that.

There are many books in Japan devoted to ikigai, but one in particular is considered definitive: *Ikigai-ni-tsuite* (About Ikigai), published in 1966. The book's author, psychiatrist Mieko Kamiya, explains that as a word, ikigai is similar to "happiness" but has a subtle difference in its nuance. Ikigai is what allows you to look forward to the future even if you are miserable right now (Kamiya, 1966).

In a 2001 research paper on ikigai, co-author Akihiro Hasegawa, a clinical psychologist and associate professor at Toyo Eiwa University, placed the word ikigai as part of everyday Japanese language. It is composed of two words: *iki*, which means life and *gai*, which describes value or worth. According to Hasegawa, the origin of the word ikigai goes back to the Heian period (794–1185). *Gai* comes from the word *kai* ("shell" in Japanese) which was deemed highly valuable, and from there ikigai derived as a word that means value in living (Mitsuhashi, 2017).

Hasegawa points out that in English, the word *life* means both lifetime and everyday life. So, ikigai translated as *life's purpose* sounds very grand. "But in Japan we have *jinsei,* which means lifetime and *seikatsu,* which means everyday life," he says. The concept of ikigai aligns more to *seikatsu* and, through his research, Hasegawa discovered that Japanese people believe that the sum of small joys in everyday life results in more fulfilling life as a whole (Mitsuhashi, 2017).

Japan has some of the longest-living citizens in the world—87 years for women and 81 for men, according to the country's Ministry of Health, Labour and Welfare (2019). Could this concept of ikigai contribute to longevity? Author Dan Buettner believes it does. He is the author of *Blue Zones: Lessons on Living Longer from the People Who've Lived the Longest* (Buettner, 2010), and has travelled the globe exploring long-lived communities around the world.

One such zone is Okinawa, a remote island with a remarkably high number of centenarians. While a unique diet likely has a lot to do with residents' longevity, Buettner says ikigai also plays a part. "Older people are celebrated, they feel obligated to pass on their wisdom to younger generations," he says. This gives them a purpose in life outside of themselves, in service to their communities (Buettner, 2010). According to Buettner, the concept of ikigai is not exclusive to Okinawans: "there might not be a word for it but in all four blue zones such as Sardinia and Nicoya Peninsula, the same concept exists among people living long lives." Buettner suggests making three lists: your values, things you like to do, and things you are good at (Buettner, 2010). The cross section of the three lists is your ikigai (Mitsuhashi, 2017). But, knowing your ikigai alone is not enough. Simply put, you need an outlet. Ikigai is "purpose in action," he says.

In a culture where the value of the team supersedes the individual, Japanese workers are driven by being useful to others, being thanked, and being esteemed by their colleagues, says Toshimitsu Sowa, CEO of HR consulting firm Jinzai Kenkyusho (Mitsuhashi, 2017). CEO of executive recruiting firm Probity Global Search Yuko Takato spends her days with highly qualified people who consider work as their ikigai and, according to Takato, they all have one thing in common: they are motivated and quick to take action (Mitsuhashi, 2017).

However, this is not to say that working harder and longer are key tenets of the ikigai philosophy—nearly a quarter of Japanese employees work more than 80 hours of overtime a month, and with tragic outcomes—the phenomenon of karoshi (death from overwork) claims more than 2,000 lives a year.

Rather, ikigai is about feeling your work makes a difference in people's lives. How people find meaning in their work is a topic of much interest to management experts. One research paper by Wharton management professor Adam Grant explained that what motivates employees is "doing work that affects the well-being of others" and to "see or meet the people affected by their work" (Grant, 2013). In one experiment, cold callers at the University of Michigan who spent time with a recipient of the scholarship they were trying to raise money for brought in 171% more money when compared with those who were merely working using a phone. The simple act of meeting a student beneficiary provided meaning to the fundraisers and boosted their performance. This applies to life in general. Instead of trying to tackle world hunger, you can start small by helping someone around you, like a local volunteering group (Mitsuhashi, 2017).

Part III

Wabi-Sabi

Two preliminary observations about the Japanese cultural tradition are relevant to the arts. First, classical Japanese philosophy understands reality as constant change, or (to use a Buddhist expression) impermanence.

The idea of mujō (impermanence) is perhaps most forcefully expressed in the writings and sayings of the 13th-century Zen master Dōgen, who is arguably Japan's profoundest philosopher, but there is a fine expression of it by a later Buddhist priest, Yoshida Kenkō, whose work '*Essays in Idleness*' (Tsurezuregusa, 1332) sparkles with aesthetic insights (Parkes and Loughnane, 2018).

It does not matter how young or strong you may be, the hour of death comes sooner than you expect. It is an extraordinary miracle that you should have escaped to this day; do you suppose you have even the briefest respite in which to relax (Brownlee and Keene, 1968)? In the Japanese Buddhist tradition, awareness of the fundamental condition of existence is no cause for nihilistic despair, but rather a call to vital activity in the present moment and to gratitude for another moment's being granted to us (Parkes and Loughnane, 2018).

The second observation is that the arts in Japan have tended to be closely connected with Confucian practices of self-cultivation, as evidenced in the fact that they are often referred to as "ways [of living]": chadō, the way of tea (tea ceremony), shōdō, the way of writing (calligraphy), and so forth. And since the scholar official in China was expected to be skilled in the "Six Arts"—ceremonial ritual, music, calligraphy, mathematics, archery, and charioteering—culture and the arts tend to be more closely connected with intellect and the life of the mind than in the western traditions. To this day, it is not unusual in Japan for the scholar to be a fine calligrapher and an accomplished poet in addition to possessing the pertinent intellectual abilities (Parkes and Loughnane, 2018).

In the aforementioned '*Essays in Idleness*' Kenkō asks, "Are we to look at cherry blossoms only in full bloom, at the moon only when it is cloudless?" (Brownlee and Keene, 1968) If for the Buddhists the basic condition is impermanence, to privilege as consummate only certain moments in the eternal flux may signify a refusal to accept that basic condition. Kenkō continues: "To long for the moon while looking on the rain, to lower the blinds and be unaware of the passing of the spring—these are even more deeply moving. Branches about to blossom or gardens strewn with faded flowers are worthier of our admiration." This is an example of the idea of wabi, understated beauty, which was first distinguished and praised when expressed in poetry. But it is in the art of tea, and the context of Zen, that the notion of wabi is most fully developed (Parkes and Loughnane, 2018).

The term sabi occurs often in the Manyōshū, where it has a connotation of desolateness (sabireru means "to become desolate"), and later on it seems to acquire the meaning of something that has aged well, grown rusty (another word pronounced sabi means "rust"), or has acquired a patina that makes it beautiful (Parkes and Loughnane, 2018).

The importance of sabi for the way of tea was affirmed by the great 15th-century tea master Shukō, founder of one of the first schools of tea ceremony. As a distinguished commentator puts it: "The concept sabi carries not only the meaning 'aged'—in the sense of 'ripe with experience and insight' as well as 'infused with the patina that lends old things their beauty'—but also that of tranquility, aloneness, deep solitude" (Hammitzsch, 1993).

The feeling of sabi is also evoked in the haiku of the famous 17th-century poet Matsuo Bashō, where its connection with the word sabishi (solitary, lonely) is emphasized. The following haiku typifies sabi(shi) in conveying an atmosphere of solitude or loneliness that undercuts, as Japanese poetry usually does, the distinction between subjective and objective (Parkes and Loughnane, 2018):

"Solitary now—
Standing amidst the blossoms
Is a cypress tree."

Contrasting with the colorful beauty of the blossoms, the more subdued gracefulness of the cypress—no doubt older than the person seeing it but no less solitary—typifies the poetic mood of sabi (Parkes and Loughnane, 2018).

As an extremely complex aesthetic value, it is difficult to find a corresponding word for Wabi-Sabi in a foreign language. Therefore, when the Japanese introduce Wabi-Sabi to the world outside of Japan, a series of short sentences and phrases are often used to make a broad, multiple, and flexible description. Leonard Koren described it as a hybrid for introducing Wabi-Sabi "a beauty of things imperfect impermanent, and incomplete. It is a beauty of things modest and humble it is a beauty of things unconventional." In short, Wabi-Sabi expresses the beauty of incompleteness, imperfections, nature, simplicity, silence, humility, etc.

Wabi-Sabi refers to an aesthetic philosophy and vision applied to objects, which alludes to beauty in imperfections and the value of the passage of time, and openly accepts the deterioration and transience of existence, both human and material. For example, a lovely porcelain teacup that has been used for many years—it is chipped and scratched from use, but has acquired value and beauty from its rich history. But, beyond the aesthetic perspective, Wabi-Sabi also has lessons for our daily actions and the way we conceive of the world and life itself.

Richard Powell, author of the book *Wabi Sabi Simple*, notes that, "Nothing lasts, nothing is finished, nothing is perfect" (Powell, 2005)—and to this I would add, that is fine. It is necessary to learn that we can find beauty in imperfection, that we must honor the fleeting nature of experiences and existence itself by savoring and living in the present moment, that life is not and will not be perfect but that it is beautiful, and that nothing is permanent, which is why every moment is sacred.

We may be frustrated with a situation, we may feel that things are not as we would like, we may wish that some things lasted longer and others were over sooner. We suffer when our plans don't go as we expected, or when an experience is not as perfect as we had hoped.

Wabi-Sabi can help us adapt in a healthy way to the changes and endless cycles of life. As Charles Darwin wrote, it is not the strongest or most intelligent species that survive, but rather the most flexible and adaptable. During this time, we are faced with a call for attention and a reminder to return to the essential—the simple and magical aspects of life. We can learn to recognize beauty and appreciate imperfection and impermanence as an opportunity to grow and to live to the fullest.

How can we start to practice Wabi-Sabi? Here are four ways to take this philosophy into everyday life.

Savor the present moment

Much is being said and written now about the practice of mindfulness—the art of living in the present—and how we can train our minds to be in the here and now, so we can enjoy the positive moments of each day. We can start by taking a few minutes daily to focus on breathing, body sensations, or emotions. Mindfulness practice invites us to be present throughout the day: to enjoy that first cup of coffee in the morning, to contemplate the clouds and their movement with amazement, to listen more deeply, and (when we can do so safely) to hug each other heart to heart.

Embrace Your Personal Story

Reflect on the path you've travelled, on all the ups and downs, and bring attention to the moments of joy, learning, and transformation (both external and internal) that you have experienced over time. Each person has a unique story with its own authentic and particular beauty. Reflecting and writing about these moments allow us to cultivate perspective and feel a sense of accomplishment and empowerment. It is equally important to give love to the scars that have marked our lives; we must not forget that each one of them adds value to our personal history.

Extract Learning

When things do not go as we expect or we are surprised by events that alter the order of our lives, what can we learn from the situation? Learning shifts us from victims to creators, allowing us to adapt and cultivate a resilient attitude toward change, loss, and transition.

Find Beauty in Simplicity

We can learn to redefine beauty, to expand our gaze, and to bring into focus elements that elicit joy and appreciation. We can do this with the objects we've gathered around us, with our everyday interactions with those we meet or live with, and also with nature. You might try taking pictures of the beauty you observe each day, and creating a Wabi-Sabi album.

The time has come to embrace change, fleetingness, and imperfection as a source of beauty, wisdom, and growth. We often speak of the "ravages of time"; we are conditioned to resist aging and seek eternal beauty and youth. Time does not wreak havoc—time shapes works of art and gives value to both objects and people. How wonderful to be able to tell stories and to have wrinkles and scars (internal and external) that have marked the path of a lifetime!

There are times when life unfolds in a very different way than we would have liked or imagined, when we have no control and are forced to face the imperfection of a situation. We are experiencing one of those times right now with COVID-19: a situation that no one expected and that has turned our lives upside down. It is in moments like these that we can return to the simple but profound philosophy of Wabi-Sabi, one of the Japanese secrets for a happy life.

Part IV

Japanese Philosophy, Life, and Knowledge

Ikigai, as an idea is becoming popular outside of Japan as a way to live longer and better. It not only facilitates people to find their purpose in life (PIL) but also provides them with an ability to integrate stressful events during the course of their lives without any ambiguity. As a natural corollary, it leads to reduced anxiety and lower sympathetic nervous system activity during psychologically and physically stressful situations.

Work-Life Balance

Work-life balance constitutes an important aspect of people's life in modern times. Notwithstanding its importance, the concept or phrase 'work-life balance' has been overused without people really understanding as to what it actually means. Theoretically, balance could suggest a 50/50 split but more often than not it does not happen that way. The focus and priority keeps shifting between family and work depending on the exigencies. However, considering the time people spend on work, it is worthwhile finding ikigai in one's work so as to sustain long-term work-related self-motivation.

Organizations relying on robust strategy of pursuing an ikigai approach can successfully instill a sense of purpose and joy in their teams which inter-alia leads to positive organizational outcomes. In a survey conducted in 2016, 82% of the Japanese men and women who responded felt they needed to feel joy at work in order to feel fulfilled.

Organizational purpose

Increasingly, the present society is acquiring a secular hue, which, in turn, is leading people to search for purpose and meaning in their work life (Taylor, 2019). Progressively, employees care less about monetary fulfillments and more about how their work seeks to fulfill a greater purpose. To illustrate, a recent study by LinkedIn found that 74 percent of job candidates want a job where they feel like their work matters (LinkedIn, 2019).

Workplace culture thrives when an organization and its employees identify and nurture their collective purpose. In the workplace, collective purpose symbolizes the shared goals and values of an organization and its people. A shared purpose serves as the driving force behind staff, encouraging them forward with a clear sense of direction and a mutually acknowledged destination (Taylor, 2019).

Job Crafting

Job crafting is the process of shaping any job to achieve better alignment to an individual's motives, strengths, and passion. It is the act of crafting and designing one's own job instead of passively accepting the job that is allocated (Berg, Dutton and Wrzesniewski, 2007). The term 'job crafting' was coined in 2001 by Jane Dutton and Amy Wrzesniewski (Wrzesniewski and Dutton, 2001). Prof Dutton says that the idea of job crafting had been going on for many years. She found that nearly 75% of the workers had already made spontaneous changes or adjustments to their jobs to satisfy their personal needs and make their jobs more fulfilling. Finding *ikigai* at work often requires us to do some form of job crafting to make the jobs more engaging and rewarding.

The Power of Flow

Psychologist Mihaly Csikszentmihalyi asserts in his book *Flow: The Psychology of Optimal Experience* that Flow is "the state in which people are so involved in an activity that nothing else seems to matter; the experience is so enjoyable that people will continue to do it even at great cost, for the sheer sake of doing it." When we flow, we are focused on a concrete task without distractions. Our mind is "in order" (Csikszentmihalyi, 1990). The ability to reach this state of 'Flow' is the key ingredient for finding happiness and living according to one's *ikigai*. In other words, it is the motivation, passion, and involvement people bring to their work which fuels their will to contribute positively to the company's goals.

Engaged employees

One day, on John F. Kennedy's first visit to NASA, he met a janitor who was mopping the floor and asked him what he did at NASA. The janitor replied, "I'm helping put the man on the moon!" He had a clear understanding of the purpose and expressed in NASA's vision that guided his actions and showed him how his work mattered. That's engagement. Multiplied across an organization, this has a ripple effect: Highly engaged teams have better customer engagement, higher productivity, fewer accidents, and 21% greater profitability. Engaged employees also have lower absenteeism and higher morale (Harter, 2018).

Companies that provide meaningful and purposeful work don't only have higher profit margins, but their employees *feel* like they make a difference. They are emotionally invested in the business—it isn't just a paycheck to them; it's an opportunity to do work that matters. Engaged employees are naturally inclined to learning and seeking new challenges, continuously investing in their work, making a clear connection between their skills and their role, and committing to improvement and alignment with the company's purpose.

It is clear therefore, that it is necessary to keep a work-life balance, which means that an equilibrium needs to be maintained between our professional and personal lives. We spend a lot of time and energy in professional organizations where we invest crucial hours in carrying out mandated tasks and discharging responsibilities; it is imperative for organizations to be sensitized to the need for 'work-life balance,' for example, a balance between the work we are doing and deriving pleasure out of and a balance between the chores we are performing and maintaining meaningful connections with our co-workers. All of this can be achieved if we inculcate this approach in corporations.

The needs of both organization and employee go hand in hand. We have studied that the organizational goals and individual goals coincide with each other and it is very important to satisfy both of them. Consider an employee who is not enjoying his work and remains dissatisfied and unhappy because of his job: He or she will not work at his full potential and his productivity will remain low. This will lead to the downfall of the firm because the efficiency of the employee is directly related to the growth of the company. On the other hand, consider an employee who appreciates his work and is satisfied with it: he'll remain self-motivated and nobody needs to waste his time in encouraging him and he'll work at his optimum level. This will lead to the advancement of the institution.

Building a strong workplace community

We all know that an organization is nothing but a collection of people working together. If the workforce of the institution is pleased with their work and are excited about it, then they will keep good and positive relations with their colleagues and this is bound to increase the sense of belongingness and teamwork among the people of the company, and this will help the management develop.

The employer can conduct various interactive sessions, several games, and fun activities as this can increase the team bonding of the workers. They can also provide numerous incentives and rewards whether monetary or non-monetary as this can give recognition to their work. For example, there is a software company named 'Engagedly' which provides Guru badges to those employees who perform well in their training and development sessions; 'Google' provides employee stock option plan to their people as it creates a sense of ownership among them; recently 'Zomato' came up with the "period leave" policy for their female workers. These are just some of the examples that can ensure that the employees not only remain engaged on a more personal level, but try and align their purpose: their "why" with that of the organization.

Also at the time of recruitment or the hiring process, the recruiter can ask the person who is applying for the job some questions such as 'What are our strengths? What are we good at? Do we know what the company needs from us?' By answering all these questions, the interviewer will understand the psychology of the person as he will be able to read his mind and this can help in making good decisions. For example, if the company wants a person who has good technical skills but the person who is applying for the job is not good at it. He is just applying for the sake of it and the employer also agrees to this. The idea is that first the person needs to understand the basics of that skill and then he'll need to master it or get proficiency in it. If he realizes that he is not suitable for this job, he might get irritated with his work and ultimately regretting his decision. In order to avoid such situations both the administration as well as the individual should apply this approach; otherwise, we will end up at the wrong place.

Sustainability, Mindfulness, and the Art of Imperfection

The effect of perfectionist aesthetics reaches the supermarket shelves as well. Another consequence of perfectionist aesthetics is the accelerated pace of the perceived obsolescence of manufactured goods, ranging from clothing to hi-tech gadgets that encourages fast fashion (Saito, 1997). This consumer action fuelled by perfectionist aesthetics is responsible for resource depletion, environmental degradation, mounting garbage, not to mention human rights violation in those developing nations where many goods are manufactured and where developed nations' garbage gets dumped. Imperfectionist aesthetics is helpful in responding to these environmental consequences of perfectionism (Haeg, 2010).

In the matter of consumer goods, there has been a growing interest in repair. Under perfectionism, repair has a negative connotation because it is associated with damage. However, in the apparel industry, which is notorious for promoting fast fashion, some designers are starting to incorporate signs and potentials for repair in their designs.

Wabi-Sabi encourages us to be content with what we have and resist the urge to constantly update or refresh our homes and wardrobes to keep up. Saving and investing in quality items, those that are likely to be passed down through generations, can help minimize environmental impact and help you find gratitude for what you own. Upcycling or adopting a 'make do and mend' attitude is also another way to embrace Wabi-Sabi and extend the lifespan of our possessions.

Wabi-Sabi is acknowledging that new isn't always more beautiful than old, and, in turn, questioning the societal pressure to constantly consume and upgrade. This is perhaps accelerated by ever-evolving technology and the idea that we need the next phone, tablet, or computer as ours is soon outdated. Challenging this compliments the principles of slow design and slow interiors, which instead champions local craftsmanship over the mass-produced and encourages being conscious of the environmental impact of our purchases. This is also particularly pertinent for fast fashion and the speed at which low quality trend-led garments are produced.

Wabi-Sabi also encourages letting go of the past. Wabi-Sabi and particularly Kintsugi place emphasis on where you are on your journey. A beautiful new bowl which becomes cracked and repaired with gold isn't damaged; instead it becomes so much more than what it was before. That being said, it can never go back to what it originally was. It's about being at peace with change and decay and seeing these as progression, learning from the cycle of nature and the seasons. As a result, Wabi-Sabi encourages mindfulness and an engaged relationship with the present.

This concept of Wabi-Sabi offers potent wisdom to help us deal with a rollercoaster year like 2020. It is an acceptance and appreciation of the impermanent, imperfect, and incomplete nature of everything, including ourselves. And when you really think about that, it's relief. We are not supposed to be perfect. We are all works-in-progress, as are our careers, and relationships, and lives. When things don't work out, we can pause, reflect, and grieve, then shapeshift, innovate, transform, or evolve, or simply choose to try again.

The principles that underlie Wabi-Sabi can teach us life lessons about letting go of perfection and accepting ourselves just as we are. They give us tools for escaping the chaos and material pressures of modern life, so we can be content with less. And they remind us to look for beauty in the everyday, allowing ourselves to be moved by it and, in doing so, feeling gratitude for life itself. The secret of Wabi-Sabi lies in seeing the world not with the logical mind but through the feeling heart. Perhaps that is the way to navigate this pandemic and come out the other side with a sense of hope.

Conclusion

Modern times are VUCA times (**V**olatile, **U**ncertain, **C**omplex, and **A**mbiguous) that describe the state of constant flux which individuals, societies, and businesses find themselves in. The manifestation can be also termed as an 'era of acceleration' wherein all types of goods can be ordered online and delivered within hours. People rely on apps for accessing and downloading instructional videos for seemingly normal activities like exercise and meditation. Then, there are apps for online ordering of meals from various restaurants and food-vending outlets. Consequence of this ever-increasing rate of technological advancement and social change is speeding up the pace of business and life itself, thereby making most of us time-starved where a 24-hour day is not enough. Exacerbating the situation is the fact that people today are under intense pressure to be "ideal workers"—totally committed to their jobs and always on call. As a natural corollary, the world is suffering the consequences emanating from a global lifestyle which calls upon them to constantly adjust their work schedules to suit different time zones across continents, which throws their biological clock out of sync. Quite logically, people are suffering from sleep disorders and encounter related health problems. With the problem assuming gargantuan dimensions, it has dawned on people that social systems should be allowed to auto-heal by slowing down or reducing the pace of life so as to enable each of us to pay attention to an easy-paced life, wellness, and time-tested food habits.

The early years of the 21st century have witnessed a worldwide epidemic of poor mental health and related illnesses. By 2030, the cost to the global economy of all mental health problems could amount to $16 trillion. How the world confronts mental health challenges, which are a blight on a growing number of people's lives as well as an economic encumbrance, was on the agenda at the World Economic Forum's Annual Meeting 2019 in Davos (Fleming, 2019).

Simplicity and finding contentment in what we have is at the heart of the slow living mindset. But, as with many ethics, slow living takes inspiration from age-old philosophies which have stood the test of time across centuries and generations of wise men and learned philosophers. Out of people all over the world, the Japanese have perfected the art of integrating ancient philosophies into their daily practices. There seems to be a piece of Japanese philosophy to suit every stress or struggle in life. Shintoism, Buddhism, and Qi, which advocate the unity of mind and body, have contributed to the Japanese philosophy of life. The practice of psychosomatic medicine emphasizes the connection between mind and body and combines the psychotherapies (directed at the mind) and relaxation techniques (directed at the body) to achieve stress management. Participation in religious activities such as preaching, praying, and meditating helps in achieving mind as well as body relaxation.

Japanese philosophies teach us how to be gentler, kinder, and more mindful, both toward ourselves and to others. For a culture that values treating others with respect so highly, these philosophies are so important. Japan has a long and rich history of wellness helped by the introduction of Buddhism and also by evolution of traditions through the centuries. The philosophy and practices behind wellness and health are woven deep into the fabric of Japanese culture. The events that shaped modern-day Japan have brought about these ideas of wellness and ultimately created a healthy society. Just like in traditional Indian healing systems, philosophy lies at the heart of *J-Wellness*.

The world has woken up to the power of Japan inspired wellness called J-Wellness, which is motored by ikigai—the Japanese word for 'a reason to live.' Ikigai is a mystical inner space of equilibrium where needs, desires, ambitions, and satisfaction come together. Then there is Kintsugi—the art of repairing 'broken pottery' and Wabi-Sabi that embraces the flawed or the imperfect—an object's use marks its value since its broken parts, cracks, and repairs reflect events in its existence akin to a human being's passage through life.

As the Global Wellness Summit 2020 Report observes, "Japan is not standing still, but rather executing exciting innovations on top of its cultural traditions of trust, exacting quality in all matters, and a deep reverence for nature." Japan's ancient esoteric healing and wellness culture is catching the imagination of the world that's constantly in search of new miracle cures. J-Wellness is a balanced state of the mind, body and soul to achieve perfect serenity and quality of life. Brilliantly marrying revered traditions with innovative technologies, Japan asserts a comprehensive culture of wellness—and encourages the world to follow suit.

To sum up, we only live once. We have one life, and therefore only one chance to live it fully, with meaning and purpose.

References

Accordino, D.B., Accordino, M.P. and Slaney, R.B. (2000). An investigation of perfectionism, mental health, achievement, and achievement motivation in adolescents. *Psychology in the Schools*, 37(6), pp.535–545.

Berg, J.M., Dutton, J.E., and Wrzesniewski, A. (2007). What is Job Crafting and Why Does it Matter?. *Positive Organisational Scholarship*, Michigan Ross School of Business [online] Available at: https:// positiveorgs.bus.umich.edu/wp-content/uploads/What-is-Job-Crafting-and-Why-Does-it-Matter1.pdf

Brownlee, J.S. and Keene, D. (1968). Essays in Idleness: The "Tsurezuregusa" of Kenkō. *Books Abroad*, 42(3), p.491.

Buetow, S. and Wallis, K. (2017). The Beauty in Perfect Imperfection. *Journal of Medical Humanities*, 40(3), pp.389–394.

Buettner, D. (2010). *The blue zones : lessons for living longer from the people who've lived the longest.* Washington, D.C.: National Geographic Society; Enfield.

Central Research Services (2010). Central Research Report (No. 636), [online] Available at: https://www.crs.or.jp/backno/No636/6362.htm.

Fleming, S. (2019). *This is the world's biggest mental health problem - and you might not have heard of it.* [online] World Economic Forum. Available at: https://www.weforum.org/agenda/2019/01/this-is-the-worlds-biggest-mental-health-problem/.

Flett, G.L. and Hewitt, P.L. (2014). A Proposed Framework for Preventing Perfectionism and Promoting Resilience and Mental Health Among Vulnerable Children and Adolescents. *Psychology in the Schools*, 51(9), pp.899–912.

Garcia, H. and Miralles, F. (2018). *Ikigai: the Japanese Secret to a Long and Happy Life.* Thorndike Press.

Grant, A.M. (2013). *Outsource Inspiration* in Dutton, J.E. and Spreitzer, G. (Eds.), *Putting Positive Leadership in Action,* [online] Available at: https://faculty.wharton.upenn.edu/wp-content/uploads/2013/12/Grant_OutsourceInspiration.pdf.

Haeg, F. (2010). *Edible estates: attack on the front lawn: a project by Fritz Haeg.* Editorial: New York: Metropolis Books.

Harter, J. (2018). *Employee Engagement on the Rise in the U.S.* [online] Gallup.com. Available at: https://news.gallup.com/poll/241649/employee-engagement-rise.aspx.

Heale, R. (2020). *Is a Crisis in Mental Health the Next Pandemic?* [online] Evidence-Based Nursing blog. Available at: https://blogs.bmj.com/ebn/2020/10/04/is-a-crisis-in-mental-health-the-next-pandemic/.

Horst Hammitzsch (1993). *Zen in the art of the tea ceremony.* New York, N.Y., U.S.A.: Arkana.

Juniper, A. (2003). *Wabi sabi: the Japanese art of impermanence.* Boston: Tuttle Pub.

Kasulis, T. (2019). *Japanese Philosophy.* Summer 2019 ed. [online] Stanford Encyclopedia of Philosophy. Available at: https://plato.stanford.edu/entries/japanese-philosophy/.

Kamiya, M. (1966). 生きがいについて / *Ikigai ni tsuite.* みすず書房, Tōkyō: Misuzu Shobō.

LinkedIn (2019). Global Talent Trends 2019, [online] LinkedIn. Available at: https://business.linkedin.com/talent-solutions/resources/talent-strategy/global-talent-trends-2019#formone

Mihaly Csikszentmihalyi (1990). *Flow : The Psychology of Optimal Experience.* New York: Harper [And] Row.

Ministry of Health, Labour and Welfare (2019). Handbook of Health and Welfare Statistics 2019, [online] Available at: https://www.mhlw.go.jp/english/database/db-hh/1-2.html.

Mitsuhashi, Y. (2017). *Ikigai: A Japanese concept to improve work and life.* [online] www.bbc.com. Available at: https://www.bbc.com/worklife/article/20170807-ikigai-a-japanese-concept-to-improve-work-and-life

Parkes, G. and Loughnane, A. (2018). *Japanese Aesthetics (Stanford Encyclopedia of Philosophy).* [online] Stanford.edu. Available at: https://plato.stanford.edu/entries/japanese-aesthetics/.

Powell, R.R. (2005). *Wabi sabi simple : create beauty, value imperfection, live deeply.* Avon, Ma: Adams Media.

Saito, Y. (1997). The Role of Imperfection in Everyday Aesthetics. *Contemporary Aesthetics* [online] Available at: https://contempaesthetics.org/newvolume/pages/article.php?articleID=797

Taylor, S. (2019). *Finding your Ikigai: how to drive organisational purpose and engagement.* [online] Inside HR. Available at: https://www.insidehr.com.au/ikigai-organisational-purpose-engagement/.

Wrzesniewski, A. and Dutton, J.E. (2001). Crafting a Job: Revisioning Employees as Active Crafters of Their Work. *Academy of Management Review*, 26(2), pp.179–201.

Yildirim, E. (2020). *Lessons To Learn From Wabi-Sabi & Ikigai.* [online] Available at: https://unlockedpotentials.com/lessons-to-learn-from-wabi-sabi-ikigai/ [Accessed 30 Aug. 2021].

PART II

Knowledge Management in the Age of Digital Technology and New Economy

8

KNOWLEDGE MANAGEMENT IN THE DIGITAL ECONOMY ERA

Challenges and Trends

Xiaoying Dong and Yan Yu

Tapscott (1996) initially proposed the concept of digital economy in 1996. In the late 1990s, the analyses were mainly concerned with the adoption of the Internet and early thinking about its economic impacts (with reference to the "Internet economy") (Brynjolfsson and Kahin, 2002). The recent discussion on digital economy focuses on "digitalization", which is defined as the transition of businesses through the use of digital technologies, products, and services (Brennen and Kreiss, 2014). In the United States, it is believed that digital economy relies on the e-commerce and information technology (IT) industries, which are composed of infrastructure, e-commerce process, and e-commerce trade (Henry et al., 1999). On the G20 Summit held in 2016, the Chinese government highlighted digital economy and considered it as the most important driver for innovation and economic growth in China (NSILG office, 2016). "Digital economy" was referred to as a system that uses digital knowledge and information as key production factors, information network as an important carrier, and effective use of information and communication technology (ICT) as an important driving force for efficiency improvement and economic structure optimization of economic activities. The definition of the digital economy has evolved, reflecting the rapidly changing nature of technology and its use by enterprises and consumers (Barefoot et al., 2018).

With the advancement of ICT, digital economy has become a new economic form after agricultural economy and industrial economy. Digital economy is a new engine of economic growth, which greatly reduces the cost of information search and information sharing in the transaction activities of social members and improves the output efficiency. In the new form of digital economy, knowledge will continue to be a key competitive differentiator when it comes to driving organizational performance. Figuring out how to effectively produce and manage knowledge in the digital economy era brings forth new challenges for both researchers and practitioners.

According to the UNCTAD report on digital economy in 2019, the digital economy continues to evolve at a breakneck speed, driven by the ability to collect, use, and analyze massive amounts of machine-readable information (digital data) about practically everything. These digital data arise from the digital footprints of personal, social, and business activities taking place on various digital platforms. This has been accompanied by an expansion of big data analytics, artificial intelligence (AI), cloud computing, and new business models (e.g., digital platforms). With more devices accessing the Internet, an ever-increasing

DOI: 10.4324/9781003112150-10

number of people using digital services and more value chains being digitally connected, the role of digital data and technologies is set to expand further. As a result, access to data and the ability to transform data into digital intelligence have become crucial for organizations to gain and sustain their competitiveness.

The expansion of the digital economy creates many new economic opportunities. Digital data can be used for development purposes and for solving societal problems, including those related to the SDGs (Sustainable Development Goals). Thus, data can help improve economic and social outcomes, and be a force for innovation and productivity growth. Platforms facilitate transactions and networking as well as information exchange. From a business perspective, the transformation of all sectors and markets through digitalization can foster the production of higher quality goods and services at reduced costs. Furthermore, digitalization is transforming value chains in different ways, and opening up new channels for value addition and broader structural change.

In the digital and hyperconnected era, organizations are collecting and generating a tsunami of data, but few are able to capitalize on its full potential. Technology has also spawned new ways of working that make the knowledge management (KM) transformation become more urgent. With the explosion of workforce conversations on digital collaboration tools, knowledge no longer sits in databases waiting to be accessed but flows dynamically across the digital communications channels that now define working relationships. To fit to these changes, organizations need to redefine how they promote KM to help maximize human potential at work. Data have become a new economic resource for creating and capturing value. Learning will be always in the flow of work. Organizations should leverage new technologies that can not only contextualize information, but push it through an organization's systems to teams in ways that support problem-solving and help workers innovate and uncover new insights (See Volini et al. 2020). Therefore, knowledge discovery, which aims to turn data into digital intelligence and bring organizations strategic value, is key for them to succeed. For example, Honda invested efforts in 2019 to better understand driver behavior for improving the driver experience. By using an AI tool called Watson Discovery from IBM Watson, Honda was able to create new knowledge from analyzing complaint patterns from drivers, enabling engineers to respond to quality challenges in vehicles more efficiently. This improved not only their own work experience, but the experience of Honda's customers as well (refer to Anderson, 2019). Furthermore, the power of people and machines working together offers an opportunity for knowledge creation.

Technologies-Driven Knowledge Management Paradigm Shift

Traditional KM Technologies and Systems

According to Nonaka (1994), knowledge is dynamic, since it is created in social interactions among individuals and organizations. Nonaka and Takeuchi (1995) conducted multiple impactful research on dynamic knowledge creation for competition in the leading Japanese companies. Knowledge is also context-specific, as it depends on a particular time and space. Therefore, KM is generally defined as performing the activities involved in discovering, capturing, sharing, and applying knowledge so as to enhance the impact of knowledge on goal achievement in organizations (Becerra-Fernandez et al., 2003). Technology is undoubtedly a big part of the growing need for more effective KM. Advanced technologies, new ways of working, and shifts in workforce composition are rendering traditional views of KM obsolete.

KM systems utilize a variety of KM mechanisms and technologies to support the KM processes (Alavi and Leidner, 2001; Dong et al., 2016). Technologies that support KM include data mining and AI technologies, encompassing those used for knowledge acquisition and case-based reasoning systems, online forums, computer-based simulations, databases, decision support systems, enterprise resource planning systems, expert systems, management information systems, expertise locator systems, videoconferencing, and information repositories, encompassing best practices databases, and lessons learned systems.

According to the knowledge processes, KM systems can be classified into KM discovery systems, KM capture systems, KM sharing systems, and knowledge application systems (Becerra-Fernandez et al., 2003). Knowledge discovery systems support the process of developing new tacit or explicit knowledge from data and information or from the synthesis of prior knowledge. Knowledge capture systems support the process of retrieving either explicit or tacit knowledge that resides within people, artifacts, or organizational entities. Knowledge-sharing systems support the process through which explicit or implicit knowledge is communicated to other individuals. Discussion groups or chat groups facilitate knowledge-sharing by enabling individuals to explain their knowledge to the rest of the group. Knowledge application systems support the process through which some individuals utilize knowledge possessed by other individuals without actually acquiring that knowledge.

KM systems are also related to function-based information systems that focus on managing organizational knowledge resources and processes (Alavi and Leidner, 2001). Sources of organizational knowledge can be both external and internal. The external sources consist of inter-organizational processes, competitors, suppliers/partners, and customers and competitors, while the major internal knowledge is from employees. Accordingly, the KM systems are embedded in different information systems such as competitive intelligence system (CIS), supply chain management system (SCMS), and customer relationship management system (CRMS) and enterprise portal. These are related to four important organizational functions, including competitive intelligence, supply chain management, customer relationship management, and internal knowledge-sharing, which concentrate on different sources of knowledge. Knowledge management is embedded in organizational functions, rather than remaining isolated from them. These systems capture the generic KM processes, such as creation, storage, retrieval, and representation of knowledge, and thus can be used for managing organizational knowledge, despite the fact that each of them has its own functional specificity for certain operations.

CIS supports the management of knowledge from competitors, government, and other public knowledge, and consists of systematic processes for the acquisition, analysis, interpretation, and exploitation of competitive information. It supports innovation processes by systematically managing the competitive intelligence and tracking fast changes in markets (Lemos and Porto, 1998). Similarly, SCMS and CRMS support the management of knowledge embedded in inter-organizational processes and exchanges with the firm's partners. SCMS enable a close inter-organizational collaboration, facilitate knowledge creation and sharing among supply partners, and subsequently enhance innovativeness. CRMS contributes to products or services innovation by enabling a closer connection between the firm and its customers and facilitating their interaction with the firm. While CIS, SCMS, and CRMS serve as efficient channels for acquiring and managing external knowledge, enterprise portals focus on internal knowledge. Enterprise portal integrates knowledge from multiple functions or systems, provide access to the knowledge repertoire, and facilitate communication throughout the organization, thus enabling/supporting the important KM processes within the organization such as facilitating new ideas generation. The appropriate usage of these KM systems can enhance organizational innovativeness (Yu et al., 2013).

CPS Redefining KM Systems

The advancement of IT, such as cloud computing, big data, Internet of things (IoT), mobile Internet, and AI in recent years have refined the KM systems and applications. The cyber-physical system (CPS) helps to analyze how KM systems should be reconfigured for organizations in the era of digital economy (Dai et al., 2018). The CPS is an algorithm-enabled system, in which physical and virtual components are closely intertwined, able to operate on different spatial and temporal scales, and interact with each other depending on the changing contexts. The architecture of CPS entails five layers. Different layers are supported by differential technologies, thus enabling the value chain of transforming data toward knowledge and differential capabilities (see Figure 8.1).

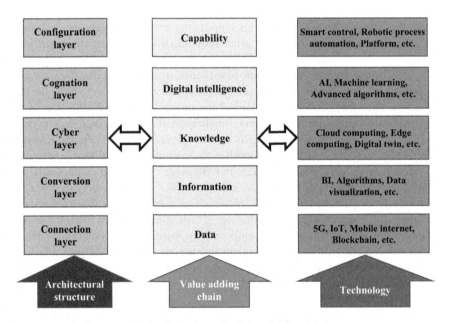

Figure 8.1 CPS Architecture-Technology along the Value-Adding Chain

(1) **The connection layer** digitizes the elements of the physical space (such as sensors, equipment, factory, process, and service), and drives the digitization of the elements and processes of the physical space, so that it has the ability of free flow and exchange in the interconnected cyberspace. The connection layer is closely related to the development of 5G, IoT, blockchains, etc. It is tightly related to data collection and storage, and further establishes the connections among the large scale of data.

(2) **The transformation layer** is to further realize the value addition of data on the basis of a large number of elements and processes in the connection layer. Data increment refers to the use of computing tools and algorithms to collect data from the connection layer. Integration, processing, analyzing, and mining help realize the transformation of data

to information. Therefore, the transformation layer is closely related to data mining and knowledge discovery.

(3) **The network layer** gathers and integrates massive data of various types and sources in cyberspace supported by cloud computing, mobile Internet, and other computing technologies. Heterogeneous digital resources interact with each other through standardized connection and heterogeneous computing methods to form a wide area data analysis basis. The aggregation of big data in the network layer breaks the information isolation between entity objects and becomes an important foundation of building digital platforms. In the network layer, knowledge, rather than data, is created and connected. Knowledge graph technologies are emerging and empower the development of a large scale of knowledge network.

(4) **The cognitive layer** uses AI and advanced algorithms to develop intelligent machines that can respond similarly as human intelligence, including natural language processing (NLP), image recognition, expert system, and deep learning. The cognitive layer can process the multi-sourced heterogeneous data (such as transaction data, user-generated data, and senor captured data) as well as knowledge (such as business rules, experience, and common knowledge). Advanced algorithms, such as machine learning and deep learning, aim to generate digital intelligence, thereby providing users with highly personalized services.

(5) **The configuration layer** entails the feedback of cyberspace information to the physical space and the guidance control of the system comprising the bidirectional interaction between the virtual world and physical world that points to the ultimate demoing market. By using preset rules and semantic norms and other control technologies, the corrective and preventive decisions made by the cognitive layer are applied to the supervised system to drive the knowledge resources to flexibly and dynamically allocate and control the underlying industrial equipment and machine components, so that the whole system has the ability of self-adaption and self-configuration. The configuration layer enables organizations to self-optimize for disturbance, self-adjust for variation, and self-configure for resilience. This is in line with the capability view of knowledge (Grant, 1996).

> ## Box 8.1: Advanced Technologies Enabling the Digital Economy
>
> **Internet of things (IoT)** refers to the growing array of Internet-connected devices, such as sensors, meters, radio frequency identification (RFID) chips, and other gadgets, that are embedded in various everyday objects enabling them to send and receive various kinds of data.
>
> **Fifth generation (5G) wireless technology** is expected to be critical for IoT due to its greater ability to handle massive volumes of data. 5G networks can process around 1,000 times more data than today's systems (Afolabi et al., 2018). In particular, it offers the possibility of connecting many more devices (e.g., sensors and smart devices).
>
> **Blockchain technologies** are a form of distributed ledger technologies that allow multiple parties to engage in secure, trusted transactions without any intermediary.
>
> **Cloud computing** is enabled by higher Internet speeds, which have drastically reduced latency between users and far away data centers. Cloud service is transforming

business models, as it reduces the need for in-house IT expertise, offers flexibility for scaling, and consistent applications rollout and maintenance (Yu et al., 2018).

Automation and robotics technologies are increasingly used in manufacturing, which could have significant impacts on employment. There are concerns that such technologies may constrain the scope for developing countries to adopt export-led manufacturing as a path to industrialization, and that the more developed economies may increasingly use robots to "reshore" manufacturing jobs.

Artificial intelligence (AI) and data analytics are enabled by the large amounts of digital data that can be analyzed to generate insights and predict behavior using algorithms, as well as by advanced computer processing power. AI is already in use in areas such as voice recognition and commercial products (such as IBM's Watson).

Digital twin consists of three distinct components, i.e., the physical product, the digital/virtual product, and connections between the two products. The connection between the physical product and the digital/virtual product is data that flow from the physical product to the digital/virtual product and information that is available from the digital/virtual product to the physical environment.

Challenges of Traditional Knowledge Management in the Digital Economy Era

Traditional KM emphasizes the process of knowledge leverage, i.e., from data to information and then to knowledge. The main activities are reflected in knowledge acquisition, processing, integration, analysis, application, and sharing. However, in the digital economy era, organizational strategy, focus, competitive approaches, value-added activities, and core knowledge appear with large changes. Traditional KM takes the organization or individual as the core, and focuses on solving the problems of knowledge acquisition, knowledge integration, knowledge application, knowledge-sharing, and knowledge creation. Among them, how to transform individual tacit knowledge into tacit and explicit knowledge at the team and organizational level, so as to improve the ability of organizational knowledge creation is the strategic goal. Traditional KM activities emphasize the influence of leaders, strategy, culture, and incentive mechanism on the effect of KM, and computer technology plays an auxiliary role. However, traditional KM encounters multiple challenges derived from the emergence of massive heterogeneous data and AI technologies in the era of digital economy. Digital data are core to all fast-emerging digital technologies, such as data analytics, AI, blockchain, IoT, cloud computing, and all Internet-based services. Data-centric business models are being adopted not only by digital platforms, but also, increasingly, by leading organizations across various sectors.

Demand for Data-driven Value Creation

Knowledge management practices are expected to result in improved productivity, improved customer and employee satisfaction, increased revenues, preparedness for AI, and effective remote work. Developing clear business value is critical for KM initiatives. In particular, the importance of proving the clear value KM offers is more important in the time of global pandemic and economic uncertainty than ever. The right KM efforts for an organization will help organizations be more agile and perform more effectively.

Business logic has changed from product dominant logic to service dominant logic (Vargo and Lusch, 2008; Vargo et al., 2010; Lusch and Nambisan, 2015; Vargo and Lusch, 2015). In the product dominant logic, enterprises impose value on commodities through a series of production activities, and then go to market to interact with consumers for product improvement. The corresponding KM practices focus on the production process and internal organization. In the service dominant logic, service is defined as "the application of specialized competences (knowledge and skills) through deeds, processes, and performances for the benefit of another entity and the entity itself" (Vargo and Lusch, 2004). Value creation is produced and completed via the proactive interaction between products/services vendors and consumers.

Interactive service shapes a process of value co-creation. Value co-creation indicates actor benefit realized from integration of resources through activities and interactions with other collaborators. Service providers offer value propositions acting as promises for stakeholders to engage in service. Value is uniquely and phenomenologically determined by service beneficiaries based on their experiences. Mining relevant knowledge from consumer data and taking it as the source of product/service innovation is crucial for value co-creation. Therefore, KM practices should expand to discover user's' potential needs in specific situations through the data-driven approach.

Demand for Heterogeneous Resource Integration

In the service dominant logic, resources are classified into operand resources and operant resources. The operand resources refer to the resources (such as land and minerals) that can be used by human beings, and their characteristics are tangible, static, and finite. Operand resources can be liquefied, unbundled, or re-bundled. Differently, operant resources refer to the resources that are capable of affecting other resources (Vargo and Lusch, 2004, 2008). Operant resources are intangible, dynamic, and infinite. The traditional economic model emphasizes the development of natural resources, such as land and material resources. In the era of digital economy, the ability to process multi-source heterogeneous data in the cyberspace has become the core competence for organizations. Barrett et al. (2015) emphasizes ITs as operant resources to enable service innovation. Advanced ITs can increase digitalization and unleash generativity to enable resource integration and create novel opportunities for value co-creation (Akaka and Vargo, 2014; Lusch and Nambisan, 2015).

Service innovation emerges when the existing resources are re-bundled or new resources are bundled to form new ways of value co-creation and develop new value (Lusch and Nambisan, 2015; Vargo and Lusch, 2015). Thus, resources integration is most important in the product/service innovation process. In a cyberspace, the integration of knowledge from different sources, structures, and characteristics will become the focus of KM. In the network layer of CPS, a large number of physical assets can be reflected and projected in cyberspace, as the so-called "digital twins". These resources are massive, diversified, volatile, heterogeneous, and so on. Leading organizations can make the large-scale and efficient integration and utilization of these resources in the cyberspace. The stronger the ability of resource integration, the greater the breadth, depth and speed of integrating resources, the higher the resource density, and the more opportunities for value co-creation among beneficiaries that can be generated. Knowledge management practices based on previous management information systems are not adequate nor competent. The advancement of AI and machine learning technologies are demanded to apply in KM practices.

Demand for Understanding the Knowledge Ecosystem and Multi-Modal Data Analytics

The increasing multi-source heterogenous data requests an improved understanding of the knowledge ecosystem, including all types of knowledge, information, and data. Organizations demand to be able to effectively capture, manage, and find everything together. Thus, KM efforts should help organizations consolidate, present, find, discover, and relate all of their different types of content (including files, data, knowledge, collaborative materials, and even people). This enables paths of discovery where an end-user can traverse content, data, and people in order to find all of the content that can help them complete their immediate mission and develop their knowledge over the longer term. The analysis and interpretation of digital assets help people understand, analyze, and make forward-looking and accurate decisions. When implementing KM practices, organizations pay more attention to how to leverage everything they have, making it easily and intuitively available to the people, connecting knowledge, and empowering people to act on the discovered knowledge.

With the integration and rapid growth of data, the capability of knowledge analysis and discovery are demanded to further improve. In the connection layer of CPS, the technology application realizes full connection, including the connection between people via social media, the connection between people and things via e-commerce platforms, the connection between things via IoT, Internet of vehicles, aeroengine data network, etc., and the connection between people and things and processes via logistics platforms. Sensors installed on physical objects can collect massive data in the product and its production process, projection of physical assets in the cyberspace to form digital twins, and present the real-time and accurate mirror images of physical objects, attributes, and states, including shape, position, state, and motion. The advancement of analytics on multi-source, multi-modal data in the cyberspace and creation of dynamic and real-time digital simulation model impose challenges to knowledge capture and discovery.

Trends of KM for Leveraging Digital Economy Development

In the era of digital economy, the importance and strategic significance of KM have been significantly recognized. Technology has a tremendous impact on KM, inspiring the development of robust platforms to leverage KM strategies. Knowledge management technologies and tools continue to evolve in response to new demands and challenges. We propose the following trends of KM development in the new era.

Change from Data Mining to Real-Time Decision-Making

Knowledge management efforts focus on initiating and realizing data-driven value creation and co-creation. Knowledge management is developed for offering decision supports to organizations. Advanced KM tools, such as dynamic digital dashboard, digital panel, and various visual tools, help employees judge, make decisions, and take countermeasures for problem-solving. Knowledge management needs to help organizations achieve their strategic objectives and better serve society. For examples, governments can effectively provide convenience services, crisis management, and social resource coordination through e-government system and smart city system; enterprises can accurately provide customized products and services to fulfill customer needs. To achieve these goals, organizations should develop data-driven decisions as organizational culture.

Change from Local Knowledge Management to Global Knowledge Management

From the architectural perspective, KM is changing from local KM to global KM at different levels of granularity. Knowledge management activities that previously developed in silos, including enterprise strategy, R&D, marketing, or production are requested to expand along the whole business processes and value chain. Also, knowledge embedded in people, equipment, processes, and activities that can be captured and analyzed at finer granularity. Therefore, organizations need to update the prior knowledge ontology and redefine the internal and external knowledge of the organizations. Knowledge ontology serves as blueprint to define the attributes and relationships of each agent in organizations.

Value Co-creation Enables Efficient Innovations in Organizations

Knowledge creation is a continuous, self-transcending process through which one transcends the boundary of the old self into a new self by acquiring a new context, a new view of the world, and new knowledge (Nonaka, 1994). The vertical and horizontal division of labor in traditional organizations has formed a large number of information silos. These silos impede knowledge dissemination and exchange, reduce knowledge-sharing efficiency, and thus result in a lower level of creativity and environmental adaptability for organizations. The digital connection in cyberspace provides unprecedented access to barrier-free knowledge flow and sharing, and creates a solid foundation for activating organizational creativity. Business insights derived from data mining and scene tracking can help organizations make quick trial and error, transform new ideas into business value, and thus continuously adapt to changing environments. In particular, large digital platform-based organizations, such as Alibaba, Tencent, and Tiktok, are able to tightly aggregate the creativity from data mining and knowledge discovery on large-scale user behaviors, as well as aggregate the demands from related stakeholders, such as product manufacturers, service providers, financial institutions, information providers, and so on. Value is co-created through the connections and interactions between consumers and relevant stakeholders, and the match between the supply side and the demand side.

Automate Unstructured Content Analysis to Drive Knowledge Discovery

Organizations are increasingly becoming insight-driven. On one hand, the development of IoT, mobile Internet, AI, and other technologies brings explosive growth of data; on the other hand, such development increases data complexity, weakens information reliability, and increases the difficulty of extracting valuable knowledge. The emerging knowledge fragmentation calls for more robust KM (Gray and Meister, 2003). Unlike structured data (tables, forms, log files), it is difficult to search for and analyze meaningful information from unstructured data. Knowledge management technologies are developed for acquiring, processing, and tagging massive unstructured content and making it available for search and analysis. The rapid development of AI technologies, such as machine learning, and NLP enables the automation processes of unstructured content analysis, including extracting entities (people, locations, companies, etc.), identifying sentiment, and categorizing topics. Therefore, the demand for AI-enabled search and analytics solutions will become more prevalent in organizations.

Build a Large-Scale Enterprise Knowledge Graph for Organization's' Intelligence

It is necessary to understand ontologies and knowledge graphs empower enterprise AI. The idea of a knowledge graph was first proposed in 2000 and developed by Google in 2012. A knowledge graph represents a collection of interlinked descriptions of entities, including objects, events, or concepts. Knowledge graphs put data in context via linking semantic metadata and, in this way, provide a framework for data integration, unification, analytics, and sharing. Foundational KM activities, such as taxonomy and tagging, content types and content cleanup, content governance, and tacit knowledge capture, are all critical to an organization's goals of connecting their knowledge, content, and data and automating ways of pushing it to the right users and assembling it for greater value and action. Enterprise knowledge graph is becoming the foundation of the navigation system to represent organizational knowledge assets in different segments, such as marketing, organizational structure, innovation, and human resources.

Traditional KM emphasizes the macro-level knowledge mapping and audit, such as developing an organizational knowledge map and competence map to reflect the knowledge asset. Knowledge objects are limited to documents and skills, and knowledge discovery is usually rule based. In the era of digital economy with massive data, organizations can use knowledge graph technology to build a large-scale, fine-grained, high-quality knowledge base. Knowledge graphs can reveal the structural relationships of people, equipment, products, and processes, and provide the support required for important decision-making, through the comprehensive use of algorithms, machine learning, graphics, information visualization technology, information retrieval, image recognition, speech recognition, and so on.

Knowledge graphs can serve as a kind of tacit knowledge elicitation and representation technology, and further establish dynamic relationships between different fields of knowledge. Knowledge graphs help to externalize the tacit knowledge of experts and transform them into organizational knowledge resources, thus helping organizations explore the value of their intellectual assets. Knowledge graphs can also enrich the knowledge-seeking experience for users. Google has pioneered question–answer capabilities in an effort to transform its "search engine" into a "knowledge engine" with the Google Knowledge Graph. The development of enterprise knowledge graphs, together with the rapid development of NLP technology, enable organizations to develop knowledge-driven intelligent businesses, such as answering highly complex questions faster and more accurately, providing innovative customer service, identifying employees for problem-solving, and predicting market trends.

Coordinate Interactions between Human and Machine Intelligence

Tacit KM has always been the difficulty and key of KM. Nonaka and other scholars (Nonaka,1994; Nonaka and Takeuchi, 1995; Nonaka et al., 2000) proposed a model of knowledge creation consisting of three elements: (i) the SECI process, including socialization, externalization, combination, internalization, for knowledge creation through conversion between tacit and explicit knowledge; (ii) ba, the shared context for knowledge creation; and (iii) knowledge assets: the input, output, and moderator of the knowledge-creating process. These three elements of knowledge creation have to interact with each other to form the knowledge spiral that creates knowledge. The SECI model emphasizes that knowledge creation can be promoted through the transformation spiral of tacit knowledge and explicit knowledge in social communication groups and situations. Tacit knowledge is shaped by the production experience, professional insight, and the practical wisdom of leader. Tacit knowledge is generated by mutual communication and collision among individual employees or groups. Tacit knowledge shapes an organization's' interpretation of the surrounding environmental changes.

In the era of digital economy, the source of tacit knowledge is further expanded into human-computer interaction. Digital twin is a real mapping of all components in the product life cycle using physical data, virtual data, and interaction data between them (Tao et al., 2019). Digital twins integrate IoT, AI, machine learning, and software analytics with spatial network graphs to create living digital simulation models that update and change as their physical counterparts change. A digital twin continuously learns and updates itself from multiple sources to represent its near real-time status, working condition, or position. This learning system learns from itself, using sensor data that conveys various aspects of its operating condition; from human experts, such as engineers with deep and relevant industry domain knowledge; from other similar machines; from other similar fleets of machines; and from the larger systems and environment of which it may be a part. A digital twin also integrates historical data from past machine usage to factor into its digital model. Therefore, digital twins foster rich human–machine interactions. As such, tacit knowledge is generated in a faster and more dynamic way, which requests robust KM to facilitate and coordinate the work between human and self-reinforcing machines.

In addition, the pandemic crisis has greatly accelerated the use of remote workers and a distributed workforce. Knowledge management should drive more effective collaboration across remote teams of workers, as well as the collaboration between workers and intelligent machines.

Concluding Remarks

In the era of digital economy, knowledge as the most important manipulative resource has become the core asset of an organization to create a competitive advantage. At the same time, we are only at the initial stage of understanding the challenges of KM with regard to concept, system, technology, and method in an era of digital economy. On the one hand, the difficulty of KM is increasing, and the requirements of users are increasing as well. The growth and dynamic changes of massive data put forward higher requirements for data acquisition and integration. Heterogeneous integration and data mining have become the key, while the accuracy, real-time, and accuracy of data to information and then to knowledge are higher. On the other hand, original KM needs to be constantly updated in technical means, and the role of human-computer interactions and AI needs to be actively explored. In order to deal with the challenges of KM in the digital economy era, more human and material resources should be invested; multi-disciplinary experts should be integrated for collaborative exploration; and KM systems and methods should be constructed to meet the requirements of the digital economy era.

Therefore, it is important for organizations to adopt agile KM that emphasizes iteration, collaboration, self-organization, and customer-centric designs. Organizations are requested to address the challenges of business and operational performance, as well as the development and implementation of a KM-based strategy in the new era.

Acknowledgment

The authors would like to acknowledge the support from the National Natural Science Foundation of China "Organizational Ambidexterity of Technology Firms: Impact of Strategic Leadership and Organizational Learning" (Grant No. 71371017) and the partial support from the National Natural Science Foundation of China (Grant No. 72172155, 91846204) and the Beijing Social Science Foundation (Grant No. 17GLC056). Dr. Yan Yu will serve as the corresponding author of this chapter.

References

Afolabi, I., Taleb, T., Samdanis, K., Ksentini, A. and Flinck, H. (2018), "Network slicing and softwarization: A survey on principles, enabling technologies, and solutions", *IEEE Communications Surveys & Tutorials*, Vol. 20 No. 3, pp. 2429–2453.

Akaka, M.A. and Vargo, S.L. (2014), "Technology as an operant resource in service (eco)systems", *Information Systems and e-Business Management*, Vol. 12 No. 3, pp. 367–384.

Alavi, M. and Leidner, D.E. (2001), "Review: Knowledge management and knowledge management systems: Conceptual foundations and research issues", *MIS Quarterly*, Vol. 25 No. 1, pp. 107–136.

Anderson, P. (2019), "IBM announces new industry-leading NLP features inside Watson Discovery", IBM.

Barefoot, K., Curtis, D., Jolliff, W., Nicholson, J.R. and Omohundro, R. (2018), Defining and measuring the digital economy. Working Paper. Bureau of Economic Analysis, United States Department of Commerce, Washington, DC.

Barrett, M., Davidson, E., Prabhu, J. and Vargo, S.L. (2015), "Service innovation in the digital age: Key contributions and future directions", *MIS Quarterly*, Vol. 39 No. 1, pp. 135–154.

Becerra-Fernandz, I., Gonzalez, A. and Sabherwal, R. (2003), *Knowledge Management: Challenges, Solutions and Technologies*, Prentice Hall, USA.

Brennen, S. and Kreiss, D. (2014), Digitalization and digitization. Culture Digitally. 8. Available at: http://culturedigitally. org/2014/09/digitalization-and-digitization/.

Brynjolfsson, E. and Kahin, B. (2002), "Understanding the digital economy [electronic resource]: Data, tools, and research", Presidents & Prime Ministers.

Dai, Y.S., Ye, L.S., Dong, X.Y. and Hu, Y.N. (2018), "CPS and the future development of manufacturing industry: A comparative study of policies and capacity building between China, Germany and the United States", *China Soft Science*, No. 02, pp. 11–20. (Chinese)

Dong, X.Y., Yu, Y. and Zhang, N. (2016), "Evolution and coevolution: Dynamic knowledge capability building for catching-up in emerging economies", *Management and Organization Review*, Vol. 12 No. 4, pp. 717–745.

Grant, G.M. (1996), "Prospering in dynamically-competitive environments: Organizational capability as knowledge integration", *Organization Science*, Vol. 7. No. 4, pp. 375–387.

Gray, P.H. and Meister, D.B. (2003), "Introduction: Fragmentation and integration in knowledge management research", *Information Technology & People*, Vol. 16 No. 3, pp. 259–265.

Henry, D.K., Buckley, P. and Gill, G. (1999), *The emerging digital economy II*, Washington, DC: US Department of Commerce.

Lemos, A.D. and Porto, A.C. (1998), "Technological forecasting techniques and competitive intelligence: Tools for improving the innovation process", *Industrial Management & Data Systems*, Vol. 98 No. 7, pp. 330–337.

Lusch, R.F. and Nambisan, S. (2015), "Service innovation: A service-dominant logic perspective", *MIS Quarterly*, Vol. 39 No. 1, pp. 155–175.

Nonaka, I. (1994), "A dynamic theory of organizational knowledge creation", *Organization Science*, Vol. 5 No. 1, pp. 14–37.

Nonaka, I. and Takeuchi, H. (1995), *The knowledge-creating company: How Japanese companies create the dynamics of innovation*, Oxford University Press.

Nonaka, I., Toyama, R. and Konno, N. (2000) "SECI, BA and leadership: A unified model of dynamic knowledge creation", *Long Range Planning*, Vol. 33, pp. 5–34.

Office of the network security and information leading group of the CPC Central Committee (NSILG office). G20 digital economy development and cooperation initiative [EB / OL]. [2016-09-29]

Tao, F., Sui, F., Liu, A., Qi, Q., Zhang, M., Song, B., Guo, Z., Lu, S.C.-Y. and Nee, A.Y.C. (2019), "Digital twin-driven product design framework", *International Journal of Production Research*, Vol. 57 No. 12, pp. 3935–3953.

Tapscott, D. (1996), *The digital economy: Promise and peril in the age of networked intelligence*, McGraw-Hill.

UNCTAD (2019), *Digital economy report 2019: Value creation and capture: Implications for developing counties*.

Vargo, S.L. and Lusch, R.F. (2004), "Evolving to a new dominant logic for marketing", *Journal of Marketing*, Vol. 68 No. 1, pp. 1–17.

Vargo, S.L. and Lusch, R.F. (2008), "From goods to service(s): Divergences and convergences of logics", *Industrial Marketing Management*, Vol. 37 No. 3, pp. 254–259.

Vargo, S.L. and Lusch, R.F. (2015), "Institutions and axioms: An extension and update of service-dominant logic", *Journal of the Academy of Marketing Science*, Vol. 44 No. 1, pp. 5–23.

Vargo, S.L., Lusch, R.F. and Akaka, M.A. (2010), "Advancing service science with service-dominant logic", *Handbook of Service Science*. Springer US.

Volini, E., Schwartz, J., Denny, B., Mallon, D., Van Durme, Y., Hauptmann, M., Yan, R. and Poynton, S. (2020), Knowledge management: Creating context for a connected world. *Deloitte Insights*.

Yu, Y., Dong, X.Y., Shen, K.N., Khalifa, M. and Hao, J.X. (2013), "Strategies, technologies, and organizational learning for developing organizational innovativeness in emerging economies", *Journal of Business Research*, Vol. 66 No. 12, pp. 2507–2514.

Yu, Y., Li, M., Li, X., Zhao, J.L. and Zhao, D. (2018), "Effects of entrepreneurship and IT fashion on SMES' transformation toward cloud service through mediation of trust", *Information & Management*, Vol. 55 No. 2, pp. 245–257.

9

DEMYSTIFYING THE LINK BETWEEN BIG DATA AND KNOWLEDGE MANAGEMENT FOR ORGANISATIONAL DECISION-MAKING

Krishna Venkitachalam and Rachelle Bosua

Introduction

The knowledge management (KM) discipline has matured significantly over the past 30 years. Evidence of this comprises a variety of models, typologies and perspectives of knowledge, i.e. tacit versus explicit and objectivist versus practice-based knowledge (Jasimuddin, Klein and Connell, 2005; Hislop et al., 2018; Marabelli and Newell, 2014), the nature of knowledge, i.e. embrained, embodied, embedded, encoded and encultured (Blackler, 1995), knowledge creation, i.e. the SECI model (Nonaka, 1991a, 1991b; Nonaka and Hirose, 2015; Nonaka and Toyama, 2005; Nonaka and Toyama, 2003), knowledge strategy (Bosua and Venkitachalam, 2013; Hansen, Nohria and Tierney, 1999), dynamics in strategic KM (Venkitachalam and Willmott, 2015), strategic shifts in knowledge (Venkitachalam and Willmott, 2016), social perspectives on networking and the flow and use of knowledge in teams, social networks and across cultures (Adler and Kwon, 2002; Bosua and Scheepers, 2007; Cross et al., 2001; Nahapiet and Ghoshal, 1998).

In contrast, the fields of big data and business analytics[1] (BA) have emerged introducing analytics as a process of developing actionable decision-making or recommendations for actions using insights gathered from historical sets of data (Chen et al., 2012; Sharda et al., 2018). Hence, in the past decade, there has been significant growth and interest in big data. The increased focus on data as an important organisational resource is not new, as data has always been the backbone of traditional business processing applications and systems since the 70s. With the introduction of Web 2.0 and Hadoop in 2005, new developments in technology (e.g. digital platforms, cloud computing, AI and machine learning) accompanying tools to collect and process large volumes of structured and unstructured data resulted in a new era of 'datafication'. Datafication is described as a technology trend whereby every possible aspect of business and human life is changed into a digital form for the sake of adding value (Lycett, 2013; Sadowski, 2019).

From a computational perspective, the focus in recent years on big data and BA (Chen and Zhang, 2016; Lycett, 2013) has sparked a growing need to analyse data to gain a deeper understanding of business needs, trends and customer requirements. Over the past two decades

 DOI: 10.4324/9781003112150-11

the new discipline 'data science' has developed significantly to complement big data processing and make sense of datafication (Lycett, 2013; Stodden, 2020). As an evolving and interdisciplinary field, data science draws on computational methods, processes, statistical algorithms, data mining techniques, machine learning and IT platforms and systems to extract 'knowledge' and insights from large sets of structured and unstructured data. Predictions are that the future of digital business will significantly draw on data science to support BA, which may provide unlimited possibilities to create business value (Gartner, 2020; Hernán et al., 2019; Vicario and Coleman, 2020).

A review of the KM literature indicates that knowledge will remain to be one of the most important resources of the 21st century (Litvaj and Stancekova, 2015; Razzaq et al., 2019). In a recent global study by Heisig et al. (2016), the authors highlight the future research areas of KM influencing many organisational aspects including knowledge creation and sharing, innovation, knowledge worker productivity and performance, decision-making and competitive advantage. One area that is of specific importance is decision-making and KM. Since KM has a unique interdisciplinary nature, there is yet a scant understanding of how organisational decision-making in the context of KM is enabled by datafication. Since datafication features strongly in a competitive landscape, there is no clear link between the fields of big data and KM yet. Therefore, the aim of this chapter is to explore this link through the literature to determine how the two areas of big data and KM in organisations for decision-making can be bridged. Hence, the research question: *What is the bridging link between big data and KM for organisational decision-making?*

In unpacking this question, we focus on insights and prior literature on big data and KM with a focus on organisational decision-making. As part of the study insight/s, we introduce the idea of *'contextual knowledge experts'* and define these *'as humans who are equipped with a specific context (dependent or bounded) of know-what and know-how, and whose collective expertise is critical to decision-making needed in different facets of an organisation'*.

This chapter is structured as follows: the next section describes the approach followed to analyse the literature. Section 'Literature Background' highlights key themes that emerged from insights based on literature review in the areas of big data and KM in organisational decision-making. 'Conceptual Model – Big Data, Knowledge Management and Organisational Decision-making' presents a conceptual model that represents the link between big data, KM, decision-making and related discussion and insights. Finally, 'Conclusions' describes limitations of the work, implications of this work for academia and practice and follow-up research.

Literature Review Method

Literature Selection

We followed a systematic approach to find, filter and analyse relevant literature, using a synthesis of the methods proposed by Wolfswinkel et al. (2013) and Webster and Watson (2002). The initial search for papers first scoped the field of study bounding the search to two disciplinary areas: big data and KM. We took into consideration that the KM discipline was at the time of writing more mature than the big data discipline in terms of frameworks, methods, processes and models. In addition, we were conscious that the link between big data and KM is an emerging field, and hence were guided by our insights in both areas to further refine our set of search keywords. In the course of our interpretation of the literature, we identified the importance of organisational decision-making through human intellectual capabilities. As a result, our keywords evolved into a final set of keywords used to search relevant literature: datafication, intellectual capabilities, BA, decision-making and big data, which were used in one or more 'AND' and 'OR' combinations with the keywords: knowledge, knowledge management, knowledge management processes, tacit knowledge, and explicit knowledge.

We conducted our search using the EBSCO and Web of Science databases and used papers that resulted from Google Scholar and the Open University search engine. In addition, we concentrated also on KM journals we were familiar with from our own research and based on Serenko and Bontis's (2022) ranking list of top 3 KM journals, e.g. *Journal of Knowledge Management* (JKM), *Knowledge Management Research and Practice* (KMRP) and *Knowledge and Process Management* (KPM). Our refined search criteria further narrowed down the papers to English, peer-reviewed papers from 2014 to 2021, but we also included highly cited papers considered topical from earlier years. Our multi-method search approach resulted in papers that were filtered on title and selected finally based on the alignment of its abstract to the paper's research question. A mix of 62 conceptual and empirical papers were used in our analysis and interpretation to shape the outcomes of this book chapter.

Analysis of the Literature

In analysing the final set of papers, a 3× step coding process proposed in Wolfswinkel et al. (2013) and used in qualitative research (Strauss and Corbin, 1998) was followed. Open themes describing the link between big data, KM and decision-making were first identified. Thereafter, we clustered the open themes into meaningful categories in line with the process suggested by Gioia and Hamilton (2013) and Strauss and Corbin (1998). We report on the interpreted themes as five relevant sub-sections in the next section.

Literature Background

Development of the KM Discipline

Central to the KM literature is the important distinction between tacit and explicit knowledge in organisations and its relation to business strategy, organisational development, the use of ICTs, protection of knowledge and organisational decision-making amongst others (Alavi and Leidner, 2001; Hislop et al., 2018; Jasimuddin et al., 2005; Venkitachalam and Busch, 2012). The sharing and transfer of knowledge within and across firm boundaries and entities enabled by ICT and human perspectives have been the most researched knowledge processes in the KM literature. Related to knowledge sharing is the ability of individuals to absorb new knowledge for decision-making and new knowledge creation (Malhotra et al., 2005; Martin-de Castro et al., 2015).

Since the beginning of the 1990s, KM has developed into an important management field that increases our understanding of the vital role of knowledge as an organisational asset (Alavi and Leidner, 2001; Ruggles, 1998). Ever since the conceptualisation of Nonaka's knowledge creation theory (1991a, 1991b, 1994), and Spender and Grant's (1996) view of knowledge as a key resource (Barney, 1991) for strategic decision-making, the KM discipline has contributed several theories and models related to identifying, capturing, sharing, evaluating, retrieving, and reusing an organisation's knowledge assets (Alavi and Leidner, 2001; Watson and Hewett, 2006). Through the application and use of these knowledge-based theories in combination with ICTs and the management literature, KM has tried to fulfil a key role in explaining the importance of knowledge for decision-making in organisations.

In the 21st century, the KM discipline emphasises knowledge as a key asset that gives organisations the capability to retain a competitive edge through product and service innovation (Grant, 1996). Subramaniam and Youndt (2005) indicate that an organisation's ability to effectively use its knowledge resources is closely linked to its ability to make timely strategic decisions to create value in the environment where it operates. More specifically, organisational decision-making relates to an organisation's collective know-how and ability to utilise its knowledge resources to create and develop new business models, routines, strategies and adapt to its environment and create value through its products and services.

The inherent nature of organisational know-how includes human tacit knowledge, which is difficult to articulate but is part of the individual and collective courses of action in decision-making that generates value in the market. Institutionalised knowledge embedded and encoded in routines and procedures over time resides as explicit knowledge in ICTs (Jasimuddin et al., 2005; Schneider, 2018). Explicit knowledge is useful for humans to recall former knowledge experiences and actions to recreate and reconstruct experiences that are valuable in organisational decision-making. In general, organisational knowledge is a firm's most valuable assets, the know-how that exists collectively in a firm's employees and their interactions constitute unique knowledge and competences that organisations apply to solve unique problems allow firms to realise and maintain its competitiveness (Bontis, 2001; Campos, Dias Teixeira and Correia, 2020).

Data and the Processing of Big Data

Data, whether a limited dataset or big data, is processed into information. Data consists of bare facts, characters or symbols that turn into information once processed by computers. Data can be structured (highly specific, stored in a predefined format) or unstructured (consists of varied types of data such as text, images, audio and web content) (Sharda et al., 2018). The processing of data into information has evolved over decades into many different tools, techniques and methods. The tools have further evolved to specifically support pre-processing and preparation of big data so that it is ready for processing into information. Examples include tools to consolidate, cleanse, transform and reduce data (the so-called data 'life-cycle', see Sharda et al., 2018). Once ready for processing, mathematical and statistical techniques have gained more recognition as enabling tools to recognise patterns in large volumes of data and solve specific business problems. At present, the three main BA types are descriptive, predictive and prescriptive, each drawing on different statistical methods to process big data (Akter et al., 2019; Sharda et al., 2018) (see Figure 9.1).

Descriptive analytics, enabled by business reports, dashboards, scorecards and large data sets from data warehouses, is used to solve problems asking: 'what is the average expenditure per household' and 'how do the means between two datasets compare'-type questions. Outcomes are averages, means or standard deviations of data sets for well-defined business problems. Predictive analytics is enabled by data, text, web mining and forecasting. More complex statistical methods such as linear and complex regression, factor analysis and forecasting models are used to predict future events through answers to questions such as: 'how many sales referrals will I get next month' and 'how many calls will I get tomorrow'? Thirdly, prescriptive analytics is enabled by optimisation and simulation techniques, decision-modelling and expert systems. Questions asked are 'what shall we do to avoid ....', 'how should we plan... ', and 'must we consider...? Outcomes are best possible business

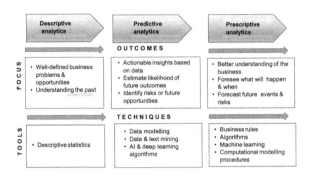

Figure 9.1 Business Analytics Types, Focus and Tools

decisions and actions for business problems. Prescriptive analytics deals with issues that raise questions about actions that need or need not be taken, what the right or wrong course of action is, or what is good or bad for a specific situation.

The data, information and knowledge hierarchy has been described frequently in the KM, organisational development and management literatures. Instead of focusing on this hierarchy, it would be more meaningful to describe the role of big data in this hierarchy. When conceptualising big data, the three 'VVV'[2] properties of big data (i.e. volume, variety and velocity) are distinguished (Akter et al., 2019; Chen, Chiang & Storey, 2012; Sharda et al., (2018). Volume refers to large quantities of data created on a daily basis worldwide. Variety refers to different types of data being created, i.e. data in traditional forms (in databases), and non-traditional forms, i.e. data created through social media, IoT devices and wearables with data as video, text, audio and graphics. Velocity refers to the speed at which data is generated with some data generated in real time (e.g. Twitter or Facebook feeds) that requires distributed processing, while other data is generated less frequently over time. The processing of big data into information, therefore, gives more insights into past experiences and trends, particularly if this data is presented visually.

From Big Data to Knowledge

Although the big data and KM link is not yet fully established from a KM perspective, recent literature acknowledges the value of big data in effective decision-making and improving business operations such as in marketing and supply chain (Chen et al., 2012 and Davenport, 2013). For example, the processing of data from social media channels can provide many new insights to marketers, e.g. how different customers react to specific advertising, what they like to see and more. This allows marketing companies to customise their advertising efforts to specific users. Big data and BA can therefore, through data mining and machine learning, provide many new insights that have not been possible before. These insights allow many organisations to make more informed decisions and help to further develop value and competitive advantage. The emergence of platform-based business models and application of BA help organisations to improve their services to customers or clients. One example is Amazon whose aim is to effectively serve customers while also learning what customers find trendy for future offerings and services.

Big data and BA have a different perspective on knowledge compared with the KM discipline. Blackler (1995) positions knowledge as embedded in human minds and embodied in human actions to differentiate between tacit and explicit knowledge. Tacit knowledge (know-how) is rooted in action and experience, is difficult to imitate, exists in human minds and has both cognitive and technical elements (Nonaka, 1994). Tacit knowledge is gained through extensive expertise that comprises interaction between knowing and doing (Jasimuddin et al., 2005; Schultze and Stabell, 2004). Tacit knowledge is therefore a unique intellectual capability and an essential cognitive resource contributing to innovation. In contrast, explicit knowledge can be articulated, uttered, codified and communicated in written, symbolic or natural language (Alavi and Leidner, 2001). Examples are routines captured in digital form, rules of thumb, heuristics, practical guidelines or any other form that can be accessed or used by others (e.g. digital artefacts). Explicit knowledge is declarative knowledge (or 'know-what') that can also exist individually or collectively, e.g. in a team or a group who has worked together and share experiences as a result of complex problem-solving as a team over time.

Explicit knowledge is a basis for new knowledge creation, and drawing on the SECI model (Nonaka, 1994), the articulation of tacit knowledge into a digital explicit form makes explicit knowledge available through ICTs to others in an organisation, enabling access to and internalising explicit knowledge. Explicit knowledge is not considered information per se, but actionable knowledge enabling its recipients to create new knowledge through knowing and acting. The internalisation of explicit knowledge can also spur the creation of new knowledge in a totally different knowledge context. Knowledge is therefore dynamic (Venkitachalam and Willmott, 2015) and processes of making tacit knowledge explicit, allows for synthesising, incorporating and applying knowledge in new scenarios. So, in the context of big data and BA, literature sources refer to computers having the ability to "… *create new knowledge on its own…*" (Muller et al., 2019), while BA techniques can '*discover*' and '*extract*' knowledge from big data through data mining algorithms, pattern matching and machine learning (Sharda et al., 2018).

Considering the definition, dimensions and nature of knowledge found in the KM literature, there is a vast difference between the conceptualisation of knowledge in big data and BA versus the meaning of knowledge in the KM discipline (Tian, 2017). Knowledge in big data and BA is an outcome of the algorithmic pattern matching and data mining that enables organisations to better understand patterns in the data. Hence, the challenge is to discern whether this 'knowledge' is indeed explicit or tacit knowledge, i.e. actionable insights that first lead to a deeper understanding of one context to another, and secondly leads to more effective decision-making in a knowledge context. At this point of contextual shift and dependency, there is no clear picture whether this context-bounded knowledge can be clearly understood from an empirical (big data) perspective.

The Context of Knowledge

One of the most important characteristics of knowledge is that it is sticky and tied to a specific context (Meacham, 1983; Tsoukas, 1996). Detached from its context, knowledge makes no sense and loses its unique value. Take for example the unique jargon that develops in a fibromyalgia health community that frequently interacts in the Reddit online social media group. The illness has unique symptoms, traits and labels for specific things, e.g. the chronic illness community uses the tag 'spoonie' to explain one's lack of energy. Too much energy spent in the morning on a day might leave one with limited energy levels (fewer 'spoons') for the afternoon/evening. The word 'spoonie' has no meaning when used alone and out of context, but in the context of chronic illness, this term has a very specific context and meaning.

The importance of a knowledge context is therefore a central underpinning of the data-information-knowledge hierarchy. Tsoukas (1996) describes an organisation as a distributed knowledge system whereby the use of knowledge is not known by a single agent alone. The knowledge an organisation needs to draw on is indeterminate and continually emerging (Venkitachalam and Willmott, 2016). As a result, knowledge is not self-contained but consists of the stock of: (i) role-related normative expectations, (ii) dispositions formed as a result of social networking and (iii) local knowledge related to specific situations or circumstances related to time and place. In this context, Tsoukas (1996) highlights four types of organisational knowledge and they are: (i) conscious explicit knowledge of an individual, (ii) objectified knowledge, which is explicit and held by the organisation (as in an organisational memory), (iii) automatic preconscious individual knowledge and (iv) collective highly context-dependent knowledge, which is present in the practices of an organisation. Of importance is thus knowledge of a specific context held individually or shared collectively in an organisation as a result of *shared practices and know-how* acquired over time through learning.

Human and Organisational Decision-Making

Extant BA literature expresses the need for practitioner knowledge in statistical methods, models, tools and techniques to improve decision-making (Muller et al., 2019). Decision-making is a complex concept rooted in psychology and comprises a higher order of thinking that involves human intellectual capabilities (Pohl, 2008). Intellectual ability is an individual's exceptional capability that evolves through a set of cognitive process, i.e. the ability to find and solve problems, reasoning, including spatial reasoning, memory use and recall, the ability to manipulate abstract ideas and make connections (Jaques, 1986). Intellectual ability evolves over time through an individual's rate of learning and experiences in a specific knowledge area, hence human cognition is often tied to a specific knowledge context resulting from prolonged exposure to problem-solving through acting and learning (Pohl, 2008).

Intellectual capability manifests as cognitive processes individuals draw on to solve complex problems through planning and carrying out goal-directed activities. Organisational decision-making therefore requires the combination of intellectual capabilities of multiple knowledge sources (both tacit and explicit). In an age of more competition, the nature of organisational problem-solving has become more complex, hence decision-making in an era of big data requires mechanisms that integrate machine knowledge with human intellectual capability. Kurzweil articulated this need way back in 1999 using Brockman's words (2002), stating '...*we are entering a new era* .... *it's a merger between human intelligence and machine intelligence*...'. With the advent of BA, there is a gap in the literature that explains how big data links to KM from an organisational decision-making perspective.

Conceptual Model – Big Data, Knowledge Management and Organisational Decision-making

Based on the preceding discussion, the conceptual model in Figure 9.2 attempts to illustrate the outcome of the BA knowledge discovery and pattern-matching activities that interprets large data sets yielding actionable insights from this data. BA is becoming increasingly adopted to support organisational decision-making (Akter et al., 2019). As explained before, the outcome of the BA process's 'machine knowledge' is used in the organisational decision-making process. This knowledge is not yet the explicit knowledge of KM that represents a specific knowledge context.

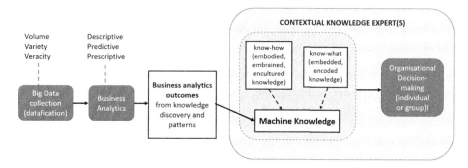

Figure 9.2   Link between Big Data and Organisational Decision-Making

Based on our analysis of the literature indicating the gap in understanding the link between big data and KM, our model illustrates that the link between machine intelligence and human intelligence needs to be brokered through the specialist know-how and know-what of *contextual knowledge experts*. Their expertise is essential to link big data and KM and solve complex business problems for organisational decision-making. To further explain this gap, we develop the following five insights derived from the literature, which are discussed in the section that follows:

Take as an example, studies as that of O'Connor and Kelly (2017) and Sumbal et al. (2017) and scholars like Pauleen's (2017) interview with one of the global experts (David Snowden) in the field of KM caution that the role of human know-how/judgement cannot be overlooked when understanding the link between big data and KM in decision-making. Snowden illustrates the case of recruitment, where there is growing evidence of using BA algorithms/big data tools to determine which candidate should attend a job interview. Snowden argues:

> *People these days are actually using algorithms to determine which CVs get put forward for an interview. You can now buy an algorithm that will improve your CV, so it's more likely to get accepted (by an algorithm designed to find acceptable CVs). This is just getting nonsensical. And it's removing human judgment from the process. And if KM is about one thing, it's about emphasizing the value of human judgment and human sensemaking*

> *(Pauleen, 2017, p.13)*

This aspect of human judgement and sensemaking a particular context/s can be effectively managed by (what we conceptualise in this chapter as) 'Contextual knowledge experts'. Hence,

Insight 1: *Contextual knowledge experts are essential to bridge the big data–KM gap for decision-making in organisations.*

When considering the limitation of raw data source/machine knowledge generated from a BA process (O'Connor and Kelly, 2017; Sumbal et al., 2017), consider the case of water engineers monitoring water pumps in reservoirs (Pauleen, 2017). Snowden explains his work with,

> *water engineers (allowed) them to report any micro anomaly they see – something they wouldn't conventionally report. They can take a picture and interpret it, for example onto a triangle, which has "it tastes wrong, it feels wrong, it looks wrong... and they're radically increasing the number of minor incidents reported by allowing the deliberate ambiguity of interpretation.*

> *(Pauleen, 2017, p. 14)*

This example is relevant evidence (deliberate ambiguity of interpretation) of how the engineers are using their years of experience and contextual know-what and know-how to make a decision concerning 'micro anomaly' or unusual developments and changes in water pump operation. To illustrate further, the water engineers as 'contextual knowledge experts' are allowed to go beyond the analytics generated machine knowledge to come to a decision-making pertaining to water quality and pump operation. Hence,

Insight 2: *Human judgement exists as actionable knowledge in the minds of contextual knowledge experts which is difficult to codify but necessary to increase the outcomes of organisational decision-making* and

Insight 3: *The resulting 'machine knowledge' from the BA process is insufficient on its own for organisational decision-making.*

Based on the above instances that emphasise the significance of context-dependent knowledge, whether the case of CV shortlisting or water pump operation, it is essential to have the human experience and judgement as the embedded and embrained qualities of human knowledge evident in contextual knowledge experts as 'recruitment specialists' and 'water engineers' in the process of decision-making. Perhaps, decisions are not entirely based on one individual's contextual (embodied) knowledge, but the distributed nature of encultured knowledge based on many 'contextual knowledge experts' that aid for better decision-making for organisational problems. Hence,

Insight 4: *The distributed nature of knowledge in the form of intellectual capability divided between different contextual knowledge experts is necessary to improve organisational decision-making* and

Insight 5: *Machine knowledge in combination with know-what and know-how of contextual knowledge experts (i.e. embrained, embodied, embedded, encoded and enculture knowledge) may significantly improve organisational decision-making.*

Conclusions

This chapter aims to explain the link between big data and KM and suggests the central role of human agency in the form of *contextual knowledge experts* to bridge the gap between big data and KM. Based on a conceptual model derived from the literature, five key arguments are proposed that explain how this gap can be bridged.

This chapter has the following limitations. First, this study is nascent and there is a need to further develop and test the proposed conceptual model. This could be tackled in two phases, first through a qualitative study involving a series of interviews with key decision-makers in a number of different competitive organisations across cultural contexts around the globe. Future research could be refined and/or the conceptual model could be extended, which could then be followed up with a larger quantitative study to further test and develop new propositions. In doing so, the coverage of the intricacies of the decision-making discipline that is currently of limited scope in this chapter can be covered in more depth in future studies.

From a research perspective, the conceptual model and the five insights have implications for academics and practitioners. For researchers, the link between BA and KM is worth exploring in particular to determine the key mechanisms that improve and impact the quality of decision-making enabled by BA. In addition, the limitations of machine knowledge can be determined in order to develop a decision-making model that bridges the big data–KM gap. For practitioners, this work has implications in the sense that contextual knowledge experts need to be identified to shape and frame the big data–KM process and to confirm their proactive role in the organisational decision-making process. Both these academic and practical implications suggest avenues for further research.

Notes

1 Business Analytics involves the analysis of data to make key business decisions in an organisation
2 Three additional V's of data (veracity, value and variability) are often added to volume, variety and velocity

References

Adler, P. S., & Kwon, S. W. (2002). Social Capital: Prospects for a New Concept. *Academy of Management Review*, 27(1), 17–40.

Akter, S., Bandara, R., Hani, U., Wamba, S. F., Foropon, C., & Papadopoulos, T. (2019). Analytics-Based Decision-Making for Service Systems: A Qualitative Study and Agenda for Future Research. *International Journal of Information Management*, 48, 85–95.

Alavi, M., & Leidner, D. E. (2001). Knowledge Management and Knowledge Management Systems: Conceptual Foundations and Research Issues. *MIS Quarterly*, 107–136.

Barney, J. (1991) Firm Resources and Sustained Competitive Advantage. *Journal of Management*. 17(1), 99–120.

Blackler, F. (1995). Knowledge, Knowledge Work and Organizations: An Overview and Interpretation. *Organization Studies*, 16(6), 1021–1046.

Bontis, N. (2001). Assessing Knowledge Assets: A Review of the Models Used to Measure Intellectual capital. *International Journal of Management Reviews*, 3(1), 41–60.

Bosua, R., & Scheepers, R. (2007). Towards a Model to Explain Knowledge Sharing in Complex Organisational Environments. *Knowledge Management Research & Practice*, 5(2), 93–109.

Bosua, R., & Venkitachalam, K. (2013). Aligning Strategies and Processes in Knowledge Management: A Framework. *Journal of Knowledge Management*, 17(3), 331–346.

Brockman J. (2002). The Singularity: a talk with Ray Kurzweil, Edge 99 – March 25, 2002, Edge Foundation, (http://www.edge.org)

Campos, S., Dias, J.G., Teixeira, M.R., & Correia, R.J. (2020). The Link Between Intellectual Capital and Business Performance: A Mediation Chain Approach. *Journal of Intellectual Capital*, DOI 10.1108/JIC-12-2019-0302

Chen, H., Chiang, R. H., & Storey, V. C. (2012). Business Intelligence and Analytics: From Big Data to Big Impact. *MIS Quarterly*, 36, 1165–1188.

Chen, C.L. Philip, & Zhang, C-Y. (2016) Data-intensive Applications, Challenges, Techniques and Technologies: A Survey on Big Data. *Information Sciences*, http://dx.doi.org/10.1016/j.ins.2014.01.015

Cross, R., Parker, A., Prusak, L., & Borgatti, S. P. (2001). Knowing What We Know: Supporting Knowledge Creation and Sharing in Social Networks. *Organizational Dynamics*, 30(2), 100–120.

Davenport, T. H. (2013). Analytics 3.0. *Harvard Business Review*, 91(12), 64–72.

Gartner (2020). 100 Data and Analytics Predictions through 2024, Accessed on 15 Dec 2020 from: https://www.gartner.com/en/information-technology/trends/100-data-and-analytics-predictions-through-2024-pd?utm_source=google&utm_medium=cpc&utm_campaign=RM_EMEA_2020_ITTRND_CPC_LG1_H2-GTS-AOC&utm_adgroup=113671253751&utm_term=data%20analytics&ad=476738599130&gclid=CjwKCAiA_eb-BRB2EiwAGBnXXu-LbRLjzHZn1DaV-ZiRm19Z3EJR-NMl55bf1ksIGa97rGx5DwZmXyhoC-w8QAvD_BwE

Gioia, D.A., Corley, K.G. & Hamilton, A.L. (2013). Seeking Qualitative Rigor in Inductive Research: Notes on the Gioia Methodology. *Organizational Research Methods*, 16(1), 15–31.

Grant, R. M. (1996). Toward a Knowledge-based Theory of the Firm. *Strategic Management Journal*, 17(S2), 109–122.

Hansen, M. T., Nohria, N., & Tierney, T. (1999). What's your Strategy for Managing Knowledge. *The Knowledge Management Yearbook 2000–2001*, 77(2), 106–116.

Heisig, P., Suraj, O.A., Kianto, A., Kemboi, C., Arrau, G.P., & Easa, N.E. (2016). Knowledge Management and Business Performance: Global Experts' Views on Future Research Needs, *Journal of Knowledge Management*, 20(6), 1169–1198,

Hernán, M. A., Hsu, J., & Healy, B. (2019). A Second Chance to Get Causal Inference Right: a Classification of Data Science Tasks. *Chance*, 32(1), 42–49.

Hislop, D., Bosua, R., & Helms, R. (2018). *Knowledge Management in Organisations: A Critical Introduction*. Oxford University Press: Oxford, UK.

Jasimuddin, S. M., Klein, J. H., & Connell, C. (2005). The Paradox of Using Tacit and Explicit Knowledge: Strategies to Face Dilemmas. *Management Decision*, 43(1), 102–112.

Jaques, E. (1986). The Development of Intellectual Capability: A Discussion of Stratified Systems Theory. *The Journal of Applied Behavioral Science*, 22(4), 361–383.

Kurzweil, R. (1999). Spiritual Machines: The Merging of Man and Machine. *The Futurist*, 33(9), 16–21.

Litvaj, I., & Stancekova, D. (2015). Decision-making, and their Relation to the Knowledge Management, Use of Knowledge Management in Decision-making. *Procedia Economics and Finance*, 23, 467–472.

Lycett, M. (2013). 'Datafication': Making Sense of (Big) Data in a Complex World. *European Journal of Information Systems*, 22(4), 1–7.

Malhotra, A., Gosain, S., & Sawy, O. A. E. (2005). Absorptive Capacity Configurations in Supply Chains: Gearing for Partner-Enabled Market Knowledge Creation. *MIS Quarterly*, 29(1), 145–187.

Marabelli, M. & Newell, S. (2014). Knowing, Power and Materiality: A Critical Review and Reconceptualization of Absorptive Capacity. *International Journal of Management Reviews*, 16(4), 479–499.

Martín-de Castro, G. (2015). Knowledge Management and Innovation in Knowledge-Based and High-Tech Industrial Markets: The Role of Openness and Absorptive Capacity. *Industrial Marketing Management*, 47, 143–146.

Meacham, J. A. (1983). Wisdom and the Context of Knowledge: Knowing That One Doesn't Know. *On the Development of Developmental Psychology*, 8, 111–134.

Muller, M., Lange, I., Wang, D., Piorkowski, D., Tsay, J., Liao, V.Q., Dugan, C., & Erikson, T. (2019). How Data Science Workers Work with Data: Discovery, Capture, Curation, Design, Creation. In *CHI 2019*, 4–9 May, Glasgow, Scotland, U.K. DOI: https: doi.org/10.11

Nahapiet, J., & Ghoshal, S. (1998). Social Capital, Intellectual Capital, and the Organizational Advantage. *The Academy of Management Review*, 23(2), 242–266.

Nonaka, I. (1991a). The Knowledge-Creating Company. *Harvard Business Review*, November–December, 96–104.

Nonaka, I. (1991b). Managing the Firm as an Information Creation Process. In Meindl, J.R., Cary, R.L., & Puffer, S.M. (Eds), *Advances in Information Processing in Organizations*. Greenwich, CT, London: JAI Press Inc., 239–275.

Nonaka, I. (1994). A Dynamic Theory of Organizational Knowledge Creation. *Organization Science*, 5(1), 14–37.

Nonaka, I. (2007). The Knowledge-Creating Company. *Managing for the Long Term, Best of HBR*, July–August, 162–171.

Nonaka, I. & Hirose, A. (2015). Practical Strategy as Co-Creating Collective Narrative: A Perspective of Organizational Knowledge Creating Theory. *Kindai Management Review*, 3, 9–24.

Nonaka, I., & Toyama, R. (2003). The Knowledge-Creating Theory Revisited: knowledge Creation as a Synthesizing Process. *Knowledge Management Research & Practice*, 1(1), 2–10.

Nonaka, I. & Toyama, R. (2005). The Theory of the Knowledge-Creating Firm: Subjectivity, Objectivity and Synthesis. *Industrial and Corporate Change*, 14(3), 419–436.

O'Connor, & Kelly, S. (2017). Facilitating Knowledge Management through Filtered Big Data: SME Competitiveness in an Agri-Food Sector. *Journal of Knowledge Management*, 21(1), 156–179.

Pauleen, D. (2017). Dave Snowden on KM and Big Data/Analytics: Interview with David J. Pauleen. *Journal of Knowledge Management*, 21(1), 12–17.

Pohl, J. (2008). Cognitive Elements of Human Decision-making. *Studies in Computational Intelligence (SCI)*, 97, 41–76.

Razzaq, S., Shujahat, M., Hussain, S., Nawaz, F., Wang, M., Ali, M., & Tehseen, S. (2019). Knowledge management, Organizational Commitment and Knowledge-Worker Performance: The neglected role of knowledge management in the public sector. *Business Process Management Journal*, 25(5), 923–947.

Ruggles, R. (1998). The State of the Notion: Knowledge Management in Practice. *California Management Review*, 40(3), 80–89.

Sadowski, J. (2019). When Data is Capital: Datafication, Accumulation, and Extraction. *Big Data & Society*, 6(1), pp. 1–12, 2053951718820549.

Schneider, M. (2018). Digitalization of Production, Human Capital, and Organizational Capital. In *The Impact of Digitalization in the Workplace* (pp. 39–52). Cham: Springer.

Schultze, U., & Stabell, C. (2004). Knowing What You Don't Know? Discourses and Contradictions in Knowledge Management Research. *Journal of Management Studies*, 41(4), 549–573.

Serenko, A., & Bontis, N. (2022). Global Ranking of Knowledge Management and Intellectual Capital Academic Journals: A 2021 Update. *Journal of Knowledge Management.* 26(1), 126–145.

Sharda, R., Delen, D., & Turban, E. (2018). *Business Intelligence, Analytics and Data Science: A Managerial Perspective*, 4th edition, Pearson Global Edition, U.K., 512 p.

Spender, J. C., & Grant, R. M. (1996). Knowledge and the Firm: Overview. *Strategic Management Journal*, 17(S2), 5–9.

Stodden, V. (2020). The Data Science Life Cycle: A Disciplined Approach to Advancing Data Science as a Science. *Communications of the ACM*, 63(7), 58–65.

Strauss, A., & Corbin, J. M. (1997). *Grounded Theory in Practice.* Thousand Oaks, CA: Sage Publications.

Subramaniam, M., & Youndt, M. A. (2005). The Influence of Intellectual Capital on the Types of Innovative Capabilities. *Academy of Management Journal*, 48(3), 450–463.

Sumbal, M., Tsui, E., & See-to, E. (2017). Interrelationship between Big Data and Knowledge Management: An Exploratory Study in the Oil and Gas Sector. *Journal of Knowledge Management*, 21(1), 180–196.

Tian, X. (2017). Big Data and Knowledge Management: A Case of Déjà Vu or Back to the Future? *Journal of Knowledge Management*, 21(1), 113–131.

Tsoukas, H. (1996). The Firm as a Distributed Knowledge System: A Constructionist Approach. *Strategic Management Journal*, 17(S2), 11–25

Venkitachalam, K., & Busch, P. (2012). Tacit Knowledge: Review and Possible Research Directions. *Journal of Knowledge Management*, 16(2), 357–372.

Venkitachalam, K., & Willmott, H. (2015). Factors Shaping Organizational Dynamics in Strategic Knowledge Management. *Knowledge Management Research & Practice*, 13(3), 344–359.

Venkitachalam, K., & Willmott, H. (2016). Determining Strategic Shifts between Codification and Personalization in Operational Environments. *Journal of Strategy and Management*, 9(1), 2–14.

Vicario, G., & Coleman, S. (2020). A Review of Data Science in Business and Industry and A Future View. *Applied Stochastic Models in Business and Industry*, 36(1), 6–18.

Watson, S., & Hewett, K. (2006). A Multi-Theoretical Model of Knowledge Transfer in Organizations: Determinants of Knowledge Contribution and Knowledge Reuse. *Journal of Management Studies*, 43(2), 141–173.

Webster, J., & Watson, R. T. (2002). Analyzing the Past to Prepare for the Future: Writing a Literature Review. *MIS Quarterly*, 26(2), xiii–xxiii.

Wolfswinkel, J. F., Furtmueller, E., & Wilderom, C. P. (2013). Using Grounded Theory as a Method for Rigorously Reviewing Literature. *European Journal of Information Systems*, 22(1), 45–55.

10

SYNTHESIS OF HUMAN KNOWLEDGE CREATION AND ARTIFICIAL INTELLIGENCE

Evolution of the SECI Spiral

Kazuo Ichijo

Introduction – A New Dimension of Human Knowledge Creation

Artificial intelligence (AI) is undergoing a third boom. Although AI dates back to the 1920s, today's boom is supported by revolutionary advancements in the abilities of computers (speed and capacity), tremendous increases in the amounts and types of digital data in use, machine learning, including deep learning technology, which has been under investigation for many years, and genetic algorithms and others. The experimental use of AI and, especially, its competitive superiority to humans first emerged in the world of games. In 2011, IBM's Watson defeated two champions on the popular quiz program "Jeopardy,"[1] suddenly accelerating the AI boom.[2] AI also continued to win against humans in shogi (AI Shogi) and go (AlphaGo). Humans were taken aback at AI's ability in the world of intellectual entertainment and performance far exceeding that of humans. For this reason, soon after Watson won "Jeopardy," many companies, hospitals, universities and other institutions sought to use it for their work and business. After implementing trial projects for applying Watson in multiple industries such as medicine and insurance, IBM decided that it could then be commercialized. The company created its IBM Watson business unit in January 2014 (Kell III et al., 2013). After the era of data processing machines and then programmable systems, we are now at the beginning of a new era in which systems using AI to learn will actively work in various fields such as pharmaceuticals, insurance, healthcare and even cooking. This is also helping expand human capabilities. It is said that after overcoming physical, information transmission and productivity limits, humans are now escaping the constraints of complexity. Cognitive capabilities of humans are growing and expanding rapidly because of AI.

On the other hand, AI is challenging human creativity in fields other than games. AI has begun to replace humans in creative activities that were human fortes. AI has already produced a newspaper article in the US (Finley, 2015). It is also being used to write novels (Kastrenakes, 2016), paint (Gershgorn, 2015) and compose music (Moss, 2015). It is debunking the traditional belief that creativity is exclusively a human domain. This trend shows no sign of stopping. Scientists predict that AI is likely to replace humans in various fields. One famous study in this area is collaborative research between Nomura Research Institute and University of Oxford Associate Professor Michael A. Osborne. The study suggests that

DOI: 10.4324/9781003112150-12

nearly 49% of Japan's labor force can be replaced by AI technology (NRI, 2015). After quantitatively analyzing data related to 601 types of jobs in Japan, the study concluded that those performing such jobs are at a high risk of being replaced as they require no special knowledge or skills, or involve data analysis and orderly and systematic operation. On the other hand, the survey also reveals that AI will have difficulties replacing people in liberal arts such as the arts, history, archeology, philosophy and theology or jobs requiring cooperation, understanding others, persuasion or negotiation, or a service-oriented mindset.

Various studies are starting to make shocking predictions about the problem of AI replacing human labor. Some indicate that the majority of routine operational jobs in banks can be entrusted to AI. Others forecast an era when humans will no longer be driving cars, provided that self-driving technology evolves and administrative procedures undergo reform. Authorization and other work that can "be done by anyone" will sooner or later likely be performed by AI. In the future, companies that introduce AI might have to think about how to deal with people who lose their jobs to AI, making this an important problem for human resource management. Moreover, it might also become necessary to take introduction of AI into consideration while making human resource recruitment plans. Even if people succeed in avoiding substitution and securing their jobs, there is also a possibility of reduction in salaries with the advancement of AI. Companies need to build business models using AI while also creating new business processes and management for AI and humans to coexist.

If a company sincerely considers using AI, its management and others in charge must explore new forms of business in which AI can coexist and collaborate with human beings. This might also necessitate a radical overhaul in the company as a whole, including cultural changes. Therefore, it is no exaggeration to say that AI is fast becoming one of the biggest problems for companies. Among specialists who emphasize the social impact AI is likely to cause, there are also those who think that the advent of the AI age will be the biggest change for Japan since its defeat in the Second World War and affect the country's fate.[3] In what way should knowledge creation by humans change in this new world where knowledge creation activities that do not depend on humans are rapidly advancing? Which part of human knowledge creation cannot be replaced by AI? This study explores the ideal form of knowledge creation activities by humans in the age of AI.

Revisiting the Knowledge Creation Theory

Professor Ikujiro Nonaka, a pioneer in knowledge creation theory, pointed out that subjective and knowledge-creating activities by humans are the very source from which the future is created. Knowledge defined as "justified true belief" indicates that knowledge creation activities by humans begin when they have strong beliefs based on their own experience. Knowledge creation by humans in an organization, which begins as the subjective view of an individual, dynamically evolves through interaction with others. Organizational knowledge creation is a social and dynamic process based on human relationships through which the individual's thought becomes justified in the organization (Nonaka and Takeuchi, 1995, Nonaka and Takeuchi, 2019).

In organizational activities, knowledge is a source of competitive advantage. If one considers the example of a corporate organization, then knowledge is created in various forms and can emerge at any point in a value chain. Knowledge can also be created as new technology in the research and development department. It is the creation of new technology that serves as an effective initiative to maintain and further develop the company's competitive advantage. Knowledge can be created in other functions. For example, because of knowledge creation in the logistic function, Amazon could be the number one ecommerce company in the world. When frequent users of the Amazon Prime service order a popular product with a Prime tag, they can get the product delivered on the same day. This is impossible to achieve without new knowledge creation by Amazon in logistics. On the other hand, Toyota created a unique manufacturing system called Toyota Production System (TPS) in manufacturing operations. This enabled the company to produce the best quality car with minimum costs. For this purpose, workers who previously would have lost their jobs if the production line stopped were allowed to pull the "Andon Cord" to stop the line if they found something wrong. This is a famous system called ANDON, and it is now widely used in manufacturing companies worldwide other than Toyota. Giving empowerment to factory workers was a paradigm shift in manufacturing companies worldwide, negating conventional knowledge in manufacturing. In the sales field, Seven-Eleven, came up with a new system of individual store management. By placing separate orders for each store, Seven-Eleven was able to create a new form of retailing, called convenience stores, in which products sought by customers at certain stores were always in stock, without any wastage. Seven-Eleven has been an industry leader by growing this new retail business.

Amazon's strength lies in logistics, Toyota's in manufacturing and Seven-Eleven's in individual store management. These companies are able to gain and maintain their competitive advantage in their respective fields as leading companies only because each company generated new methods, structures and systems, or knowledge in their core businesses. Thus, knowledge creation is the source of competitive advantage in the 21st century, characterized by a society based on knowledge and information (Drucker, 1993).

In organizational knowledge creation, knowledge is initially created as tacit knowledge. Humans generate knowledge in an intuitively tacit way through their direct experiences. As the common use of expressions such as "I cannot express that properly in words, but..." suggest, people are often unable to talk clearly about their thoughts. There is a strong tacit element in human knowledge. Tacit knowledge is the essence of human knowledge. Humans can think more than they can say. On the other hand, knowledge expressed in oral or written language is known as explicit knowledge. It is objective and shared between many groups as opposed to tacit knowledge, which is subjective and based on individual experience. Behind explicit knowledge is more abundant tacit knowledge.

Another essence of organizational knowledge creation is that it is created in a "ba," or context of knowledge creation. This context could be defined by a physical space, time or human relationships therein. Toyota, which gets its competitive advantage from problem-solving related to faults, thinks that the measures for solving the issues lie in the "ba," or the manufacturing site where the faults occur. Therefore, the company gives its workers positioned at the production line the right to stop the line and promotes exploring solutions to real issues through repeated discussions about the "why" with their superiors. Similarly, Seven-Eleven also thinks demand for a certain product can be determined only by the "ba," or each individual store. As their headquarters are away from the "ba," it is not capable of instructing individual stores about product stocking. Therefore, each store tries to determine the tacit knowledge about customer needs for particular products. This means that the store staff, including part-timers, externalize their tacit knowledge about customer needs for certain products (that is, turn tacit knowledge into explicit knowledge, i.e., numbers required for each product) based on their own observations at the store, recent sales trends, and information received from other staff members at the same store, and place orders accordingly. However, humans are not perfect. Mistakes in placing orders occur often. POS data reveal whether orders placed were appropriate. The results are then leveraged in the next knowledge creation activity (striving for an ideal product order so that there is neither a shortage nor any excess of stock). What Toyota and Seven-Eleven have in common is the establishment of a core business operation based on the human power of thinking and knowledge creation.

If knowledge remains as tacit knowledge, it is shared only within the smaller number of people and sharing it with others will take more time. Keeping knowledge tacit makes objective analysis difficult. This leads to the mistake of considering what was true in a specific "ba" in the past as knowledge in a different "ba" as well. This means that past experiences (whether of success or failure) are misunderstood as eternal and universal truths. The argument that successful companies fade away and innovators lose their competitive advantage when the times change drastically (so-called "innovator's dilemma") (Christensen, 1997) results from applying the tacit knowledge of a previous "ba" to another one without objective analysis (Tobe et al., 1991). Therefore, the key to knowledge creation in organizations is to formalize tacit knowledge, change tacit knowledge that starts from individual views into organizational knowledge and, at the same time, objectively criticize and verify it so as to move toward knowledge creation.

The SECI model for organizational knowledge creation, developed by Prof. Nonaka clearly shows how knowledge can be created within organizations. Organizational knowledge, which originates from physical experiences of individuals, is created through four processes, namely: (1) socialization, (2) externalization, (3) combination and (4) internalization (Figure 10.1).

Socialization refers to the process of generating tacit knowledge through one's own experience. The prototype of new knowledge to use in the organization consequently takes the form of new technology, business models or business operations through a person's intuitions based on his or her own experiences. New organizational knowledge that emerges as tacit knowledge can also be generated in a group when many people share a "ba." However, so far as it remains tacit, the scope of sharing is limited. Therefore, it must be shared with more

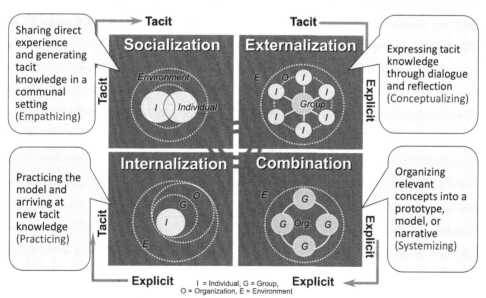

Figure 10.1   SECI Model of Organizational Knowledge Creation

Source: Nonaka I. (1994) "A Dynamic Theory of Organizational Knowledge Creation", *Organizational Science* Vol.5, No.1, February 1994, pp:14–37, Nonaka, I., Toyama, R., and Hirata, T. (2008) "Managing Flow", Palgrave

groups by expressing it in words, sentences, graphs and other forms. This occurs in the externalization process. Externalization allows wider organizational sharing of knowledge that was present with an individual or a limited group of people. Therefore, externalization of tacit knowledge is a necessary condition for combination, the next process in knowledge creation. Various visualization tools such as prototyping must be used to articulate tacit knowledge. Creating a psychologically safe environment is a necessary enabler for this articulation so that people are willing to externalize their tacit knowledge so that others can share it.

To transform new knowledge into new products or services, it is necessary to combine knowledge created in various "ba." For example, to use new technology to manufacture products and offer them to customers, new knowledge about using the new technology in production will be indispensable. Moreover, if the product is extremely innovative, it will perhaps not be accepted in the market without new knowledge about effective marketing for communicating the new value of the knowledge to the market (stakeholders, including customers). Combination synthesizes the knowledge creation activities undertaken in different departments of the organization, thereby giving rise to new products and services.

Organizational knowledge, which begins with individuals' experiences, will be created only after socialization, externalization and combination. However, the important point is that organizational activities must not stop at this. People involved in knowledge creation activities reflect on them and make them a part of their knowledge. This helps individuals internalize the results of the series of organizational knowledge creation activities, deepening each person's knowledge. These individuals, who increase their knowledge assets in this way, get involved in new knowledge creation activities, and organizational knowledge creation evolves through continuous innovation. Therefore, knowledge creation within organizations evolves through the spiral-up movement of SECI activities (Figure 10.2).

The SECI model conceptualizing organizational knowledge creation was, however, developed before the third AI boom. The knowledge creation theory is underpinned by the view that creativity is a human characteristic. It is common wisdom that only humans write, paint and compose music. However, the emergence of AI capable of writing, painting and

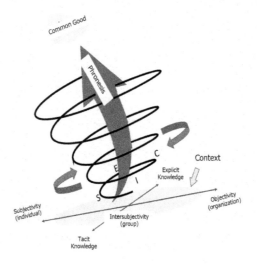

Figure 10.2 SECI Spiral

Source: I. Nonaka, H. Takeuchi, 2019, The wise company: How companies create continuous innovation, Oxford press.

composing music shows that human creativity is understood only in contrast with animals. If AI makes its way further into daily life and workplaces of humans, then organizational knowledge creation by humans must change. In that case, one must consider what could be the direction of such change. This important issue in organizational knowledge creation will be examined in IBM Watson's case in the world of cooking.

Chef Watson Project

The Chef Watson project (Bakerand Hamm, 2015), provides important suggestions for thinking about how value addition and knowledge creation activities by humans should be amid attempts to make diverse use of AI in tasks that were until now performed by humans. The common belief in the world of professional cooking was that disciples undergo training and learn on the job by working with the chef or main cook. After many years of experience, they gradually learn the "taste" the master had acquired (it can perhaps be called tacit knowledge embedded in the chef's mind and body). Transmission of tacit knowledge about cooking from the chef or master to the disciple is a common tradition in the East and the West. Therefore, becoming a disciple is a necessary process for becoming an independent chef. However, it is astonishing to think that Watson could create 100 types of new, previously unimagined recipes in a short period. What process made this possible?

The Chef Watson project began in 2011. It was born from the collaboration between the highly acclaimed American Institute of Culinary Education (AICE) and the American culinary magazine *Bon Appétit*.[4] Those in charge of IBM's Watson project input AICE's 35,000 recipes and 9,000 from *Bon Appétit* readers and used deep learning technique. Watson was fed ingredients, flavors, preservation methods, recipe categories, colors, combinations of ingredients, nutrition facts, expiry dates, molecular structure of ingredients, food-related cultural characteristics of each country and region and other data. It used all the information to learn, thereby becoming capable of producing new combinations of ingredients using a series of algorithms based on various data sets such as composition of ingredients, cultural knowledge and theory of combining food items. The combinations of food items, or recipes,

Figure 10.3 Chef Watson
Source: https://www.ibmchefwatson.com/community

were generated through attention to surprise, pleasantness and pairing. This resulted in some 100 recipes that humans had not thought of. These recipes arose from a perspective, contents and composition different from those of human chefs (Figure 10.3).

Chef Watson's recipes have already made their way to restaurants through professional chefs, and to households through homemakers. When users enter information such as main ingredients, methods of cooking and regional flavors they want in their recipes, Watson suggests complementary ingredients as well as the novelty of the combination, compatibility between ingredients, flavors and aromas. Recipe development was considered a part of "art" until now. The new attempt to perform it using Watson is being accepted in the professional world as well.[5] Even in Japan, Cook Pad, an online receipt site proposes menus based on Chef Watson's recipes. Its menus comprise new dishes and ingredient combinations that even food specialists had not thought of until now.[6]

But here is the limitation in Chef Watson's recipes. The recipes only propose unique combinations of ingredients, and the cook must decide the quantity of each.[7] The program does not provide any information about quantities of ingredients to be used or cooking procedures. Therefore, it is professional chefs who finally create the recipe by deciding on everything from ingredients to their quantities. In other words, the final decisions are still made by humans, despite Chef Watson's presence. That is why Chef Watson has been positioned as a sous-chef (the second chef in the kitchen) and is not meant to replace humans. In the first place, Chef Watson cannot function at all unless existing recipes are first fed into the program. Its aim is to increase human creativity by suggesting combinations of ingredients of which professional chefs were unable to conceive.

Watson is also being used in fields other than cooking. But in these fields, cognitive value access (CVA) is a necessary procedure for its commercialization. CVA refers to the process of determining methods of using AI to bring maximum effect of investment, based on a study of a company's vision, its strategic directions, its management policy, content and its business operations. A company's vision and strategic directions incorporate the thoughts of people involved in its management. In other words, AI is useless without the wisdom and thoughts of the leading people of the company. Before AI came into being, the purpose of computing was to support humans. Computers cannot work without humans and are not superior to them. That is because computers cannot, at present, enter the non-cognitive world of thought or handle non-rational elements essential to knowledge creation and innovation.

The Significance of Non-rationality in Knowledge Creation

The support by AI to human beings is expected to evolve in the following four stages. The first support is given by encyclopedic specialized knowledge which AI acquires (human knowledge creation support by means of AI), the second with visualization of newly discovered patterns and connections (understanding by means of AI), the third with analysis of competing perspectives (decision-making support by AI) and the fourth with creating new knowledge and discovering new value (discovery support by means of AI).[8] However, in this series of support activities, what AI decidedly lacks is common sense. It is said the brains of machines do not have the wealth of common sense that humans have acquired through experience. AI does not have common sense, which humans have obtained over their long evolution.[9] This will present a handicap in interpreting language and grasping situations. One such example involves Tay, an AI Microsoft was developing and testing, which began approving of Hitler and making discriminatory comments on Twitter. Microsoft revealed that it had decided to stop its experiment for some time.[10] Any human being with common sense is unlikely to indulge in such acts. Therefore, lack of common sense in AI has to be compensated for by humans.

Common sense refers to tacit knowledge acquired through practices. Most human decisions and acts in the real world rely on common sense. What, then, is common sense? Classical writings provide some answers for this question.

Yukichi Fukuzawa, an influential Japanese thinker in the Meiji Period, said common sense must comprise intellect and morals.[11] In Bummeiron no Gairyaku (An Outline of a Theory of Civilization), he writes that the advancement of civilization is related to the rise of intellect and morals in common people, thereby considering these the two wheels that support the advancement of culture. Moreover, he believed that intellect and morality must have two aspects – private and public. Furthermore, Fukuzawa emphasized public intellect above all. This by no means implies that he disregarded morals. He put more importance on public intellect because he feared that people in Japan had a strong inclination to interpret social problems in terms of morality (Maruyama, 1986).[12] Fukuzawa wrote that the most important condition was the fourth one, Great Knowledge (Fukuzawa, 1995). "Great knowledge" refers to distinguishing between things on the basis of their importance and judging what ought to be prioritized on the basis of time and place. This was clearly different from private or "inventive knowledge," which was defined as understanding the rationale behind things and acting accordingly. "Great knowledge" means making a distinction between big and small events, giving preference to the important over the alarming, and taking action appropriate to time and place for common goods. In other words, by "Great Knowledge," he was referring to public wisdom in judging what is important in each situation and what should receive priority (Figure 10.4).

Incidentally, Yukichi Fukuzawa's concept of Great Knowledge has some resemblance to Aristotle's phronesis. Aristotle said practical wisdom refers to the knowledge of determining the truth in a situation in which there is more than one correct answer. It refers to the knowledge of making the best judgment in the "here and now" for common goods in a world that changes at every moment. This requires calmly judging the situation one is in and applying universal principles to individual circumstances. Aristotle called this practical wisdom phronesis. "Phronesis" means "prudence" in English and can be translated into words meaning "prudence" and "discretion" in Japanese (Nonaka et al., 2008, Nonaka and Takeuchi, 2011).[13] Phronesis is the ability to consider one's virtues and merits in a grand way to live well comprehensively, not in parts. It is different from scholarship or techniques based on hypotheses and validations that can be learned logically, or, in Fukuzawa's words,

	Private	Public
Intellect	understanding the rationale behind things and acting accordingly (Inventive Knowledge)	distinguishing between things on the basis of their importance and judging what ought to be prioritized on the basis of time and place (Great Knowledge)
Moral	Integrity and Innocence	Fairness and Courageous

Figure 10.4   Intellect and Moral

"inventive knowledge." Phronesis is based on the knowledge about the individual along with the universal and is, therefore, refined through understanding of that many situations. Experience is the mechanism that cultivates such knowledge that originates from practical wisdom, making age a significant factor. Practical wisdom is refined with experience.

A focus on the computing and AI boom could suggest that rational intellect is the core of knowledge creation. However, if one looks deeper, one notices that the non-rational plays an extremely important role in this world. The real world and rationality do not necessarily deal with each other on a one-on-one basis. For example, the story[14] in "Buridan's Ass" shows the foolishness in seeking one-dimensional rationality. The story suggests that too much rationality can paralyze humans, making them unable to act. Similarly, the famous "prisoner's dilemma" teaches that the concept of trust, which contains extremely non-rational elements, can be mutually beneficial for the involved parties (Poundstone, 1992). The two prisoners being questioned in separate cells do not know what the other will say, and the only way both can benefit is by trusting each other. Thinking only about self-interest will amount to betraying the partner and saying what suits oneself could help in escaping the worst situation. However, if the partner, too, acts rationally, then saying what suits oneself leads to betraying the other. This results in their betraying one another, with neither achieving the best possible outcome. However, trusting the other and believing that the other will not do anything to harm oneself can help achieve a win–win situation in which neither says anything that harms the other. Rational choice will not result in the Pareto optimal here. The prisoner's dilemma teaches that trusting others, which can be considered non-rational faith, benefits all involved parties. Similarly, for human society to advance, it is important to make decisions while keeping rationality aside at some point. However, the decision must go beyond self-interest and contribute to the common goods of society as a whole. For this reason, even though AI is in the midst of evolution, it is necessary for humans to make judgments based on what Fukuzawa calls Great Knowledge and Aristotle calls Phronesis. AI can provide "inventive knowledge," while humans will have to obtain Great Knowledge by themselves. One must not forget the significance of the non-cognitive power of Great Knowledge and Phronesis. Even though this is the age of AI, one must avoid placing too much importance on cognitive knowledge. Sharing non-cognitive knowledge and practicing human understanding is as important now as before.

Evolution of the SECI Model of Knowledge Creation in the Age of AI

When one thinks about the constraints of AI and the significance of Great Knowledge and Phronesis, it is interesting to find a growing interest in "belief" in companies striving to build new business models using AI or digital technology. GE's Chairman and CEO Jeff Immelt abandoned the management structure established under his predecessor Jack Welch that unified the diverse and global company through shared values (principles for employee conduct). Immelt decided to unify the company on the basis of "belief" and not "value." This means that he started a revolution, radically changing the mechanism GE followed for over 20 years. His move can be called a revolution because it was GE that taught companies around the world that original shared values are effective in unifying an organization that diversifies and gets more complex as it globalizes.

In the background of Immelt's attempt to unify the diverse GE under the word "belief" lies GE's ongoing transformation into a connected industrial company using digital technology. To build Industry Internet or a new business model leveraging the Internet and achieve new growth, it is necessary to radically change the employees' thought process and conduct. To this end, GE thought that the word "belief" was more appropriate than "value" (Krishnamoorthy, 2015). Just like knowledge defined as "justified true belief," innovation originates from strong belief based on experience. Encouraging employees to engage in innovation with a strong belief and unifying them with belief, and not value, to achieve this – these are the GE management's reasons for the transformation.

On the other hand, it is also necessary to negate past beliefs to innovate. It is believed that whether the company will succeed in building a new business model using digital technology depends on whether it can negate its own past beliefs (de Jong and van Dijk, 2015). As the debate about dilemma of innovation shows, new knowledge cannot be created by sticking to past beliefs obtained in a specific "ba" that existed in the past.

While interests rise in explicit knowledge such as digitalization and AI, it is also important not to overlook heightening interest in tacit knowledge in the corporate world. Design thinking, which began in the Silicon Valley with IDEO in the center, has expanded beyond regions and territories in recent years. IDEO is considered as the most inventive industrial design company in the world. Design thinking employs designers to develop new products and services from the human perspective of users. Indeed, design is nothing but making tacit knowledge explicit. In essence, it is visualization. IDEO has been developing the know-how for it, such as a brainstorming method called Deep Dive and making use of prototyping (Kelly and Littman, 2001). This know-how has crossed the boundaries of the design world and is beginning to be used in consulting. In May 2015, McKinsey bought the American design consulting company Lunar. Founded in 1984, Lunar is a top design firm boasting clients such as Apple, HP and SanDisk. The reason why a consulting company bought a design company is that design thinking has reached beyond the world of design and is contributing to determining and seeking solutions for problems in companies (Brown, 2019).

This increase of interest in tacit knowledge, belief and design thinking in the digital and AI age suggests the roles humans must play in knowledge creation even in the current digital era. If one goes back to the SECI model of knowledge creation, the subjective role humans play in the socialization process remains the same. Because there is a rise in interest in explicit knowledge such as digital technology and AI, increasing tacit knowledge becomes all the more significant in the socialization process.

However, the prospect of drastically reducing the time taken by humans to create knowledge by using AI is expanding. This could speed up the SECI process itself. The chef of a Michelin two-star restaurant commented on Chef Watson, saying innovation takes time. Adding a new dish to the menu (if only a human is working) could easily take a year and a half.[15] Selecting and arranging ingredients is tough in itself, and is followed by repeated tasting until the chef is satisfied. The use of AI could also shrink such time-consuming processes to a large extent. This has already been validated in recipe development and holds true for other fields too. In a joint project with the Baylor College of Medicine, six new proteins that affect p53, the protein with a strong connection to cancer, were discovered in only a few weeks. In the past 30 years, only about one was discovered per year in the entire world. It is an astonishing achievement for one college to discover six proteins in only a few weeks. It is said that Watson used over 70,000 studies as a database to reach this finding, whereas humans cannot possibly go through such a large number of studies in a few weeks. Human knowledge starts working with tacit knowledge that transforms into organizational knowledge after first turning into explicit knowledge. This process takes time. However, the capabilities of computers and the explosion of knowledge have the potential to radically change this process

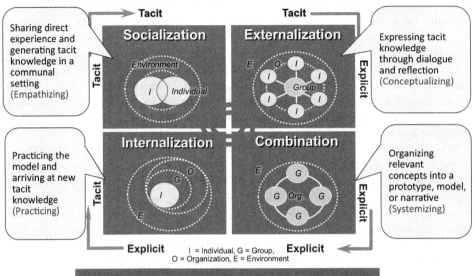

Figure 10.5 Integration in SECI Model

Source: Nonaka I. (1994) "A Dynamic Theory of Organizational Knowledge Creation", *Organizational Science* Vol.5, No.1, February 1994, pp:14–37, Nonaka, I., Toyama, R., and Hirata, T. (2008) "Managing Flow", Palgrave

and its speed. The E (externalization) and C (combination) processes of the SECI model of knowledge creation could become faster and more accurate than they are now (Figure 10.5).

IBM Research points out that Watson is strong at logical analysis, a function handled by the left brain in humans. Future challenges involve finding ways to handle right brain functions, such as art, intuition and image processing, using a computer system. To solve this problem, researchers are trying to develop a brain chip with an electronic circuit of synapses and neurons found in human brain nerves to create a completely new computer system. Neuroscientist Yuji Ikegaya says the brain reflexively provides reasons for human behavior and has a built-in reflexive process that takes place unconsciously. This is called intuition.[16] Therefore, an important issue for AI research is whether computers will be able to process this intuition. However, at the present stage, even IBM's cognitive computing is certainly not aimed at being superior to humans. Instead, it is positioned as an assisting tool. As mentioned previously, AI can offer what Yukichi Fukuzawa calls "inventive knowledge." It can do what humans are not very good at – calculation and memorizing. It can quickly analyze data that humans could not possibly process. By using the learning function, it can further improve the accuracy of analyses and interpretations. This will allow humans to obtain "inventive knowledge" at a greater speed. The purpose of AI should not be to replace human judgment and creativity, but to provide a tool for acquiring knowledge faster. It is very important that humans subjectively engage in knowledge creation with great knowledge. The world looks forward in anticipation to new knowledge creation arising from collaboration between human beings and AI.

Notes

1 Jeopardy is a popular quiz program aired in the US for over 50 years. It airs for 30 minutes in the evening from Mondays to Fridays. A panel displays 30 questions divided into six fields and five levels. Two such panels are used in the show, presenting 60 questions in all. Three contestants attempt to answer the questions in a rapid-fire round. If an answer is correct, prize money for the question is added to the contestant's score. The contestant with the highest score in the end wins. Watson competed with 74-game champion Ken Jennings and the winner of 300-million-yen's worth in prizes, Brad Rutter, and defeated both of them. Jeopardy does not repeat questions, so no amount of memorization can help in answering. Watson analyzed the questions using high-level natural language processing and found the correct answers from its 200-million-page text database. These 200 million pages included various kinds of data including Wikipedia, newspapers, the Bible and other materials.

2 IBM does not position Watson as AI. The company calls it cognitive computing aimed at more practical application of the technology. This study, however, uses the generic term AI in a broad sense. For details about the development of Watson in IBM: Kelly III, John E. and Hamm, Steve. 2013, *Smart Machines: IBM's Watson and the Era of Cognitive Computing, Columbia Business School Publishing*, NY.

3 For example, "AI de Shitsugyo Suru Hito ni Ukezara wo, Sugakusha ga Keisho (A Place Necessary for People Rendered Unemployed by AI, Warning from a Mathematician)," Statement made by Ms. Noriko Arai, Professor at National Institute of Informatics, Information and Society Research Division, *The Nikkei*, 2016.

4 Information about Chef Watson is based on the interviews with Mr. Kazushi Kuse on April 15, May 17 and 27, 2016 and the following material: http://www.ibm.com/systems/be/inspire/interview-sous-chef-watson-ajb1x, https://www-03.ibm.com/press/is/en/presskit/46500.wss

5 http://www.ibm.com/systems/be/inspire/interview-sous-chef-watson-ajb1x

6 http://cookpad.com/pr/tieup/index/694

7 However, in Bon Appétit and Cook Pad, cooking methods and quantities are provided by chefs.

8 Interview at IBM Head Office on May 17, 2016.

9 "AI, Jakuten ha Joshiki Shirazu (AI's Weakness is Lack of Common Sense)," *The Nikkei*, February 21, 2016.

10 *The Asahi Shimbun*, March 25, 2016.

11 The information about Yukichi Fukuzawa's views on intellect and morality is based on Professor Takenori Inoki's lecture on June 11, 2016, at the Knowledge Forum.

12 Yukichi Fukuzawa's fear about putting greater importance on the private aspect of intellect and morality as compared with relatively lower importance on the public aspect during the Meiji era seems true even today in light of recent scandals by politicians.

13 The following book by Aristotle has a summary about phronesis: *Nichomachean Ethics*, Parts 1 and 2. The first real research on phronesis in management: Nonaka, Ikujiro, Toyama, Ryoko, and Hirata, Toru. (2008), *Managing Flow: A Process Theory of the Knowledge-based Firm*), Palgrave Macmillan, New York, The writing that determined phronesis development by others as an important ability of knowledge-creating leaders: Nonaka, Ikujiro and Takeuchi, Hirotaka. (2011), The Wise Leader, *Harvard Business Review*, May 2011, pp. 2–11.

14 The story goes that the road on which the ass is walking forks into two. Exactly equal amounts of straw are kept at exactly the same distance on both roads. Even after a lot of deliberation about which road to take, the ass is unable to proceed on either and dies from starvation.

15 http://www.ibm.com/systems/be/inspire/interview-sous-chef-watson-ajb1x

16 Lecture by Professor Yuji Ikegaya on April 9, 2016, at the Knowledge Forum in Tokyo, Japan.

References

Baker, S. and Hamm, S., (2015), *Cognitive Cooking with Chef Watson: Recipes for Innovation from IBM and the Institute of Culinary Education*, SourceBooks, Naperville, IL.

Brown, T. (2019), *Change by Design, Revised and updated*, Harper Business, New York.

Christensen, C. (1997), *The Innovator's Dilemma: When New Technologies Cause Great Firms to Fail*, Harvard Business Review Press, Boston.

de Jong, Marc and van Dijk, Menno. (2015), "Disrupting Beliefs: A New Approach to Business-Model Innovation", *McKinsey Quarterly*, July 2015.

Drucker, P. F. (1993), *Post-Capitalist Society*, Harper Business, New York.

Finley, K. (2015), "This News-Writing Bot Is Now Free for Everyone," *Wired*, October 20, 2015. available at https://www.wired.com/2015/10/this-news-writing-bot-is-now-free-for-everyone/

Fukuzawa, Y. (1995), *Bunmeiron no Gairyaku (An Outline of a Theory of Civilization)*, Iwanami Bunko, page 120.

Gershgorn, D. (2015), "These Are What the Google Artificial Intelligence's Dreams Look Like", *Popular Science*, Jun 20, 2015, available at http://www.popsci.com/these-are-what-google-artificial-intelligences-dreams-look

Kastrenakes, J. (2016), "Google has AI Writing 'rather dramatic' Fiction as it Learns to Speak Naturally", available at http://www.theverge.com/2016/5/15/11678142/google-ai-writes-fiction-natural-language-neural-network.

Kelly, T. and Littman, J. (2001), *The Art of Innovation: Lessons in Creativity from IDEO, America's Leading Design Firm,* Currency, New York, NY.

Kelly III, John E. and Hamm, S. (2013), *Smart Machines: IBM's Watson and the Era of Cognitive Computing*, Columbia Business School Publishing, New York.

Krishnamoorthy, R. (2015), "GE's Culture Challenge After Welch and Immelt", *Harvard Business Review*, January 25, 2015, available at https://hbr.org/2015/01/ges-culture-challenge-after-welch-and-immelt

Maruyama, M. (1986), *"Bunmeiron no Gairyaku" wo Yomu* (Reading *"An Outline of a Theory of Civilization"*), Part 2, Iwanami Shinsho, first edition published in 1986, page 138.

Moss, R. (2015), "Creative AI: Computer Composers Are Changing How Music Is Made", *NEW ATLAS*, January 26, 2015, available at http://www.gizmag.com/creative-artificial-intelligence-computer-algorithmic-music/35764/

Nomura Research Institute, Ltd (NRI), (2015), "Nihon no Roudou Jinkou 49% ga Jinkou Chinou ya Robot tou de Daitai Kanou ni (49% of Japan's working population can be replaced by artificial intelligence and robots)*, Nomura Research Institute News Release*, December 2, 2015, available at https://www.nri.com/jp/news/2015/151202_1.aspx

Nonaka, I., Toyama, R., and Hirata, T. (2008), *Managing Flow: A Process Theory of the Knowledge-Based Firm*, Palgrave Macmillan, New York.

Nonaka, I. and Takeuchi, H. (1995), *The Knowledge Creating Company: How Japanese Companies Create the Dynamics of Innovation*, Oxford University Press, New York.

Nonaka, I. and Takeuchi, H. (2011), The Wise Leader. Boston, MA, USA: *Harvard Business Review*, May 1, 2011.

Nonaka, I. and Takeuchi, H. (2019), *The Wise Company: How Companies Create Continuous Innovation*, Oxford University Press, New York.

Poundstone, W. (1992), *Prisoner's Dilemma: John von Neumann, Game Theory, and the Puzzle of the Bomb*, Oxford University Press, New York.

Tobe, R., Teramoto, Y., Suginoo, Y., Murai, T., and Nonaka, I. (1991), *Shippai no Honshitsu* (The Essence of Failure), Chuokoronsha. First edition published in 1984.

11

ARTIFICIAL INTELLIGENCE-ENABLED KNOWLEDGE MANAGEMENT

Xuyan Wang, Xi Zhang, Yihang Cheng, Fangqing Tian,
Kai Chen and Patricia Ordóñez de Pablos

Introduction

Due to human-like thought and action, AI technologies have made tremendous changes in all aspects of production and life, including knowledge management (KM). KM is widely acknowledged by various organizations around the world, as a kind of activity to explore the principles of knowledge activities within or between organizations, which helps to comprehensively manage organizational knowledge (Alavi & Leidner, 2001; Nonaka & Peltokorpi, 2006). With the development of AI technologies, it seems to be very accessible to acquire knowledge, control knowledge activities, and even identify potential needs (Faraj et al., 2018; Faraj et al., 2016). Besides, AI technologies help process data, such as text, images, and videos, enabling which to share and exchange knowledge without interruption and hindrance (Yan et al., 2018). AI can also adapt to new situations, detect and infer models.

There is significant meaning in paying attention to AI-enabled KM. For example, there is much unstructured data with high value in the digital age, which is difficult to identify in traditional KM (Khan & Vorley, 2017). With the breakthrough of AI, organizations can even quantify accurately the various stages of knowledge creation (KC), so as to deeply analyse the current situation of organizational KC and prepare for the future in advance. In addition, AI has the abilities of learning, reasoning, memory, and decision-making (Andersen & Ingram Bogusz, 2019; Leicht-Deobald et al., 2019). It will expand the knowledge reuse and innovation in the process of KM (Huang & Zhang, 2016).

This chapter is organized as follows: First, we describe the relevant background of AI and KM, including the related concepts of AI, the development stage of KM and new phenomenon of AI-enabled KM. Second, we explain the dual influence of AI on KM, including positive and negative effects of AI on KM. Next, we point out the future research trends of AI-enabled KM, including the study of new questions, new technologies/mechanisms, and new theories. The final section comprises the conclusion of this chapter.

AI and KM

AI and Algorithm Technologies

The conception of AI was first proposed in 1955, which means, all aspects of learning or any other characteristics of intelligence can in principle be accurately described, so that machines

DOI: 10.4324/9781003112150-13

can be made to simulate it (McCarthy et al., 2006). Nowadays, massive amounts of data from enterprises, governments, and society make data available everywhere; the self-learning capabilities of machines (such as deep learning) are constantly increasing, and as a result, the capabilities of AI are also constantly being improved. These three forces promote each other and promote the rapid development of AI (Anthes, 2017).

AI is an interdisciplinary scientific field that intersects with psychology, linguistics, mathematical methods, and computer science (Bobrow & Stefik, 1986; Sokolov, 2019). Therefore, AI has different definitions in different subject areas. For example, in management research, AI is regarded as a new generation of technology that can interact with the environment in the following ways: (a) collect information from outside (including natural language) or other computer systems; (b) interpret information, recognize patterns, summarize rules, or predict events; (c) produce results, answer questions, or issue instructions to other systems; (d) evaluate the results of their actions and improve their decision-making systems to achieve specific goals (Ferras-Hernandez, 2018). Since the environment that stimulates functions of AI is usually highly complex and partially random, the behaviour of AI is uncertain and complex, and has multiple levels (Glikson & Woolley, 2020). The decision-making process of AI is usually opaque (Danks & London, 2017). It means that decisions made by AI may be difficult to predict, and the logic behind each decision is often difficult to understand.

There are three ways of AI presented to humans, which are AI-enabled robots, AI-enabled virtual agents, and embedded AI (Glikson & Woolley, 2020). First of all, AI-enabled robots may have multiple functions with different mechanical or human-like representations. And they can perform social-oriented mechanical tasks orderly. Second, an AI-enabled virtual agent is a representation is one in the AI does not exist in physical form but in a unique identity, such as a chatbot (Ben Mimoun, Poncin, & Garnier, 2012). This virtual representation can exist on any electronic device and can have features, such as face, body, voice, or text capabilities. Besides, this type of AI is used commercially today, and there are lots of empirical researches on interface design. At last, embedded AI is invisible to the user, which means it has no visual representation or unique identity. It can be embedded in different types of applications, such as search engines or GPS maps, and people may not be aware of its existence.

Development Tendency of KM

At present, the three stages of the KM development process and their comparisons are shown in Table 11.1.

According to Table 11.1, in the KM1.0 era, knowledge resources were abundant for most organizations, so the focus of KM was mainly on how to effectively manage it and promote KC (Nonaka, 1994). With the rapid development of Internet technology and globalization, KM entered the era of 2.0. It was no longer sufficient to only focus on KM within the organizations. It's also necessary to use Internet technology to effectively utilize global knowledge outside the organizations (Bell & Loane, 2010; Provost & Fawcett, 2013). In recent years, big data has brought new trends in the global economy, which is digital transformation. Traditional knowledge and innovation activities have undergone major changes, and KM has been in the 3.0 era. With the development of AI technologies, acquiring and using the knowledge implicit in different types of data began to become research hotspots (Jin et al., 2015). There are a lot of uncertainties in the KM 3.0 era, for example, the uncertainty of the process of KC, the uncertainty of knowledge acquisition channels, the uncertainty of knowledge partners and mechanisms (Wang et al., 2020). The emergence of AI will match

Table 11.1 Development tendency of KM 1.0, KM 2.0, and KM 3.0

The development process of KM	Characteristics	Background	Research focus
KM1.0	Knowledge management within the organizations	Knowledge creation theories of famous companies in Europe, US, and Japan	Knowledge creation, sharing, and storage process within organizations
KM2.0	Global knowledge transferring	Internet and globalization	Improve the efficiency of global knowledge transfer and cooperation through information technologies
KM3.0	Artificial intelligence (AI)-enabled knowledge management	Digital transformation; reverse globalization trends	Deep mining and micro mechanisms of the knowledge creation process driven by AI

Source: Adapted from Wang et al. (2020).

the best modern technologies to the KM process and assist its development (Ordóñez de Pablos & Lytras, 2018). Therefore, the main characteristic of this era is AI-enabled KM.

Specifically, AI brings huge possibilities to solve the problems faced by the KM 3.0 era (Wang et al., 2020), as follows:

AI drives knowledge creation process. In this stage of KM, people have to constantly search the knowledge they want, as simply sharing the existing knowledge resource management may no longer meet the needs of KM. Only combining the advanced AI technical methods, various process of KC can be effectively predicted and managed.

AI promotes rich knowledge acquisition platforms. In the era of KM 3.0, the trend of reverse globalization has made knowledge transfer between multinational companies more difficult (Kuang et al., 2019). Yet on the flip side, AI technologies promote the use of a large number of open communities and communication platforms by people, and provide rich knowledge acquisition platforms (Eseryel, 2014). The developing countries in the world, especially China, have begun to consider vigorously developing crowdsourcing or other open innovation models to stimulate knowledge innovation in the future.

AI helps build knowledge cooperation mechanism and identify knowledge partners. In the KM 3.0 era, it is crucial to find accurately the knowledge partners distributed all over the world. However, most small and micro enterprises cannot obtain the necessary information support, which prevents them from accurately matching knowledge partners and not merely conducive to their further development. Due to the low-cost characteristics of AI technologies, it can help establish good and efficient models for these disadvantaged companies to carry out knowledge sharing activities (Teodoridis, 2018).

AI accelerates digital transformation. The emergence of big data technology has effectively improved the status quo of enterprise KM. But enterprises are still facing many inevitable problems at present, such as the slowdown of overall economic growth, more personalized customer demand, and intensified industry competition (Wang et al., 2020). Digital transformation can effectively alleviate these thorny problems (Bharadwaj et al., 2013; Khanagha et al., 2014). The essence of digital transformation is that enterprises need to carry out business transformation according to their own equipment, capital, and other conditions (Vial, 2019). AI can help enterprises become intelligent and have the core competitiveness against other enterprises in the context of big data, thereby achieving the acceleration of digital transformation (Magistretti et al., 2019).

New Phenomena in AI-Enabled KM

Many new phenomena are generated in AI-enabled KM. For example, not only does the traditional KM scene change within the organization, but also new knowledge scenes are generated outside the organizations (Chae, 2019). With the advent of the AI age, many companies are following the strategy of digital transformation, simultaneously proposing numerous AI platforms such as digital communities, intelligent talent management systems, and intelligent recruitment systems (Yablonsky, 2020). Many intelligent systems and AI technologies have changed the internal environment of the organizations. It will have huge impacts on the process and effects of KM. In the digital age, the knowledge within the organizations is rich in the characteristics of big data. There is a large amount of organizational knowledge, and the growth of data is exponential. Moreover, there are various forms of organizational knowledge, such as semi-structured and unstructured text and images. The change of organizational knowledge is rapid, and the generation of new knowledge can be completed in a very short time. Through enhancing firms' knowledge search and knowledge reuse, AI-enabled KM benefit firms' innovation performance (Ruan & Chen, 2017).

In the age of AI, many advanced information and communication technologies have been developed outside the enterprises, forming many new virtual interactive communities, such as social Q&A sites, digital enterprise social media, and online communities with AI functions (Barker, 2015; Kaba & Ramaiah, 2017). These online communities may contain high-quality group tacit knowledge. Once they are converted into organizational knowledge, it will be beneficial to the development of organizations (Erden et al., 2008). In a specific dynamic environment, knowledge can be created and refined into wisdom (Nonaka & Toyama, 2007; Nonaka et al., 2018). And the stronger the resource integration ability, the more opportunities organizations have to gain a core competitive advantage (Nonaka et al., 1996). Under the influence of these new interactive activities, KC will have a certain degree of change.

Knowledge creation has been the main topic of concern in AI-enabled KM research due to its significant impact, yet there are still gaps in AI-enabled KC (Alavi & Leidner, 2001; Eseryel, 2014; Kane et al., 2014; Nonaka & Peltokorpi, 2006). For example, the theoretical understanding of KM empowered by AI needs to be improved. After Nonaka put forward the KC theory-SECI model, he proposed the concept of the KC scene – 'Ba'. He believes that tacit knowledge needs to be continuously interacted in a specific social scene to create new knowledge (Corno et al., 1999; Nonaka & Konno, 1998; Nonaka et al., 2000; Peltokorpi et al., 2007). Later, some scholars discovered that 'Ba' can exist in a virtual team or community, providing a social scene for KC (Martin-Niemi & Greatbanks, 2010). However, the KC process may be different in different social scenarios (Nonaka et al., 2014; Nonaka & Krogh, 2009; Nonaka et al., 2006; Zhao et al., 2018). However, current research has not extended to the change of the KC theory yet, and the understanding of KM enabled by AI needs to be improved. The current KM practice that focuses on managing explicit data and information technology is not enough, and tacit knowledge, such as subjective insights or emotions, must also be considered (Nonaka et al., 1998). However, it is difficult to achieve it through traditional manual ways and simple management systems in the organization. Thus some scholars turned to new situations such as community-based KC or learning in open source communities (Hemetsberger & Reinhardt, 2006; Lee & Cole, 2003). From the perspective of participants, scholars also studied the influence of communication behaviour, individual characteristics, feedback characteristics, and many other behaviours such as turnover on KC in virtual environments (Majchrzak & Malhotra, 2016; Ransbotham & Kane, 2011). Nevertheless, these studies only reveal the sociality and the re-practice of KC in the virtual environment, and there are still gaps in explaining specific KC processes in AI environments.

Dual Influence of AI on KM

AI has a dual influence on KM. On the one hand, due to the maturity of data mining and neural network technology based on big data, AI can help people search for knowledge more effectively and improve the efficiency of KM. For example, Starbucks has developed a smartphone app which is essentially a question answering robot, which can effectively improve the efficiency of counter service staff and improve customers' satisfaction with the company by saving on their wait time (Warnick, 2020). On the other hand, since most of the algorithm systems involved in AI are regarded as proprietary technology property rights, AI is unexplainable and not transparent, which further brings puzzling moral and ethical issues. For instance, ProPublica (an authoritative and nonprofit newsroom in the US) once analysed a system that can predict the possibility of criminals committing a crime again, but found that the system discriminated against blacks while helping judges make more correct judgements (Larson et al., 2016).

AI Improves the Efficacy of KM

AI can integrate explicit knowledge effectively and improve the utilization of knowledge. It is because AI can not only accurately identify static features, such as text and pictures, but also accurately identify and capture dynamic features, such as body language. Through data mining technology, people can find and effectively integrate their related explicit knowledge (Dick Stenmark, 2015). And AI technologies, such as machine learning, can process and analyse explicit knowledge efficiently and generate new knowledge (Peltokorpi et al., 2007).

AI can also help analyse large-scale and multi-dimensional data to mine potential knowledge. After acquiring data, the main problem people face is how to analyse these massive amounts of data and obtain results to assist decision-making. Thus the accuracy and timeliness of the entire process are crucial. Traditional data analysis technologies can no longer meet the huge data volume analysis requirements. Yet, natural language processing, deep learning, or other AI-related technologies can simplify data efficiently process data from multiple dimensions and perform predictive analysis on data. AI turns data into information and then knowledge, which becomes an essential core competence of an organization (Hu et al., 2018). In other words, AI improves the possibility and efficiency of discovering tacit knowledge, lays the knowledge foundation for KM, constructs multiple knowledge acquisition channels, and ultimately promotes knowledge exchange between organizations. For example, expert systems based on neural networks and other AI technologies can effectively transform tacit knowledge into explicit knowledge (Tan et al., 2010).

Social and Ethical Issues Related to AI-Enabled KM

While AI improves efficiency and effectiveness, it also eliminates the transparency, interpretability, predictability, teachability, and auditability of machine behaviour, and hides it in opaque and unexplainable methods (van der Waa et al., 2020). Not only the participants do not know the logic of programs, but even the creators of the programs do not know it. When people and algorithms participate in the KM process as different decision-making bodies, algorithms must also comply with some moral rules as the decision-making body (Martin, 2019). Ethics refers to the philosophy of dealing with human values, right and wrong behaviour, and good or bad motivations (Leicht-Deobald et al., 2019). Management ethics refers to the active fulfilment of obligations and responsibilities to stakeholders, such as investors, employees, customers, governments, and society, with regard to the operations of the management in high compatibility with social ethics (Woods & Lamond, 2011). The ethical risks of AI and algorithm technologies are mainly reflected in the fact that while AI improves efficiency and improves results, it also raises privacy and interpretative questions (Mujtaba & Mahapatra, 2019). As AI and algorithm technologies make more and more important decisions for humans, the transparency and predictability of decision-making is likely to become difficult. In addition, intelligent machines based on data-driven learning algorithms are prone to biased and discriminatory decision-making, which violates human ethics and values (Leicht-Deobald et al., 2019). Therefore, once humans lose control of AI, the consequences will be serious, such as large-scale social problems (Mujtaba & Mahapatra, 2019).

Future Research Tendency of AI-Enabled KM

Based on the above introduction and discussion of AI-enabled KM, this section outlines possible future research trends. First, we put forward the questions that require urgent attention in three aspects: tacit KM, knowledge network, and personalized knowledge. Second, we describe several new technologies or mechanisms, to respond to these questions from a technical point of view. Finally, we put forward new theoretical directions and try to study these issues from the heuristic perspective of theories. That is, Human–AI collaborative knowledge management systems (KMSs) should be established from a technical perspective and AI-enabled KC theories should be built from a management perspective.

New Research Questions

Question 1: How to facilitate tacit KM?

Explicit knowledge refers to the knowledge fully expressed by human beings (such as language, mathematical formula). People know their tacit knowledge, but it is not easy to describe it through personal experience (Q. Huang et al., 2011; P. M. Leonardi & Bailey, 2008). In the past, the focus with regard to knowledge in enterprises was on explicit knowledge. Actually, tacit knowledge plays an important role in maintaining competitive advantage and continuous KC of enterprises (Chen et al., 2021). According to the SECI theory, the mutual conversion of tacit knowledge and explicit knowledge can create new knowledge (Nonaka, 1994). And it can be transformed into valuable knowledge assets through appropriate management and leadership approaches (von Krogh et al., 2012). Many literatures emphasize that tacit knowledge can not only make innovation successful, but also bring new scientific discoveries to support strategic decision-making (Nonaka & von Krogh, 2009). Therefore, how to accurately acquire knowledge and convert tacit knowledge for use in organizations is a key challenge (Kawamura and Nonaka, 2016).

How to use the advantages of AI to process and analyse information to identify and mine tacit knowledge is an important issue. Tacit knowledge is difficult to be captured, so some scholars believe that only by showing it can we better discover, preserve, and spread it (Erden et al., 2008; Nonaka & von Krogh, 2009). But the possibility of failure in this process is very high and it is not easy to achieve. Nonaka and Takeuchi (2011) believe that through analogy and metaphor in social interaction, tacit knowledge can be gradually familiarized by people through the process of externalization. Tacit knowledge can only be used after this process, and experimental cooperation among designers is usually related to the emergence and dissemination of it (Nonaka, 1994). In the digital age, knowledge within organizations is rich in the characteristics of big data. There is a large amount of organizational knowledge, and the growth of data is exponential (Ruan & Chen, 2017). Thus, the externalization of tacit knowledge in AI environments becomes obvious, and the types of knowledge continue to increase and appear on various digital platforms, etc. For example, when people find experts with professional knowledge in specific fields within or among organizations, AI technologies can record the experience and ideas of these experts, thereby forming a knowledge base. And the next time people encounter similar problems, AI technologies can use corresponding solutions to solve problems faster. Thus, tacit knowledge is transformed into explicit knowledge and can be managed easily.

Question 2: How to Build an Intelligent Knowledge Network?

Nonaka's SECI theory interprets the process of how to integrate internal knowledge resources from the perspective of creating information and knowledge (Corno et al., 1999; Krogh et al., 1997; Nonaka & Yamanouchi, 1989). This kind of knowledge can be understood as the category of domain knowledge. There is another kind of knowledge, which also plays an important role in KM, which is meta-knowledge (Engelbrecht et al., 2019). Early research has not formed a unified definition of meta-knowledge, but it is generally believed that meta-knowledge is the knowledge about knowledge, which describes the content, structure, and general characteristics of known knowledge. Meta-knowledge is the memory with location and tag information about other members (Ren et al., 2011). Later, according to Leonardi (2015), meta-knowledge is defined as the accuracy of who knows who and who knows what. Since then, the definition of meta-knowledge has gradually become clear, and its connotation and extension are basically determined.

Meta-knowledge is a very important knowledge structure for individuals (Engelbrecht et al., 2019). Many studies have shown that the meta-knowledge of individuals like professional managers is usually incomplete (Foss & Jensen, 2019). The increase of meta-knowledge can help enhance their understanding of team members' knowledge and skills, thereby assigning tasks to team members in a more reasonable way. So team members can perform their respective responsibilities and improve the efficiency of remote office and collaborative learning.

In the AI environments, social network extensions are greatly improved. Thus, knowledge networks have become intersected, fragmented, and complicated, and the identification and measurement of meta-knowledge become more difficult. Many companies encourage workers to use online social platforms when they are not easily in contact with others, which can enhance mutual understanding among employees (Engelbrecht et al., 2019). Interactions with people of various knowledge capabilities can enhance the capacity of individuals to define a situation or problem, and apply their own knowledge to the required action and specifically solve problems (Ikujiro Nonaka et al., 2006). Besides, the use of AI technologies can capture the trajectory of people's use on digital social platforms, and identify and improve meta-knowledge networks by mining communication networks between people. Thereby, it will help manage people's fragmented knowledge and build effective knowledge networks.

Question 3: How to Design Personalized Knowledge Recommendation Systems?

Differentiated knowledge refers to the specialized knowledge possessed by individuals or organizations (Barley et al., 2018). The main goal of maintaining differentiated knowledge in the organizations is to enable organizations to retain broader knowledge and protect different forms of knowledge to provide them with a competitive advantage. It can promote important organizational processes, such as coordinating actions, supporting organizational learning and adaptation, and stimulating innovation (Barley et al., 2018). The process of creating differentiated knowledge is also the process in which an organization highlights its particularity and specialization. Differentiated knowledge that belongs to organizations or individuals are extracted from the knowledge shared by organizations to complete specific tasks. Individuals or organizational units will use this knowledge in novel ways to apply or develop in order to engage in other specific tasks, namely the production of new knowledge and the creation of value. So, the creation of differentiated knowledge is the ultimate goal of KM (Barley et al., 2018).

In the past, with regard to enterprises, the management process of differentiated knowledge focuses on dealing with the conflict of individual knowledge among employees (Barley et al., 2018; Faraj & Xiao, 2006). Although there are many kinds of knowledge in enterprises, the discovery of differentiated knowledge is lacking. And it is difficult to achieve the efficient use of differentiated knowledge. However, differentiated knowledge becomes measurable in AI environments. It's closely related to the appearance and wide application of a personalized knowledge recommendation system. This kind of system has the characteristics of initiative and timeliness, involving a variety of technologies, among which the data mining technology and collaborative filtering technology are relatively more applied. For example, this kind of system will be developed according to collaborative filtering technology and content-based technology, which can not only provide users with matching documents but also establish close contact with relevant knowledge owners, so as to achieve long-term progress (Wang & Chang, 2007). Personalized knowledge recommendation system can not only collect individual performance, individual characteristics, and other knowledge, but also adjust recommendations according to these data, so as to achieve efficient KM. For enterprises, the management of differentiated knowledge not only has to deal with the conflicts of individual knowledge, that is, to meet the needs of the individual; it also needs to be considered from an organizational level, such as organizational strategic goals. Therefore, how to make personalized knowledge recommendation from the perspective of multi-agent needs is an important issue (Wang et al., 2020).

New Technologies and Mechanisms

New Technologies – Knowledge Tracing

Initially, knowledge tracing refers to a technology that models the learners' knowledge mastery based on learners' past answering conditions, so as to obtain the current knowledge state of the students (Corbett & Anderson, 1994). It aims at predicting accurately the learners' mastery of various knowledge concepts and the performance of learners' learning behaviour in the future. In a further abstract expression, knowledge tracing refers to an empirical statistical model based on past behaviours (Romer, 1990). Through extensive training of the model, it can clearly show the current state of the subject, thereby providing part of the basis for predicting specific classification content and inferring future performance behaviour. What's more, it's a process of dynamic interaction. The model obtains information from the subject and composes its own prediction mechanism, and then infers the subject's development status through this prediction mechanism. This kind of model composed of information from the same object can produce future predictions after analysing existing information to influence the source of the information.

Knowledge tracing can help improve tacit knowledge and differentiated knowledge. For instance, it is difficult to track the knowledge status of each learner in the face of a growing group of learners. That is, for the knowledge supplier, it is impossible to determine the demand status of the knowledge demander. So there are difficulties in providing knowledge training and guidance. Knowledge tracing is currently widely used in online learning systems to accurately predict learners' performance and assess ability levels. Similarly, this technique can be applied to employee training. This is an important part of employees' personal KM.

In organizations, when training employees with the help of KMS, such as digital online learning platforms, knowledge tracing technologies can be used to evaluate employees' learning and ability levels, thereby improving the level of employees' differentiated knowledge. In other words, AI-based knowledge tracing technologies can automatically trace the learner's knowledge mastery, and trace the real-time status and changes of the learner's tacit knowledge. This will then dig out the learning rules and make it better to provide personalized knowledge recommendations. On the one hand, it can provide an analysis of the knowledge mastery based on model construction, so that the education provider or the system itself has a more comprehensive understanding of each learner. Thereby they can judge the learner's knowledge weaknesses based on this analysis, and provide more efficient feedback on learning path and resources. On the other hand, learners can also train the system in a targeted manner, so as to deeply mine the resource library, fully schedule the resources in the system, and realize the special knowledge needs of learners.

New Technologies: Knowledge Graph

Knowledge graph was first formally proposed as a concept in 2012, aiming at improving the functions of search engines (Nickel, Murphy, et al., 2016). Although the definition is controversial, knowledge graph can be regarded as a knowledge network constructed based on the semantic database of entities (Qi et al., 2017). And the semantic database is essentially a graph-based data structure for storing knowledge.

Compared with the earlier semantic network, knowledge graph has its own characteristics (Nickel, Rosasco, et al., 2016; Qi et al., 2017). Above all, the knowledge graph focuses on the relationship between entities and their attribute values. First, knowledge graphs have conceptual hierarchical relationships, but the number of these relationships is much smaller than the number of relationships between entities. Second, an important source of knowledge graph is encyclopedia, especially the semi-structured data extraction in encyclopedia. Encyclopedia acquires high-value knowledge as kernel knowledge, using knowledge mining tools to quickly build a large-scale, high-value knowledge graph. Third, the construction of the knowledge graph focuses on solving the knowledge fusion and data cleaning technology from different sources.

Taking advantage of knowledge graph technologies can help extract fragmented knowledge, tap tacit knowledge, and discover connections between various sources of knowledge. Based on the above characteristics, knowledge graph can refine knowledge from heterogeneous multi-layer structure data and information by using AI technologies, such as machine learning, to build a graphical knowledge base (Nickel, Murphy, et al., 2016). It can be seen that an important value of knowledge graphs is to extract useful information from massive amounts of data, and aggregate scattered information fragments, and organize them together in the form of graphs to become relatively reference information and insightful knowledge to aid decision-making. Therefore, for KM, knowledge graph technology can better dig out the explicit and implicit value of knowledge. For example, it can be used in knowledge search, knowledge question and answer, knowledge recommendation, etc.

New Mechanisms – Knowledge Spillover

Knowledge spillover was a way of knowledge diffusion (Feldman & Kelley, 2006). Romer (1990) proposed a knowledge spillover model, which is used to explain the knowledge produced by any manufacturer can increase the productivity of the whole society. It is manifested that the change of any individual knowledge increases the scale of the overall knowledge, which is realized through the influence of the knowledge of a certain unit on the knowledge change of the surrounding unit body. In a broader way, knowledge spillover can be expressed as a product's own output leading to changes in the surrounding environment, and this environmental change is reflected in the corresponding increase in the output of other similar products in the environment, that is, product promote changes in the scale of products of the same species and different genera. Jaffe (1986) originally introduced the process of knowledge spillover into the knowledge process, and linked this process with the impact that corporate knowledge may have on its industry. Knowledge spillover contributes to the diffusion and re-creation of knowledge.

Knowledge spillover has a high spontaneity in daily life, so it does not need to be promoted by related parties to a greater extent. But to deconstruct this effect, it can be found that the knowledge spillover effect is essentially an indirect promotion under the influence of the environment. The following examples can help understand the process of knowledge spillover. Governments in some regions may set up R&D subsidies to encourage companies in different industries in the market to promote their own R&D, enhance market vitality, and speed up technological progress. When some companies have won awards, other companies that have not received funding in the industry have also increased their own funds from other sources (Feldman & Kelley, 2006). These funds are the performance of companies seeking breakthroughs, and at the same time, they make the R&D projects of these companies classified as environmental more feasible. In other words, companies that receive government subsidies have knowledge spillover effects on other companies in the industry. It can be seen that knowledge spillover not only promotes the diffusion of knowledge, but also helps promote the development of organizational innovation activities.

The development of AI technologies makes the knowledge spillover effect more obvious and measurable. As large-scale social networks are becoming more common, the scale of knowledge networks has also expanded. In this case, the knowledge spillover effect will become more obvious. In addition, due to the development of virtual AI, such as robots, the carrier of knowledge spillover is no longer limited to communication between people, but can also be spread through explicit machine language (Gu & Li, 2020). What's more, AI can accelerate enterprise KC and technology spillover, improve organizational learning and knowledge absorption capabilities, and bring technological innovation to enterprises (Liu et al., 2020). Therefore, even if AI is applied in a few companies, it will undoubtedly promote the KM level of the entire industry.

New Theories

Technical Perspective: Human-Machine Collaborative KMS

From a technical perspective, in order to better promote tacit knowledge, build intelligent knowledge networks, and promote differentiated knowledge, human-machine collaborative KMS can be built. Enterprises usually use KMS to mine and manage user knowledge and the emergence of AI makes KMS more intelligent. It can transfer information between human and machine intelligence through logical algorithm, and transform knowledge (Alavi & Leidner, 2001). This kind of human-machine collaborative KMS can not only store a large amount of data, but also perform efficient calculations, logical predictions, adjustments, and optimization decisions, and meet the requirements of current KM. However, in the digital age, the design of KMS has become more and more complicated. Due to the opacity and other characteristics of AI, the system can easily exceed human reasoning and analysis capabilities and lose control. For example, there is an algorithmic ethics problem. Therefore, how to establish a KMS based on human-machine collaboration from the perspective of design science has become very important.

The goal of design science is to improve the human condition by shaping IS solutions (Gregor & Hevner, 2013). The application of AI in the design of socio-technical systems often creates complex (opaque) solutions to important research challenges. Intelligent control means knowing all levels of system behaviour in all use cases. Therefore, it is necessary to design the rules of human-machine common behaviour in KMS not only according to the development law and evolution characteristics of AI, but also to meet the needs of humans and society. In addition, after discovering system problems and deficiencies, it is necessary to continuously iteratively update, so as to effectively design a KMS based on human-machine collaboration.

Management Perspective: AI-Enabled Knowledge Creation Theory

From a management perspective, new theories can be built to further explore the questions discussed above, for AI is changing the variables, mechanisms, and boundaries of KC (Avdeenko et al., 2016; Fowler, 2000; Pee et al., 2019). In the era of AI, tacit knowledge is no longer just a concept, it may also become variables that can be identified and measured, and it is constantly being explored and expanded. The essence of the KC process is the mutual transformation of different kinds of knowledge when people interact with others (Nonaka & Toyama, 2003). The rapid advancement of algorithm technologies undoubtedly provides excellent tools for mining deep-level information in data and efficiently using knowledge. As mentioned above, tacit knowledge can be visualized through knowledge graph technologies, and real-time changes of tacit knowledge can be measured through knowledge tracing. The research of Stenmark (2000) who attempted to exploit tacit knowledge using recommender systems is a good example. Meta-knowledge can also reflect the level of tacit knowledge to a certain extent. Therefore, it can be further explored in the direction of measurement and visualization of tacit knowledge constructs.

Second, new mechanisms can be explored to build the process of AI-enabled KC. Given the process of KC will become more rapid and even predictable, its development may have a state of leaps and mutations. For example, the ubiquitous social network makes every stage of KC have a social characteristic. With the help of algorithm tools, we can accurately identify the various information, quantify the various stages of KC, and better grasp the process of KC. For example, AI technologies can accelerate the process of KC through reconstructing the knowledge network, thus achieving a breakthrough in innovation (Kneeland et al., 2020).

Finally, it is possible to explore the boundaries of KC in different scenarios, for the reason that the boundaries of KC have become blurred, due to the creation of multiple AI-enabled knowledge scenarios. For example, some open innovation platforms with large-scale users are using digital technologies to gather collective wisdom to realize KC and innovation (Germonprez et al., 2017; Yan et al., 2018). In other words, large-scale KC has become possible. Besides, digital transformation has made the organizations more virtual, and the boundaries of KC within the organizations have also become blurred due to the introduction of AI. It makes the KM process a dynamic process, which matches the creative and adaptive aspects of dynamic capabilities, including knowledge that is constantly updated over time (Nonaka et al., 2016). Therefore, future research can also explore the process of organizational KC in new scenarios such as digitalization.

Conclusion

This chapter reviews the background of AI and KM, and elaborates what happens in the KM process under the influence of AI. The future research direction of AI-enabled KM has also been elaborated. It can be seen that KM has undergone tremendous changes due to the influence of AI technologies. It means that the role of AI in KM should not be ignored, whether in the practice or research of KM. And AI-enabled KM will become a focus of KM research in the future.

Acknowledgement

The study is funded by funds from National Key R&D Program of China (No. 2020YFA0908600), National Natural Science Foundation of China (No. 71722005, No. 71571133, No. 71790590 and No. 71790594), and Tianjin Natural Science Foundation (No. 18JCJQJC45900).

References

Alavi, M., & Leidner, D. E. (2001). Review: Knowledge Management and Knowledge Management Systems: Conceptual Foundations and Research Issues. *Mis Quarterly, 25*(1), 107–136. doi:10.2307/3250961

Andersen, J. V., & Ingram Bogusz, C. (2019). Self-Organizing in Blockchain Infrastructures: Generativity Through Shifting Objectives and Forking. *Journal of the Association for Information Systems, 20*(9), 1242–1273. doi:10.17705/1jais.00566

Anthes, G. (2017). Artificial Intelligence Poised to Ride a New Wave. *Communications of the ACM, 60*(7), 19–21. doi:10.1145/3088342

Avdeenko, T. V., Makarova, E. S., & Klavsuts, I. L. (2016). Artificial Intelligence Support of Knowledge Transformation in Knowledge Management Systems. *2016 13th International Scientific-Technical Conference on Actual Problems of Electronic Instrument Engineering (Apeie), Vol 3*, 195–201.

Barker, R. (2015). Management of Knowledge Creation and Sharing to Create Virtual Knowledge-Sharing Communities: A Tracking Study. *Journal of Knowledge Management, 19*(2), 334–350. doi:10.1108/jkm-06-2014-0229

Barley, W. C., Treem, J. W., & Kuhn, T. (2018). Valuing Multiple Trajectories of Knowledge: A Critical Review and Agenda for Knowledge Management Research. *Academy of Management Annals, 12*(1), 278–317. doi:10.5465/annals.2016.0041

Bell, J., & Loane, S. (2010). 'New-wave' Global Firms: Web 2.0 and SME Internationalisation. *Journal of Marketing Management, 26*(3–4), 213–229. doi:10.1080/02672571003594648

Ben Mimoun, M. S., Poncin, I., & Garnier, M. (2012). Case study—Embodied virtual agents: An analysis on reasons for failure. *Journal of Retailing and Consumer Services, 19*(6), 605–612. https://doi.org/10.1016/J.JRETCONSER.2012.07.006

Bharadwaj, A., El Sawy, O. A., Pavlou, P. A., & Venkatraman, N. (2013). Digital Business Strategy: Toward a Next Generation of Insights. *MIS Quarterly*, 471–482.

Bobrow, D. G., & Stefik, M. J. (1986). Perspectives on Artificial-Intelligence Programming. *Science, 231*(4741), 951–957. doi:10.1126/science.231.4741.951

Chae, B. K. (2019). A General Framework for Studying the Evolution of the Digital Innovation Ecosystem: The Case of Big Data. *International Journal of Information Management, 45*, 83–94.

Chen, J., Wang, L., & Qu, G. (2021). Explicating the Business Model from a Knowledge-Based View: Nature, Structure, Imitability and Competitive Advantage Erosion. *Journal of Knowledge Management, 25*(1), 23–47. doi:10.1108/jkm-02–2020–0159

Corbett, A. T., & Anderson, J. R. (1994). Knowledge Tracing - Modeling the Acquisition of Procedural Knowledge. *User Modeling and User-Adapted Interaction, 4*(4), 253–278.

Corno, F., Reinmoeller, P., & Nonaka, I. (1999). Knowledge Creation within Industrial Systems. *Journal of Management and Governance, 3*, 379–394.

Danks, D., & London, A. J. (2017). *Algorithmic Bias in Autonomous Systems*. Paper presented at the Proceedings of the 26th International Joint Conference on Artificial Intelligence.

Engelbrecht, A., Gerlach, J. P., Benlian, A., & Buxmann, P. (2019). How Employees Gain Meta-Knowledge Using Enterprise Social Networks: A Validation and Extension Of Communication Visibility Theory. *The Journal of Strategic Information Systems, 28*(3), 292–309.

Erden, Z., von Krogh, G., & Nonaka, I. (2008). The Quality of Group Tacit Knowledge. *Journal of Strategic Information Systems, 17*(1), 4–18. doi:10.1016/j.jsis.2008.02.002

Eseryel, U. Y. (2014). IT-Enabled Knowledge Creation for Open Innovation. *Journal of the Association for Information Systems, 15*(11), 805–834. doi:10.17705/1jais.00378

Faraj, S., Pachidi, S., & Sayegh, K. (2018). Working and Organizing in the Age of the Learning Algorithm. *Information and Organization, 28*(1), 62–70. doi:10.1016/j.infoandorg.2018.02.005

Faraj, S., von Krogh, G., Monteiro, E., & Lakhani, K. R. (2016). Special Section Introduction Online Community as Space for Knowledge Flows. *Information Systems Research, 27*(4), 668–684. doi:10.1287/isre.2016.0682

Faraj, S., & Xiao, Y. (2006). Coordination in Fast-Response Organizations. *Management Science, 52*(8), 1155–1169. doi:10.1287/mnsc.1060.0526

Feldman, M. P., & Kelley, M. R. (2006). The Ex Ante Assessment of Knowledge Spillovers: Government R&D Policy, Economic Incentives and Private Firm Behavior. *Research Policy, 35*(10), 1509–1521. doi:10.1016/j.respol.2006.09.019

Ferras-Hernandez, X. (2018). The Future of Management in a World of Electronic Brains. *Journal of Management Inquiry, 27*(2), 260–263. doi:10.1177/1056492617724973

Foss, N. J., & Jensen, H. (2019). Managerial Meta-Knowledge and Adaptation: Governance choice when firms don't know their capabilities. *Strategic Organization, 17*(2), 153–176. doi:10.1177/1476127018778717

Fowler, A. (2000). The Role of AI-Based Technology in Support of the Knowledge Management Value Activity Cycle. *Journal of Strategic Information Systems, 9*(2–3), 107–128. doi:10.1016/s0963–8687(00)00041-x

Germonprez, M., Kendall, J. E., Kendall, K. E., Mathiassen, L., Young, B., & Warner, B. (2017). A Theory of Responsive Design: A Field Study of Corporate Engagement with Open Source Communities. *Information Systems Research, 28*(1), 64–83. doi:10.1287/isre.2016.0662

Glikson, E., & Woolley, A. W. (2020). Human Trust in Artificial Intelligence: Review of Empirical Research. *Academy of Management Annals, 14*(2), 627–660. doi:10.5465/annals.2018.0057

Gregor, S., & Hevner, A. R. (2013). Positioning and Presenting Design Science Research for Maximum Impact. *MIS Quarterly, 37*(2), 337–355.

Gu, L., & Li, J. (2020). Research on the Influence of Artificial Intelligence on Enterprise Knowledge Management. *Academia Bimestrie*(06), 39–44. doi:10.16091/j.cnki.cn32–1308/c.2020.06.008

Hemetsberger, A., & Reinhardt, C. (2006). Learning and Knowledge-Building in Open-Source Communities - A Social-Experiential Approach. *Management Learning, 37*(2), 187–214. doi:10.1177/1350507606063442

Hu, S., Zou, L., Yu, J. X., Wang, H. X., & Zhao, D. Y. (2018). Answering Natural Language Questions by Subgraph Matching over Knowledge Graphs. *IEEE Transactions on Knowledge and Data Engineering, 30*(5), 824–837. doi:10.1109/tkde.2017.2766634

Huang, P., & Zhang, Z. (2016). Participation in Open Knowledge Communities and Job-Hopping: Evidence from Enterprise Software. *MIS Quarterly, 40*(3), 785–806. doi:10.25300/misq/2016/40.3.13

Huang, Q., Davison, R. M., & Gu, J. (2011). The Impact of Trust, Guanxi Orientation and Face on the Intention of Chinese Employees and Managers to Engage in Peer-To-Peer Tacit and Explicit Knowledge Sharing. *Information Systems Journal, 21*(6), 557–577. doi:10.1111/j.1365-2575.2010.00361.x

Jaffe, A. (1986). Technological Opportunity and Spillovers of R&D: Evidence from Firms' Patents, Profits and Market Value. *American Economic Review, 76*(5), 984–1001.

Jin, X., Wah, B. W., Cheng, X., & Wang, Y. (2015). Significance and Challenges of Big Data Research. *Big Data Research, 2*(2), 59–64. doi:10.1016/j.bdr.2015.01.006

Kaba, A., & Ramaiah, C. K. (2017). Demographic Differences in Using Knowledge Creation Tools among Faculty Members. *Journal of Knowledge Management, 21*(4), 857–871. doi:10.1108/jkm-09-2016-0379

Kane, G. C., Johnson, J., & Majchrzak, A. (2014). Emergent Life Cycle: The Tension Between Knowledge Change and Knowledge Retention in Open Online Coproduction Communities. *Management Science, 60*(12), 3026–3048. doi:10.1287/mnsc.2013.1855

Kawamura, K. M., & Nonaka, I. (2016). Kristine Marin Kawamura, PhD interviews Ikujiro Nonaka, PhD Preface. *Cross Cultural & Strategic Management, 23*(4), 637–656. doi:10.1108/ccsm-06-2014-0056

Khan, Z., & Vorley, T. (2017). Big Data Text Analytics: An Enabler of Knowledge Management. *Journal of Knowledge Management, 21*(1), 18–34.

Khanagha, S., Volberda, H., & Oshri, I. (2014). Business Model Renewal and Ambidexterity: Structural Alteration and Strategy Formation Process during Transition to a Cloud Business Model. *R&D Management, 44*(3), 322–340.

Kneeland, M. K., Schilling, M. A., & Aharonson, B. S. (2020). Exploring Uncharted Territory: Knowledge Search Processes in the Origination of Outlier Innovation. *Organization Science, 31*(3), 535–557. doi:10.1287/orsc.2019.1328

Krogh, G., Nonaka, I., & Ichijo, K. (1997). Develop Knowledge Activists. *European Management Journal, 15*, 475–483.

Kuang, L., Huang, N., Hong, Y., & Yan, Z. (2019). Spillover Effects of Financial Incentives on Non-Incentivized User Engagement: Evidence from an Online Knowledge Exchange Platform. *Journal of Management Information Systems, 36*(1), 289–320. doi:10.1080/07421222.2018.1550564

Larson, J., Mattu, S., Kirchner, L., & Angwin, J. (2016, May 23). How We Analyzed the COMPAS Recidivism Algorithm. *ProPublica.* Retrieved from https://www.propublica.org/article/how-we-analyzed-the-compas-recidivism-algorithm

Lee, G. K., & Cole, R. E. (2003). From a Firm-based to a Community-Based Model of Knowledge Creation: The Case of the Linux Kernel Development. *Organization Science, 14*(6), 633–649. doi:10.1287/orsc.14.6.633.24866

Leicht-Deobald, U., Busch, T., Schank, C., Weibel, A., Schafheitle, S., Wildhaber, I., & Kasper, G. (2019). The Challenges of Algorithm-Based HR Decision-Making for Personal Integrity. *Journal of Business Ethics, 160*(2), 377–392. doi:10.1007/s10551-019-04204-w

Leonardi, P. (2015). Ambient Awareness and Knowledge Acquisition: Using Social Media to Learn "Who Knows What" and "Who Knows Whom". *MIS Quarterly, 39*, 747–762.

Leonardi, P. M., & Bailey, D. E. (2008). Transformational Technologies and the Creation of New Work Practices: Making Implicit Knowledge Explicit in Task-Based Offshoring. *MIS Quarterly, 32*(2), 411–436.

Liu, J., Chang, H., Forrest, J., & Yang, B. (2020). Influence of Artificial Intelligence on Technological Innovation: Evidence from the Panel Data of China's Manufacturing Sectors. *Technological Forecasting and Social Change, 158*, 120142.

Magistretti, S., Dell'Era, C., & Petruzzelli, A. M. (2019). How Intelligent is Watson? Enabling Digital Transformation Through Artificial Intelligence. *Business Horizons, 62*(6), 819–829.

Majchrzak, A., & Malhotra, A. (2016). Effect of Knowledge-Sharing Trajectories on Innovative Outcomes in Temporary Online Crowds. *Information Systems Research, 27*(4), 685–703. doi:10.1287/isre.2016.0669

Martin-Niemi, F., & Greatbanks, R. (2010). The BA of Blogs: Enabling Conditions for Knowledge Conversion in Blog Communities. *Vine, 40*, 7–23.

Martin, K. (2019). Designing Ethical Algorithms. *Mis Quarterly Executive, 18*(2), 129–142. doi:10.17705/2msqe.00012

McCarthy, J., Minsky, M. L., Rochester, N., & Shannon, C. E. (2006). A Proposal for the Dartmouth Summer Research Project on Artificial Intelligence, August 31, 1955. *AI Magazine, 27*(4), 12-12.

Mujtaba, D. F., & Mahapatra, N. R. (2019). Ethical Considerations in AI-Based Recruitment. In M. Cunningham & P. Cunningham (Eds.), *2019 IEEE International Symposium on Technology and Society*.

Nickel, M., Murphy, K., Tresp, V., & Gabrilovich, E. (2016). A Review of Relational Machine Learning for Knowledge Graphs. *Proceedings of the IEEE, 104*(1), 11–33. doi:10.1109/jproc.2015.2483592

Nickel, M., Rosasco, L., Poggio, T., & Aaai. (2016). *Holographic Embeddings of Knowledge Graphs. AAAI'16: Proceedings of the Thirtieth AAAI Conference on Artificial Intelligence,* February 2016, Pages 1955–1961.

Nonaka, I. (1994). A Dynamic Theory of Organizational Knowledge Creation. *Organization Science, 5*(1), 14–37. doi:10.1287/orsc.5.1.14

Nonaka, I., Hirose, A., & Takeda, Y. (2016). "Meso'-Foundations of Dynamic Capabilities: Team-Level Synthesis and Distributed Leadership as the Source of Dynamic Creativity. *Global Strategy Journal, 6*(3), 168–182. doi:10.1002/gsj.1125

Nonaka, I., Kodama, M., Hirose, A., & Kohlbacher, F. (2014). Dynamic Fractal Organizations for Promoting Knowledge-Based Transformation@ A New Paradigm for Organizational Theory. *European Management Journal, 32*, 137–146.

Nonaka, I., & Konno, N. (1998). The Concept of "Ba": Building a Foundation for Knowledge Creation. *California Management Review, 40*(3), 40–54.

Nonaka, I., & Krogh, G. (2009). Perspective - Tacit Knowledge and Knowledge Conversion: Controversy and Advancement in Organizational Knowledge Creation Theory. *Organization Science, 20*, 635–652.

Nonaka, I., Krogh, G. v., & Voelpel, S. (2006). Organizational Knowledge Creation Theory: Evolutionary Paths and Future Advances. *Organization Studies, 27*, 1179–1208.

Nonaka, I., & Peltokorpi, V. (2006). Objectivity and Subjectivity in Knowledge Management: A Review of 20 Top Articles. *Knowledge and Process Management, 13*(2), 73–82. doi:10.1002/kpm.251

Nonaka, I., Reinmoeller, P., & Senoo, D. (1998). The 'ART' of Knowledge: Systems to Capitalize on Market Knowledge. *European Management Journal, 16*, 673–684.

Nonaka, I., & Takeuchi, H. (2011). The Wise Leader. *Harvard Business Review, 89*(5), 58–+.

Nonaka, I., & Toyama, R. (2003). The Knowledge-Creating Theory Revisited: Knowledge Creation as a Synthesizing Process. *Knowledge Management Research & Practice, 1*, 2–10.

Nonaka, I., & Toyama, R. (2007). Strategic Management as Distributed Practical Wisdom (Phronesis). *Industrial and Corporate Change, 16*(3), 371–394. doi:10.1093/icc/dtm014

Nonaka, I., Toyama, R., & Konno, N. (2000). SECI, Ba and Leadership: A Unified Model of Dynamic Knowledge Creation. *Long Range Planning, 33*(1), 5–34.

Nonaka, I., Umemoto, K., & Senoo, D. (1996). From Information Processing to Knowledge Creation: A Paradigm Shift in Business Management. *Technology in Society, 18*, 203–218.

Nonaka, I., & von Krogh, G. (2009). Tacit Knowledge and Knowledge Conversion: Controversy and Advancement in Organizational Knowledge Creation Theory. *Organization Science, 20*(3), 635–652. doi:10.1287/orsc.1080.0412

Nonaka, I., von Krogh, G., & Voelpel, S. (2006). Organizational Knowledge Creation Theory: Evolutionary Paths and Future Advances. *Organization Studies, 27*(8), 1179–1208. doi:10.1177/0170840606066312

Nonaka, I., & Yamanouchi, T. (1989). Managing Innovation as a Self-Renewing Process. *Journal of Business Venturing, 4*, 299–315.

Nonaka, I., Yokomichi, K., & Nishihara, A. H. (2018). *Unleashing the Knowledge Potential of the Community for Co-creation of Values in Society.*

Ordóñez de Pablos, P., & Lytras, M. (2018). Knowledge Management, Innovation and Big Data: Implications for Sustainability, Policy Making and Competitiveness. *Sustainability, 10*(6), 2073. doi:10.3390/su10062073

Pee, L. G., Pan, S. L., & Cui, L. L. (2019). Artificial Intelligence in Healthcare Robots: A Social Informatics Study of Knowledge Embodiment. *Journal of the Association for Information Science and Technology, 70*(4), 351–369. doi:10.1002/asi.24145

Peltokorpi, V., Nonaka, I., & Kodama, M. (2007). NTT DoCoMo's Launch of i-mode in the Japanese Mobile Phone Market: A Knowledge Creation Perspective. *Journal of Management Studies, 44*(1), 50–72. doi:10.1111/j.1467-6486.2007.00664.x

Provost, F., & Fawcett, T. (2013). Data Science and its Relationship to Big Data and Data-Driven Decision Making. *Big Data, 1*(1), 51–59. doi:10.1089/big.2013.1508

Qi, G., Gao, H., & Wu, T. (2017). The Research Advances of Knowledge Graph. *Technology Intelligence Engineering, 3*(1), 4–25. doi:10.3772/j.issn.2095–915x.2017.01.002

Ransbotham, S., & Kane, G. C. (2011). Membership Turnover and Collaboration Success in Online Communities: Explaining Rises and Falls from Grace in Wikipedia. *Mis Quarterly, 35*(3), 613–627.

Ren, Y., Harper, F. M., Drenner, S., Terveen, L., Kiesler, S., Riedl, J., & Kraut, R. E. (2011). Building Member Attachment in Online Communities: Applying Theories of Group Identity and Interpersonal Bonds. *MIS Quarterly, 36*(3), 841–864.

Romer, P. M. (1990). Endogenous Technological-Change. *Journal of Political Economy, 98*(5), S71–S102. doi:10.1086/261725

Ruan, A., & Chen, J. (2017). Does Formal Knowledge Search Depth Benefit Chinese Firms' Innovation Performance? Effects of Network Centrality, Structural Holes, and Knowledge Tacitness. *Asian Journal of Technology Innovation, 25*(1), 79–97. doi:10.1080/19761597.2017.1302546

Sokolov, I. A. (2019). Theory and Practice of Application of Artificial Intelligence Methods. *Herald of the Russian Academy of Sciences, 89*(2), 115–119. doi:10.1134/S1019331619020205

Stenmark, D. (2015). Leveraging Tacit Organizational Knowledge. *Journal of Management Information Systems, 17*(3), 9–24. doi:10.1080/07421222.2000.11045655

Tan, K., Baxter, G., Newell, S., Smye, S., Dear, P., Brownlee, K., & Darling, J. (2010). Knowledge Elicitation for Validation of a Neonatal Ventilation Expert System Utilising Modified Delphi and Focus Group Techniques. *International Journal of Human-Computer Studies, 68*(6), 344–354. doi:10.1016/j.ijhcs.2009.08.003

Teodoridis, F. (2018). Understanding Team Knowledge Production: The Interrelated Roles of Technology and Expertise. *Management Science, 64*(8), 3625–3648. doi:10.1287/mnsc.2017.2789

van der Waa, J., Schoonderwoerd, T., van Diggelen, J., & Neerincx, M. (2020). Interpretable Confidence Measures for Decision Support Systems. *International Journal of Human-Computer Studies, 144*, 102493.

Vial, G. (2019). Understanding Digital Transformation: A Review and a Research Agenda. *The Journal of Strategic Information Systems, 28*(2), 118–144.

von Krogh, G., Nonaka, I., & Rechsteiner, L. (2012). Leadership in Organizational Knowledge Creation: A Review and Framework. *Journal of Management Studies, 49*(1), 240–277. doi:10.1111/j.1467-6486.2010.00978.x

Wang, C., Zhu, H., Zhu, C., Zhang, X., Chen, E., & Xiong, H. (2020). *Personalized Employee Training Course Recommendation with Career Development Awareness*. Paper presented at the Proceedings of The Web Conference 2020, Taipei, Taiwan. https://doi.org/10.1145/3366423.3380236

Wang, H. C., & Chang, Y. L. (2007). PKR: A Personalized Knowledge Recommendation System for Virtual Research Communities. *Journal of Computer Information Systems, 48*(1), 31–41.

Wang, X., Zhang, X., Xiong, H., & de Pablos, P. O. (2020). KM 3.0: Knowledge Management Computing Under Digital Economy. 207–217. doi:10.1007/978-3-030-40390-4_13

Warnick, J. (2020, January 10). AI for Humanity: How Starbucks Plans to Use Technology to Nurture the Human Spirit. Retrieved from https://stories.starbucks.com/stories/2020/how-starbucks-plans-to-use-technology-to-nurture-the-human-spirit/

Woods, P. R., & Lamond, D. A. (2011). What Would Confucius do?–Confucian Ethics and Self-Regulation in Management. *Journal of Business Ethics, 102*(4), 669–683.

Yablonsky, S. A. (2020). AI-Driven Digital Platform Innovation. *Technology Innovation Management Review, 10*(10).

Yan, J., Leidner, D. E., & Benbya, H. (2018). Differential Innovativeness Outcomes of User and Employee Participation in an Online User Innovation Community. *Journal of Management Information Systems, 35*(3), 900–933. doi:10.1080/07421222.2018.1481669

Zhao, Y., Liu, Z., & Song, S. (2018). *Why Should I Pay for the Knowledge in Social Q&A Platforms?* Paper presented at the International Conference on Information.

12

EVOLVING DYNAMICS OF KNOWLEDGE IN INDUSTRY 4.0

*Nikolina Dragičević, André Ullrich, Eric Tsui,
and Norbert Gronau*

Introduction and Outline

Advances in digital technologies (i.e., combinations of information, communication, computing, and connectivity technologies, c.f., Bharadwaj et al., 2013), the pervasiveness of digital transformation (i.e. an integrated set of change and strategy initiatives involving both technology and people, c.f., Nadkarni & Prügl, 2020) and the availability of large amounts of data are revolutionizing society, organizations, and industries. Big data – increasingly gathered by the data sensing Internet of Things smart devices – is the most critical resource of the 21st century, comparable to the importance of land in ancient times, and machines and factories in 19th and 20th centuries (World Economic Forum, 2018). Driven by these technological advances, fourth industrial revolution (i.e., Industry 4.0) emerges and drives innovation in various sectors, such as manufacturing, health, electricity, or logistics.

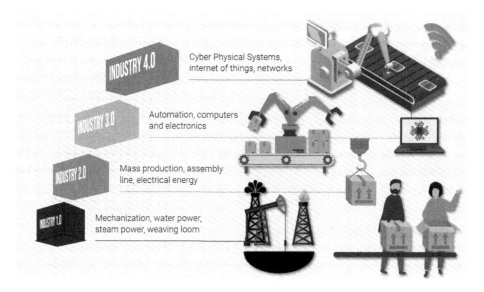

Figure 12.1   Stages of Industrial Developments

DOI: 10.4324/9781003112150-14

While the first three revolutions have been declared ex-post, the fourth was proclaimed to be revolution ex-ante, which led to a vast variety of different understandings and characterizations of the concept Industry 4.0 (e.g., Kagermann et al., 2013; Drath & Horch, 2014; Lasi et al., 2014; Pfeiffer, 2017) (see Figure 12.1). In the 18th century, the first industrial revolution was the first to change the economic landscape. It was characterized by the mechanization of processes, steam power usage, and the weaving loom. The mass production via the installation of assembly lines and the use of electrical energy marked the second industrial revolution at the end of the 19th century. The third industrial revolution (the 1970s) was driven by the automation of processes using computer technology and electronics. The usage of information technology leads to new services and automated control of manufacturing, logistics, and marketing, which resulted in extensive information gathering and exchanges between enterprises, suppliers, and customers.

At its core, the fourth industrial revolution (i.e., Industry 4.0) describes a shift from the automated industrial systems – which produce large quantities of similar products based on central production plans – to the vision of the self-organized industrial systems (Lee, 2015), in which intelligent and semi-autonomous objects adapt (Gronau, 2019) and enable individualization of products with the advantages of mass production (Kagermann et al., 2013). The main underlying technology of Industry 4.0 includes cyber-physical systems (CPS) – "systems of collaborating computational entities, which are in intensive connection with the surrounding physical world and its on-going processes, providing and using, at the same time, data-accessing and data-processing services available on the internet" (Monostori, 2014, p. 9). CPS technology is embedded in smart objects (SOs), i.e., networked embedded devices, such as machines in factories and meters in homes, and objects of everyday use at the network edges, such as refrigerators and air-conditioners. Distributed artificial intelligence (AI) embedded in SOs allows their collective self-organization, self-learning, and self-healing, and leads to increasingly decentralized and complex industrial systems (Lasi et al., 2014; Monostori, 2014). Examples of Industry 4.0 scenarios include smart grids, smart logistics, smart healthcare, and smart manufacturing (Alahakoon & Yu, 2016; Leitao et al., 2016).

Enabling digital technologies of Industry 4.0 are changing the dynamics of knowledge. Vast amounts of data become available across industrial systems with CPS's sensing and computational ability. Due to AI and analytics embedded in SOs distributed across the ecosystem, decision-making can, to a great extent, be handled automatically. For example, in smart grid scenarios, smart meters collect real-time, contextual consumption data in households, provide relevant information – customized consumption behaviour reports and enable automated turning on and off of appliances such as air-conditioners or refrigerators. However, Industry 4.0 is a socio-technical system, and SOs seek interactive feedback from customers. Customers or employees interact with SOs via user interfaces (UI), make sense of incoming data and make decisions on energy consumption that reflect their tacit knowledge – personal needs, preferences, and judgements.

The majority of Industry 4.0 knowledge management research work addresses to a large extent the vital role of big data and AI-driven analytics for future industrial systems (e.g., Lugmayr et al., 2017; Pauleen & Wang, 2017; Sumbal et al., 2017). However, the role of humans-in-the-loop, i.e., the role of interacting human actors with SOs, as a critical vehicle for unlocking the potential value of big data was not sufficiently considered (cf. Dragičević et al., 2020). Therefore, the Industry 4.0 vision raises several important questions regarding the relationship between humans and technology and the role of knowledge in supporting value co-creation. From the humans-in-the-loop point of view, the primary issue revolves around utilizing the resources and functionalities offered by SOs via UI in the form of data and information in a way that leverages their knowledge and capabilities and supports their decision-making.

The following objectives emerge, which this chapter will aim to address:

- To discuss what is the role of data, information, and knowledge in Industry 4.0
- To demonstrate how knowledge-based activities of human and non-human actors lead to value co-creation in different Industry 4.0 scenarios

This chapter addresses these objectives by elaborating the nature of knowledge, discussing the knowledge dynamics in Industry 4.0, outlining examples of human and machine knowledge-based interactions in different Industry 4.0 scenarios, and drawing implications of adopting a knowledge-based perspective for the evolvement of new ecosystems. This chapter is organized as follows. Towards an Understanding of the Concept Industry 4.0 introduces the concept of Industry 4.0 and its main characteristics. Knowledge Dynamics: Background to a Concept examines the knowledge dynamics theories and overviews the role of knowledge in the Industry 4.0 ecosystem based on constructivist epistemology. Modelling knowledge dynamics in Industry 4.0 Scenarios elaborates on the main actors and their knowledge-based activities in Industry 4.0 ecosystems and provides the exemplary smart factory, smart manufacturing, and smart logistics scenarios. Discussing the Dynamics of Knowledge in Industry 4.0 and Drawing Implications discusses vital points on knowledge dynamics in Industry 4.0 and draws implications for practice and research in Industry 4.0 from the knowledge perspective. Conclusions provides a conclusion and ends with a discussion on the future research and development in the field.

Towards an Understanding of the Concept Industry 4.0

Understanding of the concept Industry 4.0 and its main characteristics is still evolving among researchers and practitioners. The report which first described Industry 4.0 (Kagermann et al., 2013) identified CPS and Internet of Things and Services as its core drivers. Nevertheless, rather than on a specific characterization of what it is and how it is realized, the focus was on what Industry 4.0 can do or lead to – meeting individual customer demands, flexible business and engineering processes, optimized decision-making, resource productivity and efficiency, new business models. In another seminal paper, Lasi et al. (2014) identified two development directions that characterize Industry 4.0. According to these authors, the first driving force of Industry 4.0 is a considerable application-pull which induces changes such as short development periods, individualization on demand, flexibility, decentralization, and resource efficiency. The second driving force of Industry 4.0 is a tremendous technology-push characterized by mechanization and automation, digitalization and networking, and miniaturization.

The literature describes the following common features of Industry 4.0: (1) the technical integration of CPS in an industrial context; (2) the horizontal integration through value networks; (3) end-to-end digital integration of engineering across the value chain; (4) the vertical integration and networked industrial system (Kagermann et al., 2013; Wang et al., 2018). In a recent literature review, Beier et al. (2020) synthesized the key features of Industry 4.0 according to the three categories: (1) humans – where they, for example, emphasize how new technologies affect the future of work and job design, and discuss some of the characteristics of human and machine interaction; (2) organization – where they identify main features of Industry 4.0 systems through, for example, decentralization and flexibility;

(3) technology – where they note key elements to be automation and big data. Some of the common features across the three categories, Beier et al. (2020), similarly to other studies, discuss through the interconnectedness, integration, customization, Internet of Things and CPS keywords.

We will explain some of the main features of Industry 4.0, mentioned above, in the next paragraphs. The vertical and horizontal integration is in Industry 4.0 enabled by the CPS and the Internet of Things and Services network that connects them. CPS integrate their physical function with a digital representation for the physical part in the digital world, allowing them to exhibit both deterministic and probabilistic, optimized behaviours (Leitao et al., 2016). Monitoring physical processes via the virtualization leads to many opportunities in assisting users (operations, management, customers) across domains. New generation CPS integrate with service-oriented architecture principles, i.e., they have embedded the intelligent logic control that is exposed as a service in a standalone mode, to other CPS, or to the third-party applications in the cloud systems (Karnouskos et al., 2012; Leitao et al., 2016). Internet of Things and Services is a "self-configuring, adaptive, complex network" of the Internet of Things (Minerva et al., 2015, p. 74) and Services that connects CPS-enabled SOs, customers and providers – to offer a service (Hermann et al., 2016).

The integration and connection via CPS-enabled SOs in Industry 4.0 leads to a dissolution of the classical hierarchical automation pyramid in industrial systems (Salazar et al., 2019). In this pyramid, data and information were streaming upwards from the devices and sensors. They were passing over the control level using Programmable Logic Controller (PLC) and the process control level using Supervisory Control and Data Acquisition (SCADA) system to arrive to the plant management level and the Manufacturing Execution System (MES). From there, they were heading to the enterprise resource planning (ERP) level and from there downwards again.

In Industry 4.0 environment, in contrast, there is a networked structure of the entities (humans and SOs such as machinery, equipment and work pieces) and data is directly gained from sensors which share it further without the strict hierarchical order (Figure 12.2). Such a de-hierarchization leads to a situation where the previous decision-making hierarchy, consisting of people and functions of information systems, is replaced to a considerable extent with direct coordination and communication between participating entities. For example, direct communication between the equipment warehouse, the supplier and the final assembly department in smart manufacturing scenarios allows to significantly shorten the frozen zone, which otherwise would not allow changes to the product configuration for several weeks.

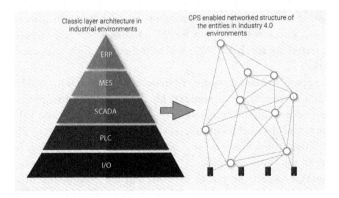

Figure 12.2 Dissolution of the Classical Automation Pyramid (cf., Salazar et al., 2019)

This new networked structure induces some crucial changes in knowledge dynamics in Industry 4.0. For instance, it may be possible to use real-time data from the field to readjust the SOs' (smart meters' or smart machines') actions. A change in customer preferences, gained by the big data analytics on their consumption behaviours, can be used to recalculate the production volume of different product alternatives. For example, American car manufacturers use social media analysis to find out the most wanted colour combinations of their cars and transfer this information directly to job shop scheduling of the paint shop (Boler-Davis, 2016). All these data-based feedback can be directed to their intended recipients (e.g., employees or other SOs) directly without going through information systems' hierarchy. Moreover, data that was typically stored only to fulfil traceability requirements can in new industrial systems be analysed and combined with data from other internal or external sources.

As it can be seen from the preceding discussion, reduction in organizational hierarchies enables faster, real-time decision-making based on the complexity of big data generated by SOs in dispersed parts of Industry 4.0 ecosystem and big data analytics (Lasi et al., 2014). However, as already emphasized, Industry 4.0 is a socio-technical system. Hence, the potential value of big data can only be fully realized when leveraged to support knowledge-based activities of humans-in-the-loop who interact with these data via UI embedded in SOs or third-party applications. UI play a significant role since they are mediators between human and machine-generated intelligence. In Industry 4.0, they become intelligent, i.e. dynamic, context-aware and consisting of features such as eye-tracking and object detection (Sonntag et al., 2017).

Some research work has already been done regarding the role of humans in new, digitalized systems. Such literature mostly focuses on the development of new competences and respective qualification measures. Morrar et al. (2017), for example, point out that employees need new knowledge, skills and qualifications to purposefully use and apply the latest technologies which are changing their work processes. Gronau et al. (2017) emphasize that competences regarding organization, processes, and interaction among human and technical entities become relevant in this new environment. Grzybowska and Łupicka (2017) further identify creativity, efficiency orientation, research skills, analytical skills and entrepreneurial thinking as relevant managerial skills in the new working environments.

However, as Beier et al. (2020) stressed, most of the current Industry 4.0 literature is concerned with technological aspects while the human factor and implications for human work and knowledge are still insufficiently investigated. The motivation for this chapter mainly stems from the identified gap in the knowledge dynamics area; hence, we will aim to contribute by providing a holistic view on the interactions among knowledge-based activities of both human and non-human actors – SOs and diverse computational entities. But, first, we will discuss the nature of knowledge and the dynamics among big data, information, and knowledge. We will start with this since we trust that "questions of method are secondary to questions of paradigm, which we define as the basic belief system or worldview that guides the investigator, not only in choices of the method but in ontologically and epistemologically fundamental ways" (Guba & Lincoln, 1994, p. 105).

Knowledge Dynamics: Background to a Concept

Duality of Knowledge: A Pianist Illustration

More than 50 years ago, Polanyi (1966), the scientist and philosopher, started to think of knowledge in terms of the duality, i.e., he pondered tacit and explicit knowledge as being inseparable and mutually constituted. Such a constructivist epistemological stance stands in contrast to the one rooted in positivism – which adopts the view of the tacit – explicit dualism, i.e., that knowledge can be divided into two types with distinct features. Whereas dualism suggests either/or thinking and is associated with classifications and taxonomies, duality suggests both and thinking is related to the epistemology of practice (Schultze & Stabell, 2004). Herein lies a critical distinction: the fundamental positivist premise is that knowledge is conceived as an artefact that people or machines can possess, which can be deconstructed into discrete units (e.g., Hansen, 1999; Kogut & Zander, 1992). The constructivist premise, on the contrary, is that knowledge is embodied (i.e., it does not exist outside the knower), socially constructed (i.e., co-created by interacting individuals and social groups engaged in action), tied to practice (i.e., it is inseparable from the activities that humans undertake), and culturally embedded (i.e., shaped to some extent by values and beliefs of the sociocultural context in which humans act) (e.g., Brown & Duguid, 1991; Lave & Wenger, 1991; Hislop, 2002).

Let us illustrate the duality of knowledge assumption, as imagined by Polanyi since we will follow it in our discussions about the role of knowledge in Industry 4.0 (see Figure 12.3). A simple example makes the point. Imagine a pianist. He has the ability to play the piano, i.e., his tacit knowledge enables him to perform the action of playing the piano. However, the pianist is only aware of such knowledge on a subsidiary level – *he knows more than he can tell* (Polanyi, 1966). The object of his focal awareness, i.e., the focal target, is the music itself. An attempt to focus on the technical ability, for example, on how to move his fingers, would make his "performance clumsy to the point of paralyzing it" (Tsoukas, 2005, p. 6), i.e., such focus would deprive these tacit components of meaning (Polanyi & Prosch, 1977). As Polanyi (1958, p. 56) has noted: "If a pianist shifts [his] attention from the piece [he] is playing to the observation of what [he] is doing with [his] fingers while playing it, [he] gets confused and may have to stop." Thus, instead of attending to the tacit components, the knower – for his action to be effective – only subsidiarily relies on them (attends *from* them) and switches his focal attention (attends *to*) to something else – the music itself (Polanyi, 1966; Tsoukas, 2005). Thus, there are two kinds of awareness in tacit knowing – subsidiary and focal awareness.

Since the integration of the subsidiaries to the focal target relies on the internal tacit act, tacit knowledge is inherently inarticulable (Polanyi & Prosch, 1977). What occurs as a result of articulation is a new artefact, which is mutually constitutive with the tacit background

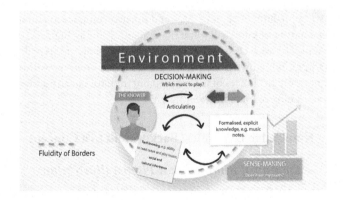

Figure 12.3 Dynamic Relations that Comprise Human Knowing

but is not articulated tacit knowledge *per se*. As Polanyi (1966, p. 20) elaborates, even what is often considered to be the detached, objective knowledge, such as music notes, "can be only constructed by relying on prior tacit knowing and can function as a theory only within an act of tacit knowing." Polanyi's (1967, p. 314, italics in original) description of the interaction between the tacit and explicit (articulate) usefully encapsulates the duality of knowledge:

> *All knowledge falls into one of these two classes: it is either tacit or rooted in tacit knowledge. The idea of an explicit knowledge is indeed self-contradictory; deprived of their tacit coefficients, all spoken words, all formulae, all maps, and graphs, are meaningless. An exact mathematical theory means nothing unless we recognize an inexact non-mathematical knowledge on which it bears and a person whose judgment upholds this bearing.*

Hence, knowledge in a formalized form cannot be a wholly formalized system (Tsoukas, 2005) since it cannot be independent of tacit knowing: "All knowing is personal knowing – participation through indwelling" (Polanyi & Prosch, 1977, p. 44).

Thus, in the case of our pianist, the sense-making of his music will depend on the context of a knowledgeable audience, that is, the music will be "heard" differently in the middle of the Amazon jungle and the concert hall, and differently "heard" by every individual depending on his tacit knowledge (Stenmark, 2002). Equally, the sense he will make of music notes will vary from other pianists depending on his tacit knowledge, including personal commitments and judgements. The pianist's decision-making, regarding, for example, repertoire selection, would rely on the same factors. What we know as formalized, explicit, and articulated knowledge cannot be conceived separately from the unarticulated cultural, social, cognitive, and emotional background on which it is based (Tuomi, 1999; Stenmark, 2000; Tsoukas, 2005). Further critical argument emphasized perpetually by Polanyi (e.g., 1969, see also Hislop, 2002; Tsoukas, 2005) is that knowing is not merely a cognitive process; instead, it is a whole-body activity involving our senses. He (1969, p. 147) noted: "the way the body participates in the act of perception can be generalized further to include the bodily roots of all knowledge and thought. [...] Parts of our body serve as tools for observing objects outside and for manipulating them."

It could be, therefore, more fruitful to follow those researchers who call for a focus on "knowing" activity rather than on "knowledge," since the former term more helpfully expresses the emergent and dynamic nature of the underlying construct (cf. Thompson & Walsham, 2004). As Cook and Brown (1999) pointed out, whereas "knowledge" is about possession, "knowing" is about relation: it is about the interaction between the knower and social and physical world. Knowing is hence the act of relating (cf. Stacey, 2000), a dynamic capability inseparable from doing. Rejecting the merely cognitive basis of knowing and challenging mind-body dichotomy leads to the notion of knowing as occurring in activities and tasks that humans undertake on an on-going basis (Hislop, 2002).

Differentiating (Big) Data, Information, and Knowledge

In the knowledge management literature, when discussing the relationship between knowledge and technology, it is often emphasized how valuable it is to differentiate data, information, and knowledge (cf. Tuomi, 1999; Stenmark, 2002). However, definitions of these entities and their relationships vary among authors; the terms are sometimes even used interchangeably (Stenmark, 2002).

In providing our understanding of these terms, we need to remind ourselves of a critical difference between the positivist and constructivist views on knowledge discussed earlier. The positivists argue that human knowledge can be objectified and codified and handling such knowledge representations can be looked into via technology. On the contrary, the constructivists say that human knowledge cannot be separated from the knower and that formalized and explicit forms of knowledge could only exist as data and information (Stenmark, 2002). In other terms, whereas humans deal with knowledge, machines carry only the manifestations or representations of knowledge, which are "at least one step lower in the chain of abstraction from reality" (Spiegler, 2003, p. 535).

The constructivists further argue that data and information processed by machines require tacit knowledge not only to be understood but as well to be created. Tacit knowledge is needed to define data structure embedded in an instrument used to collect phenomena sensed from the environment and determine relations that define the meaning of what data is (Tuomi, 1999). Hence, the term "raw data" is an oxymoron (Bowker, 2005; Gitelman, 2013), the essence of which might be depicted well by Geertz's (1973, p. 9) description: "What we call our data are really our own constructions of other people's constructions of what they and their compatriots are up to."

Following the constructivist rationale, we provide our understanding of the relevant terms. Table 12.1 shows definitions, properties, and knowledge-based activities related to human and smart object knowledge based on Dragičević et al. (2020). We define data as symbols that represent the properties of objects and events (Ackoff, 1989). Big data, then, refers to large volumes of diverse types of data generated at frequent intervals. Big data has characteristics such as volume, variety, velocity, and veracity, signifying magnitude of data, structural heterogeneity, the rate at which data are generated, and unreliability of data, respectively (Gandomi & Haider, 2015). Information refers to processed data into usable

Table 12.1 Machine and human knowledge: definitions, properties, and activities (Dragičević et al., 2020)

Machine domain (data space)			Human domain (experience space)
Data	*Information*	*Machine knowledge and intelligence*	*Tacit knowing*
Data: Symbols that represent properties of objects, events	Descriptions, processed data into usable form	Ability to apply algorithms, learn, and predict	The act of relating, dynamic capability
Big data: Large volumes of diverse types of data generated at frequent intervals			
Big data sensing (*based on predefined data structure embedded in the sensor*)	Big data management (*processing, integration, and aggregation of data to create information*)	Big data analytics (*modelling and analysis; including the application of artificial intelligence fields such as supervised and unsupervised machine learning; deep learning*)	Dialoguing with data, sense-making, and decision-making (*involving personal needs, beliefs, values, know-how, and emotions*)
Based on the logic that can be automated		Emergent	

form or descriptions, having functional difference (rather than structural) from data (Ackoff, 1989). Smart object knowledge is machine knowledge, whose logic can be articulated and, thus, programmed and automated (Ackoff, 1989). In the Industry 4.0 context, SOs have learning capabilities based on the application of AI fields such as supervised and unsupervised machine learning. Application of big data analytics and AI enables higher-level learning capabilities of machines, used to identify non-obvious, hidden relationships and patterns in big data (Sumbal et al., 2017). SOs also exhibit deep-learning capabilities, referring to the exploitation of neural networks that aim to mimic humans' thought and decision-making processes (cf. Lee et al., 2016; Sonntag et al., 2017).

View on knowledge based on the assumption of duality has critical implications for the perception of the relationship between human knowledge, SO-generated data and information, and SO knowledge. Since the "act of personal insight" is tacit, that is, it is inherent to the knower and the attributes of personal and social context, the sense-making and interpretation of the data and information provided by SO via UI rely on active human involvement. Hence, in "a process of dialogue rather than one of discovery"; insights are "evoked by the data" rather than "explained from the data" (Bryant & Raja, 2014). Figure 12.4 depicts differences in perceptions of how insights are gained, and value is created in "big data environment" according to the positivist and constructivist perspective (cf. Dragičević et al., 2020).

In Industry 4.0, SOs have abilities such as self-learning and self-organizing intelligence. However, humans, the main stakeholders in Industry 4.0 environments, make sense of the data and information provided by SO intelligence indifferently. This could include testing assumptions, tracing backwards the analysis, discarding some aspects of the data and focusing on others, more data gathering, and analysing to support initial insights (Labrinidis & Jagadish, 2012). As well, SOs can pick up and learn about only the isolated features of the environment. Hence, the broader context, comprising human factors and their tacit knowledge, their specific needs, judgements, and values stays out of the smart object reach and requires human involvement.

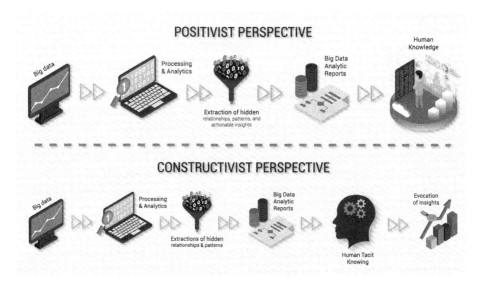

Figure 12.4 Differences in Perceptions of How Insights Are Gained According to the Positivist and Constructivist Perspective (cf., Dragičević et al., 2020)

Knowledge Dynamics Models and Ba

In the context of Industry 4.0, we define knowledge dynamics as interdependent knowledge-based activities performed by the multiplicity of actors of the socio-technical world – including SOs, computational entities, and human actors – which lead to value co-creation (cf., Dragičević et al., 2020), such as specified in Table 12.1. Knowledge management literature provided several knowledge dynamics models, rooted either in the positivist or in the constructivist logic. The positivist logic, rooted in the Cartesian body-object split or the Newtonian logic guided researchers to propose models that perceive knowledge dynamics, for example, through the metaphor of a flow (Nissen, 2002), stock-and-flow (Bolisani & Oltramari, 2012), or as a process (e.g., Gronau et al., 2016). A distinct feature of such understanding of knowledge is that tacit knowledge can be articulated, operationalized, or transferred (e.g., Ambrosini & Bowman, 2001; Hansen, 1999). Following this rationale, some authors contemplated knowledge dynamics in digital or technology-mediated environments (Alavi & Tiwana, 2002; Faraj et al., 2016; Pan & Leidner, 2003). For example, Faraj et al. (2016) propose that in online communities, socialization of knowledge (tacit to tacit conversions) is mediated by digital means, that is, without a physical presence, through repeated online interactions (asking questions, validating answers, presenting ideas, etc.). However, as discussed in the previous paragraph, such conceptualizations disregard the inherent allusiveness and inarticulability of the tacit knowledge, which decides what is shared in the virtual space and how it will be interpreted.

The constructivist logic guided some researchers to address these issues by conceiving knowledge relationally, an idea which was already known from the philosophers who objected to the Cartesian subject-object split. For example, Heidegger (1962) explains the human existential mode with the concept of *Dasein*, that is, being there, which is characterized by the inherent relationships with the environment. Kimura (1988) introduces a similar idea of Aida, space "in-between." To emphasize its emergent property, Bratianu and others (e.g., Bratianu & Bejinaru, 2019), proposed to use the energy metaphor of knowledge as an energy field, characterized by its continuous relational interaction and transformation, and co-existing cognitive, emotional, and spiritual dimensions.

Based on the dynamic and relational understanding of the nature of knowledge – by building on the work of the Japanese philosophers Kitaro Nishida and Shimizu – Nonaka and Konno (1998, p. 40) put forward the concept of *ba* as a shared space for emerging relationships and knowledge creation. According to these authors, *ba* can be understood as a sort of "frame (made up of the borders of space and time) in which knowledge is activated as a resource for creation" (Nonaka & Konno, 1998, p. 41). The implication is the following: "If knowledge is separated from ba, it turns into information, which can then be communicated independently from ba. The information resides in media and networks. It is tangible. In contrast, knowledge resides in ba. It is intangible" (Nonaka & Konno, 1998, p. 41). The concept of *ba* is based on the understanding that systems such as organizations or industrial ecosystems do not merely process information but create knowledge through action and interaction (Nonaka et al., 2000, p. 6).

Since it can reflect the relational nature of knowledge, and in this sense is relatable to Polanyi's notion of duality of knowledge (cf. Grant, 2007), Dragičević et al. (2020) used it as a central building component to develop a conceptual model of knowledge dynamics in smart grids. We build on these ideas in this chapter. In particular, we follow the understanding of these authors that there are three interrelated accounts of *ba*:[1] 1) a location where knowledge-based interactions take place, which involves mental (e.g., values, emotions,

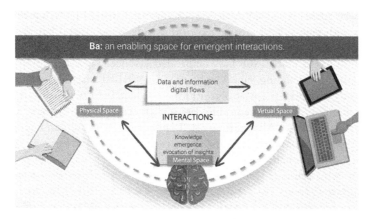

Figure 12.5   Ba: A Relational Space for Emergent Interactions through Physical, Virtual, and Mental Space

needs), virtual (e.g., networks), and physical (e.g., factory, home) components; 2) an existential space in which human actors engage their tacit knowing through time and space-sensitive, unique configurations of interactions (Nonaka & Toyama, 2003) to evoke insights and create meanings out of data and information embedded in, for example, big data analytics reports; 3) an enabling context or conditions for actors' interactions and knowledge creation (cf. Wei Choo & Correa Drummond de Alvarenga Neto, 2010).

Utilizing *ba* as a building component has implications for depicting knowledge dynamics in Industry 4.0. Based on such an understanding, we utilize *ba* to account for *humans-in-the-loop* and their tacit contribution as a necessary component of value co-creation and a prerequisite of the emergence of new (tacit) knowledge and insights in Industry 4.0 scenarios. Big data analytics and AI are applied to address objectives specific to Industry 4.0 and create value out of big data across the various parts of the ecosystems. However, as Figure 12.5 shows, whereas big data and information are automatically processed and can digitally flow through the virtual and physical systems, insights emerge only through the tacit human involvement in the mental space.

Modelling Knowledge Dynamics in Industry 4.0 Scenarios

Actors

In this chapter, we define main actors in Industry 4.0 as entities which perform knowledge-based activities – *humans*, *SOs*, and *computational systems embedded in the cloud-based IoT&S* (cf. Dragičević et al., 2020). Industry 4.0 ecosystem has both technical and social actors; SOs interact with humans via embedded multimodal UI which allow for complex ways of human-machine interaction, for example through different kinds of prompts and gestures (Beverungen et al., 2019). Hence, SOs create value by themselves, through their data sensing, analysing, and learning capabilities, as well as by additional value, which is co-created with interacting human actors, for example, when they seek knowledge input from humans via UI (see Industry 4.0 Scenarios – an Illustration for the value co-creation illustration through different Industry 4.0 scenarios). In the next paragraphs, we introduce the main actors.

SOs are networked embedded devices of the material world such as smart machines or smart meters with embedded learning algorithms (rule- or statistical-based), which allow them to sense and analyse data, and act according to the rules and limitations imposed by these algorithms. For example, SOs have embedded advanced big data mining and machine learning algorithms, including supervised and unsupervised machine learning and deep learning. Greatly improved machine algorithms embedded in SOs are used to "learn" from the massive amount of heterogeneous big data sets allowing for the creation of preemptive and individualized service (Allmendinger & Lombreglia, 2005; Kagermann et al., 2014). SOs form a highly configurable network of Internet of Things and Services of which they are building blocks (Hermann et al., 2016).

Other important actors in Industry 4.0 ecosystems are *computational components of the cloud-based Internet of Things and Services* (cloud-based IoT&S). IoT&S acts as a facilitator of actor-to-actor combinations, connecting SOs, human actors and systems, allowing for the establishment of value networks and value configurations (Kagermann et al., 2014). Actors who perform knowledge-based activities are computational entities embedded in IoT&S, such as big data analytics blocks, visualization tools, and an integrated service-oriented architecture (SOA) (Dragičević et al., 2020).

In the Industry 4.0 ecosystem, actors interact with one another for the primary purpose of supporting *humans-in-the-loop* – interacting humans such as employees or customers who are producers or consumers of products and services. Industry 4.0 ecosystem enables customers to monitor and make decisions regarding their services and products, even down to separate devices, which brings more awareness into their consumption behaviour. On the other hand, service providers can better understand their customers and profile them for targeted services and higher loyalty. Therefore, one key to design Industry 4.0 scenarios is to understand customers and their needs. Such an understanding increasingly relies on customer consumption and behaviour data, collected by sensors embedded in SOs (Lim et al., 2018). The design to support the integration of humans-in-the-loop depends on the application domain, the type of operation performed, and the kind of data to be exchanged between humans and the system (Leitao et al., 2016).

Different Layers of Knowledge Dynamics

The Industry 4.0 ecosystem can be viewed as a dual-loop system; one loop involving the physical layer (*SOs*) and the virtual layer (*cloud-based IoT&S*), and the other loop involving the interface layer (*humans-in-the-loop*)[2] and the virtual layer (*cloud-based IoT&S*) (Dragičević et al., 2020) (see Figure 12.6). Industry 4.0 ecosystem is dynamic and evolving. The interactivity of actors enables data and information flow in the physical and virtual layer, and the activation of *ba* and the engagement of (tacit) knowing in the interface layer.

SOs with embedded CPS components in the physical layer sense their surroundings, allowing for real-time data collection. For example, these are smart machines in factories, smart meters in homes, or autonomous vehicles in logistics. They analyse data and offer their functionality as a service in a standalone mode or via third-party applications, enabling continuous communication and interaction with them.

The virtual layer's computational systems collect and analyse massive amounts of data from SOs in the physical layer and other data from the system's distributed points. The virtual layer also generates customized statistical reports (information) that are fed back upstream and delivered to various web-based or mobile applications devices (e.g., user applications,

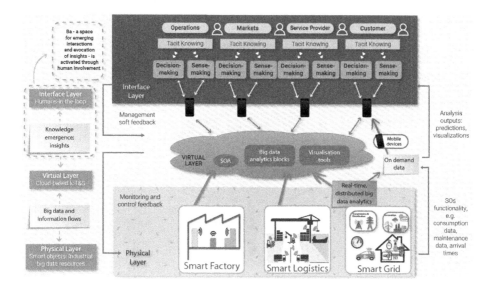

Figure 12.6   Knowledge-Based Activities across the Three Layers: Physical, Virtual, and Interface Layer

supervisory systems) and accessed by humans via UI embedded in in-home display or other mobile or web-based applications.

Humans-in-the-loop in the interface layer perform tacit knowledge-based activities – they make sense of incoming data and information via UI and make decisions regarding various aspects of Industry 4.0 ecosystem, such as balancing demand and supply in the grid, troubleshooting in the factory, or decision on route optimization alternatives (see Figure 12.7). User interface denotes a contact point between a human actor and smart meter (machine); at UI, the knowledge-based interactions between humans and machines occur and a dialogue (involving tacit knowledge) with data and information takes place. During sense-making, humans organize, manipulate, and filter received data and information into a cohesive structure, leading them to generate insights. Human sense-making is tied to the senses, skills, action, tactile experiences, intuition, unarticulated mental models, or implicit rules of thumb (Nonaka et al., 2000; Nonaka & Von Krogh, 2009).

In a dialogical process, tacit human knowledge shapes the meaning of data (i.e., adds meaning to data) but at the same time is shaped by the sense-making and interpretation of new data (cf., Tuomi, 1999). Industry 4.0 scenarios enable human more direct and visible physical connection to the data generated in the physical layer, which provides an opportunity for their increased engagement with those data at dispersed parts of the ecosystem.

The physical-virtual-interface layer conceptualization used in the model may be related to the systems theory approach according to which any complex system is made of three subsystems: a physical subsystem, a decision subsystem, and an information subsystem (cf. Romero & Vernadat, 2016). However, by acknowledging the duality of knowledge and building on the Nonaka and Konno's (1998) concept of *ba*, the main distinction of our conceptualization lies in the emphasis on how different layers in Industry 4.0 merge and how only through such a symbiosis and tacit involvement of the human-in-the-loop in the interface layer and insights can be evoked. Value is co-created in the symbiosis of the

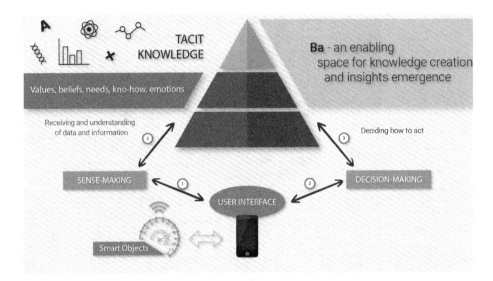

Figure 12.7   Human Tacit Knowledge-Based Activities via the User Interface

knowledge-based activities of different actors across the physical–virtual–interface layers, as we will illustrate through the various Industry 4.0 scenarios in the next section.

Industry 4.0 Scenarios – an Illustration

Smart Grid Scenario

We locate our first example of the knowledge dynamics in the smart grid service ecosystems. Industry 4.0 smart grid scenario offers a vision of smart energy systems that connects energy producers, energy facilities, smart grid management, and energy consumers with one another in a complex system of systems (Greer et al., 2014). Smart grids are power networks enabled by "smart" technologies that allow bidirectional energy and communication among participating actors (Alahakoon & Yu, 2016). An advanced metering infrastructure is the core component of a smart grid, consisting of a system of connected smart meters and other *SOs* such as smart refrigerators and air-conditioners. They are employed in smart grid utilities such as smart homes, allowing for collection and analysis of contextual consumption data from members of the household (in the *physical layer*). In the smart grid service ecosystem, human and SOs interact with one another for the primary purpose of supporting customers who are consumers of energy and for whom the smart grid ecosystem is created.

Some of the advantages of using smart metering AI in the exemplary smart grid scenario are automated meter reading and data processing, early fraud detection, real-time pricing schemes, and customer profiling (Alahakoon & Yu, 2016). Furthermore, complementing the AI embedded in the cloud (computational entities in the *virtual layer*) further enhances their capabilities. For example, fine-grained consumption data collected in smart homes can be merged with environmental and financial data to calculate the energy impact of business processes, which leads to system-wide optimizations (Karnouskos, 2014).

Due to the symbiosis of the physical and virtual worlds provided by CPS, data about energy usage is available to the consumer even down to the level of separate appliances, increasing in that way the possibility of better consumption awareness. In the dynamic Industry 4.0

scenarios, sense-making of data and wide-area monitoring are critical functions and crucial in effective decision-making. For example, customers' sustainable energy usage is highly dependent on their assessment of the many interrelated and changing factors such as energy supply and demand in the system, energy prices, environmental conditions, and household energy consumption.

To exemplify the knowledge dynamics in smart grid scenario, imagine a household where energy consumer (*human-in-the-loop* in the *interface layer*) needs to make use of the reports (e.g., consumption data analysis, merged with other data such as energy prices or weather conditions) provided by UI integrated into the in-home display or mobile phone to decide how much energy to use daily. Whereas analysis of consumption and other data can be automated to a great extent by using big data analytical tools (enabling, for example, generation of granulated trend and cycle analysis of consumption data, cf. Alahakoon & Yu, 2016), on consumers' tacit knowledge – such as personal needs, beliefs, and values – it will depend on what sense they will make out of analytics reports and what kind of decisions they will make.

Consumers (different household members), driven by their personal needs, purposes, and knowledge, make sense of the information provided by the UI and affordances differently and correspondingly utilize the possibilities provided by in-home displays and mobile applications in their unique way. They can download consumption data or geographic information system data to understand their consumption behaviour better and improve it to save energy. In attempting to make sense of available data, they will attend to other household members' needs and personal and household income. Accordingly, they might set automated alerts based on these specific consumption patterns, particular lifestyles, and preferences to track consumption progress against these goals. In other words, the dialogic activity between consumer and information provided by UI – due to tacit personal and social components involved in it – is inherently indeterminate and irredeemably local (Tsoukas, 1996, p. 19, 20). Due to consumers' tacit context – biographical components and social conditions – consumers' sense-making activities make reports received via UI relevant in concrete situations. That is, consumer activities are a part of the "social context the details of which cannot be fully described *ex-ante*" (Tsoukas, 1996, p. 19).

By opening data and analytics to customers via UI, smart grid ecosystem offers customers an opportunity to have a more active role by becoming co-creators of a service provided to them. Since they have empowered positions, they get the chance to engage in managing their energy usage and express their unique preferences to the level of single appliances more actively. A service provider is connected in real-time with their customers and understands their consumption behaviour and needs better. Data analytics based on the real-time consumption data and "hard field intelligence" (Allmendinger & Lombreglia, 2005) enables them to understand consumption usage patterns, offering new billing and payment options and automated service, such as predictions of usage of the next bill, understanding of household electricity distribution, and comparing consumption with neighbours (benchmarking). For example, such infrastructure allows for new customized pricing schemes and services and tips for energy saving to match lifestyle choices.

Smart Factory Scenario

The second scenario for describing the knowledge dynamics is located in the smart factory ecosystem. The successful integration of CPS provides significant benefits for the manufacturing industry, subsumed under the concept of a smart factory (Lee, 2015). Smart factories can handle "complexity, are less prone to disruption and can manufacture goods more efficiently" (Kagermann et al., 2013, p. 19). In comparison with conventional factories, machinery and equipment are equipped with sensors, processing units, and actuators to collect data from their environment, analyse and transmit these data via controllers; due to such CPS-enabled capabilities of these SOs, the production system is to a large extent able to configure, maintain, and organize itself (Lee, 2015). For example, prognostics systems are in place for isolated machine equipment, bringing self-awareness to the equipment (Lee, 2015). Condition-monitoring systems intervene if parameters diverge from reference values (Guillén et al., 2016). However, occasional human intervention is necessary. For example, if a grinding station notifies a worker regarding the need to refill lubricants or that a grinding head needs to be replaced, coordination and a verbal consultation between the machine setter and another process employee regarding the quick intervention in the process might be necessary.

As an illustration, assume the production of femur prosthesis in a smart factory, typically produced in small numbers with a range of variants. There are occasionally late adjustments necessary, and it is possible that an urgent order needs to be fulfilled and therefore incorporated into the production programme. In this smart factory scenario, the prothesis order comes in via a standardized electronic data interface (EDI) (*interface layer*) and a sales representative (*human-in-the-loop*) checks in the ERP system whether and when there would be some leeway in the production plan. He confirms the order and sends via the ERP system a note regarding this to the production foremen (*human-in-the-loop*), responsible for the producing powder-coated variants. A cloud-solution consisting various information systems (*computational entities* in the *virtual layer*) connects data from the different machine equipment (*SOs*) collected in the factory (*physical layer*) and analyses it (Lee et al., 2015; Wang et al., 2016). Therein, historical data and compared data from all the machine components act as a basis for predictive analytics and maintenance techniques (Lee et al., 2015; Wang et al., 2016). Furthermore, decision systems and visualization applications are implemented to support a human-machine interaction via UI (Lee, 2015).

The priority lot order appears on the foremen's AR glasses, together with product specifications, due date, and instructions for necessary manufacturing process changes. According to the product specifications, a small series of a product variant with powder coating needs to be produced. The specified due date indicates to him when this lot has to be executed. The foreman considers the current production schedule and due dates and decides when to incorporate the hot rocket lot. Based on his experience and know-how (i.e., his tacit knowledge), he assesses the feasibility and runs a simulation of the production programme. Whereas his decision-making is increasingly supported by analytics, the final decision will still depend on his tacit knowledge, that is on his experience with the machines and employees currently working the shift. Afterwards, he passes the task via tablet to the machine setter on site. The machine setter has to calibrate CPS via a tablet and trigger their implementation in the current process flow. When trying to implement the workstations, the machine setter directly receives a notification on the AR glasses. A decision regarding further proceeding is required. There is a variety of information based on the analytics received via UI embedded in production support application on his smart tablet, which could assist the setter in his decisions, such as delivery date variations, occupancy times, degree of employment, and overall equipment efficiency about the best time for discharging the old production lot and others. If the setter needs assistance for this decision, he will contact the foreman via a smart tablet. After the verbal consultation, the machine setter sends an implementation prompt.

Triggered by the executed intervention, a group of workpieces notifies the process employee on his AR glasses about the implementation plan. The process employee checks the machine utilization plan via tablet and sends his decision as a notification to a production software that controls the workpieces. The workpieces follow the decision; after the products pass the quality control conducted via sensors, they are transferred to rapid commissioning, after which they are promptly dispatched to the customer.

Value is co-created in the symbiosis of different layers of the factory and actors. Vertical (connectedness of manufacturer and customer via EDI) and horizontal integration (information exchange on maintenance intervals and special occurrences) allow information provision through big data analytics and support employees' decision-making. Through connected information systems and virtual platforms, vertical integration of the value chain enables late modifications of products and, therefore, creates additional value for customers.

Smart Logistics Scenario

The third scenario for describing the knowledge dynamics brought about by Industry 4.0 is located in the smart logistics ecosystem. In this scenario, all members and components are connected over wired or wireless digital networks (Oh & Jeong, 2019), creating a digital community of partners and enabling more coordinated operations, based on distributed data and quick information exchange. The key technologies are IoT, CPS, cloud computing, big data analytics, sensors, AI, and robotics (Merlino & Sproģe, 2017; Oh & Jeong, 2019). Essential stakeholders in the scenario are a distributor and a wholesaler who are in charge of logistic operations within the supply chain. Their main activities include order management, warehouse management and transportations, and goods management (McFarlane et al., 2016, p. 105; Lee et al., 2018, p. 2756). A retailer operates as the last part of the downstream site and sells finished products to customers – who are the most important stakeholders, for whom the network was created. He does primarily order management, including order receipt, assignment, scheduling, order execution, and tracking (McFarlane et al., 2016, p. 105). At the point of sale, technology-specific data on customer and their demands can be collected and analysed, providing information for retailers and producers and customers.

Today's supply chains and distribution systems are facing transformations caused by technological advances. Near or even real-time data and information flows between all supply chain members are enabled by IoT&S and service networks (Kagermann et al., 2014). The manufacturer can acquire "accurate and reliable data" (Lee et al., 2015, p. 19), e.g., on the current status of production, or necessary maintenance measures for machinery and equipment through sensors implemented in factory objects (*SOs* in the *physical layer*) and share them to distributors, wholesalers, or directly to customers (*humans-in-the loop* in the *interface layer*). The underlying *computational entities* in those digital networks (*virtual layer*) use big data technology and analyse these data. Products (also SOs) are equipped with radio frequency identification (RFID) as well as GPS tags for communication, identification, and tracking purposes (Abdel-Basset, 2018). Warehouse management, especially inventory management was thoroughly transformed with the introduction of identification systems such as RFID, for example, the goods on the storage place can be designated more efficiently. For the transportation and order tracking of goods between the different actors of the supply chain, big data analytics is employed (Rozados & Tjahjono, 2014). On this basis, stakeholders are aware of the current delivery status and can, thus, plan activities better.

Technological advancements can solve different supply chain phenomena. For example, CPS usage in supply chains presents a possible solution to mitigate the bullwhip effect by allowing real-time data and information flows between actors. The bullwhip effect refers to the increase of demand from the downstream site (retailer) to the upstream site (factory) (Shukla et al., 2009, p. 6479), that is, "orders to the supplier tend to have a larger variance than sales to the buyer (i.e., demand distortion), and the distortion propagates upstream in an amplified form (i.e., variance amplification)" (Lee et al., 1997, p. 546). In traditional supply chains, the main problem pertains to no direct communication between the actors due to which data and information cannot flow freely between them. In turn, this leads to insufficient qualitative information about the demands of the actors of a supply chain and, thus, to solely locally optimal decisions and finally to the bullwhip effect.

In smart logistics scenarios, however, the use of the CPS at different stages of a supply chain (e.g., production or distribution) as well as the connection of various systems through technical interfaces brings relevant changes (Geisberger & Broy, 2012, p. 20). All members and components are connected over wireless digital networks, enabling more coordinated operations and collaboration among relevant stakeholders. CPS components enable more efficient operations, better use of the warehouse capacity, more accurate inventory management in real-time and reduction of shipment time. Such capabilities could aid in resolving the bullwhip effect. Large amounts of data from different sources are collected and can be transformed into information within the computational systems near or even in real-time. All actors and the sales systems are connected through, for example, a cloud service due to which they have better and timely access to the information available on orders. Therefore, horizontal and vertical integration of the different supply chain units is achieved (Kagermann et al., 2013, p. 24). One stakeholder in the supply chain does not depend on the information about the order from the preceding supply chain member and can make sense of this information to complete production and order decisions more accurately.

However, while CPS resolves real-time data and information flow and visibility issue, there is still an issue regarding the decision-maker when he hides what he knows or has decision biases. Hence, the role of tacit knowledge is again critical. A simple example illustrates the point. Imagine a retailer (*human-in-the-loop*) who has exclusive knowledge on the customer based on the experience and the contextualization (sense-making) of different information, which cannot easily be transferred to the others throughout the digital system. For example, he could use his knowledge of product turnover rates in different seasons and make sense of the inventory stock, but potentially hide this information to gain a competitive advantage towards others, such as negotiating better purchase price.

Moreover, various studies argue that the bullwhip effect cannot be alleviated by addressing merely the operational issues and that the role of human behaviour is overlooked. Nienhaus et al. (2006) suggest that humans tend to employ strategies of "safe harbour" and "panic," which lead to increase of orders, even when there are no price changes and bottlenecks. Moreover, they argue that humans tend to undervalue the information they receive and act as an obstacle to information flow. Haines et al. (2017) also found that, in predicting performance in the supply chain, the use of information is more important than its availability. Decision-making success depends on the relevancy of the selected information and how effectively this information is converted to a decision.

Discussing the Dynamics of Knowledge in Industry 4.0 and Drawing Implications

The presented knowledge dynamics Industry 4.0 scenarios provide a new perspective on how through the interaction of actors – entities which perform knowledge-based activities (humans, SOs, and computational systems embedded in the cloud) – value co-creation in new industrial ecosystems is achieved vertically, i.e. cross-level within the physical, virtual, and interface layers, and horizontally, i.e. cross-domain through value networks.

Due to the wide use of the advanced CPS and computational approaches, Industry 4.0 allows for a variety of actor-to-actor combinations and value networks across the physical, virtual, and interface layer, either as dyads, such as machine-to-machine; triads, such as (human-to-human)-to-machine or as networks, such as many humans-to-machines. A symbiosis of the physical layer and the virtual layer enables bidirectional interaction among participating entities. It promises to equip physical resources with adaptive emergent capabilities that commonly characterize social and biological systems (Leitao et al., 2016). Importantly, it re-shapes actor-to-actor interactions by allowing increasing substitution of human-based interactions with machine-to-machine and machine-to-cloud interactions. Heterogeneous SOs exhibit self-organizing behaviour and learning derived from such interactions. Autonomous and real-time decision-making is enabled with no easily visible external interventions. The cloud (consisting of computational entities and information systems as actors) serves as the mediator of interactions between humans and machines.

As our exemplary scenarios demonstrated, the mass employment of SOs (machine actors) in the physical layer results in flows of data and information in dispersed parts of industrial ecosystems, the potential value of which is realized when leveraged to enable and support decisions or to create additional benefits. However, SOs and computational entities in the cloud deal with data generation, transfer, processing, machine-based analysis, and learning. The tacit contribution of humans-in-the-loop in the interface layer, nevertheless, is not replaceable by machines. Whereas SOs handle automated activities (data and information processing and analytics), the broader context, comprising human factors and their tacit knowledge, their specific needs, judgements, values, and emotions stay out of the SOs outstretch. Ecosystems in which smart services are provided are socio-technical systems, which heavily rely on machine learning capabilities. For example, our empirical illustrations through the three scenarios have shown how learning algorithms make use of sensor data, e.g. from a smart meter, allow for customer profiling based on the fine-grained data collected by SOs. However, our epistemological assumptions guide our conclusions that Industry 4.0 ecosystems, as any socio-technical systems, need human participation – their mental activity of learning and making sense – for value determination and value co-creation.

Unlike data and information embedded in UI, tacit knowledge is shaped by values, beliefs, and judgements. Instructive is Aristotle's concept of *phronesis* as "a true and reasoned state of capacity to act concerning the things that are good or bad for man" (Aristotle, *Nicomachean Ethics* VI. 6). Nonaka and Takeuchi (2011), building on the *phronesis*, proposed the concept of practical wisdom as "tacit knowledge acquired from experience that enables people to make prudent judgements and take actions based on the actual situation, guided by values and morals." Hence, it is tacit knowledge that guides decisions in industrial ecosystems, such as the implementation of ideas that would lead to more sustainable behaviour or that would reflect personal, deep customer needs. Despite the decisive role of technologies and AI in Industry 4.0, according to World Economic Forum (Tasaka, 2020), skills such as the ability to show deep empathy to customers, ability to realize new ideas in an organization, and ability to perform collective intelligence management could never be replaced by AI.

The implication for the knowledge dynamics study in Industry 4.0 is the following. Emerging from the constructivist rationale, we develop the argument that instead of attempting to operationalize or formalize tacit knowledge, knowledge dynamics models should, as a first step, account for spaces of human-to-machine interaction and identify its enabling conditions. Hence, we propose the concept of *ba* as a critical analytical unit for understanding and managing knowledge dynamics, which indicates that insights are gained only through human involvement, that is, their relational acts, for example, when interacting with UI and making sense of information in analytical reports. To facilitate tacit engagement of the humans-in-the-loop in the Industry 4.0 ecosystem, one would particularly need to consider how to design enabling contexts – *ba* – that support this objective (Dragičević et al., 2020).

Value creation in Industry 4.0 ecosystems then emerges from interactions within an organic configuration of multiple *ba* (Nonaka & Toyama, 2003) coming from many possible and time-sensitive combinations of interactions involving humans and other non-human actors, that is, through an "on-going, nonlinear, fluid process of interaction of participating actors oriented towards other actors and/or systems" (Kakihara & Sørensen, 2002, p. 7).

Implications for Research

The contribution of this chapter to academic research mainly addresses two aspects. First, we demonstrate how different constructions rooted in the diverse epistemological traditions pose critical theoretical implications for studying knowledge dynamics. The study rests on the assumption that a clear understanding of the nature of knowledge is necessary to develop a holistic view of the overall knowledge dynamics and suggest appropriate strategies for supporting the underlying knowledge-based activities. Namely, adherents of the positivist epistemological assumption arguing that knowledge can be formalized might lead to the understanding of industrial systems as information processing artefacts that depend on data availability and the ability of analytical tools to extract value from these data. The constructivist assumption that knowledge is an outcome of dynamic and emergent processes of knowing, on the contrary, necessarily leads to accounting for the humans-in-the-loop in modelling knowledge dynamics. While machines carry out automated knowledge-based activities, such as data processing and analytics, humans carry out emergent knowledge-based activities, such as biographically and context-dependent sense-making and decision-making.

Second, by discussing in theoretical terms the constructs underlying knowledge dynamics, we provide a vocabulary that both academics and practitioners can use to identify and study these and associated constructs in industrial ecosystems to increase the comparability of future theoretical and empirical work. In this sense, the identified constructs underlying knowledge dynamics contribute to creating theory-based knowledge on this topic in the Industry 4.0 field. In this endeavour, we particularly aimed to bridge the gap between the methods mainly relying on the systematic literature analysis-based identification of the relevant concepts and the methods focusing on merely practical experience to describe knowledge dynamics phenomena.

It is important to emphasize that Industry 4.0 is still evolving and that despite the successful implementation, it is still in its early stages of evolution in many world industries (Wilkesmann & Wilkesmann, 2018). Contributions to research such as the present study aim to highlight the importance of strategic choices which will make organizations bring the Industry 4.0 vision to real-world contexts. Supporting this argument, consider as well Wilkesmann and Wilkesmann (2018) research. These authors demonstrated how existing Industry 4.0 applications use different types of organizing. On one side of the continuum, there is a work environment that supports highly qualified humans with a broad leeway and a high degree of autonomy necessary to enable design and innovations. On the other side of the continuum is a work environment with a narrow leeway, little autonomy, and a top-down structure of control authority predetermined by digital applications. This and similar research show how both theoretical and practical understanding of the consequences of different implementation decisions is necessary.

Implications for Practice

While algorithms can automate many routine tasks, data-driven AI's narrow nature implies that many other tasks will require human involvement. Individual customer needs can be met in new smart service ecosystems (e.g. Kagermann et al., 2014) – not only because of smart use of analytics but also because the architecture enables more opportunities for human tacit engagement in product or service design and execution as well as more reliable sense-making. This allows for more purposefully addressing unique and variable individual needs. Such a lens instructs us that despite the propositional value of smart technologies, their successful implementation and creation of *value-in-use* still necessitates understanding of tacit needs' and behaviours of the humans who use them, whether customers, service providers, or others. Since the smart technologies and their properties do not have value by themselves but only in use according to actors' interpretations that are driven by their unique knowledge, they need to be well integrated into the practice of social entities – humans who interact with them.

For example, customers have their needs which in most cases cannot be controlled by a producer of goods or service providers; attempts of smart service could fail due to customers rejecting them. In other words, the effect of service provision will be mediated by customers' practice through which they will determine its value. To design or to choose properties of SOs and platform-based applications (e.g. UI or mobile application) through which employee or customers access its functionalities, the producer or service provider needs to be attentive both to the technical aspects of the artefact and to the social context within which the smart sensor is performing. Considering technological artefacts as linked with the technology use aids with the understanding of why some technologies succeed in some contexts and others not (Akaka & Vargo, 2014).

Based on the preliminary analysis of the knowledge dynamics in digitalized environments, we explicate a guideline to unlock the potential of knowledge dynamics that could direct practitioners activities (Table 12.2).

Nevertheless, the role of technology and non-human actors in industrial ecosystems remains critical and drives efficiency gains. IoT&S platforms enable the establishment of value networks by connecting various actors (beyond the traditional provider-customer divide) and allow sharing information and creating knowledge in different contexts. Non-human actors prompt engagement of human actors, i.e., can affect change in actors' (routine) behaviour. In this sense, leveraging the use of technology allows the creation of differential value (Bharadwaj et al., 2013, p. 472) and shifts the organizing logic and innovation of the companies (Yoo et al., 2010). Some of the main issues in this area pertain to, for example, addressing heterogeneous data sets coming from multiple sources (e.g., different types of sensors), which requires standardization of big data formats, semantic descriptions of their content (meta-data), models and architectures (Dragičević et al., 2020).

Table 12.2 Guidelines to support value co-creation in Industry 4.0 ecosystems

Element	Guidelines
Human actors	Consider incentive or reward systems that can be introduced to support employees' and customers' engagement effectively.
	Think about different types of training that can be created to support employees', customers', and service providers' use of smart technologies.
	Support elicitation of human actors' – employees, customers, and service providers' needs, and means of continuous learning about these needs in on-going service practice.
	Design interfaces according to employee or customer need focusing on high usability and solely provide the necessary information.
Technological actors (smart object)	Design or choose smart objects and applications (e.g. affordances embedded in user interfaces) via which employees or customers would access their functionalities in a way that supports usage, participation, and engagement.
	Consider and decide consciously which data should be collected and how it should be analysed, applied, and presented to support employees and more sustainable consumption behaviour.
Activities	Design the flow of the activities and tasks performed via user interfaces so that employees' or customers' personal needs and roles could come to the surface.
	Integrate smart objects into the practice of social entities – humans who interact with them by taking into account their different (tacit) personal and social characteristics.
	Enable and motivate human actors to voice their opinions about and via digital platforms.
Organizational	Create enabling spaces for tacit engagement and the emergence of knowledge.
	Allow for information flows and exchange of ideas and solutions.
	Make use of technologies to gather data and distribute information.

Conclusions

The explosion of digital connectivity and the advances of information and communication technology are revolutionizing industrial sectors. The fourth industrial revolution comes with a value ecosystem which represents a tremendous impetus to move the industries forward with higher-quality products and services with more efficient processes at reduced costs.

Despite the critical importance of using technology for value co-creation in Industry 4.0 scenarios, it is essential to remember that contemporary industrial value ecosystems have social and technical dimensions. Given the intangible, relational, and continuous nature of knowledge (Kakihara & Sørensen, 2002; Tsoukas, 2005), in this chapter, we concur with the view that the study of Industry 4.0 should take into account the complexity of both the social and technical entities. This chapter assumes that new industrial ecosystems (as any other socio-technical systems) cannot be reduced to the value of big data, algorithmic transformations, and learning capabilities of smart technologies. Technology matters as long as it fulfils the purpose of benefiting humans.

We conclude with some observations about the future research and evolvement of digital industrial ecosystems. As we have discussed in this chapter, the value that industries can obtain from big data analytics is contingent on using the proper tools to convey the analytics processes to those who make decisions. Therefore, the questions arise how to design for human interaction with data and how to represent data analysis to allow their most purposeful use. Further developments in this sense will occur on visual representations which promise to be useful tools for supporting reasoning (both perceptual and analytical) in complex Industry 4.0 ecosystems. In this sense, research on the value of the human-centred design process might help identify the tasks humans perform and their decisions in the overall context of their work. This could involve observing and interviewing the key decision-makers involved in the scenario under analysis and using predefined 'cognitive' probes to identify the information needed to develop situational awareness and make decisions on specific tasks (cf. Fioratou et al., 2016). Subsequently, these insights can be used to create visual representations of data and information that would help humans see and interpret data and information that resembles the way they think and that fits their needs better (cf., Sultanow et al., 2017).

The human-machine interaction via UI in Industry 4.0 will be researched further regarding the embodied nature of human cognition. Namely, cognition is intentional, situated activity since most of the thinking and action happens in a particular, often complex environment has a practical end, and utilizes the possibility of interaction and props from the environment (Anderson, 2003). Humans are embodied agents, and cognition is situated in interactions with the physical, social, and cultural background. In this sense, the potential lies in implementing virtual reality and augmented reality technologies in visual representations. Decision-makers' immersion into virtual models of the real operational and management environment would allow the making sense of data in all three dimensions available to the human perception in real-time. This would support them in achieving the mental state of flow in which they would perform activities by being fully immersed in virtual models of the environment in which they make their choices.

In digital industrial environments, augmented and virtual reality technologies and wearables and audio-based assistant systems provide employees with the supportive or necessary information within the work processes. These changes prompt research and development in the areas such as new competence establishment, job design, and qualification requirements lying in the disciplines of information systems, computer science, and engineering, which would enable employees to cope within these new environments (cf., Enke et al., 2018; Pfeiffer, 2017; Prifti et al., 2017).

In the end, we would like to emphasize how smart value ecosystems are unfolding with us humans as their active shapers; this gives us a unique opportunity to ensure they become "empowering and human-centred, rather than divisive and dehumanising" (Schwab, 2017, p. 4). Our assumptions about the world shape our research interests and lead us towards specific questions and types of investigations. The personal motivation for this study stems from recognizing this important need and the opportunity to make a difference in academic theory and practice. In today's digital economy, it also becomes vital to create ecosystems that enable people to live better.

Notes

1 Nonaka et al. (2000) distinguished four types of *ba* (i.e., originating, dialoguing, exercising, and systemizing) that correspond to different types of interactions (combinations of face-to-face, virtual, individual, and collective interactions). Since this line of thought has a rationale in knowledge conversions (e.g., that tacit could be converted to explicit knowledge), which is not consistent with Polanyi's notion of duality of knowledge, at least in this chapter, we don't attempt to adapt this framework for depicting knowledge dynamics in Industry 4.0.

2 For the purpose of depicting knowledge dynamics in this chapter, we take into account only the human-to-machine interaction through UI (i.e., we account for *human-in-the-loop*) and not the human-to-human interaction. Hence, instead of the mental layer, we call it an interface layer.

References

Abdel-Basset, M., Manogaran, G., & Mohamed, M. (2018). Internet of Things (IoT) and its impact on supply chain: A framework for building smart, secure and efficient systems. *Future Generation Computer Systems, 86*, 614–628

Ackoff, R. L. (1989). From data to wisdom. *Journal of Applied Systems Analysis, 16*(1), 3–9.

Akaka, M. A., & Vargo, S. L. (2014). Technology as an operant resource in service (eco)systems. *Information Systems and E-Business Management, 12*(3), 367–384.

Alahakoon, D., & Yu, X. (2016). Smart electricity meter data intelligence for future energy systems: A survey. *IEEE Transactions on Industrial Informatics, 12*(1), 425–436.

Alavi, M., & Tiwana, A. (2002). Knowledge integration in virtual teams: The potential role of KMS. *Journal of the American Society for Information Science and Technology, 53*(12), 1029–1037.

Allmendinger, G., & Lombreglia, R. (2005). Four strategies for the age of smart services. *Harvard Business Review, 83*(10), 131.

Ambrosini, V., & Bowman, C. (2001). Tacit knowledge: Some suggestions for operationalization. *Journal of Management Studies, 38*(6), 811–829.

Anderson, M. L. (2003). Embodied cognition: A field guide. *Artificial Intelligence, 149*(1), 91–130.

Beier, G., Ullrich, A., Niehoff, S., Reißig, M., & Habich, M. (2020). Industry 4.0: How it is defined from a sociotechnical perspective and how much sustainability it includes–A literature review. *Journal of Cleaner Production, 259*, 120856. https://doi.org/10.1016/j.jclepro.2020.120856

Beverungen, D., Müller, O., Matzner, M., Mendling, J., & vom Brocke, J. (2019). Conceptualizing smart service systems. *Electronic Markets, 29*(1), 7–18. https://doi.org/10.1007/s12525-017-0270-5

Bharadwaj, A., El Sawy, O. A., Pavlou, P. A., & Venkatraman, N. (2013). Digital business strategy: Toward a next generation of insights. *MIS Quarterly, 37*(2), 471–482.

Boler-Davis, A. (February 2016). How GM uses social media to improve cars and customer service. *Harvard Business Review*, https://hbr.org/2016/02/how-gm-uses-social-media-to-improve-cars-and-customer-service (last accessed Dec 13, 2020)

Bolisani, E., & Oltramari, A. (2012). Knowledge as a measurable object in business contexts: A stock-and-flow approach. *Knowledge Management Research & Practice, 10*(3), 275–286.

Bowker, G. C. (2005). *Memory practices in the sciences* (Vol. 205). Cambridge, MA: MIT Press.

Bratianu, C., & Bejinaru, R. (2019). Knowledge dynamics: A thermodynamics approach. *Kybernetes, 49*(1), 6–21.

Brown, J. S., & Duguid, P. (1991). Organizational learning and communities-of-practice: Toward a unified view of working, learning, and innovation. *Organization Science, 2*(1), 40–57.

Bryant, A., & Raja, U. (2014). In the realm of Big Data. *First Monday, 19*(2). doi: 10.5210/fm.v19i2.4991.

Cook, S. D., & Brown, J. S. (1999). Bridging epistemologies: The generative dance between organizational knowledge and organizational knowing. *Organization Science, 10*(4), 381–400.

Dragicevic, N., Ullrich, A., Tsui, E., & Gronau, N. (2020). A conceptual model of knowledge dynamics in the industry 4.0 smart grid scenario. *Knowledge Management Research & Practice, 18*(2), 199–213.

Drath, R., & Horch, A. (2014). Industrie 4.0: Hit or hype?[industry forum]. *IEEE industrial Electronics Magazine, 8*(2), 56–58.

Enke, J., Glass, R., Kreß, A., Hambach, J., Tisch, M., & Metternich, J. (2018). Industrie 4.0–Competencies for a modern production system: A curriculum for learning factories. *Procedia Manufacturing, 23*, 267–272.

Faraj, S., von Krogh, G., Monteiro, E., & Lakhani, K. R. (2016). Special Section Introduction—online community as space for knowledge flows. *Information Systems Research, 27*(4), 668–684. https://doi.org/10.1287/isre.2016.0682

Fioratou, E., Chatzimichailidou, M. M., Grant, S., Glavin, R., Flin, R., & Trotter, C. (2016). Beyond monitors: Distributed situation awareness in anaesthesia management. *Theoretical Issues in Ergonomics Science, 17*(1), 104–124. https://doi.org/10.1080/1463922X.2015.1106620

Gandomi, A., & Haider, M. (2015). Beyond the hype: Big data concepts, methods, and analytics. *International Journal of Information Management, 35*(4), 137–144.

Geertz, C. (1973). *The interpretation of cultures* (Vol. 5019). New York: Basic Books.

Geisberger, E., & Broy, M. (2012). *AgendaCPS*. Berlin Heidelberg: Springer.

Gitelman, L. (2013). *Raw data is an oxymoron*. Cambridge, MA: MIT Press.

Grant, K. A. (2007). Tacit knowledge revisited – We can still learn from Polanyi. *The Electronic Journal of Knowledge Management, 5*(2), 173–180.

Greer, C., Wollman, D. A., Prochaska, D. E., Boynton, P. A., Mazer, J. A., Nguyen, C. T., ... Pillitteri, V. Y. (2014). NIST framework and roadmap for smart grid interoperability standards, release 3.0 (No. Special Publication (NIST SP)-1108r3).

Gronau, N. (2019). Determining the appropriate degree of autonomy in cyber-physical production systems. *CIRP Journal of Manufacturing Science and Technology, 26*, 70–80

Gronau, N., Thim, C., Ullrich, A., Vladova, G., & Weber, E. (2016). A proposal to model knowledge in knowledge-intensive business processes. In *BMSD* (Vol. 16, pp. 98–103). Rhodes, Greece.

Gronau, N., Ullrich, A., & Teichmann, M. (2017). Development of the industrial IoT competences in the areas of organization, process, and interaction based on the learning factory concept. *Procedia Manufacturing, 9*, 254–261.

Grzybowska, K., & Łupicka, A. (2017). Key competencies for Industry 4.0. *Economics & Management Innovations, 1*(1), 250–253.

Guba, E. G., & Lincoln, Y. S. (1994). Competing paradigms in qualitative research. *Handbook of Qualitative Research, 2*(2), 105.

Guillén, A. J., Crespo, A., Macchi, M., & Gómez, J. (2016). On the role of prognostics and health management in advanced maintenance systems. *Production Planning & Control, 27*(12), 991–1004.

Haines, R., Hough, J., & Haines, D. (2017). A metacognitive perspective on decision making in supply chains: Revisiting the behavioral causes of the bullwhip effect. *International Journal of Production Economics, 184*, 7–20. https://doi.org/10.1016/j.ijpe.2016.11.006

Hansen, M. T. (1999). The search-transfer problem: The role of weak ties in sharing knowledge across organization subunits. *Administrative Science Quarterly, 44*(1), 82. https://doi.org/10.2307/2667032

Heidegger, M. (1962). *Being and time*. UK: Basil Blackwell.

Hermann, M., Pentek, T., & Otto, B. (2016). Design principles for industrie 4.0 scenarios. In *2016 49th Hawaii International Conference on System Sciences (HICSS)* (pp. 3928–3937). Koloa, HI: IEEE.

Hislop, D. (2002). Mission impossible? Communicating and sharing knowledge via information technology. *Journal of Information Technology, 17*(3), 165–177.

Kagermann, H., Riemensperger, F., Hoke, D., Helbig, J., Stocksmeier, D., Wahlster, W., Scheer, A.W., & Schweer, D. (March 2014). SMART SERVICE WELT Recommendations for the Strategic Initiative Web-based Services for Businesses.

Kagermann, H., Wahlster, W., & Helbig J. (2013). Recommendations for implementing the strategic initiative INDUSTRIE 4.0: Securing the future of German manufacturing industry; final report of the Industrie 4.0 Working Group. Forschungsunion.

Kakihara, M., & Sørensen, C. (2002). Exploring knowledge emergence: From chaos to organizational knowledge. *Journal of Global Information Technology Management, 5* (3), 48–66.

Karnouskos, S. (2014). The cloud of things empowered smart grid cities. In G. Fortino & P. Trunfio (Eds.), *Internet of things based on smart objects* (pp. 129–142). Switzerland: Springer.

Karnouskos, S., Colombo, A. W., Bangemann, T., Manninen, K., Camp, R., Tilly, M., ... & Eliasson, J. (2012, October). A SOA-based architecture for empowering future collaborative cloud-based industrial automation. In *IECON 2012-38th Annual Conference on IEEE Industrial Electronics Society* (pp. 5766–5772). IEEE.

Kimura, B. (1988). Aida (in-between). *Japanese, Kobundo.*

Kogut, B., & Zander, U. (1992). Knowledge of the firm, combinative capabilities, and the replication of technology. *Organization Science, 3*(3), 383–397.

Labrinidis, A., & Jagadish, H. V. (2012). Challenges and opportunities with big data. *Proceedings VLDB Endowment, 5*(12), 2032–2033.

Lasi, H., Fettke, P., Kemper, H.-G., Feld, T., & Hoffmann, M. (2014). Industry 4.0. *Business & Information Systems Engineering, 6*(4), 239–242.

Lave, J., & Wenger, E. (1991). *Situated learning: Legitimate peripheral participation*. Cambridge: Cambridge University Press.

Lee, H. L., Padmanabhan, V., & Whang, S. (1997). Information distortion in a supply chain: The bullwhip effect. *Management Science, 43*(4), 546–558.

Lee, J. (2015). Smart factory systems. *Informatik-Spektrum, 38*(3), 230–235

Lee, J., Bagheri, B., & Jin, C. (2016). Introduction to cyber manufacturing. *Manufacturing Letters, 8*, 11–15.

Lee, J., Bagheri, B., & Kao, H.-A. (2015). A cyber-physical systems architecture for Industry 4.0-based manufacturing systems. *Manufacturing Letters, 3*, 18–23.

Lee, C., Lv, Y., Ng, K., Ho, W., & Choy, K. L. (2018). Design and application of Internet of things-based warehouse management system for smart logistics. *International Journal of Production Research, 56*(8), 2753–2768.

Leitao, P., Karnouskos, S., Ribeiro, L., Lee, J., Strasser, T., & Colombo, A. W. (2016). Smart agents in industrial cyber–physical systems. *Proceedings of the IEEE, 104*(5), 1086–1101.

Lim, C., Kim, M.-J., Kim, K.-H., Kim, K.-J., & Maglio, P. P. (2018). Using data to advance service: Managerial issues and theoretical implications from action research. *Journal of Service Theory and Practice, 28*(1), 99–128. https://doi.org/10.1108/JSTP-08-2016-0141

Lugmayr, A., Stockleben, B., Scheib, C., & Mailaparampil, M. A. (2017). Cognitive big data: Survey and review on big data research and its implications. What is really 'new' in big data? *Journal of Knowledge Management, 21*(1), 197–212.

McFarlane, D., Giannikas, V., & Lu, W. (2016). Intelligent logistics: Involving the customer. *Computers in Industry, 81*, 105–115.

Merlino, M., & Sproġe, I. (2017). The augmented supply chain. *Procedia Engineering, 178*, 308–318.

Minerva, R., Biru, A., & Rotondi, D. (2015). Towards a definition of the Internet of Things (IoT). *IEEE Internet Initiative, 1*, 1–86.

Monostori, L. (2014). Cyber-physical production systems: Roots, expectations and R&D challenges. *Procedia CIRP, 17*, 9–13.

Morrar, R., Arman, H., & Mousa, S. (2017). The fourth industrial revolution (Industry 4.0): A social innovation perspective. *Technology Innovation Management Review, 7*(11), 12–20.

Nadkarni, S., & Prügl, R. (2020). Digital transformation: A review, synthesis and opportunities for future research. *Management Review Quarterly.* https://doi.org/10.1007/s11301-020-00185-7

Nienhaus, J., Ziegenbein, A., & Schoensleben, P. (2006). How human behaviour amplifies the bull-whip effect. A study based on the beer distribution game online. *Production Planning & Control, 17*(6), 547–557. https://doi.org/10.1080/09537280600866587

Nissen, M. E. (2002). An extended model of knowledge flow dynamics. *Communications of the Association for Information Systems, 8*(1), 18.

Nonaka, I., & Konno, N. (1998). The concept of "ba": Building a foundation for knowledge creation. *California Management Review, 40*(3), 40–54.

Nonaka, I., & Takeuchi, H. (2011). The wise leader. *Harvard Business Review, 89*(5), 58–67.

Nonaka, I., & Toyama, R. (2003). The knowledge-creating theory revisited: Knowledge creation as a synthesizing process. *Knowledge Management Research & Practice, 1* (1), 2–10.

Nonaka, I., Toyama, R., & Konno, N. (2000). SECI, Ba and leadership: A unified model of dynamic knowledge creation. *Long Range Planning, 33*(1), 5–34.

Nonaka, I., & Von Krogh, G. (2009). Perspective—Tacit knowledge and knowledge conversion: Controversy and advancement in organizational knowledge creation theory. *Organization Science, 20*(3), 635–652.

Oh, J., & Jeong, B. (2019). Tactical supply planning in smart manufacturing supply chain. *Robotics and Computer-Integrated Manufacturing, 55*, 217–233.

Pan, S. L., & Leidner, D. E. (2003). Bridging communities of practice with information technology in pursuit of global knowledge sharing. *The Journal of Strategic Information Systems, 12*(1), 71–88.

Pauleen, D. J., & Wang, W. Y. C. (2017). Does big data mean big knowledge? KM perspectives on big data and analytics. *Journal of Knowledge Management, 21*(1), 1–6.

Pfeiffer, S. (2017). The vision of "Industrie 4.0" in the making—a case of future told, tamed, and traded. *Nanoethics, 11*(1), 107–121.

Polanyi, M. (1958). *Personal knowledge. Towards apostcritical philosophy.* London: University of Chicago Press.

Polanyi, M. (1967). Sense-giving and sense-reading. *Philosophy, 42*(162), 301–325.

Polanyi, M. (1966). *The tacit dimension.* New York: Doubleday & Company.

Polanyi, M., & Prosch, H. (1977). *Meaning.* London: University of Chicago Press

Prifti, L., Knigge, M., Kienegger, H., & Krcmar, H. (2017). A competency model for "Industrie 4.0" employees.

Romero, D., & Vernadat, F. (2016). Enterprise information systems state of the art: Past, present and future trends. *Computers in Industry, 79*(Supplement C), 3–13.

Rozados, I. V., & Tjahjono, B. (2014). Big data analytics in supply chain management: Trends and related research. *6th International Conference on Operations and Supply Chain Management.*

Salazar, L. A. C., Ryashentseva, D., Lüder, A., & Vogel-Heuser, B. (2019). Cyber-physical production systems architecture based on multi-agent's design pattern—comparison of selected approaches mapping four agent patterns. *The International Journal of Advanced Manufacturing Technology, 105*(9), 4005–4034.

Shukla, V., Naim, M. M., & Yaseen, E. A. (2009). 'Bullwhip'and 'backlash'in supply pipelines. *International Journal of Production Research, 47*(23), 6477–6497.

Schultze, U., & Stabell, C. (2004). Knowing what you don't know? Discourses and contradictions in knowledge management research. *Journal of Management Studies, 41*(4), 549–573.

Schwab, K. (2017). *The fourth industrial revolution*. New York, NY: Crown Business.

Sonntag, D., Zillner, S., van der Smagt, P., & Lörincz, A. (2017). Overview of the CPS for smart factories project: Deep learning, knowledge acquisition, anomaly detection and intelligent user interfaces. In *Industrial internet of things* (pp. 487–504). Cham, Switzerland: Springer.

Spiegler, I. (2003). Technology and knowledge: Bridging a "generating" gap. *Information & Management, 40*(6), 533–539.

Stacey, R. (2000). The emergence of knowledge in organization. Emergence. *A Journal of Complexity Issues in Organizations and Management, 2*(4), 23–39.

Stenmark, D. (2000). Leveraging tacit organizational knowledge. *Journal of Management Information Systems, 17*(3), 9–24.

Stenmark, D. (2002). Information vs. knowledge: The role of intranets in knowledge management. In *System sciences, 2002. HICSS. Proceedings of the 35th Annual Hawaii International Conference on Big Island, HI* (pp. 928–937).

Sultanow, E., Tobolla, M., Ullrich, A., & Vladova, G. (2017). Visual Analytics Supporting Knowledge Management. In *i-KNOW*. http://ceur-ws.org/Vol-2025/paper_hci_1.pdf

Sumbal, M. S., Tsui, E., & See-to, E. W. (2017). Interrelationship between big data and knowledge management: An exploratory study in the oil and gas sector. *Journal of Knowledge Management, 21*(1), 180–196.

Tasaka, H. (2020, October 23). *These 6 skills cannot be replicated by artificial intelligence*. World Economic Forum. https://www.weforum.org/agenda/2020/10/these-6-skills-cannot-be-replicated-by-artificial-intelligence/

Thompson, M. P. A., & Walsham, G. (2004). Placing knowledge management in context. *Journal of Management Studies, 41*(5), 725–747.

Tsoukas, H. (1996). The firm as a distributed knowledge system: A constructionist approach. *Strategic Management Journal, 17*(S2), 11–25.

Tsoukas, H. (2005). Do we really understand tacit knowledge? In S. Little & T. Ray (Eds.), *Managing knowledge: An essential reader* (p. 107). Thousand Oaks: SAGE Publications Ltd.

Tuomi, I. (1999). Data is more than knowledge: Implications of the reversed knowledge hierarchy for knowledge management and organizational memory. In *Systems sciences, 1999. HICSS-32. Proceedings of the 32nd Annual Hawaii International Conference on Hawaii*, USA (p. 12).

Wang, S., Wan, J., Di Li, & Zhang, C. (2016). Implementing smart factory of Industrie 4.0: An outlook. *International Journal of Distributed Sensor Networks, 12*(1), 1–10.

Wang, Y., Chen, Q., Gan, D., Yang, J., Kirschen, D. S., & Kang, C. (2018). Deep learning-based socio-demographic information identification from smart meter data. *IEEE Transactions on Smart Grid, 10*(3), 1.

Wei Choo, C., & Correa Drummond de Alvarenga Neto, R. (2010). Beyond the BA: Managing enabling contexts in knowledge organizations. *Journal of Knowledge Management, 14*(4), 592–610.

Wilkesmann, M., & Wilkesmann, U. (2018). Industry 4.0–organizing routines or innovations?. *VINE Journal of Information and Knowledge Management Systems, 48*(2) 238–254.

World Economic Forum. (2018). *Will the Future Be Human? - Yuval Noah Harari*. https://www.youtube.com/watch?v=hL9uk4hKyg4 (last accessed Dec. 22, 2020)

Yoo, Y., Henfridsson, O., & Lyytinen, K. (2010). Research commentary—The new organizing logic of digital innovation: An agenda for information systems research. *Information Systems Research, 21*(4), 724–735.

13

DYNAMICS OF ENTERPRISE KNOWLEDGE GENERATION SYSTEM BASED ON THE SECI FRAMEWORK

Xirong Gao

Background

As Nonaka and Takeuchi (1995) argue, there are many factors that influence the success of a company, and too many of them often make a company get lost in them. In this context, these two scholars suggest that knowledge is the ultimate resource for companies to gain a competitive advantage, and that knowledge creation is the primary factor that determines whether or not a company can achieve excellence ("Make It Better", in the Chinese sense). Thus, a company that pursues this should and must create knowledge and ultimately become a "knowledge-creating company".

The question is, how do companies go about creating knowledge? Nonaka and Takeuchi (1995) constructed a SECI (Socialization-Externalization-Combination-Internalization) framework for enterprises to create knowledge based on the experience of Japanese company innovation and transformation, and argued the principle and mechanism of creating new knowledge by interconversion between tacit and explicit knowledge, thus providing a conceptual model for how enterprises create knowledge. However, the SECI framework is only a qualitative conceptual model; the two authors justify it mainly by case illustrations, and fail to translate it into a dynamic model that can operate on its own, which is undoubtedly a shortcoming of the SECI framework.

Based on the above background, we reconstruct the SECI knowledge spiral system into a dynamic model of knowledge generation system similar to the "eye of storm" with the aid of the storm generation principle, and train it to dynamically simulate the enterprise knowledge generating mechanism. This will help move the SECI framework from a black-box qualitative conceptual model to a mathematical model that can peek into the internal structure and simulate its operation, thus explaining at a subtler level the mechanism whereby knowledge is created by enterprises.

Literature Review

Regarding the value and utility of knowledge, the academic consensus is that knowledge is an enterprise's most important intangible resource that is rooted and scattered in all aspects of its organization system, difficult to imitate and socially complex, and hence can bring sustainable competitive advantage to enterprises. The mainstream view of enterprise

DOI: 10.4324/9781003112150-15

knowledge is that the more important resource of an enterprise than the knowledge it possesses is the ability to use its knowledge effectively, in particular, the ability to use existing knowledge to create new knowledge. Therefore, how to improve the knowledge creation capability of enterprises has become an important topic of widespread academic interest.

More recently, system dynamics have been increasingly applied to knowledge management research (Alavi & Leidner, 2001). Xiaolan He and Xianyu Wang (2012) divided the tacit knowledge management task of organizations into three parts, designed a system dynamics model accordingly, simulated and analyzed the logical cause-effect and feedback relationships among the factors, and proposed several measures to help organizations improve their tacit knowledge management efficiency; Yumei Wang and Jing Zhang (2009) used a system dynamics approach to analyze the internal and external support subsystems of organization knowledge innovation, investigated the contributory factors of organization knowledge innovation and its operation mechanism, and obtained the results that can be drawn on; Xiuhong Wang and Yuan Liu (2006) established a system dynamics model for the transformation of subjective tacit knowledge, and described from a quantitative perspective the influence of each factor on enterprise knowledge stock; Xin Wang and Bing Sun (2012) built a system dynamics model for the internal knowledge transfer of enterprises, and conducted causality analysis, and provided a theoretical foundation for enterprises to formulate effective knowledge transfer strategies.

As it is widely recognized, modern society is virtually a knowledge explosion society where new knowledge emerges at an increasingly rapid pace. However, there is scanty literature that systematically examines and maps the dynamic trajectory of knowledge creation in modern society from the perspective of knowledge explosion at present. This is precisely the topic that this chapter hopes to explore.

The "Eye of Storm" Model of Enterprise Knowledge Generation Based on the SECI Framework

The "Eye of Storm" Model of Enterprise Knowledge Generation

For the SECI knowledge spiral system, we can borrow the concept of storm generation to systematically describe its intrinsic operation mechanism. In the development course of the storm, there are three decisive factors: a huge source of water vapor supply — seawater, an immense source of energy — solar radiation, and a smooth and vast space arena — ocean surface. Similarly, the knowledge generation process requires three major elements: first, enterprises should have a large enough stock of knowledge; second, enterprises should have adequate incentive for knowledge transformation; and third, enterprises should have a loose enough environmental space for knowledge transformation. On these grounds, we can build the "eye of storm" model of enterprise knowledge generation as shown in Figure 13.5d. In Figure 13.1, the four types of knowledge in the outer circle represent enterprise knowledge stock; the four processes such as socialization, externalization, combination, and internalization among the four types of knowledge represent the knowledge transformation dynamics of enterprises, and the smooth connection among the four types of knowledge; the four processes and the new knowledge represents the environmental space of knowledge transformation. The operation principle of the model is that the four types of knowledge generate new knowledge through the mutual transformation of the four processes; the generated new knowledge returns to the four types of knowledge and participates in the next round of knowledge transformation process; as the circle repeats, more and more new knowledge is generated, more and more knowledge stocked, and knowledge transformation impetus becomes stronger and stronger until a super-scale storm of new knowledge is formed. In addition, the external knowledge base in Figure 13.2 is also an important source of enterprise knowledge stocks, and the knowledge in the external knowledge base will continue to flow into enterprises at an accelerated rate as the storm of new knowledge continues to strengthen. Of course, in Figure 13.1, if there is a drastic decline in the enterprise's knowledge stock, or if the enterprise's knowledge transformation drive is substantially weakened, or if the enterprise's connection with the external knowledge base is interrupted, the enterprise's new knowledge generation process is reversed and eventually tends to stagnate. The above bifurcation process can be expressed graphically as Figure 13.2.

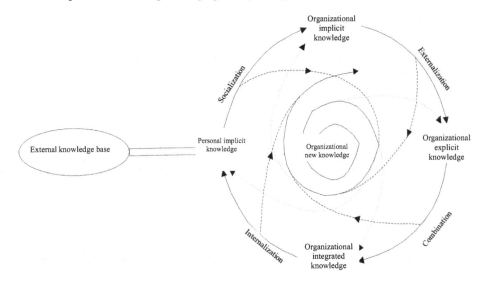

Figure 13.1 The "Eye of Storm" Model for Organizations to Generate New Knowledge

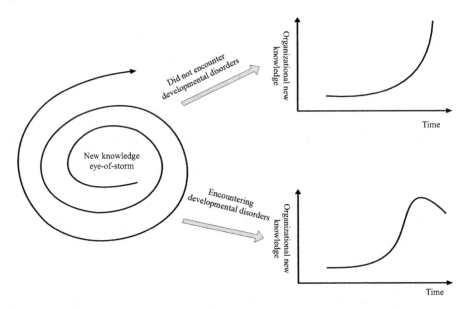

Figure 13.2 Bifurcation Diagram of the Evolutionary Path of the Knowledge Generation Process

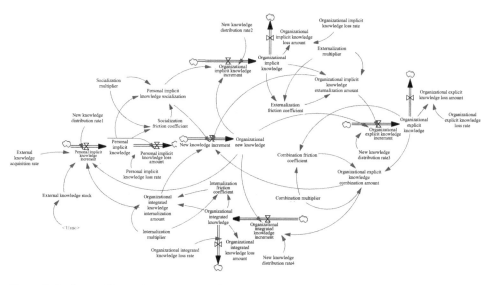

Figure 13.3 System Dynamics Expression of Enterprise Knowledge Generation Model

System Dynamics Expression of Enterprise Knowledge Generation Model

To simulate the enterprise knowledge generation model shown in Figure 13.2, Figure 13.1 needs to be transformed into a system dynamics model. Figure 13.3 shows the system dynamics expression of the enterprise knowledge generation model. In Figure 13.3, the four transformation processes namely socialization, externalization, combination, and internalization among the four types of knowledge are positively facilitated by the socialization multiplier, externalization multiplier, combination multiplier, and internalization multiplier, and negatively inhibited by the socialization friction coefficient, externalization friction coefficient, combination friction coefficient, and internalization friction coefficient, respectively. To reflect the knowledge flow between organization and environment, variables such as external knowledge acquisition rate, individual implicit knowledge loss rate, organizational implicit knowledge loss rate, organizational explicit knowledge loss rate, and organizational integrated knowledge loss rate are also set in Figures 13.5f. For the quantitative relationship between these variables, please refer to the appendixes below.

System Dynamics Simulation of Enterprise Knowledge Generation Model

Model Training

To check the simulation effect of the system dynamics model of enterprise knowledge generation in Fig. 3, the real data of representative enterprises can be used to train the model. Given trade secrecy and data availability considerations, national data may be used as an agent for simulation training. In this chapter, we propose to use the actual data collected in China during 2002–2011 to train the model, whereby the external knowledge stock is proxied by the number of global patent applications (source: *China Statistical Yearbook 2002–2011*); the personal implicit knowledge is proxied by the education level and age structure of company employees in China (source: *China Labour Statistical Yearbook 2002–2011*); organizational implicit knowledge is proxied by the number of organizations in China and

199

their scale (source: *China Statistical Yearbook 2002–2011*); organizational explicit knowledge is proxied by the number of vocational training personnel of all enterprises in China (source: *China Labor Statistical Yearbook 2002–2011*); organizational integrated knowledge is proxied by the number of new product projects, R&D projects and personnel of all enterprises in China (source: *China Statistical Yearbook on Science and Technology 2002–2011*); and organizational new knowledge is proxied by the number of patents granted to all enterprises in China (source: *China Statistical Yearbook 2002–2011*). The agent relationship equation is presented in Appendix 5.2.

In terms of the exogenous variables in the model, the following initial values are to be assigned: (1) socialization multiplier, externalization multiplier, combination multiplier, and internalization multiplier, which are defined in the range of [0, 1], and their initial values may be set to the median of 0.5; (2) personal implicit knowledge loss rate, organizational implicit knowledge loss rate, organizational explicit knowledge loss rate, and organizational integrated knowledge loss rate, which are defined in the range of [0, 1], and their initial values may be set to the median of 0; (3) new knowledge allocation rates 1, 2, 3, and 4, which are defined in the range of [0, 1], but the sum of the four is identically equal to 1, so their initial values may be set to the same value of 0.25; (4) external knowledge acquisition rate, which is defined in the range of [0, 1], and their initial values may be set to a sufficiently small initial value of 0.001 due to its complexity.

Based on the above data, system dynamics simulation training is conducted for six state variables, including external knowledge stock, personal implicit knowledge, organizational implicit knowledge, organizational explicit knowledge, organizational integrated knowledge and organizational new knowledge, and finally the training is completed when the simulated values of the six state variables are sufficiently close to the real values. Figure 13.4 shows the final simulation results of the six state variables.

As seen in Figure 13.4, the simulated values of external knowledge stock, personal implicit knowledge, organizational implicit knowledge, organizational explicit knowledge, organizational integrated knowledge and organizational new knowledge (dashed line in Figure 13.4) are sufficiently close to the real values (solid line in Figure 13.4), indicating that the fit of the model is high enough so that it can be used in the next step of simulation analysis.

Simulation of the Formation Process of Enterprise Knowledge Generation Storm

When an enterprise has a large enough knowledge stock, strong enough knowledge transformation impetus, and loose enough knowledge transformation environment space, the four types of knowledge, namely, personal implicit knowledge, organizational implicit knowledge, organizational explicit knowledge, and organizational integrated knowledge, will generate new organizational knowledge through the mutual transformation of four processes, i.e., socialization, externalization, combination, and internalization. The new organizational knowledge thus generated will return to the four types of knowledge to participate in the next round of the knowledge transformation process. New organizational knowledge will show an explosive growth as the above cycle repeats itself ad infinitum.

Using the system dynamics model of enterprise knowledge generation trained in Figure 13.4, the growth process of new organizational knowledge is simulated in the time span between 2002 and 2022, and the generation trajectory of enterprise knowledge storm is obtained, as shown in Figure 13.5a. The result shown in Figure 13.5a is the evolutionary path of the knowledge generation process when a company is not "developmentally challenged" (see the upper right part of Figure 13.5e).

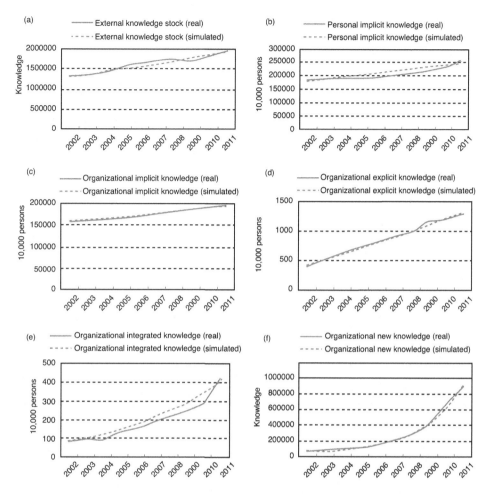

Figure 13.4 Training Effect of System Dynamics Simulation for Real Values of Six State Variables

A mathematical fit to the organizational new knowledge growth curve shown in Figure 13.5a yields a mathematical expression for this curve, as in Equation (1).

$$y = 44821\,e^{0.4855\,t} \tag{1}$$

where new organizational knowledge (y) explodes as an exponential function, with a growth rate of nearly 50% per unit of time (t). If a company has one unit of new knowledge in 2002, at this rate of growth, it will have 3,300 units of new knowledge in 2022, or an expansion of 3,300 times in 20 years, certainly akin to an explosion.

Simulation of the Disappearing Process of Enterprise Knowledge Generation Storm

The lower right part of Figure 13.5e suggests that when companies "encounter developmental barriers", their new knowledge generation process reverses and eventually stalls.

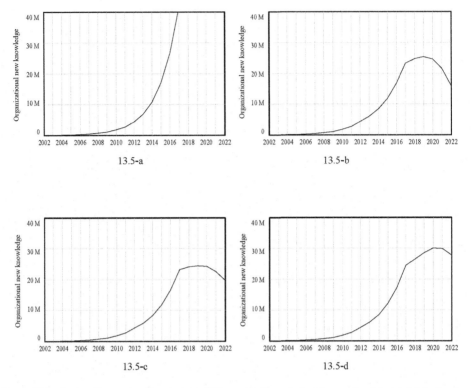

Figure 13.5 System Dynamics Simulation of Enterprise Knowledge Generation Model (M Indicating a Million)

These developmental barriers include: a dramatic decline in the company's knowledge stock; a significant weakening of its knowledge transformation dynamics; and a blockage of its connection to the external knowledge base. The subsiding process of enterprise knowledge generation storm under the above three scenarios is modeled below respectively.

Demise of Knowledge Generation Storm Caused by the Decline in Enterprise Knowledge Stock

Enterprise knowledge stock refers to the sum of personal implicit knowledge, organizational implicit knowledge, organizational explicit knowledge, and organizational integrated knowledge possessed by the enterprise. If the knowledge stock increases, it will accelerate four transformation processes of new knowledge and thus generate more new knowledge. But conversely, if the knowledge stock reduces, it will inhibit the four transformation processes and thus impede new knowledge generation.

The declining enterprise knowledge stock can be expressed by the increase in the loss rate of the four types of knowledge. To simulate the hindering effect of declining enterprise knowledge stock on knowledge generation, we can take Figure 13.5a as the basis and increase the loss rate of the four types of knowledge by 0.1 units in equal amounts every three years at four time points of 2012, 2015, 2018, and 2021, respectively, finally making the loss rate increase from its initial value of 0 to its final value of 0.4, as indicated by step equations (2)–(5).

$$\text{Personal implicit knowledge loss rate} = 0 + \text{STEP}(0.1, \ 2012) + \text{STEP}(0.1, \ 2015) \\ + \text{STEP}(0.1, \ 2018) + \text{STEP}(0.1, \ 2021) \tag{2}$$

$$\text{Organizational implicit knowledge loss rate} = 0 + \text{STEP}(0.1, 2012) + \text{STEP}(0.1, 2015) \\ + \text{STEP}(0.1, 2018) + \text{STEP}(0.1, 2021) \tag{3}$$

$$\text{Organizational explicit knowledge loss rate} = 0 + \text{STEP}(0.1, 2012) + \text{STEP}(0.1, 2015) \\ + \text{STEP}(0.1, 2018) + \text{STEP}(0.1, 2021) \tag{4}$$

$$\text{Organizational integration knowledge loss rate} = 0 + \text{STEP}(0.1, 2012) + \text{STEP}(0.1, 2015) \\ + \text{STEP}(0.1, 2018) + \text{STEP}(0.1, 2021) \tag{5}$$

At this point, Figure 13.5a evolves into Figure 13.5b. As seen in Figure 13.5b, the growth momentum of new organizational knowledge is suppressed as the four types of knowledge loss rate increases and peaks roughly in 2019, after which it begins to decline sharply and eventually tends to die out.

Disappearance of the Knowledge Generation Storm Caused by the Weakening of Enterprise Knowledge Transformation Impetus

The knowledge transformation dynamics of enterprises are reflected in four types of transformation multipliers, i.e., socialization multiplier, externalization multiplier, combination multiplier, and internalization multiplier. The rise of these four types of transformation multipliers will promote the four transformation processes of new knowledge and thus generate more new knowledge; conversely, if these four types of transformation multipliers fall, they will inhibit the four transformation processes of new knowledge and thus set back the generation of new knowledge.

The weakening motivation of enterprise knowledge transformation can be expressed by the decline of the four types of transformation multipliers. To simulate the hindering effect of the weakening driving power of enterprise knowledge transformation on knowledge generation, we can take Figure 13.5a as the basis and reduce the four types of transformation multipliers by 0.1 units in equal amounts every three years at four time points of 2012, 2015, 2018, and 2021, respectively, making the four types of transformation multipliers decrease from their initial value of 0.5 to their final value of 0.1, as indicated by step equations (6)–(9).

$$\text{Socialization multiplier} = 0.5 - \text{STEP}(0.1, 2012) - \text{STEP}(0.1, 2015) \\ - \text{STEP}(0.1, 2018) - \text{STEP}(0.1, 2021) \tag{6}$$

$$\text{Externalization multiplier} = 0.5 - \text{STEP}(0.1, 2012) - \text{STEP}(0.1, 2015) \\ - \text{STEP}(0.1, 2018) - \text{STEP}(0.1, 2021) \tag{7}$$

$$\text{Combination multiplier} = 0.5 - \text{STEP}(0.1, 2012) - \text{STEP}(0.1, 2015) \\ - \text{STEP}(0.1, 2018) - \text{STEP}(0.1, 2021) \tag{8}$$

$$\text{Internalization multiplier} = 0.5 - \text{STEP}(0.1, 2012) - \text{STEP}(0.1, 2015) \\ - \text{STEP}(0.1, 2018) - \text{STEP}(0.1, 2021) \tag{9}$$

At this point, Figure 13.5a evolves into Figure 13.5c. As seen in Figure 13.5c, the growth momentum of organizational new knowledge is suppressed as the four types of knowledge loss rate falls and peaks roughly in 2019, after which it begins to decline sharply and eventually tends to die out.

Disappearance of Knowledge Generation Storm Caused by the Impeded Connection between Enterprises and External Knowledge Bases

The connection of enterprises and external knowledge bases is mainly reflected in a company's external knowledge acquisition rate. An increase in external knowledge acquisition rate will facilitate the four transformation processes of new knowledge and thus generate more new knowledge. Conversely, if the external knowledge acquisition rate goes down, the four transformation processes of new knowledge will be inhibited to frustrate the generation of new knowledge.

The hindered connection between enterprises and external knowledge bases can be expressed by the decline of the external knowledge acquisition rate. To simulate the hindering effect of the obstructed connection between enterprises and external knowledge bases on knowledge generation, we can take Figure 13.5a as the basis and reduce the external knowledge acquisition rate by an equal amount of 0.0002 units every three years at four time points of 2012, 2015, 2018, and 2021, respectively, making the external knowledge acquisition rate decrease from its initial value of 0.001 to the final value of 0.0002, as indicated by step equations (5)–(11).

$$\text{External knowledge acquisition rate} = 0.001 - \text{STEP}(0.0002, 2012) - \text{STEP}(0.0002, 2015)$$
$$- \text{STEP}(0.0002, 2018) - \text{STEP}(0.0002, 2021) \tag{5–11}$$

At this point, Figure 13.5a evolves into Figure 13.5d. As seen in Figure 13.5d, as the external knowledge acquisition rate slows down, the growth momentum of organizational new knowledge is suppressed and peaks roughly in 2020, after which it begins to decline sharply and eventually tends to die out.

Conclusion and Insights

An "eye of storm" model of enterprise knowledge generation is constructed based on SECI and the "eye of storm" generation principle and expressed as a system dynamics model. The model is trained with the empirical data of related Chinese enterprises from 2002 to 2012, and the following results are obtained using the trained model to simulate the enterprise knowledge generation mechanism:

1   When a company has a large enough knowledge stock, a strong enough knowledge transformation drive and a relaxed enough knowledge transformation environment, it can absorb more and more external knowledge and implement an increasingly strong positive feedback loop of knowledge transformation internally, so as to generate infinite new knowledge and finally achieve an explosive growth of organizational new knowledge.

2   When a company encounters obstacles such as the decline of its own knowledge stock, or the weakening of internal knowledge transformation impetus, or the obstruction of external knowledge absorption, the new knowledge generation process will be reversed and eventually at a standstill, leading to the arrested development and even disappearance of the enterprise knowledge generation storm.

The above results suggest that to stand out in knowledge creation, enterprises must take strong measures to enhance their own ability to absorb external knowledge, improve their own knowledge transformation capability, and prevent knowledge loss caused by talent flow or technology spillover.

In the next step, we can make in-depth sensitivity analysis on the key contributing factors in the process of enterprise knowledge generation to provide more precise quantitative results for the study of enterprise knowledge generation mechanism.

Appendix 1 Quantitative Relationship between the Variables in Figure 13.3

1   State Variable Equation

Personal implicit knowledge = INTEG[Personal implicit knowledge increment
−personal implicit knowledge loss amount]

Organizational Implicit Knowledge = INTEG[Organizational implicit knowledge increment
−organizational implicit knowledge loss amount]

Organizational explicit knowledge = INTEG[Organizational explicit knowledge increment
−organizational explicit knowledge loss amount]

Organizational integrated knowledge = INTEG[Organizational integrated knowledge increment
−organizational integrated knowledge loss amount]

Organizational new knowledge = INTEG[Organizational new knowledge increment]

2   Rate Variable Equation

Personal implicit knowledge increment = DELAY1 [Organizational integrated knowledge
internalization amount + organizational new
knowledge × new knowledge distribution
rate1 + external knowledge stock × external
knowledge acquisition rate, 1]

Organizational implicit knowledge increment = DELAY2 [Personal implicit knowledge
socialization amount + organizational
new knowledge × new knowledge
distribution rate2, 2

Organizational explicit knowledge increment = DELAY3 [Organizational implicit knowledge
externalization amount
+ organizational new knowledge
× new knowledge distribution rate3, 2

Organizational integrated knowledge increment = DELAY4 [Organizational explicit
knowledge combination amount
+ organizational new knowledge
× new knowledge distribution rate4,

Organizational new knowledge increment = Personal implicit knowledge socialization amount
+ organizational implicit knowledge externalization
amount + organizational explicit knowledge
combination amount + organizational integrated
knowledge internalization amount

Personal implicit knowledge loss = Personal implicit knowledge
$$\times \text{ personal implicit knowledge loss rate}$$

Personal implicit knowledge loss = Organizational implicit knowledge
$$\times \text{ organizational implicit knowledge loss rate}$$

Organizational explicit knowledge loss = Organizational explicit knowledge × organizational
$$\text{explicit knowledge loss rate}$$

Organizational integrated knowledge loss = organizational integrated knowledge
$$\times \text{ organizational integrated knowledge loss rate}$$

3. Auxiliary Variable Equation

Personal implicit knowledge socialization amount = Personal implicit knowledge × socialization
multiplier × (1– socialization friction
coefficient^2)

Organizational implicit knowledge externalization amount = Organizational implicit knowledge
× externalization multiplier
× (1– externalization friction
coefficient^2)

Organizational explicit knowledge combination amount = Organizational explicit knowledge
combination multiplier
× (1–combination friction coefficient^2)

Organizational integrated knowledge internalization amount = Organizational integrated
knowledge × internalization
multiplier × (1– internalization
friction coefficient^2)

Socialization friction coefficient = $(1 - \text{socialization multiplier})^2$
$$\times \text{EXP}\Big(A \times \text{LN}\Big(\text{IF THEN ELSE}\big(\text{personal implicit knowledge}$$
$$<= \ 0, \ 1, \ \text{personal implicit knowledge}\big)\Big)\Big)$$

Externalization friction coefficient = $(1 - \text{externalization multiplier})^2$
$$\times \text{EXP}\Big(A \times \text{LN}\Big(\text{IF THEN ELSE}\big(\text{organizational implicit}$$
$$\text{knowledge} <= \ 0, \ 1, \ \text{organizational implicit knowledge}\big)\Big)\Big)$$

Combination friction coefficient = $(1 - \text{combination multiplier})^2$
$$\times \text{EXP}\Big(A \times \text{LN}\Big(\text{IF THEN ELSE}\big(\text{organizational explicit}$$
$$\text{knowledge} <= 0, \ 1, \ \text{organizational explicit knowledge}\big)\Big)\Big)$$

Internalization friction coefficient = $(1 - \text{internalization multiplier})^2$
$$\times \text{EXP}\Big(A \times \text{LN}\Big(\text{IF THEN ELSE}\big(\text{organizational integrated}$$
$$\text{knowledge} <= 0, \ 1, \ \text{organizational integrated knowledge}\big)\Big)\Big)$$

External knowledge stock = $a \times \text{EXP}\big(b \times \text{Time}\big)$

Appendix 2 Agent Relationship Equation for Each State variable in Model Training in Figure 13.4

1 External knowledge stock = global patent applications (in piece)

2 Personal implicit knowledge = $\alpha \times A \times \beta^{\mathrm{T}}$ (in 10,000 people). In the equation, $A = \{a_{ij}\}$ is the composition matrix of the educational level of employees nationwide by age group, and a_{ij} is the number of employees in the ith age group with the jth level of education (in 10,000 people), wherein i ($i = 1, 2,..., 11$) represents the 11 age groups of employees (in descending order: 16–19, 20–24, 25–29, 30–34, 35–39, 40–44, 45–49, 50–54, 55–59, 60–64 years old, and above 65+), and j ($j = 1, 2,..., 7$) represents 7 types of educational attainment (from low to high: illiterate, elementary school diploma, middle school diploma, high school diploma, junior college graduate, bachelor's degree, master's degree and above); vector $\alpha = (1\ 2\ 3\ 4\ 5\ 6\ 7\ 8\ 9\ 10\ 11)$ is the weight vector of the 11 age groups of employed persons; vector $\beta = (2^0\ 2^1\ 2^2\ 2^3\ 2^4\ 2^5\ 2^6)$ is the weight of the 7 types of educational attainment.

3 Organizational implicit knowledge = $B \times \gamma^{\mathrm{T}} \times \bar{x}$ (in 10,000 people). In the equation, $B = \{b_{ij}\}$ is the panel matrix of enterprise scale structure in China, b_{ij} is the number of the ith scale enterprises in year i, wherein i ($i = 1, 2,..., 10$) represents 10 years (from small to large: 2002, 2003, 2004, 2005, 2006, 2007, 2008, 2009, 2010, 2011), and j ($j = 1, 2, 3$) represents 3 types of enterprise scales (from small to large: small-sized, medium-sized, and large-sized); vector $\gamma = (2^0\ 2^2\ 2^4)$ denotes enterprise scale weight; $\bar{x}$ the average number of company employees in China (unit: 10,000 employees/company).

4 Organizational explicit knowledge = the number of vocational training personnel of all enterprises in China (in 10,000 people).

5 Organizational integrated knowledge = (the number of new product projects of all enterprises in China + the number of R&D projects of all enterprises in China) × the average number of R&D personnel of all enterprises in China (in 10,000 people).

6 Organizational new knowledge = $C \times \delta^{\mathrm{T}}$ (in unit). In the equation, $C = \{c_{ij}\}$ is the panel matrix of patent grants for enterprises in China, c_{ij} is the quantity of patents granted in type j in year i (unit: piece), wherein i ($i = 1, 2,..., 10$) represents 10 years (from small to large: 2002, 2003, 2004, 2005, 2006, 2007, 2008, 2009, 2010, 2011), and j ($j = 1, 2, 3$) represents three types of enterprises patents granted (in order: design, utility model, invention); vector $\delta = (2^0\ 2^1\ 2^2)$ represents the weight of enterprise patent types.

References

Alavi, M., Leidner, D. Knowledge Management and Knowledge Management Systems: Conceptual Foundations and Research Issues. *MIS Quarterly*, 2001, 25 (1): 107–136.

He, X., Wang, X. System Dynamics Analysis of Tacit Knowledge Management Based on Organization Perspective. *Library and Information Service*, 2012, 56 (10): 107–112. (In Chinese)

Nonaka, I., Takeuchi, H. *The Knowledge – Creating Company: How Japanese Companies Create the Dynamics of Innovation*. New York: Oxford University Press, 1995.

Wang, X., Liu, Y. System Dynamic Model of Tacit Knowledge Transferring. *Science of Science and Management of S & T*, 2006, 27 (5): 90–94. (In Chinese)

Wang, X., Sun, B. Modeling and Simulation of System Dynamics on Knowledge Transfer in Enterprise. *Information Science*, 2012, 30 (2): 173–177, 195. (In Chinese)

Wang, Y., Zhang, J. Analysis of the Innovation Factors of Knowledge Organization Based on the System Dynamics. *Journal of Qingdao University of Science and Technology (Social Sciences)*, 2009, 25 (4): 58–62. (In Chinese)

PART III

Knowledge Management in Practice

14

HOW KNOWLEDGE MANAGEMENT DIFFERS ACROSS NATIONAL CULTURES

A Systematic Literature Review

Gang Liu, Eric Tsui, and Aino Kianto

Introduction

Knowledge management (KM) significantly affects organizational development and performance, especially in today's highly globalized environments (Inkinen, 2016; Liu et al., 2020a; Liu et al., 2020b). As a socially embedded activity (e.g., Nonaka and Takeuchi (1995); Nonaka et al. (2000); Liu et al. (2019)), KM is strongly impacted by the cultural context in which it takes place. While most of the studies addressing the role of culture in KM have addressed culture from the perspective of the focal organization (Mueller, 2012) and mapped the characteristics of knowledge-friendly organizational culture (KFOC) (e.g., Kayas and Wright (2018)), this chapter focuses on the relatively neglected issue of national culture. Because KM is developed, practiced, and researched around the globe, it is important to understand how the dispositions embedded in wider national-level cultures may impact its boundary conditions and characteristics. Therefore, this chapter aims to summarize the existing knowledge on how national culture impacts KM and to outline the related issues in which further research is needed.

To provide a comprehensive understanding of the role of national culture in KM, we apply the systematic literature review methodology. To the best of the authors' knowledge, this is the first study to provide such an overarching examination concerning the role of national culture in KM. To understand how cultural dispositions are likely to impact KM, we lean on the most established categorization of cultural dispositions, that of the cultural values put forward by Hofstede et al. (2010).

Even though many previous studies have examined KM among different national cultures, the generalizability of an individual study is limited to the country or countries involved in the given study because a comprehensive examination of the previous studies about KM across national cultures has been lacking so far. As a consequence, a systematic understanding of KM differences in different national cultures remains unexplored. To address the outlined research gap, this study examines how KM differs across various cultures and thereby provides a deeper understanding of KM from the perspective of cultural context.

National culture is "the pattern of enduring personality characteristics found among the populations of nations" (Clark, 1990 p. 66), which affects KM activities due to its influence

DOI: 10.4324/9781003112150-17

on individuals' behavior (King, 2007). National culture reflects people's underlying thoughts about knowledge and their behavior toward knowledge-related activities. This is because people have unique cultural values and beliefs about the way they conduct knowledge-related activities, such as how knowledge acquisition, sharing, creation, application, and protection are implemented (King, 2007; Inkinen et al., 2017). These understandings also impact institutional arrangements, including managerial philosophies, governance systems, and norms for competition (North, 1990).

The current studies concerning KM and national culture can be classified into three categories. The first group of studies focuses on KM in multi-national companies (MNCs) or joint ventures (e.g., Ahammad et al., 2016); Dhir et al. (2020); Pauluzzo and Cagnina (2019); Pauluzzo and Cagnina (2019)); the second group examines KM differences by comparing KM across countries or regions (e.g., Geppert, 2005; Kianto et al., 2011), and the third one investigates KM differences from the perspective of different national cultural dimensions (e.g., Cegarra-Navarro et al., 2011; Boone et al., 2019). This research only examines studies from the second and third categories, because the studies in the first category mainly examined the impacts of cultural differences between head companies and subsidiaries rather than between different cultures, and they therefore were not useful in identifying the KM differences in different cultures.

The next section of the chapter discusses cultural dispositions and their role in KM, and the subsequent section presents the research methodology and procedures applied in this study. The findings are discussed in the section that follows, and the future research directions and implications are presented in the subsequent section. The chapter ends with conclusive remarks.

National Culture and KM

There is a widespread understanding that there is no best universal method for implementing KM (e.g., Inkinen et al., 2017), which implies that the appropriate KM choices need to be selected that best fit the specific circumstances (Handzic, 2017). National culture, as a highly important environmental factor, is attracting the attention of many scholars and practitioners in KM research and practices (e.g., Liu et al., 2021a). National culture refers to the collective programming of the mind that distinguishes people in one nation from another (Hofstede, 1993; Hofstede et al., 2010). For example, people in different national cultures are likely to analyze and respond to the same managerial issues in different ways (Schneider and De Meyer, 1991). It has also been found that firms with people of different national cultural backgrounds manage knowledge differently (Cegarra-Navarro and Sánchez-Polo, 2010; Cegarra-Navarro et al., 2011). Such differences can be interpreted by the fact that, first, national cultures mirror people's cognition about knowledge and their behavior toward knowledge-related activities, such as knowledge acquisition, sharing, creation, application, and protection (King, 2007); second, national culture reflects differences in social contingencies, such as relationship development, trust, social hierarchy, status, leadership, power, and politics (Beesley and Cooper, 2008), which affect the way knowledge is managed (Kim, 2020); and thirdly, institutions across national cultures differ, for example, in the extent to which they favor and support shared decision-making and participation (Putnam et al., 1993).

Cross-cultural research has been, to a great extent, guided by the seminal framework of Geert Hofstede (Hofstede, 2002; Hofstede et al., 2010) for the past several decades (Tsui et al., 2016). Hofstede and his colleagues (2010) contributed a deeper understanding of the way differences in national culture affect values, behavior, institutions, and organizations, from different perspectives, such as social norms, families, education systems, work and organizations, political systems, religions, and so on. In addition, their work has stimulated fruitful argument and provided a solid foundation for developing cross-cultural research (Chapman, 1997), including studies addressing KM (e.g., Li, 2010; Strese et al., 2016). Although, during the past few decades, Hofstede's epistemology of national culture has been criticized (McSweeney, 2002, 2020; Minkov, 2018), it remains the most valid framework for generating fruitful insights in cultural and business research (Hofstede, 2002; Kirkman et al., 2006; Beugelsdijk et al., 2015). Therefore, the present study adopted Hofstede et al.'s (2010) national culture framework to analyze earlier KM research on cross-cultural backgrounds.

Hofstede et al. (2010) identified six dimensions of national culture, namely, power distance (PD), individualism versus collectivism (IC), masculinity versus femininity (MF), uncertainty avoidance (UA), long-term orientation versus short-term orientation (LS), and

Table 14.1 Hofstede's National Culture Dimensions and KM

Dimension	Definition	How does it affect KM?
Power distance	Power distance reflects the extent of inequality in power between a less powerful person and a more powerful other within the same society (Hofstede, 2001; Hofstede et al., 2010).	Organizational hierarchy and the power of leaders facilitate/hinder KM activities. The leader–subordinates relationship plays an important role in KM.
Individualism versus collectivism	Individualism and collectivism portray the relationship between the individual and group in a specific society (Hofstede, 2001; Hofstede et al., 2010).	In-/out-group membership is critical for KM. Training and learning are effective based on the individual or collective orientation of a nation.
Masculinity versus femininity	Femininity versus masculinity represents the differences in the genders that are reflected in the national culture.	KM is affected by the degree of equality of the genders. Females and males are (un)equal participating in KM activities.
Uncertainty avoidance	Uncertainty avoidance refers to the degree of ambiguity tolerance in society and indicates people's comfort level in unstructured environments (Hofstede, 2011).	Ambiguity tolerance affects the objectives of KM and the adoption of KM solutions.
Long-term orientation versus short-term orientation	Long-term orientation versus short-term orientation reflects people's values and beliefs toward the past, present, and future (Hofstede et al., 2010).	Long-term orientation versus short-term orientation influences people's view of KM and its potential benefits.
Indulgence orientation versus restraint orientation	Indulgence refers to a society that permits the relatively free gratification of basic and natural human desires related to enjoying life and having fun, while restrained culture refers to a society that controls and regulates the gratification of needs by employing strict social norms (Hofstede, 2011, p. 15).	Indulgence orientation versus restraint orientation affects the attitudes of people toward learning and entertainment, as well as the way KM is implemented.

indulgence versus restrained (IR) culture. PD reflects the extent of inequality in power between a less powerful person and a more powerful other within the same society (Hofstede, 2001; Hofstede et al., 2010). PD affects KM because differences in organizational hierarchies and power distributions can either facilitate or hinder KM activities. The leader-subordinates relationship also plays a critical role in KM activities. IC portrays the relationship between the individual and the group in a specific society (Hofstede, 2001; Hofstede et al., 2010). In-/out-group membership is critical in collective societies, and it affects trust-building, communication, and social network development, thereby influencing KM activities. Training and learning are more effective at the group level in collective societies but more effective at the individual level in individualistic societies. MF represents the differences in the genders that are reflected in the national culture. For example, females and males participate unequally in KM activities when the society is masculine oriented. UA refers to the degree of ambiguity tolerance in a society and indicates people's comfort level in unstructured environments (Hofstede, 2011), which affects the objectives of KM and the adoption of KM solutions. LS reflects people's values and beliefs toward the past, present, and future (Hofstede et al., 2010), which influences their view of KM and its potential benefits. Indulgence refers to a society that permits the relatively free gratification of basic and natural human desires around enjoying life and having fun, while a restrained culture is one that controls and regulates the gratification of needs by employing strict social norms (Hofstede, 2011, p. 15). Indulgence orientation versus restraint orientation affects the attitudes of people toward learning and entertainment, as well as the way KM is deployed. Table 14.1 provides a summary of Hofstede's national culture dimensions and their impact on KM.

Research Method

To explore the impact of national culture on KM, this study applies the systematic literature review methodology, as this approach provides new understanding and identifies research gaps from the existing body of research literature based on a reliable and transparent scientific procedure (Hempel, 2020).

This study conformed with Hempel's (2020) nine steps in reviewing the present literature concerning the national culture and KM, as shown in Table 14.2. After defining the research objective (detailed in the previous section), the study adopted the Scopus database, as most KM-related journals are indexed in this database. The search was initiated in July 2020. The terms "knowledge management" and "national culture" were coupled in the literature search to locate where they appeared in the titles, abstracts, or keywords of articles. In addition, the scope of the search was limited to English-written papers, no matter their source, in order to obtain as many appropriate studies as possible. In this phase, 1,478 relevant papers were obtained. After eliminating papers based on titles and abstracts, 97 remained for full-text screening. Among the 97 papers, 64 papers were excluded for the following reasons: the full text of four papers could not be found; 15 papers were purely conceptual; and 10 papers investigated KM in MNCs or joint ventures. The conceptual papers did not provide empirical evidence, and the papers concerning the KM of MNCs and joint ventures did not provide enough knowledge about the KM differences between their native country and the designated countries. Therefore, the papers in those two categories were excluded. In addition, 35 papers were excluded as they did not fit the scope of our study. Finally, 33 papers either ascribed national culture dimensions to or directly analyzed the differences of KM in different regions by means of empirical tests or case studies. Among these 33 papers, two papers were deleted due to similar findings based on the same dataset, and one paper was

Table 14.2 Research Procedures

SN	Step	Application in this study
1	Define the research objective	What are the differences in KM in different national cultures?
2	Select database	Scopus database
3	Formulate a search strategy	Search string: *knowledge management* and *national culture* of English-written papers
4	Define inclusion (exclusion) criteria	Included studies that are evidence-based and compared KM differences across national cultures
5	Organize material	Used endnote to manage the studies
6	Extract information from the literature	Extracted authors' names, research methods, findings, and conclusions
7	Evaluate material	Examined the selected studies
8	Synthesize findings	Synthesized the findings into tables
9	Write up the literature review	Wrote this chapter

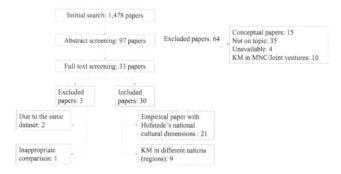

Figure 14.1 Paper Selection and Exclusion Procedures

excluded because of inappropriate comparisons. Finally, as shown in Figure 14.1, 21 studies were identified that analyzed KM with Hofstede's national culture index and nine papers that compared KM across different regions. In order to consolidate the findings consistently, the findings of the nine studies were transformed according to Hofstede's national culture index based on the regions that these studies explored. The detailed transformation method can be found in Appendix B.

Findings of Current Studies

Descriptive Findings

Two categories of studies with respect to KM across national cultures were found. As shown in Figure 14.2, the first category of studies (denoted by red squares) compares KM in different countries (regions), while the second category (denoted by blue dots) examines KM according to Hofstede's national culture index, an increasingly utilized approach. Therefore, this study adopted Hofstede's national culture dimensions to review KM in different national cultural contexts. This review revealed that the number of studies has fluctuated year by year and that the citations of these studies vary, with most having less than 40. This indicates that the

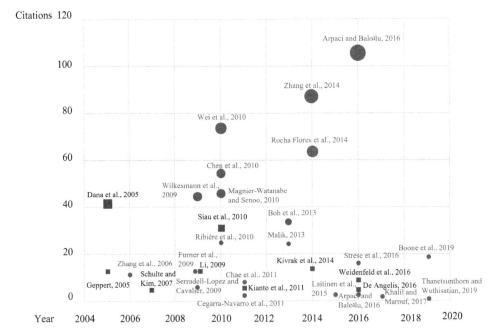

Figure 14.2 Citations of Publications

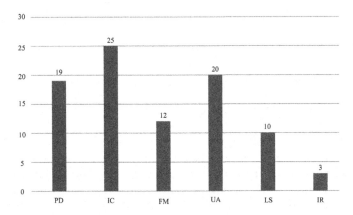

Figure 14.3 Number of Studies for Each National Culture Dimension

impact of national culture on KM is attracting researchers' attention as a promising research field, one that calls for a deeper investigation. Figure 14.3 illustrates that previous studies have paid more attention to investigating the impacts of IC, UA, and PD on KM than femininity versus masculinity, long-term orientation versus short-term orientation (LS), and IR culture.

KM and Hofstede's National Culture

National cultures influence KM activities because they affect the behavior of all people living in a particular country (King, 2007). National cultures reflect people's ideas about knowledge and their behavior toward knowledge processes, such as knowledge acquisition, sharing, creation, application, and protection (King, 2007). National cultures also shape KM practices (Hussinki et al., 2017; Liu et al., 2019) and influence KM solution adoption (Ang and Massingham, 2007). Hofstede et al.'s (2010) dimensions of national culture are widely used in organizational research (Tsui et al., 2016), including in many KM studies, e.g., Liu et al. (2021b). As previous studies mainly adopted Hofstede et al.'s (2010) national culture indexes to measure national culture in their research, this study reviewed the findings with respect to different knowledge processes and KM practices in the previous literature, based on Hofstede's national culture dimensions. In reviewing the various findings of the literature review, this study found that different national culture dimensions play a distinct role in affecting knowledge processes and KM practices.

4.2.1 Power Distance and KM

Power distance reflects the extent of inequality in power between a less powerful person and a more powerful other within the same society (Hofstede, 2001; Hofstede et al., 2010), which might affect knowledge processes and KM practices. The previous research revealed that high PD within a culture hindered knowledge sharing (Siau et al., 2010; Kivrak et al., 2014). However, Chang et al. (2016) claimed that knowledge-sharing behavior in low PD regions was mediated by reciprocal benefits for employees who obeyed their supervisors. Wilkesmann et al. (2009) found that high PD was an obstacle for knowledge transfer, but Boh et al. (2013) suggested that the impacts of PD on knowledge sharing were insignificant. In addition, Cegarra-Navarro et al. (2011) argued that knowledge transfer was easier for small and medium-sized enterprises (SMEs) in high PD societies than in low PD societies. Boone et al. (2019) provided empirical evidence that low PD societies facilitated the knowledge creation (innovation) of MNCs with diversified top management teams. In contrast, Malik (2013) reported that knowledge creation (patents) was not affected by regional PD differences. Magnier-Watanabe and Senoo (2010) suggested that different degrees of PD could facilitate different types of knowledge acquisition. For instance, obtaining opportunistic knowledge was easier in low PD regions, whereas obtaining focused knowledge was easier in high PD regions (Magnier-Watanabe and Senoo, 2010).

Moreover, the evidence shows that employees are more open-minded (Cegarra-Navarro et al., 2016) and willing to trust each other in low PD regions (Thanetsunthorn and Wuthisatian, 2019). It seems that KFOC can be more easily fostered in low PD regions. On the other hand, Strese et al. (2016) did not find any effect of PD on the relationship between organizational culture and absorptive capability. Kianto et al. (2011) found that firms in high PD regions had a higher maturity level of strategic KM, a greater use of KM-supportive information technologies (IT), and more knowledge-based organizational structures than firms in low PD regions. However, Chae et al. (2011) suggested that the degrees of PD did not affect KM-supportive IT applications, such as the adoption of human resource information systems. In addition, Cegarra-Navarro et al. (2011) claimed that learning and collaboration were positively related to the PD index in Spanish SMEs.

4.2.2 Individualism versus Collectivism and KM

Individualism and collectivism portray the relationship between the individual and group in a specific society (Hofstede, 2001; Hofstede et al., 2010). Earlier studies showed that a higher degree of regional collectivism supported knowledge sharing (Dana et al., 2005; Geppert, 2005; Kivrak et al., 2014; Zhang et al., 2014; Arpaci and Baloǧlu, 2016). Distinctions in knowledge-sharing characteristics between individualistic and collective societies

Table 14.3 Typical Differences in KM Between Low- and High-Power Distance Societies

Low power distance	High power distance	Empirical evidence
Knowledge is openly shared among all employees	Knowledge is difficult to share	Kivrak et al. (2014); Siau et al. (2010)
Knowledge transfer is less easy in SMEs	Knowledge transfer is much easier in SMEs	Cegarra-Navarro et al. (2011)
Knowledge can be more easily created	Knowledge creation has to overcome hierarchy	Boone et al. (2019)
Opportunistic knowledge acquisition is facilitated	Focused knowledge acquisition is facilitated	Magnier-Watanabe and Senoo (2010)
Employees with a high score of PD share knowledge through reciprocal benefits	Power distance score of employees had no impact on knowledge sharing	Chang et al. (2016)
Employees trust each other	Employees are less likely to trust each other	Thanetsunthorn and Wuthisatian (2019)
Employees are more open-minded	Employees are less open-minded	Cegarra-Navarro et al. (2016)
A lower maturity level of strategic KM, fewer KM-supportive information technologies (IT), and less knowledge-based organizational structures	A higher maturity level of strategic KM, more KM-supportive IT, and more knowledge-based organizational structures	Kianto et al. (2011)
Learning and collaboration were less supported in SMEs	Learning and collaboration were more strongly supported in SMEs	Cegarra-Navarro et al. (2011)

have also been found. For instance, Wei et al. (2010) argued that people in individualistic societies share knowledge in order to demonstrate their determinations, whereas people in collective societies share knowledge in order to build harmonious social networks. Similarly, Chang et al. (2016) observed that employees in individualistic societies share knowledge on the basis of organizational rewards, while employees in collective societies share knowledge due to reciprocal benefits. Flores et al. (2014) noted that the organizational structure was more important for sharing security knowledge in individualistic societies, whereas the organizational procedures were more important for sharing security knowledge in collective societies. In addition, Li (2009) and Siau et al. (2010) argued that employees in collective regions dislike and are afraid of sharing knowledge with their foreign colleagues on IT platforms. Similarly, Zhang et al. (2006) reported that both Chinese and American students were more willing to share knowledge with in-group members than with out-group members. Some studies, such as Wilkesmann et al. (2009), Cegarra-Navarro et al. (2011), Chen et al. (2010), and Schulte and Kim (2007), supported the view that collectivism in societies enables a smoother transfer of knowledge; however, Boh et al. (2013) pointed out that trust and openness rather than differences in IC affected the success of knowledge transfer. Magnier-Watanabe et al. (2011) showed that the degree of individualism played a significant role in affecting knowledge retention, whereas Malik (2013) found that knowledge creation was not related to the degree of individualism.

The KM practices in societies with different degrees of individualism are inconstant. Employees are more open-minded in individualistic societies (Cegarra-Navarro et al., 2011), whereas employees are more likely to trust each other in collective societies

Table 14.4 Typical Differences in Knowledge Management Between Individualistic and Collective Societies

Individualistic societies	Collective societies	Empirical evidence
People are unlikely to share knowledge	People are more likely to share knowledge with in-group members	Arpaci and Baloılu (2016); Dana et al. (2005); Geppert (2005); Kivrak et al. (2014); Zhang et al. (2014)
Tend to share knowledge in order to manifest their determinations	Tend to share knowledge in order to create harmonious social networks	Wei et al. (2010)
Interested in reading non-English posts on IT platforms and like sharing knowledge on IT platforms	Dislike sharing knowledge with foreign colleagues but like sharing knowledge with domestic colleagues on IT platforms	Li (2009); Siau et al. (2010)
Security knowledge sharing is facilitated by organizational structure	Security knowledge sharing is facilitated by organizational procedures	Flores et al. (2014)
Employees with a high score on individualism share knowledge through organizational rewards	Employees with a high score on collectivism share knowledge through reciprocal benefits	Chang et al. (2016)
Knowledge transfer is less easy	Knowledge transfer is much easier	Wilkesmann et al. (2009); Cegarra-Navarro et al. (2011); Chen et al. (2010); and Schulte and Kim (2007)
Knowledge retention is more facilitated	Knowledge retention is less facilitated	Magnier-Watanabe et al. (2011)
Employees are less likely to trust each other	Trust is easily developed among employees	Thanetsunthorn and Wuthisatian (2019); Kivrak et al. (2014)
People are more open-minded	People are less open-minded	Cegarra-Navarro et al. (2011)
More KM-supportive IT activities were deployed	Fewer KM-supportive IT activities were deployed	Khalil and Marouf (2017); Laitinen et al. (2015)
People like to learn by themselves	People like to learn together	Furner et al. (2009)

(Kivrak et al., 2014; Thanetsunthorn and Wuthisatian, 2019). Furner et al. (2009) found that people in individual societies liked to learn by themselves, while people in collective societies liked to learn together. Studies have also revealed that more KM-supportive IT activities were implemented in individualistic societies than in collective societies (Laitinen et al., 2015; Khalil and Marouf, 2017).

4.2.3 Femininity versus Masculinity and KM

Femininity and masculinity describe the differences in genders that are reflected in national cultures (Hofstede, 2011). The findings of the study by Magnier-Watanabe and Senoo (2010) implied that masculinity positively affected prescribed knowledge transfer, while femininity positively affected adaptive knowledge transfer. Additionally, Cegarra-Navarro

Table 14.5 Typical Differences in Knowledge Management Between Masculine and Feminine Societies

Masculine societies	Feminine societies	Empirical evidence
Positively affect prescribed knowledge transfer	Positively affect adaptive knowledge transfer	Magnier-Watanabe and Senoo (2010)
Knowledge transfer is not easy	Knowledge transfer is easier	Cegarra-Navarro et al. (2011)
More problems for knowledge sharing	Fewer problems for knowledge sharing	Kivrak et al. (2014)
More emphasis on knowledge protection	Less concern with knowledge protection	Serradell-Lopez and Cavalier (2009)
Security knowledge sharing is facilitated by organizational structure	Security knowledge sharing is facilitated by organizational procedures	Flores et al. (2014)
People are more open-minded	People are less open-minded	Cegarra-Navarro et al. (2011)
Learning and collaboration are more difficult	Learning and collaboration are easier	Cegarra-Navarro et al. (2011)
More like group learning and unstructured learning	Fewer like group learning but like structured learning	Furner et al. (2009)

et al. (2011) reported that femininity facilitated knowledge transfer for SMEs. Kivrak et al. (2014) found that knowledge sharing in high femininity cultures had fewer difficulties, while Serradell-Lopez and Cavalier (2009) found that cultural levels of masculinity were significantly associated with knowledge protection. Cegarra-Navarro et al. (2011) reported that employees were more open-minded in masculine societies, whereas learning and collaboration were easier in feminine societies. Moreover, Furner et al. (2009) found that in masculine societies, employees preferred group learning in seeking management opportunities.

4.2.4 Uncertainty Avoidance and KM

Uncertainty avoidance refers to the degree of ambiguity tolerance in a society and indicates people's comfort level in unstructured environments (Hofstede, 2011). Differences in KM exist between strong and weak UA regions. Kivrak et al. (2014) found that people had more difficulty sharing knowledge in strong UA regions than in weak UA regions. Likewise, Li (2009) and Siau et al. (2010) revealed that employees disliked sharing knowledge on IT platforms more in strong UA regions than in weak UA regions. Chang et al. (2016) argued that employees in strong UA societies shared knowledge because of reciprocal benefits, but this finding was not supported in weak UA societies. Wilkesmann et al. (2009) suggested that effective knowledge transfer depended on clearly defined regulations in strong UA societies, whereas in weak UA societies, knowledge transfer would be more effective, with fewer rules. Magnier-Watanabe and Senoo (2010) claimed that weak uncertainty societies focused on explorative knowledge application, while strong uncertainty societies focused on exploitative knowledge application. Serradell-Lopez and Cavalier (2009) concluded that firms in more masculine societies paid more attention to knowledge protection. Additionally, Malik (2013) showed that knowledge creation was not affected by national UA. Kianto et al. (2011) reported that KFOC was more mature in a strong UA country, e.g., Russia, but Thanetsunthorn and Wuthisatian (2019) found that employees were less likely to trust each

Table 14.6 Typical Differences in Knowledge Management Between Weak and Strong Uncertainty Avoidance Societies

Weak uncertainty avoidance societies	Strong uncertainty avoidance societies	Empirical evidence
Fewer problems for knowledge sharing	More problems for knowledge sharing	Kivrak et al. (2014)
More like sharing knowledge on IT platforms	More dislike sharing knowledge on IT platforms with their foreign colleagues	Li (2009); Siau et al. (2010)
Uncertainty avoidance score of employees had no impact on knowledge sharing	Employees with a low score on UA share knowledge through reciprocal benefits	Chang et al. (2016)
Mainly focused on explorative knowledge application	Mainly focused on exploitative knowledge application	Magnier-Watanabe and Senoo (2010)
Knowledge transfer is supported, without strict rules	Knowledge transfer is supported by rules	Wilkesmann et al. (2009)
Pay less attention to knowledge protection	Pay more attention to knowledge protection	Serradell-Lopez and Cavalier (2009)
People are more open-minded	People are less open-minded	Cegarra-Navarro et al. (2011)
Learning and collaboration are more difficult	Learning and collaboration are easier	Cegarra-Navarro et al. (2011)
People prefer less structure in learning	People prefer more structure in learning	Furner et al. (2009)
The use of technology has a non-effect on knowledge transfer	The use of technology is a disadvantage for knowledge transfer	Weidenfeld et al. (2016)
Negatively affected KM-supportive IT deployment	Positively affected KM-supportive IT deployment	Chae et al. (2011); Ribière et al. (2010); Khalil and Marouf (2017)

other in strong UA regions. Cegarra-Navarro et al. (2011) argued that people were more open-minded in weak UA regions but were more focused on learning and collaboration in strong UA regions. Furner et al. (2009) found that people in strong uncertainty regions preferred structured learning. Weidenfeld et al. (2016) highlighted the use of KM-supportive IT-facilitated knowledge transfer in strong UA regions, but this finding was not supported in weak UA regions. Chae et al. (2011) revealed that KM-supportive IT was more deployed in strong UA regions than in weak UA ones.

4.2.5 Long-Term versus Short-Term Orientation and KM

Long-term versus short-term orientation reflects people's values and beliefs toward the past, present, and future (Hofstede et al., 2010). It was found that knowledge sharing, learning (Geppert, 2005), and knowledge transfer (Schulte and Kim, 2007) were more intensive in long-term orientation societies. Studies also revealed that people were more open-minded and trusted each other more (Laitinen et al., 2015; Thanetsunthorn and Wuthisatian, 2019) in long-term orientation societies. In addition, KM-supportive IT adoption was more widely implemented in long-term orientation societies (Ribière et al., 2010; Khalil and Marouf, 2017).

Table 14.7 Typical Differences in Knowledge Management Between Long-Term and Short-Term Orientation

Long-term orientation societies	Short-term orientation societies	Empirical evidence
Knowledge sharing is much easier	Knowledge sharing is less easy	Geppert (2005)
Learning is more popular in firms	Learning is less popular in firms	Geppert (2005)
Knowledge transfer is much easier	Knowledge transfer is less easy	Schulte and Kim (2007)
Trust is more easily created	Development of trust is difficult	Thanetsunthorn and Wuthisatian (2019); Laitinen et al. (2015)
KM-supportive IT activities are more deployed	KM-supportive IT activities are less deployed	Khalil and Marouf (2017)
Decision-making of government is more affected by knowledge	Decision-making of government is more affected by culture	De Angelis (2016)

Table 14.8 Typical Differences in Knowledge Management Between Indulgence-Oriented and Restraint-Oriented Cultures

Indulgence-oriented cultures	Restraint-oriented cultures	Empirical evidence
Knowledge sharing is less intensive	Knowledge sharing is more intensive	Geppert (2005)
Less focus on learning	More focus on learning	Geppert (2005)
Strategic KM, KM-supportive IT, and knowledge-based organizational structure are less mature	Strategic KM, KM-supportive IT, and knowledge-based organizational structure are more mature	Kianto et al. (2011)

De Angelis (2016) claimed that governments in long-term oriented regions made decisions that were more dependent on knowledge, while decision-making in short-term oriented regions was more affected by culture.

4.2.6 Indulgence-Oriented versus Restraint-Oriented Cultures and KM

An indulgent society is one that permits the relatively free gratification of basic and natural human desires related to enjoying life and having fun, while a restrained culture refers to a society that controls and regulates the gratification of needs by employing strict social norms (Hofstede, 2011, p. 15). So far, limited attention has been paid to examining the differences in KM between indulgence-oriented and restraint-oriented cultures; however, some empirical findings can be indirectly found in earlier scholarly works. For example, Geppert (2005) found that in restraint-oriented cultures, knowledge sharing was more intensive, with a greater focus on learning. The study of Kianto et al. (2011) showed that the maturity level of strategic KM, KM-supportive IT, and knowledge-based organizational structure was higher in restrained nations than in indulgence-oriented cultures. In addition, Thanetsunthorn and Wuthisatian (2019) claimed that the degree of indulgence in nations had an effect on trust in organizations.

Future Directions and Implications

Future Directions

The present study has thoroughly reviewed the KM research across different national cultures over the past 15 years. By drawing a holistic picture and identifying research gaps, the study points out future directions in this area. First, the findings of some earlier studies showed that high PD is an obstacle for KM because the flow of knowledge is difficult in a high hierarchy organization; on the other hand, some studies found that high PD is an enabler for KM. The reasons for such inconsistency deserve further exploration. KM leadership refers to the capability of leaders to influence others on KM processes and activities, but current studies have neglected the role of KM leadership in affecting KM in different cultural contexts. Therefore, future studies could examine whether differences in KM leadership styles exist between high and low PD regions and how these differences are manifested and operate in different situations. Many organizations appoint chief knowledge officers (CKOs) or establish corporate universities (Liu et al., 2018) to support KM. It would be interesting to scrutinize the impacts of national PD on the KM benefits of the changes created as new positions and departments alter the power structure of organizations. Further, future research could link in the upper echelons theory (Hambrick and Mason, 1984) to examine the influence of personality characteristics, such as overconfidence and narcissism on the part of chief executive officers and CKOs, on decisions related to KM projects in different PD societies.

Second, many studies have examined the differences in KM between individualistic and collective societies. These studies suggest that people in collective societies are more likely to share knowledge within their groups. It seems to be the case that some KM activities are easier in more collective societies, but it would be worthwhile to further examine the border of collective knowledge sharing, how the border evolves, and whether it induces any disadvantages for KM. It is also noted that some KM activities, such as knowledge retention, the open-mindedness of employees, and KM-supportive IT are more enabled by individualistic cultures. Future research might be designed to find a balance point to take advantage of IC across different regions.

Third, earlier studies mainly found that KM can be more easily carried out in feminine societies than in masculine societies. Since gender inequality is greater in masculine societies, further work needs to be done to investigate whether females are unequally treated in KM activities, whether the inequality of genders is stronger in masculine societies than in feminine societies, and how females handle discrimination in KM participation if they encounter this problem in different degrees of masculine societies.

Fourth, UA is related to rules and the ambiguity tolerance of societies (Hofstede, 2001; Hofstede et al., 2010). KM can help organizations mitigate business risks through strategic KM but initiating KM projects might bring risks if the organizations are not well prepared. However, an understanding of strategic KM in different UA societies is lacking in the earlier literature. It is therefore recommended that further studies be undertaken to assess the effects of UA on strategic KM development. More research is also required to provide greater insight into the effects of UA on different KM initiatives.

Fifth, limited attention has been paid to examining KM between long-term and short-term oriented cultures. In addition, how much time it takes for KM to benefit organizations is still poorly understood. The previous literature shows that people in long-term oriented societies are more patient about obtaining KM benefits, but how long they are willing to wait for these benefits is worth exploring. Further studies could also focus on evaluating whether any other differences in terms of knowledge application, protection, and retention, as well as strategic KM and KM leadership styles, exist between long-term and short-term oriented societies.

Similarly, the impacts of indulgence-oriented versus restraint-oriented cultures on KM have not been systematically studied. It is suggested that future studies thoroughly ascertain the differences in KM between indulgence-oriented and restraint-oriented cultures, as well as the influence of these different cultures on KM initiatives.

Finally, previous studies have mainly shown the impacts of national culture on knowledge sharing and transfer. Future research is also needed to examine the impacts of national culture on other knowledge processes, such as knowledge creation, protection, and retention, as well as on KM practices, such as KFOC, KM leadership, KM strategies, strategic KM, knowledge-based human resource management, KM-supportive IT, and organizational learning. A weakness of some previous studies is the small number of nations included in the data collection. It is recommended that future research expand the scope of nations for collecting data, so that the generalizability and validity of the findings can be improved. Further work is also needed to shed light on the underlying mechanism of national culture in terms of affecting KM. Future cross-cultural research should consider the impacts of other factors, such as organizational inertia, types of industries, national economy, etc. on KM. Hofstede's national culture dimensions have been criticized in the sense that their values do not represent the current situation, as Minkov (2018) argued. For instance, Confucian countries are becoming more individualism-oriented nowadays. Further studies might therefore adopt updated national culture values to produce novel knowledge. For example, a newly developed national culture dimension, flexibility versus monumentalism (Minkov et al., 2018), might be added to the future research models. As the COVID-19 pandemic is dramatically changing our way of carrying out KM activities, further cross-cultural investigations into KM activities, especially in the post-COVID-19 pandemic era, is strongly recommended.

Implications for Researchers and Practitioners

This study notably contributes to cross-cultural research into KM in several ways. First, it is the first systematic literature review with respect to KM and national culture to demonstrate a holistic picture of the current research. Second, it reveals that national culture significantly affects knowledge processes and KM practices, indicating that cultural context does indeed matter for KM. Third, it shows that differences in KM processes and practices are manifested in different national cultural conditions, which demonstrates how specific aspects of culture impact various KM boundary conditions, requirements, and methods. These findings have, therefore, deepened our understanding of the relationship between national culture and KM. Finally, this study has highlighted the need for greater attention by KM scholars to the identified knowledge gaps of KM in cross-cultural research in the future.

This study also offers several practical implications for knowledge managers, especially for those who work in MNCs. First, it informs practitioners that the cultural context matters for KM. Practitioners should therefore understand the cultural uniqueness of local subsidiaries in order to define feasible KM procedures and practices. Second, this study provides an understanding of how managers should condition and contextualize the KM approaches and methods they apply to manage knowledge in different cultural contexts. For instance, managers could encourage face-to-face in-group knowledge sharing by emphasizing the mutual benefits in a collective society, but encourage knowledge sharing on IT platforms with a bonus in an individualistic society. Finally, this study helps practitioners who manage diversified teams with members from various nations. In particular, managers could define clear responsibilities and rules for members who are from strong UA societies while allowing for some ambiguities in KM in weak UA societies in order to provide flexibility.

Limitations

This study is subject to the following limitations. Its scope is limited by only choosing papers written in English from the Scopus database, which might have caused some studies to be missed due to language bias or database bias. Some potential studies might also have been missed due to the selected keywords, without considering different dimensions of national culture in terms of the literature retrieved. The inclusion of papers based on the title, abstract, and full content strictly complied with the pre-defined criteria, but the reviewers' subjective decisions might have elicited different choices. Additionally, some findings are limited by the transforming of studies comparing KM in different countries into KM comparisons in terms of the different national culture dimensions. This study followed Hofstede et al.'s (2011) national culture dimensions to analyze KM in cross-cultural research. Applying other national culture classifications, such as the cultural dimensions of the Global Leadership and Organizational Behavior Effectiveness (GLOBE) project (Dorfman et al., 2012), may produce a slightly different analysis, even with the same studies.

Conclusions

Determining the influence of national culture on KM activities is important for both KM theory and practice. Prior to this research, knowledge about the role of national culture in affecting KM was scattered in the literature. This study was the first to systematically audit the current knowledge with respect to KM research in cross-cultural contexts. It reveals that national culture significantly impacts some knowledge processes and KM practices and also demonstrates how various cultural dispositions tend to impact KM. These findings deepen our understanding of the interaction of KM and national culture. However, several essential research questions remain unanswered in the earlier literature. These identified knowledge gaps are of broad relevance to management research communities in terms of sparking further investigations.

Acknowledgments

The authors of this chapter appreciate the Research Committee of the Hong Kong Polytechnic University for the provision of a scholarship (project code: RUNQ) to complete this research.

References

Ahammad, M. F., Tarba, S. Y., Liu, Y., & Glaister, K. W. (2016). Knowledge transfer and cross-border acquisition performance: The impact of cultural distance and employee retention. *International Business Review, 25*(1), 66–75. doi:10.1016/j.ibusrev.2014.06.015

Ang, Z., & Massingham, P. (2007). National culture and the standardization versus adaptation of knowledge management. *Journal of Knowledge Management, 11*(2), 5–21. doi:10.1108/13673270710738889

Arpaci, I., & Baloɪlu, M. (2016). The impact of cultural collectivism on knowledge sharing among information technology majoring undergraduates. *Computers in Human Behavior, 56*, 65–71. doi:10.1016/j.chb.2015.11.031

Beesley, L. G. A., & Cooper, C. (2008). Defining knowledge management (KM) activities: Towards consensus. *Journal of Knowledge Management, 12*(3), 48–62. doi:10.1108/13673270810875859

Beugelsdijk, S., Maseland, R., & van Hoorn, A. (2015). Are scores on Hofstede's dimensions of national culture stable over time? A cohort analysis. *Global Strategy Journal, 5*(3), 223–240. doi:10.1002/gsj.1098

Boh, W. F., Nguyen, T. T., & Xu, Y. (2013). Knowledge transfer across dissimilar cultures. *Journal of Knowledge Management, 17*(1), 29–46. doi:10.1108/13673271311300723

Boone, C., Lokshin, B., Guenter, H., & Belderbos, R. (2019). Top management team nationality diversity, corporate entrepreneurship, and innovation in multinational firms. *Strategic Management Journal, 40*(2), 277–302. doi:10.1002/smj.2976

Cegarra-Navarro, J. G., & Sánchez-Polo, M. T. (2010). Linking national contexts with intellectual capital: A comparison between Spain and Morocco. *The Spanish Journal of Psychology, 13*(1), 329–342.

Cegarra-Navarro, J. G., Soto-Acosta, P., & Wensley, A. K. P. (2016). Structured knowledge processes and firm performance: The role of organizational agility. *Journal of Business Research, 69*(5), 1544–1549. doi:10.1016/j.jbusres.2015.10.014

Cegarra-Navarro, J. G., Vidal, M. E. S., & Cegarra-Leiva, D. (2011). Exploring the role of national culture on knowledge practices: A comparison between Spain and the UK. *Spanish Journal of Psychology, 14*(2), 808–819. doi:10.5209/rev_SJOP.2011.v14.n2.28

Chae, B., Prince, J. B., Katz, J., & Kabst, R. (2011). An exploratory cross-national study of information sharing and human resource information systems. *Journal of Global Information Management, 19*(4), 18–44. doi:10.4018/jgim.2011100102

Chang, Y. W., Hsu, P. Y., Shiau, W. L., & Cheng, Y. S. (2016). The effects of individual and national cultures in knowledge sharing: A comparative study of the U.S. And China. *Journal of Global Information Management, 24*(2), 39–56. doi:10.4018/JGIM.2016040103

Chapman, M. (1997). Preface: Social anthropology, business studies, and cultural issues. *International Studies of Management & Organization, 26*(4), 3–29.

Chen, J., Sun, P. Y. T., & McQueen, R. J. (2010). The impact of national cultures on structured knowledge transfer. *Journal of Knowledge Management, 14*(2), 228–242. doi:10.1108/13673271011032373

Clark, T. (1990). International marketing and national character: A review and proposal for an integrative theory. *Journal of Marketing, 54*(4), 66–79.

Dana, L. P., Korot, L., & Tovstiga, G. (2005). A cross-national comparison of knowledge management practices. *International Journal of Manpower, 26*(1), 10–22. doi:10.1108/01437720510587244

De Angelis, C. T. (2016). The impact of national culture and knowledge management on governmental intelligence. *Journal of Modelling in Management, 11*(1), 240–268. doi:10.1108/JM2–08–2014–0069

Dhir, S., Rajan, R., Ongsakul, V., Owusu, R. A., & Ahmed, Z. U. (2020). Critical success factors determining performance of cross-border acquisition: Evidence from the African telecom market. *Thunderbird International Business Review.* 63(1), 43–61. doi:10.1002/tie.22156

Dorfman, P., Javidan, M., Hanges, P., Dastmalchian, A., & House, R. (2012). GLOBE: A twenty year journey into the intriguing world of culture and leadership. *Journal of World Business, 47*(4), 504–518. doi:10.1016/j.jwb.2012.01.004

Flores, W. R., Antonsen, E., & Ekstedt, M. (2014). Information security knowledge sharing in organizations: Investigating the effect of behavioral information security governance and national culture. *Computers and Security, 43*, 90–110. doi:10.1016/j.cose.2014.03.004

Furner, C. P., Mason, R. M., Mehta, N., Munyon, T. P., & Zinko, R. (2009). Cultural determinants of leaning effectiveness from knowledge management systems: A multinational investigation. *Journal of Global Information Technology Management, 12*(1), 30–51. doi:10.1080/1097198x.2009.10856484

Geppert, M. (2005). Competence development and learning in British and German subsidiaries of MNCs: Why and how national institutions still matter. *Personnel Review, 34*(2), 155–177. doi:10.1108/00483480510579402

Hambrick, D. C., & Mason, P. A. (1984). Upper echelons: The organization as a reflection of its top managers. *The Academy of Management Review, 9*(2), 193–206.

Handzic, M. (2017). The KM times they are a-changin'. *Journal of Entrepreneurship, Management and Innovation, 13*(3), 7–27. doi:10.7341/20171331

Hempel, S. (2020). *Conducting your literature review: Concise guides to conducting behavioral, health, and social science research.* Washington, DC: American Psychological Association.

Hofstede, G. (1993). Cultural constraints in management theories. *The Executive, 7*(1), 81–94.

Hofstede, G. (2001). *Culture's consequences: Comparing values, behaviors, institutions, and organizations across nations.* Thousand Oaks, CA: Sage Publications.

Hofstede, G. (2002). Dimensions do not exist: A reply to Brendan McSweeney. *Human relations (New York), 55*(11), 1355–1360.

Hofstede, G. (2011). Dimensionalizing cultures: The Hofstede model in context.

Hofstede, G., Hofstede, G. J., & Minkov, M. (2010). *Cultures and organizations: Software of the mind.* New York: McGraw-Hill.

Hussinki, H., Kianto, A., Vanhala, M., & Ritala, P. (2017). Assessing the universality of knowledge management practices. *Journal of Knowledge Management, 21*(6), 1596–1621. doi:10.1108/jkm-09–2016–0394

Inkinen, H. (2016). Review of empirical research on knowledge management practices and firm performance. *Journal of Knowledge Management, 20*(2), 230–257. doi:10.1108/JKM-09–2015–0336

Inkinen, H., Kianto, A., Vanhala, M., & Ritala, P. (2017). Structure of intellectual capital – an international comparison. *Accounting, Auditing & Accountability, 30*(5), 1160–1183. doi:10.1108/aaaj-11–2015–2291

Kayas, O. G., & Wright, G. (2018). Knowledge management and organisational culture. In J. Syed, P. A. Murray, D. Hislop, & Y. Mouzughi (Eds.), *The Palgrave handbook of knowledge management* (pp. 131–149). Cham: Springer International Publishing.

Khalil, O., & Marouf, L. (2017). A cultural interpretation of nations' readiness for knowledge economy. *Journal of the Knowledge Economy, 8*(1), 97–126. doi:10.1007/s13132-015-0288-x

Kianto, A., Andreeva, T., & Shi, X. (2011). Knowledge management across the globe - an international survey of KM awareness, spending, practices and performance. *12th European Conference on Knowledge Management, ECKM 2011*, 514–523.

Kim, S. S. (2020). Exploitation of shared knowledge and creative behavior: The role of social context. *Journal of Knowledge Management, 24*(2), 279–300. doi:10.1108/jkm-10–2018–0611

King, W. R. (2007). A research agenda for the relationships between culture and knowledge management. *Knowledge and Process Management, 14*(3), 226–236. doi:10.1002/kpm.281

Kirkman, B. L., Lowe, K. B., & Gibson, C. B. (2006). A quarter century of culture's consequences: A review of empirical research incorporating Hofstede's cultural values framework. *Journal of International Business Studies, 37*(3), 285–320. doi:10.1057/palgrave.jibs.8400202

Kivrak, S., Arslan, G., Tuncan, M., & Birgonul, M. T. (2014). Impact of national culture on knowledge sharing in international construction projects. *Canadian Journal of Civil Engineering, 41*(7), 642–649. doi:10.1139/cjce-2013–0408

Laitinen, J. A., Pawlowski, J. M., & Senoo, D. (2015) A study on the influence of national culture on knowledge sharing. In *Vol. 224. Lecture notes in business information processing* (pp. 160–175): Springer Verlag.

Li, W. (2009). Online knowledge sharing among Chinese and American employees: Explore the influence of national cultural differences. *International Journal of Knowledge Management, 5*(3), 54–72. doi:10.4018/jkm.2009070104

Li, W. (2010). Virtual knowledge sharing in a cross-cultural context. *Journal of Knowledge Management, 14*(1), 38–50. doi:10.1108/13673271011015552

Liu, G., Kianto, A., & Tsui, E. (2020a). A comprehensive analysis of the importance of intellectual capital elements to support contemporary developments in Chinese firms. In P. O. de Pablos & L. Edvinsson (Eds.), *Intellectual capital in the digital economy* (pp. 62–73). London, UK: Routledge.

Liu, G., Tsui, E., & Kianto, A. (2018). *The myth of the presence of chief knowledge officers.* Paper presented at the European Conference on Knowledge Management, Padua, Italy.

Liu, G., Tsui, E., & Kianto, A. (2020b). *A meta-analysis study on the relationship between strategic KM and organisational performance.* Paper presented at the 21st European Conference on Knowledge Management, Coventry, UK, 477–483.

Liu, G., Tsui, E., & Kianto, A. (2021a). Knowledge-friendly organisational culture and performance: A meta-analysis. *Journal of Business Research, 134*, 738–753. doi: https://doi.org/10.1016/j.jbusres.2021.05.048

Liu, G., Tsui, E., & Kianto, A. (2021b). Revealing deeper relationships between knowledge management leadership and organisational performance: A meta-analytic study. *Knowledge Management Research & Practice*. doi:10.1080/14778238.2021.1970492.

Liu, Y., Chan, C., Zhao, C., & Liu, C. (2019). Unpacking knowledge management practices in China: Do institution, national and organizational culture matter? *Journal of Knowledge Management, 23*(4), 619–643. doi:10.1108/JKM-07–2017–0260

Magnier-Watanabe, R., Benton, C., & Senoo, D. (2011). A study of knowledge management enablers across countries. *Knowledge Management Research & Practice, 9*(1), 17–28. doi:10.1057/kmrp.2011.1

Magnier-Watanabe, R., & Senoo, D. (2010). Shaping knowledge management: Organization and national culture. *Journal of Knowledge Management, 14*(2), 214–227. doi:10.1108/13673271011032364

Malik, T. H. (2013). National institutional differences and cross-border university-industry knowledge transfer. *Research Policy, 42*(3), 776–787. doi:10.1016/j.respol.2012.09.008

McSweeney, B. (2002). Hofstede's model of national cultural differences and their consequences: A triumph of faith - a failure of analysis. *Human relations (New York), 55*(1), 89–118.

McSweeney, B. (2020). Hofstede's model of national cultural differences and their consequences: A triumph of faith - a failure of analysis. In D. K. Boojihawon, J. Mordaunt, M. D. Domenico, N. Nik Winchester, & S. Vangen (Eds.), *Organizational collaboration: Themes and issues.* United Kingdom: Taylor & Francis.

Minkov, M. (2018). A revision of Hofstede's model of national culture: Old evidence and new data from 56 countries. *Cross Cultural & Strategic Management, 25*(2), 231–256.

Minkov, M., Bond, M. H., Dutt, P., Schachner, M., Morales, O., Sanchez, C.,... Mudd, B. (2018). A reconsideration of Hofstede's fifth dimension: New flexibility versus monumentalism data from 54 countries. *Cross-cultural Research, 52*(3), 309–333.

Mueller, J. (2012). The interactive relationship of corporate culture and knowledge management: A review. *Review of Managerial Science, 6*(2), 183–201. doi:http://dx.doi.org/10.1007/s11846-010-0060-3

Nonaka, I., & Takeuchi, H. (1995). *The knowledge-creating company: How Japanese companies create the dynamics of innovation.* New York: Oxford University Press.

Nonaka, I., Toyama, R., & Nagata, A. (2000). A firm as a knowledge-creating entity: A new perspective on the theory of the firm. *Industrial and Corporate Change, 9*(1), 1–20.

North, D. C. (1990). *Institutions, institutional change, and economic performance.* Cambridge: Cambridge University Press.

Pauluzzo, R., & Cagnina, M. R. (2019). A passage to India: Cultural distance issues in IJVs' knowledge management. *Knowledge Management Research and Practice, 17*(2), 192–202. doi:10.1080/14778 238.2019.1599496

Putnam, R. D., Leonardi, R., & Nanetti, R. (1993). *Making democracy work: Civic traditions in modern Italy.* Princeton, NJ: Princeton University Press.

Ribière, V. M., Haddad, M., & Vande Wiele, P. (2010). The impact of national culture traits on the usage of web 2.0 technologies. *VINE Journal of Information and Knowledge Management Systems, 40*(3), 334–361. doi:10.1108/03055721011071458

Schneider, S. C., & De Meyer, A. (1991). Interpreting and responding to strategic issues: The impact of national culture. *Strategic Management Journal, 12*(4), 307–332.

Schulte, W. D., & Kim, Y. K. (2007). Collectivism and expected benefits of knowledge management: A comparison of Taiwanese and US perceptions. *Competitiveness Review, 17*(1–2), 109–117. doi:10.1108/10595420710816650

Serradell-Lopez, E., & Cavalier, V. (2009). National culture and the secrecy of innovations. *International Journal of Knowledge and Learning, 5*(3–4), 222–234. doi:10.1504/IJKL.2009.031197

Siau, K., Erickson, J., & Nah, F. F. H. (2010). Effects of national culture on types of knowledge sharing in virtual communities. *IEEE Transactions on Professional Communication, 53*(3), 278–292. doi:10.1109/TPC.2010.2052842

Strese, S., Adams, D. R., Flatten, T. C., & Brettel, M. (2016). Corporate culture and absorptive capacity: The moderating role of national culture dimensions on innovation management. *International Business Review, 25*(5), 1149–1168. doi:10.1016/j.ibusrev.2016.02.002

Thanetsunthorn, N., & Wuthisatian, R. (2019). Understanding trust across cultures: An empirical investigation. *Review of International Business and Strategy, 29*(4), 286–314. doi:10.1108/RIBS-12–2018–0103

Tsui, A. S., Nifadkar, S. S., & Amy Yi, O. (2016). Cross-national, cross-cultural organizational behavior research: Advances, gaps, and recommendations. *Journal of Management, 33*(3), 426–478. doi:10.1177/0149206307300818

Wei, J., Liu, L., & Francesco, C. A. (2010). A cognitive model of intra-organizational knowledge-sharing motivations in the view of cross-culture. *International Journal of Information Management, 30*(3), 220–230. doi:10.1016/j.ijinfomgt.2009.08.007

Weidenfeld, A., Björk, P., & Williams, A. M. (2016). Cognitive and cultural proximity between service managers and customers in cross-border regions: Knowledge transfer implications. *Scandinavian Journal of Hospitality and Tourism, 16*, 66–86. doi:10.1080/15022250.2016.1244587

Wilkesmann, U., Fischer, H., & Wilkesmann, M. (2009). Cultural characteristics of knowledge transfer. *Journal of Knowledge Management, 13*(6), 464–477. doi:10.1108/13673270910997123

Zhang, Q., Chintakovid, T., Sun, X., Ge, Y., & Zhang, K. (2006). Saving face or sharing personal information? A cross-cultural study on knowledge sharing. *Journal of Information and Knowledge Management, 5*(1), 73–79. doi:10.1142/S0219649206001335

Zhang, X., De Pablos, P. O., & Xu, Q. (2014). Culture effects on the knowledge sharing in multi-national virtual classes: A mixed method. *Computers in Human Behavior, 31*(1), 491–498. doi:10.1016/j.chb.2013.04.021

APPENDICES

Appendix 14A: Descriptive Statistics

Table 14A.1 Studies in Each Culture Dimension

Culture dimension	Studies	Quantity
Power distance	Boh et al., 2013; Boone et al., 2019; Cegarra-Navarro et al., 2011; Chae et al., 2011; Chang et al., 2016; Chen et al., 2010; Furner et al., 2009; Khalil and Marouf, 2017; Kianto et al., 2011; Kivrak et al., 2014; Magnier-Watanabe and Senoo, 2010; Malik, 2013; Ribière et al., 2010; Serradell-Lopez and Cavalier, 2009; Siau et al., 2010; Strese et al., 2016; Thanetsunthorn and Wuthisatian, 2019; Wilkesmann et al., 2009; Zhang et al., 2014	19
Individualism versus collectivism	Arpaci and Baloǧlu, 2016; Boh et al., 2013; Cegarra-Navarro et al., 2011; Chang et al., 2016; Chen et al., 2010; *Dana et al., 2005*; Furner et al., 2009; *Geppert, 2005*; Khalil and Marouf, 2017; Kivrak et al., 2014; Laitinen et al., 2015; Li, 2009; Magnier-Watanabe and Senoo, 2010; Malik, 2013; Ribière et al., 2010; *Flores et al., 2014; Schulte and Kim, 2007*; Serradell-Lopez and Cavalier, 2009; Siau et al., 2010; Strese et al., 2016; Thanetsunthorn and Wuthisatian, 2019; Wei et al., 2010; Wilkesmann et al., 2009; Zhang et al., 2006; Zhang et al., 2014	25
Masculinity versus femininity	Cegarra-Navarro et al., 2011; Furner et al., 2009; Khalil and Marouf, 2017; Kivrak et al., 2014; Magnier-Watanabe and Senoo, 2010; Malik, 2013; Ribière et al., 2010; *Flores et al., 2014*; Serradell-Lopez and Cavalier, 2009; Siau et al., 2010; Thanetsunthorn and Wuthisatian, 2019; Wilkesmann et al., 2009;	12
Uncertainty avoidance	Cegarra-Navarro et al., 2011; Chae et al., 2011; Chang et al., 2016; Chen et al., 2010; Furner et al., 2009; Khalil and Marouf, 2017; *Kianto et al., 2011*; Kivrak et al., 2014; Li, 2009; Magnier-Watanabe and Senoo, 2010; Malik, 2013; Ribière et al., 2010; Serradell-Lopez and Cavalier, 2009; Siau et al., 2010; Strese et al., 2016; Thanetsunthorn and Wuthisatian, 2019; Wei et al., 2010; Weidenfeld et al., 2016; Wilkesmann et al., 2009; Zhang et al., 2014	20
Long-term orientation versus short-term orientation	Cegarra-Navarro et al., 2011; De Angelis, 2016; Geppert, 2005; Khalil and Marouf, 2017; Laitinen et al., 2015; Malik, 2013; Ribière et al., 2010; Schulte and Kim, 2007; Thanetsunthorn and Wuthisatian, 2019; Zhang et al., 2014	10
Indulgence versus restraint	Geppert, 2005; Kianto et al., 2011; Thanetsunthorn and Wuthisatian, 2019	3

Note: The italics denotes indirect empirical evidence

Appendix 14B: Method of Finding Transformation

Take the study of Kianto et al. (2011) as an example.
Step 1: Obtain Hofstede's national culture index

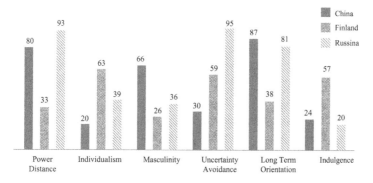

Note: Obtained from https://www.hofstede-insights.com/product/compare-countries/
Figure 14B.1: Hofstede's National Culture Index of China, Finland, and Russia

Step 2: Compare empirical findings with Hofstede's national culture index
As shown in Table 5 of Kianto et al. (2011, p. 521), for the power distance index, Russia > China > Finland; for the strategic KM score, Russia > China > Finland. Therefore, it can be assumed that strategic KM was more deployed in high power distance regions than in low power distance regions. A similar finding can also be revealed for the strategic KM in indulgence-oriented and restraint-oriented cultures, but the score sequence of the strategic KM in each country cannot match the index of other dimensions of national culture. Thus, it remained unknown concerning the impacts of other dimensions of national culture on strategic KM.

Appendix 14C: Finding Summaries of Earlier Studies

Table 14C.1 Findings Based on Knowledge Processes

SN	National culture dimension	Knowledge sharing	Knowledge transfer
1	Power distance (High)	-: Kivrak et al., 2014; Siau et al., 2010	NS: Boh et al., 2013 -: Wilkesmann et al., 2009; + Cegarra-Navarro et al., 2011 *for SMEs*
	Power distance (Low)	+ Siau et al., 2010 share knowledge through reciprocal benefits (Chang et al., 2016)	NS: Boh et al., 2013
2	Individualism	Share knowledge through organizational rewards (Chang et al., 2016); share knowledge due to manifesting their individual determinations (Wei et al., 2010); knowledge sharing is facilitated by organizational structure (Flores et al., 2014)	NS: Boh et al., 2013
	Collectivism	+: Arpaci and Baloılu, 2016; Kivrak et al., 2014; Zhang et al., 2014; *Dana et al., 2005; Geppert, 2005* + dislike sharing with out-group members Li, 2009; Siau et al., 2010; share knowledge through reciprocal benefits (Chang et al., 2016); share knowledge due to creating harmonious social networks (Wei et al., 2010); knowledge sharing is facilitated by organizational procedures (Flores et al., 2014)	NS: Boh et al., 2013 +: Wilkesmann et al., 2009; Cegarra-Navarro et al., 2011, Chen et al., 2010; + Schulte and Kim, 2007
3	Femininity	Knowledge sharing is facilitated by organizational procedures (Flores et al., 2014)	+ Cegarra-Navarro et al., 2011 for SMEs
	Masculinity	- Kivrak et al., 2014; knowledge sharing is facilitated by organizational structure (Flores et al., 2014)	+ prescribed K. diffusion Magnier-Watanabe and Senoo, 2010
4	Uncertain avoidance (Strong)	-: Kivrak et al., 2014, Li, 2009; share knowledge through reciprocal benefits (Chang et al., 2016)	+ Cegarra-Navarro et al., 2011 for SMEs Depends on rules (Wilkesmann et al., 2009)
	Uncertain avoidance (Weak)		
5	Long-term orientation	+ *Geppert, 2005*	+ *Schulte and Kim, 2007*
	Short-term orientation		
6	Indulgence-oriented		
	Restrained	+ *Geppert, 2005*	

Note: The italics denotes indirect empirical evidence

Knowledge creation	Knowledge acquisition	Knowledge application	Knowledge protection	Knowledge retention
NS: Malik, 2013 (Patent count)	+ (focused KA) Magnier-Watanabe and Senoo, 2010			
+ Boone et al., 2019				
NS: Malik, 2013 (Patent count)				+ (private) KR Magnier-Watanabe and Senoo, 2010
NS: Malik, 2013 (Patent count)			+: Serradell-Lopez and Cavalier, 2009 (secrecy)	
NS: Malik, 2013 (Patent count)		+ (exploitative) KA Magnier-Watanabe and Senoo, 2010	+: Serradell-Lopez and Cavalier, 2009 (secrecy)	
NS: Malik, 2013 (Patent count)				

Table 14C.2 Findings based on Knowledge Management Practices

SN	National culture dimension	KFOC	Leadership	Strategic KM
1	Power distance (High)	-: Trust, Thanetsunthorn and Wuthisatian, 2019; ns organizational culture-absorptive capability Strese et al., 2016		+ (Kianto et al., 2011)
	Power distance (Low)	+ Open-minded Cegarra-Navarro et al., 2011		
2	Individualism	+ Open-minded Cegarra-Navarro et al., 2011		
	Collectivism	+: Trust, Thanetsunthorn and Wuthisatian, 2019; Kivrak et al., 2014; ns organizational culture-absorptive capability Strese et al., 2016		
3	Femininity			
	Masculinity	+ Open-minded Cegarra-Navarro et al., 2011		
4	Uncertainty avoidance (Strong)	-: Trust, Thanetsunthorn and Wuthisatian, 2019; ns organizational culture-absorptive capability Strese et al., 2016 + (Kianto et al., 2011)		
	Uncertainty avoidance (Weak)	+ Open-minded Cegarra-Navarro et al., 2011		
5	Long-term orientation	+: Trust, Thanetsunthorn and Wuthisatian, 2019; Laitinen et al., 2015 + open-minded Cegarra-Navarro et al., 2011	Decision-making of government is more affected by knowledge (De Angelis, 2016)	
	Short-term orientation			
6	Indulgence-oriented			
	Restrained			+ (Kianto et al., 2011)

Note: The italics denotes indirect empirical evidence

Knowledge. strategy	KM-supportive IT	Organizational learning	Knowledge structure	Knowledge-based HRM
	NS human resource information system adoption Chae et al., 2011 *+ (Kianto et al., 2011)*	+ Cegarra–Navarro et al., 2011 for SMEs	*+ (Kianto et al., 2011)*	
	+ Khalil and Marouf, 2017 -: Laitinen et al., 2015	Learning by themselves Furner et al., 2009 + Cegarra–Navarro et al., 2011 for SMEs *+ Geppert, 2005*		
	+: Chae et al., 2011 (HRIS), Khalil and Marouf, 2017 +: Ribière et al., 2010 (expressive usage of Web2.0);	+ Cegarra–Navarro et al., 2011 for SMEs Like group earning Furner et al., 2009 Learning in structure Furner et al., 2009 + Cegarra–Navarro et al., 2011 for SMEs		
	+ Khalil and Marouf, 2017; + Ribière et al., 2010 (instrumental usage of Web 2.0)	*+ Geppert, 2005*		
	+ (Kianto et al., 2011)	*+ Geppert, 2005*	*+ (Kianto et al., 2011)*	

15

IMPLEMENTATION OF KNOWLEDGE MANAGEMENT STRATEGIES

Regina Lenart-Gansiniec

Knowledge

Knowledge has been widely recognized to be the most crucial competitive asset. Knowledge refers to a theoretical or practical understanding of a subject. Based on one of the most recognized definitions, knowledge is a dynamic human resource of justification of the personal beliefs to obtain the truth (Nonaka, 1994). Knowledge is a concept, skill, experience, and vision that provides some framework for creating, evaluating, and using information. Knowledge is believed to be an organizational resource that may lead to obtaining a competitive advantage (Wang & Noe, 2010) and that may be used to solve organizational problems, to adjust organization's key resources to requirements of the market and to increase effectiveness and productivity. It is also an organization's strategic resource, a success factor (Nahapiet & Ghoshal, 2009) and an element that allows organizations for surviving in turbulent and competitive times (Asrar-ul-Haq & Anwar, 2016).

Knowledge can be distinguished as two different types – tacit and explicit knowledge. Tacit knowledge is the personal and context-specific knowledge of a person. It is bound to the person and is thus difficult to formalize and communicate (Nonaka & Takeuchi, 1995). In turn, explicit knowledge is represented by words, numbers, signs, symbols, a set of general rules, rules of conduct, procedures, reports, statements, and codes. According to Nonaka and Takeuchi (1995), this type of knowledge is not the most important resource. It is a piece of knowledge that can be applied in an organization.

Absorptive Capacity

Absorptive capacity is the mechanism that makes external knowledge available to and usable within an organization. The very notion of absorptive capacity in the organizational context was firstly defined by Cohen and Levinthal (1990, p. 128) as recognition of the value of new, external information, its assimilation, and application to commercial ends. Moreover, Zahra and George (2002) offer a reconceptualization of this construct as a dynamic capability. They defined absorptive capacity as a set of organizational routines and strategic processes by which firms acquire, assimilate, transform, and exploit knowledge for the purpose of value creation.

DOI: 10.4324/9781003112150-18

In order for knowledge to contribute to building a competitive advantage, it should be renewed, updated, and modified. This determines its usefulness and value. The ability to allocate these resources and assimilate them is essential. This comes down to the fact that the organization should create proportions between exploited and explored knowledge, define the knowledge that is to be a strategic asset of the organization and create a synergy effect and become valuable for the organization. Creating knowledge on your own concentrates risk and extends the time it takes to create a knowledge base. For knowledge to be used effectively, it must be managed. This means that knowledge management is just as important to an organization as managing other resources. Knowledge that is not well managed corrodes easily.

Absorptive capacity is recognized to be a major dynamic competence Zahra and George (2002) that allows organizations for acquiring knowledge to use it to increase adaptation to changes in their environment and to be competitive (Daghfous, 2004). Absorptive capacity is a key to organizational competitive advantage (Cohen & Levinthal, 1990; Prahalad & Hamel, 2006), innovative performance (Chen et al., 2015), and flexibility (Sterman, 2002), and it also allows for reconfiguring knowledge resources in order to help organizations adjust to changing environments (Zahra & George, 2002). What is more, absorptive capacity supports organizational learning (van den Bosch et al., 2003; Zahra & George, 2002).

Knowledge Management

Knowledge management results from reflection on the factors of productivity of knowledge workers and knowledge-based organizations, being a synthesis of quality management regarding the internal customer, open processes and common goals; strategic management as an attempt to formalize processes related to the management of intellectual capital; human resource management, focused on individual competences; information management, dealing with information separate from technology, and the economy in which the concept of learning in action was developed. Bukowitz and Williams (1999) define knowledge management as a process by which an organization generates a wealth of knowledge based on intellectual and knowledge-based organizational assets.

Knowledge management is defined in literature in different ways: Japanese, resource oriented and process oriented. The Japanese approach emphasizes the so-called spiral of knowledge, (SECI model). The SECI model depicts the four processes, i.e. socialization, externalization, combination, and internalization which conversion modes generated by the switching process from one type of knowledge to another (Nonaka, 1994). Nonaka and Takeuchi (1995) suggested that knowledge management is a set of methods for the collection, combination, and transfer of knowledge assets, and more importantly, for the creation of new knowledge, after taking stock of and leveraging the available knowledge assets. In this context, knowledge management is a repeating cycle of processes, where tacit and formal knowledge is compiled. However, the organizations create and manage knowledge in a very dynamic fashion (Nonaka et al., 2000). The dynamic theory of knowledge creation posits that knowledge is created by the creative tension between tacit and explicit know-how, leading to a dynamic flow of activities that facilitates the generation, transfer, and application of knowledge (the dynamic theory of knowledge creation developed by Nonaka and Takeuchi, also known as the SECI model). The SECI model (Nonaka, 1994; Nonaka et al., 1994; Nonaka and Takeuchi, 1995; Nonaka et al., 2000; Nonaka, Nishiguchi, 2001; Nonaka, Toyama, 2003; Nonaka, von Krogh, 2009) includes knowledge creation as a dynamic process, in which the continuous dialog between tacit and explicit knowledge generates new knowledge and amplifies it across individual, organizational, and inter-organizational levels. It implies that an organization aiming to increase and transform its knowledge should simultaneously promote many and diverse policies and related practices. After compiling them, cyclic processes of knowledge conversion are obtained:

- socialization consisting in changing tacit knowledge into tacit knowledge;
- externalization, i.e., the transformation of tacit knowledge into formal knowledge;
- combination, i.e., creating formal knowledge from formal knowledge;
- internalization corresponding to the transformation of formal knowledge into tacit knowledge.

The resource approach assumes that for efficient knowledge management, key skills are important, and they include: physical and technical systems, management, employees' skills and knowledge, standards and values, joint problem-solving, implementation and integration of new tools and technologies, and experimenting and importing knowledge. Knowledge management focuses its attention on the key competences, skills, and knowledge of employees as well as standards and technology implementation. These elements will facilitate the transfer of knowledge from the environment to the organization. In the process approach, the sub-processes that make up knowledge management are important. In this approach, knowledge management consists of all the processes that enable the creation, dissemination, and use of knowledge for the purposes of the organization. The knowledge management model developed by Davenport and Prusak (2000) is based on three processes: creation, codification, and knowledge transfer. The process of creating knowledge involves increasing the amount of knowledge that is inside and outside the organization. Knowledge codification consists in giving knowledge a new form that would be accessible to users. The knowledge transfer process involves its transmission and absorption.

Knowledge creation involves developing of new content or the replacing of the existing content within the tacit and explicit knowledge. Also, knowledge creation is process of enabling people to create new insights such as eureka moments or additional or alternative views of long existing knowledge. In short, knowledge creation represents a focus on the content of the knowledge that has been and is being created. This refers to different types of knowledge that can be created individually and collectively through different social and cognitive processes of action and interaction (Nonaka et al., 2014). According to Nonaka and Takeuchi (1995), knowledge creation often occurs as a result of two kinds of learning which supplement each other, that is, learning how to deal with dilemmas arising from current conditions and subsequently creating a new set of conditions where the dilemmas do not occur.

Knowledge storage refers to the process of recording knowledge and storing it in the repositories, such as archives, databases, and filing systems. In this context, storage is the mechanism which stores the knowledge created and transfers it within the firm, and between firms, after a knowledge creation process. It aims at transferring the knowledge to the individual, groups, or units that need to apply it (Johannsen, 2000). Argote (2011) and Argote and Ingram (2000) state that stored knowledge can effectively safeguard the organization from the distracting effects of turnover.

Knowledge transfer is a purposeful and one-direction process that involves communicating knowledge to be applied (Ko et al., 2005). This is observed in any organization on a daily basis in employees' daily operations. Knowledge transfer aims at delivering knowledge to places where the knowledge in question is indispensable. This process is of major importance for the success of the knowledge transfer process because the transfer in question results in changes in the knowledge base (Argote & Ingram, 2000).

Knowledge sharing is a multi-directional process that aims at knowledge exchange and the purpose is not always unequivocally stated. This is also "a social interaction culture, involving the exchange of employee knowledge, experiences and skills through the whole department or organization" (Lin, 2007, p. 315). At the core of knowledge sharing are collective activities aimed at exchanging knowledge within teams, organizational units, and organizations. This process is necessary to transform individual knowledge into organizational knowledge.

Knowledge application refers to the actualizing of knowledge (Newell et al., 2004), and applying of knowledge to make good use of the created knowledge. The main objective of knowledge application is to integrate knowledge obtained from internal and external sources to manage organizational targets (Shin et al., 2001). Knowledge application makes knowledge more active and relevant for the creation of firm value (Young Choi et al., 2010). In this context, when organizations correctly apply relevant knowledge, they reduce the likelihood of making mistakes, reduce redundancy, increase efficiency and continuously translate their organizational expertise into products (Chen & Huang, 2009), increase the efficiency of organizations, and innovation performance (Young Choi et al., 2010).

Knowledge, Absorptive Capacity, Knowledge Management

Absorptive capacity has been applied in a diverse range of research streams, such as knowledge management. The relationship between absorptive capacity and knowledge management seems undisputed. Only then will they allow to maximize benefits and improve the ways of working in the organization. It should also be emphasized that it is difficult to indicate at what process of knowledge management, absorptive capacity is important – this is due to the ambiguity and multiplicity of approaches. It should also be emphasized that it is difficult to indicate at what stage of absorptive capacity is important – this is due to the ambiguity and multiplicity of approaches. On the one hand, it is pointed out that absorptive capacity is necessary only in the early stages of knowledge management processes. It is also debatable that processes of knowledge management like creation, sharing, and application of knowledge crucially drive the absorption of external knowledge. In addition, knowledge source and prior knowledge constitute the antecedents of absorptive capacity (Cohen & Levinthal, 1990; Todorova & Durisin, 2007).

As a result, knowledge processes are central components of the absorptive capacity construct. However, other authors believe that knowledge management is intrinsically related to knowledge acquisition, assimilation, and application processes (Cohen & Levinthal, 1990). Liao et al. (2007) stated that knowledge sharing influences the absorptive capacity of employees with higher education level. Therefore, acquisition of new knowledge from external sources tends to be more successful when an organization possesses existing knowledge related to the new knowledge being acquired. The research conducted in this context shows a fundamental role absorptive capacity plays in knowledge management, particularly including a possibility to use external sources of knowledge and strategies of knowledge management (Mariano & Walter, 2015). Besides, absorptive capacity is important for better understanding the way organizations can manage knowledge. Additionally, "knowledge management, knowledge transfer, and innovation were the major research themes connected to absorptive capacity, together with other closely aligned concepts such as knowledge transfer and sharing, and knowledge creation and learning" (Mariano & Walter, 2015, p. 375). Research has found that absorptive capacity closely relates to knowledge management processes, such as acquisition, creation, utilization, and sharing.

What Is a Knowledge Management Strategy?

Knowledge management strategies are indispensable when organizations focus their attention on knowledge and when they deem knowledge to be the most important and strategic asset. In short, knowledge management strategies concentrate on knowledge and they point to different methods of acquiring strategic knowledge by organizations that wish to obtain and sustain their competitive advantage. The literature review indicates that there are many definitions of knowledge management strategies. For example, a knowledge management strategy is defined to be the creation and subsequent management of an environment, which encourages knowledge to be created, shared, learnt, enhanced, organized, and utilized for the benefit of the organization and its customer. In this context, knowledge management strategy is the attempt to formulate intentional plans for explicitly managing knowledge and a sort of roadmap for the knowledge management department of an organization. From the perspective of the knowledge management strategy research that has been conducted so far, it is clear that the phenomenon has many advantages for organizations. Knowledge management strategy is critical to the success of knowledge management initiatives in organizations (Choi et al., 2008). Here, let me focus on five of those advantages, i.e. specified know-how, operational efficiency, organizational learning and improvement, and customer success with self-service and reduction of operating costs. More advantages should emerge as more knowledge management strategies research is conducted.

Knowledge management strategy mainly deals with specific and detailed organizational, managerial, and technical arrangements that a company adopts for its knowledge management programs. Knowledge management strategies focus on adopting specific practices and knowledge management systems, in particular, planning and implementing tools and operational methods of knowledge management, identifying key knowledge management processes and assigning related tasks to employees, selecting practices and computer tools that will be used in knowledge management. Therefore, it is necessary to define what a knowledge management system is. As it has already been mentioned, knowledge management strategies aim, among other things, at adopting knowledge management systems, which include databases, organizational language, networks, and knowledge transfer. Knowledge management systems can be defined as principles, methods, sets of information, IT systems, networks of connections, and relations allowing to improve organizational processes of knowledge management.

Knowledge Management Strategy and Knowledge Strategy

In the literature, the concept of knowledge accompanies a knowledge management strategy. The knowledge strategy is not the same as the knowledge management strategy. Knowledge management strategies are considered lower-level strategies. Knowledge management strategy is a general plan that provides guidelines for making decisions and attaining results of knowledge management initiatives. These strategies show how the knowledge management system works. They are linked to process and infrastructure, and a combination of goals, rules, relationships, and measures. On the other hand, the knowledge strategy is a refinement of the organization's strategy with information on what resources the organization should acquire to achieve its goals. It is also a consequence and a premise for recognizing the strategic importance of knowledge.

The goals of knowledge strategy are to optimize knowledge creation and to transform it to competitive advantage in the enterprise, to formulate for filling the existing knowledge gap and the needed knowledge gap, and to answer the strategic questions that emphasize the competitive intelligence and internal retrieving systems of knowledge (Zack, 1999). A knowledge strategy identifies knowledge, either existing in the firm or required for a projected situation, and draft ways to develop and/or capitalize on it. Knowledge strategy is directed at shaping knowledge resources and learning processes. In this context, knowledge strategy relates to guidelines and to practical application of processes, to make the best out of existing or new knowledge domains and should result in plans to manage existing knowledge or creating new ones. For example, Zack's (1999, p. 135) defined knowledge strategy as an overall approach that an organization takes to align its knowledge resources and capabilities to the intellectual requirements of its business strategy. Similarly, for von Krogh et al. (2001), the ultimate purpose of a knowledge strategy is the application of knowledge processes to an existing or new knowledge domain to achieve a strategic goal. For Kasten (2011), a knowledge strategy can be referred to as the general guidelines that shape the organization's capability to manipulate its cognitive resources, with the ultimate goal of making the best use of these assets for competitive advantage. In that approach, knowledge strategy as an element of a business strategy ensures some connection between strategical decisions of an organization and its structures of knowledge and actions.

Shannak et al. (2012) suggest that there are at least three different meanings associated between knowledge management strategy and knowledge strategy: (1) knowledge management strategy is seen as the attempt to formulate intentional plans for explicitly managing knowledge and a sort of roadmap for the knowledge management department of an organization;

(2) knowledge management strategy mainly deals with specific and detailed organizational, managerial, and technical arrangements that an organization adopts for its knowledge management programs. In this view, knowledge management strategy deals with the way knowledge can support competitive advantage in general, while knowledge strategy focuses on specific implementation details of methods, managerial practices, and infrastructure.

Dimensions of a Knowledge Management Strategy

As it has already been stated, knowledge management strategies are a combination and amalgamation of objectives set for the system of knowledge management. The strategies in question concentrate on knowledge and they point to ways of actions to be undertaken within the system of knowledge management. At the same time, a strategy of knowledge management is a multi-dimensional notion. In the available literature, there are different suggestions concerning dimensions of knowledge management, particularly including the following : (1) type of task (routine/non-routine), type of knowledge (tacit/explicit), interaction (individual/group), business strategy (innovation/efficiency), type of a problem, type of a problem-solving method, competitive advantage, an organizational level (manager/staff), a goal priority (innovation along with efficiency/efficiency along with innovation), sources of knowledge (external/internal). For instance, Bhatt (2002) and Greiner et al. (2007) emphasize the type of a task i.e., routine or non-routine. In another approach, Hansen et al. (1999) identify the type of knowledge (tacit/explicit) and business strategy (innovation/efficiency).

Even more detailed, Gottschalk (2006) identified the type of problem, problem-solving methods, competitive advantage, and the method of the problem faced by the organization to determine the appropriate knowledge management strategy. Interaction, i.e., individual or group, which is used in the research of Bhatt (2002) and Donoghue et al. (1999) determines whether knowledge management is focused on the individual or if there is a need to involve several people in the organization. On the other hand, Greiner et al. (2007) focused on business strategy (innovation/efficiency), whereby organizations with an innovation strategy use a personalized method to enhance the creation of innovation, while the efficiency strategy uses the codification strategy to increase the utilization of existing knowledge. Type of knowledge, i.e., tacit or explicit, was used in Greiner et al. (2007), Hansen et al. (1999), and Ng et al. (2012).

Types of a Knowledge Management Strategies

The knowledge management strategies based on types of knowledge most often referred to in the literature include the following two strategies: codification and personalization (Hansen et al., 1999). These strategies are focused on knowledge, in particular taking into account its availability and transformation. They also take into account of the division into explicit and implicit knowledge (Nonaka & Takeuchi, 1995) and are some expression of the use of tools for acquiring, transmitting, and accumulating knowledge. The primary goal of the codification strategy is to collect, store, archive, process, share open knowledge, and then document and codify it. Additionally, this strategy includes the creation, implementation, and use of databases, computer networks, software, document management systems, and workflow. It is also assumed that the codification strategy will be successful for those organizations whose business strategy requires the re-use of existing knowledge (Hansen et al., 1999). In the case of codification strategies, knowledge is collected and saved in the form of databases available to other employees. This requires employees to be able to use information technology. Attention is also paid to the economy of multiple use, which refers to the fact that a one-time investment in knowledge is supposed to lead to its multiple use. This approach enables all authorized employees to download codified knowledge and share their knowledge via electronic devices. Codified knowledge is acquired, reused, saved, refined and improved, which ultimately can lead to organizational innovation, learning, and improvement of existing opportunities.

The personalization strategy is based on a person-to-person approach. This strategy aims at transferring, communicating, and exchanging knowledge through knowledge networks such as discussion forums. This strategy assumes that knowledge is related to humans. This strategy does not focus on storing or gathering knowledge but creating a network of connections between people. It is also focused on improving knowledge-sharing processes and creating learning opportunities for employees. Information technology is used to communicate with one another, to share knowledge or skills. This allows individuals for eliminating barriers in the communication process. It is also oriented towards a creative and analytical approach to solving organizational problems. In short, organizations that apply a personalization strategy emphasize the "knowledge economy" and developing highly personalized solutions to complex problems, thus using direct contact and personal interaction to solve problems, new or customer-specific solutions, or product innovations using creativity and design (Hansen et al., 1999). As suggested by Zanjani et al. (2008), the personalization strategy is more suitable for SMEs conducting tasks that are more innovative in nature.

As an intermediary to personalization and codification strategy, other research focused on adding two new strategies: relation strategy and substitution strategy. Relation strategy is a knowledge management strategy that is focused on the relationships between individuals to be able to share and increase innovation through the creation of new knowledge. This strategy is used if the organization places more priority on the creation of innovation, in line with the increased efficiency in the creation of the innovation. The substitution strategy is a knowledge management strategy that is focused on the utilization of information and communication infrastructure as a back-up of knowledge possessed by the experts. This approach is used if the organization is prioritized on efficiency by utilizing existing knowledge or new knowledge, in line with the creation of innovation in organizations.

However, Bloodgood and Salisbury (2001) identify knowledge creation, knowledge transfer, and knowledge protection. The creation-related strategy aims at acquiring new knowledge and generating knowledge that could be useful while launching innovative solutions. This strategy concentrates on creativity, experimentation, and, to a significant extent, creating a shared understanding within the creating group to construct new knowledge that can be used to develop new products and services. The transfer-related strategy concentrates, however, on obtaining the latest knowledge that is available in the organization's environment and utilizing it to its fullest extent as quickly as possible. The protection-related strategy involves sustaining already generated or acquired knowledge and the knowledge has to be sustained in its original and creative condition. Organizations that use a strategy of knowledge protection focus on maintaining knowledge in its original and constructive state, i.e., not losing it or allowing it to become altered or obsolete and keeping.

In another approach von Krogh et al. (2001) identify four strategies that are distinguished based on the domain of already existing or new knowledge and a process of knowledge concentrated on transfer or creation. In this approach, a domain of knowledge contains data, information, articulated knowledge including handbooks, manuals, presentations, or lists of key persons and groups that have some tacit knowledge and professional experience that could be valuable for an organization. However, knowledge processes involve transfer and creation. Taking the above into consideration, the following strategies of knowledge are discussed: a leveraging strategy, an expanding strategy, appropriation strategy, and a probing strategy. The leveraging strategy concentrates on knowledge transfer between different areas of organizational domains it sets out from existing knowledge domains and focuses on transferring that knowledge throughout the organization. This strategy is orientated toward achieving efficiency in operations, reducing risks in operations. The strategy ensures that the co-organization internally transfers existing knowledge from various knowledge domains, for example in areas such as product development, manufacturing, marketing and sales, human resources, purchasing, and finance. The expanding strategy aims at creating new knowledge based on already existing knowledge domains in an organization. The emphasis is on increasing the scope and depth of knowledge by refining what is known and by bringing in additional expertise relevant for knowledge creation. Creating new knowledge is carried out in research laboratories or during group meetings, workshops, formal, and informal trainings. Appropriation strategy provides for developing a new knowledge domain based on external sources in order to combine the domain with knowledge that already exists in the organization in question. This strategy builds up a new knowledge domain by transfer of knowledge from external sources by means of acquisitions or a strategic partner. The probing strategy involves creating new knowledge – tacit and explicit, individual and social – through collective work. This requires identification of team participants who would be interested in developing their own community focused on loose ideas and visions of a potential knowledge domain. In this context, gathering or developing new relevant data sets, creating new information, and new tacit and explicit, individual and social knowledge, are important parts of probing.

According to Gottschalk (2006), the strategy selection is based on the current business characteristics, which depend on the type of problem encountered, the type of problem-solving method, and the competitive advantage. Gottschalk (2006) classified the knowledge management strategy into the following three categories: stock, flow, and growth strategy. In this context, if organizations are facing new and complex issues, they will require a new problem-solving method anyway and if the organization's competitive advantage is innovation, then the organizations are categorized as an expert-driven business. In this goal, the organization advised using the growth strategy, which is focused on developing new knowledge and emphasized access to a network of experts and learning environments. The flow strategy shall be a better option when the organization is facing a new problem, but it can be solved using the existing problem-solving method. Organizations are categorized as experience-driven businesses with a competitive advantage on the effective adaptation of problem-solving methodologies and techniques. The growth strategy is for organizations that are focused on developing new knowledge and it emphasizes access to a network of experts and learning environment.

Implementation of a Knowledge Management Strategy

Implementation of a knowledge management strategy may contribute to improvement in organization's learning capacity and to combination knowledge-based opportunities and better knowledge utilization. In this meaning, new resources and generated opportunities are difficult to imitate and the strategy of knowledge makes them the nucleus of a competitive advantage, resulting in higher profitability. The implementation of the knowledge management strategy can be carried out in two ways: (1) concentration on one strategy and (2) combination of several strategies. When focusing on one strategy (Gottschalk, 2006; Greiner et al., 2007; Hansen et al., 1999), the organization chooses one knowledge management strategy and, on its basis, identifies the business characteristics of the organization. It also uses the infrastructure needs. In turn, the implementation of a strategy by combining several strategies that are appropriate for the business (Bhatt, 2002; Donoghue et al., 1999; Ng et al., 2012) aims at integrating different types of knowledge, i.e., combinations of tacit and explicit knowledge. The implementation of a knowledge management strategy can be stimulated or shaped by various factors, including knowledge audit, organizational culture, organizational structure, support of management and masters, IT infrastructure, and community of practices.

Before designing an implementation plan and implementing a knowledge management strategy, a knowledge audit is required. Knowledge audit allows for the qualitative assessment of the organization in terms of knowledge management capabilities. A knowledge audit is carried out to identify knowledge needs, make an inventory of existing knowledge resources, analyze knowledge flows, and create knowledge mapping. A typical knowledge audit allows you to answer the following questions (Choy et al., 2004):

- What are the knowledge needs of the organization?
- What resources or knowledge resources does the organization have and where are they located?

- What are the gaps in the knowledge of the organization?
- How does knowledge flow throughout the organization?
- What blockages are there in this flow (i.e., to what extent people, processes, and technology currently support or hinder the effective flow of knowledge)?

Organizational culture is defined as a set of rules, norms, values, assumptions, and beliefs that are shared by employees within an organization and that affect the way decisions are made; culture is the most important success factor for organizational knowledge. Organizational culture conducive to the implementation of a knowledge management strategy should support the creation and sharing of knowledge, as well as the trust and openness of the organization to new knowledge (Alavi et al., 2005). In particular, an open organizational culture enables an organization to transform tacit knowledge into explicit knowledge.

The implementation of a knowledge management strategy is also favored by a flat organizational structure, with dynamically created ad hoc task teams composed of units that trust each other, where there are real possibilities of flexible change of roles of individual employees-specialists. Importantly, teams should be open to sharing knowledge, in particular specialist knowledge. It is also important to build management support into knowledge management strategies. Identification of an influential person in the organization combined with strong leadership is considered to be factors supporting the implementation of a knowledge management strategy.

A knowledge management strategy is a formula that includes a combination of goals, principles, and resources for a knowledge management system. In this approach, the knowledge management strategy should be related to the overall strategy of the organization. In this context, the knowledge management strategy depends on way the company serves its clients, the economics of its business, and the people it hires (Hansen et al., 1999). Thus, the knowledge management strategy should be closely related to the goals and business strategy of the organization or sub-units of the organization (Zack, 1999). Implementation of an acknowledged management strategy involves establishing positions and appointing individuals who would be responsible for managing knowledge in a particular organization (Chief Knowledge Officer, CKO). The CKO is a unique and integrated or hybrid manager, processing skills and attributes that include an ability to think conceptually, manage people and projects, communicate effectively both internally and externally, and very importantly persuade and advocate. The CKO works as a change agent to build a cultural climate that rewards sharing behavior (Earl & Scott, 1999). The CKO job is to ensure that the organization profits from the effective use of knowledge resources. Investments in knowledge may include employees, processes, and intellectual property. The CKOs can help an organization maximize the returns on investment in knowledge (people, processes, and intellectual capital), exploit their intangible assets (know-how, patents, customer relationships), repeat successes, share best practices, improve innovation, and avoid knowledge loss after organizational restructuring.

Implementation of a knowledge management strategy should involve investment in infrastructure and applications that facilitate employees' communication and knowledge sharing, storing, updating, enhancing, and developing. In a knowledge management strategy, technology is also an instrument in a collection of processes that govern the creation, dissemination, and utilization of knowledge to fulfill organizational objectives. In this context, Dixon (2000) and Nonaka and Takeuchi (1995) discuss technology as a means of transfer of explicit knowledge that will allow internalization of that knowledge and thereby its incorporation into the understanding and experience of the individual. Dixon (2000) particularly identifies technological tools as facilitators and as a practical means of national and global knowledge integration.

Finally, community of practices (CoP) is also important for the implementation of knowledge management strategies. Wenger (2000) defines CoP as groups of people who share a concern or a passion for something they do and learn how to do it better as they interact regularly. Such communities are typically based on the affinity created by common interests or experience, where practitioners face a common set of problems in a particular knowledge area and have an interest in finding or improving the effectiveness of solutions to those problems. Their emergence may be spontaneous, and they are held together by informal relationships and a common purpose, they share common knowledge or a specific domain, expertise, and tools and learn from one another. They possess knowledge which is crucial to the success of the organization. It is through the process of sharing information and experiences with the group that the members learn from each other and have an opportunity to develop themselves personally and professionally (Wenger, 2000). CoP also stimulates interaction, fosters learning, creates new knowledge, socializes with new members, identifies and shares best practices (Dei & van der Walt, 2020), and connects people who might not otherwise have the opportunity to interact. The community of practices (CoP) enhance in sharing and transferring tacit knowledge by individuals and groups, create expand and exchange knowledge and to develop individual capabilities.

References

Alavi, M., Kayworth, T. R. and Leidner, D. E. (2005). An empirical examination of the influence of organizational culture on knowledge management practices. *Journal of Management Information Systems*, 22(3), pp. 191–224.

Argote, L. (2011). Organizational learning research: Past, present and future. *Management Learning*, 42(4), pp. 439–446.

Argote, L. and Ingram, P. (2000). Knowledge transfer: A basis for competitive advantage in firms. *Organizational Behavior and Human Decision Processes*, 82(1), pp. 150–169.

Asrar-ul-Haq, M. and Anwar, S. (2016). A systematic review of knowledge management and knowledge sharing: Trends, issues, and challenges. *Cogent Business and Management*, 3(1), pp. 1–17.

Bhatt, G. D. (2002). Management strategies for individual knowledge and organizational knowledge. *Journal of Knowledge Management*, 6(1), pp. 31–39.

Bloodgood, J. M. and Salisbury, W. D. (2001). Understanding the influence of organizational change strategies on information technology and knowledge management strategies. *Decision Support Systems*, 31(1), pp. 55–69.

Bukowitz, W., & Williams, R. (1999). The knowledge management fieldbook. *Business Digest*.

Chen, C. J. and Huang, J. W. (2009). Strategic human resource practices and innovation performance – The mediating role of knowledge management capacity. *Journal of Business Research*, 62(1), pp. 104–114.

Chen, J., Zhao, X. and Wang, Y. (2015). A new measurement of intellectual capital and its impact on innovation performance in an open innovation paradigm. *International Journal of Technology Management*, 67(1), pp. 1–25.

Choi, B., Poon, S. K. and Davis, J. G. (2008). Effects of knowledge management strategy on organizational performance: A complementarity theory-based approach. *Omega*, 36(2), pp. 235–251

Choy, S. Y., Lee, W. B. and Cheung, C. F. (2004). A systematic approach for knowledge audit analysis: Integration of knowledge inventory, mapping and knowledge flow analysis. *Journal of Universal Computer Science*, 10(6), pp. 674–682.

Cohen, W. M. and Levinthal, D. A. (1990). Absorptive capacity: A new perspective on learning and innovation. *Administrative Science Quarterly*, 35(1), pp. 128–152.

Daghfous, A. (2004). Absorptive capacity and the implementation of knowledge-intensive best practices. *S.A.M. Advanced Management Journal*, 69(2), pp. 21–27.

Davenport, T. and Prusak, L. (2000). *Working knowledge: Managing what your organization knows*. Boston: Harvard Business School Press.

Dei, D.-G. J. and van der Walt, T. B. (2020). Knowledge management practices in universities: The role of communities of practice. *Social Sciences & Humanities Open*, 2(1), 100025.

Dixon, N. M. (2000). *How companies thrive by sharing what they know*. Boston: Harvard Business School Press.

Donoghue, B. L. P., Harris, J. G. and Weitzman, B. (1999). Knowledge management strategies that create value. *Outlook*, 1. pp. 48–53.

Earl, M. and Scott, I. (1999). What is a chief knowledge officer? *Sloan Management Review*, https://sloanreview.mit.edu/article/what-is-a-chief-knowledge-officer.

Gottschalk, P. (2006). Stages of knowledge management systems in police investigations. *Knowledge-Based Systems*, 19(6), 381–387.

Greiner, M. E., Bohmann, T. and Krcmar, H. (2007). A strategy for knowledge management. *Journal of Knowledge Management*, 11(6), pp. 3–15.

Hansen, M. T., Nohria, N. and Tierney, T. (1999). What's your strategy for managing knowledge? *Harvard Business Review*, https://www.hbs.edu/faculty/Pages/item.aspx?num=7313

Johannsen, C. G. (2000). Total quality management in a knowledge management perspective. *Journal of Documentation*, 56(1), pp. 42–54.

Kasten, J. (2011). Knowledge strategy and its influence on knowledge organization. *Proceedings of the North American Symposium on Knowledge Organization*, 1, p. 44–54.

Ko, D. G., Kirsch, L. J., and King, W. R. (2005). Antecedents of knowledge transfer from consultants to clients in enterprise system implementations. *MIS Quarterly: Management Information Systems*, 29(1), pp. 59–85.

Liao, S. H., Fei, W. C., & Chen, C. C. (2007). Knowledge sharing, absorptive capacity, and innovation capability: An empirical study of Taiwan's knowledge-intensive industries. *Journal of Information Science*, 33(3), pp. 340–359.

Lin, H. F. (2007). Knowledge sharing and firm innovation capability: An empirical study. *International Journal of Manpower*, 28(3/4), pp. 315–332.

Mariano, S. and Walter, C. (2015). The construct of absorptive capacity in knowledge management and intellectual capital research: Content and text analyses. *Journal of Knowledge Management*, 19(2), pp. 372–400.

Nahapiet, J. and Ghoshal, S. (2009). Social capital, intellectual capital, and the organizational advantage. *Academy of Management Review*, 23(2), pp. 242–267.

Newell, S., Tansley, C. and Huang, J. (2004). Social Capital and knowledge integration in an ERP project team: The importance of bridging and bonding. *British Journal of Management*, 15(1), pp. 43–57.

Ng, A. H. H., Yip, M. W., Din, S. and Bakar, N. A. (2012). Integrated knowledge management strategy: A Preliminary literature review. *Procedia - Social and Behavioral Sciences*, 57, pp. 209–214.

Nonaka, I. (1994). A dynamic theory of organizational knowledge creation. *Organization Science*, 5(1), pp. 14–37.

Nonaka, I. and Nishiguchi, T. (2001). *Knowledge Emergence: Social, Technical, and Evolutionary Dimensions of Knowledge Creation*. Oxford: Oxford University Press.

Nonaka, I. and Takeuchi, H. (1995). *The Knowledge-Creating Company: How Japanese Companies Create the Dynamics of Innovation*. New York: Oxford University Press.

Nonaka, I. and von Krogh, G. (2009). Perspective-tacit knowledge and knowledge conversion: Controversy and advancement in organizational knowledge creation theory. *Organization Science*, 20(3), pp. 635–652.

Nonaka, I., Byosiere, P., Borucki, C. C. and Konno N. (1994). Organizational knowledge creation theory: A first comprehensive test. *International Business Review*, 3(4), pp. 337–351.

Nonaka, I., Kodama, M., Hirose, A. and Kohlbacher, F. (2014). Dynamic fractal organizations for promoting knowledge-based transformation - A new paradigm for organizational theory. *European Management Journal*, 32(1), pp. 137–146.

Nonaka, I., Toyama, R. (2003). The knowledge-creating theory revisited: Knowledge creation as a synthesizing process. *Knowledge Management Research & Practice*, 1, pp. 2–10.

Nonaka, I., Toyama, R. and Konno, N. (2000). SECI, Ba and leadership: A unified model of dynamic knowledge creation. *Long Range Planning*, 33(1), pp. 5–34.

Prahalad, C.K. and Hamel, G. (2006). *The Core competence of the corporation*. In: Hahn, D., Taylor, B. (Eds.), *Strategische unternehmungsplanung – Strategische Unternehmungsführung*, Berlin, Heidelberg: Springer.

Shannak, R., Masadeh, R. and Ali, M. (2012). Knowledge management strategy building: Literature review. *European Scientific Journal*, 8(15), pp. 143–168.

Shin, M., Holden, T. and Schmidt, R. A. (2001). From knowledge theory to management practice: Towards an integrated approach. *Information Processing and Management*, 37(2), pp. 335–355.

Sterman, J. D. (2002). System dynamics modeling: Tools for learning in a complex world. *California Management Review*, 43(4), pp. 8–25.

Todorova, G. and Durisin, B. (2007). Absorptive capacity: Valuing a reconceptualization. *Academy of Management Review*, 32(3), 774–786.

van den Bosch, F., van Wijk, R. and Volberda, H. (2003). Absorptive capacity: Antecedents, models and outcomes. *ERIM Report Series Research in Management*.

Von Krogh, G., Nonaka, I. and Aben, M. (2001). Making the most of your company's knowledge: A strategic framework. *Long Range Planning*, 34(4), pp. 421–439.

Wang, S. and Noe, R. A. (2010). Knowledge sharing: A review and directions for future research. *Human Resource Management Review*, 20(2), pp. 115–131.

Wenger, E. (2000). Communities of practice and social learning systems. *Organization*, 7(2), pp. 225–246.

Young Choi, S., Lee, H. and Yoo, Y. (2010). The impact of information technology and transactive memory systems on knowledge sharing, application, and team performance: A field study. *MIS Quarterly: Management Information Systems*, 34(4), pp. 855–870.

Zack, M. H. (1999). Developing a knowledge strategy. *California Management Review*, 41(3), pp. 125–145.

Zahra, S. A. and George, G. (2002). Absorptive capacity: A review, reconceptualization, and extension. *Academy of Management Review*, 27(2), pp. 185–203.

Zanjani, M. S., Mehrasa, S. and Mandana, M. (2008). Organizational dimensions as determinant factors of KM approaches in SMEs. In: *Proceedings of World Academy of Science, Engineering and Technology*, 45, pp. 394–289. Available at: http://citeseerx.ist.psu.edu/viewdoc/download?doi=10.1.1.193.348&rep=rep1&type=pdf (accessed on 18 March 2022).

16

EXPANDING THE WORKPLACE TO PROMOTE KNOWLEDGE CREATION

Dai Senoo and Bach Q. Ho

Introduction

The Importance of Space in Knowledge Creation

In the research field of knowledge management, there are multiple topics such as knowledge acquisition, sharing, utilization, and accumulation. Among these, this chapter focuses its attention on knowledge creation.

Changing of the major trend in how corporates create value can be seen as the transition from "value creation through production" to "value creation through innovation". The raison d'etre of a company is to create value for customers, employees, shareholders, and society. This is true regardless of the times that we are in, but the time has come for change in methods of value creation. For commercial capitalism during the Age of Exploration, geographical differences were the source of profits, and for industrial capitalism in the 20th century, the difference between the value of labor and the value of products was the source of profits. However, in the 21st century, where there is a higher degree of homogenization and globalization, such naturally occurring differences are unlikely to happen. Thus, society's attention is turned toward "knowledge creation".

Knowledge is the source of innovation. The creation of new knowledge leads to new products, services, organizations, and business models. Traditionally, most of the work in companies was "information processing" and their main task was problem solving. However, creativity is required to derive innovative value in modern times. It is not possible to create new value simply by following manuals and relying on prior experience as before. The knowledge possessed by business owners and employees has become the focus of our attention as a source of innovation. Up to now, it is usually regarded that there are four main management resources that are indispensable for corporate activities: people (labor force), goods (production facilities and raw materials), money (capital), and information. However, as the importance of innovation in economic activities increases, in addition to these four management resources, knowledge possessed by business owners, managers, employees, and customers has come to draw attention as a source of innovation.

In the process of knowledge creation, individual knowledge is transformed through interaction with others to create value. The ideas needed to create new knowledge are not

DOI: 10.4324/9781003112150-19

achieved in an individual's mind, but are realized by mixing disparate knowledge. This is what J. A. Schumpeter calls "innovation" (Neue Kombination), and it is the activity of innovation itself that involves knowledge creation.

Space is necessary for the existence of relationships between people who possess knowledge. Until now, offices in companies have often been designed around information-processing tasks by individuals. However, when aiming to promote knowledge creation, it is necessary to prepare a workplace designed with an emphasis on relationships, that is, with a focus on group work.

Leading companies are already making various changes. For example, many of the newly created workplaces have more space for eating and drinking, and are equipped with table tennis and billiard tables. These can be regarded as welfare benefits aimed at taking a break and improving the health of working individuals, but they can also be regarded as a mechanism for creating new relationships. Innovative ideas do not come up even if you talk formally and seriously. You may notice something while doing an activity which you do not normally do, or you may come up with new ideas while talking to people you do not usually meet. Similarly, talking to people you meet all the time in an outdoor tent compared to talking to them in the same meeting room as you normally do offers a different "Ba" (human-to-human relationship), which may lead to new discoveries.

Changes in Specifications Required for Workplace

The focal point of workplace design is changing from individual work to group work. In order to get new ideas for innovation, it is recommended to improve group work with colleagues and activate communication. Rather than silently creating documents, it is becoming more important to talk to customers and people in the company to whom you have never talked before and to collect information. Work done in collaboration with a team is becoming more important than work done alone.

There are three reasons to emphasize group work: (1) group work creates higher value than individual work; (2) the proportion of knowledge work is increasing; (3) due to the development of information and communications technology (ICT) and cost reduction (and the impact of the spread of the COVID-19 virus), workplaces suitable for individual work has become something which has to be designed by each individual, instead of being homogeneously created by companies.

In the subsequent sections of this chapter, a workplace designed with an emphasis on knowledge creation work by a group will be called a "knowledge creation workplace". The concept of "Ba" is useful for analyzing this kind of workplace. This is because it is more efficient to use the relationship between workers as an unit of analysis than to use each individual worker as an unit of analysis. From a systematic point of view, it means switching the focus of our attention from a node (single element) to a link (relationship).

Technologies in Work Space

In today's world where technology is developing and there is a fusion of the real and virtual worlds, it is important to assume that the process of knowledge creation can include artifacts (man-made objects) when we are considering space. In addition to human-centered analysis of "who and who act in collaboration", it is also fruitful and productive to design a knowledge-creating workplace using the framework of "actor network theory" which analyzes artifacts such as instruments, machines, and artificial intelligence by treating them in the same way as humans (as far as the research is concerned).

The COVID-19 virus spread worldwide in 2020 and has not stopped spreading as of 2021. To prevent the spread of infections, companies have accelerated teleworking from home, and remote video-conferencing systems such as Zoom and Skype have become widespread overnight. It also has become clear that the real physical office performed a function that video-conferencing systems cannot replace for now.

For example, in a physical office, when an idea comes to mind, it is possible to involve not only the person who is talking with you, but also the person who happened to be there or the person who passed by, and try the idea with them. Some virtual office systems are attempting to enable such "accidental" involvement by having people in the vicinity as well as online meeting attendees reflected in the background, or by making avatars always existent on the screen.

Furthermore, in the physical office, it has become clear that humans are observing each other. While it may seem that humans do not seem to be very conscious of each other when gathered in the same space, the fact is they often closely look at other people. For example, when someone is angry at a meeting, normally it is impossible to tell whether he/she is really angry or just making an angry pose just based on the information you can gather at the scene, somehow you will be able to tell the difference when you have been with him/her in the same space for a couple of months before that. Based on a person's utterances, it is difficult to understand the true meaning of what he/she is saying without background information and context, and the surrounding environment such as facial expressions, postures, and movements. This is an essential requirement in order to have deep conversations which are necessary for knowledge creation.

The Question of This Chapter

Having established the importance of space in knowledge creation, the expectations that society has for workspace for team-based knowledge creation, and how technology is fusing the real and virtual, we formulate a question for this chapter as follows.

The question is "How can we expand the knowledge creation workplace?" A more detailed way to express this question would be "In what direction should we expand the working space so as to effectively enable the creation and activation of the Ba (relationships) that encourages knowledge creation?" In addressing this question, the authors regard the utilization of the current continuously evolving ICT as a premise.

For readers who wish to read the conclusion first, the answer to this question is the hypothesis that "An effective direction to work towards is the utilization of external knowledge and the ability to provide a improvisational response". This chapter proposes the use of external knowledge as a policy for geographical expansion, and responding in an improvisational manner as a policy for temporal expansion. The discussions leading up to such proposals will be described below.

The Theory of Ba

Definition of Ba

A "Ba" is a context-sharing relationship for the emergence of knowledge, and the state of such Ba and the degree of connection between Ba influence the organizational knowledge creation process. Establishing and activating this relationship is a requirement for promoting knowledge creation. Other requirements for promoting knowledge creation include leadership and knowledge assets, but since space is the theme of this chapter, we focus on the Ba here. As mentioned in 'Changes in Specifications Required for Workplace', it is convenient to use the concept of Ba when considering the knowledge creation workplace.

Outline of Knowledge Creation Theory

I. Nonaka has advocated "organizational knowledge creation theory". Knowledge creation refers to the circulatory interaction between tacit knowledge and explicit knowledge, which "makes thoughts into words, words into shapes, shapes into practice, and practice into further thoughts". The premise of organized knowledge creation theory is the assumption that all knowledge can be reduced to two types: tacit knowledge and explicit knowledge. "Tacit knowledge" is subjective and embodied knowledge that is difficult to express in language or numerical values, and more specifically this includes beliefs, viewpoints, well-honed skills, and know-how. On the other hand, "explicit knowledge" is objective and rational knowledge that can be expressed in languages and numerical values, and more specifically this includes texts, equations, specifications, and manuals.

We will explain the four-mode knowledge creation process called SECI for each mode. Socialization is a mode in which individuals share tacit knowledge through shared experiences. Under the apprenticeship system, which has a policy of "skills are not learned but stolen", disciples acquire the values and skills of their masters through observation and imitation during shared experiences. An example of socialization is when members from the development team visit the site where a product is used and experience the user's sense of everyday life and cultural climate when developing a product. This mode requires the full utilization of the five senses in order to acquire non-verbal knowledge.

Externalization is a mode in which an individual or group transforms tacit knowledge into explicit knowledge through metaphors and dialogues. The verbalization of tacit knowledge which resists such attempts at verbalization, can open up a new possibility where knowledge can spread without being limited to the scope of shared experience. It also opens up the possibility of creating value that goes beyond merely trying to please the customer by keeping an objective distance from reality which facilitates an in-depth and thorough form of conceptualization. Examples of this mode can be seen when trying to capture advanced skills embodied in an individual into a manual, or when a product development team tries to determine the concept of a new product.

Combination is a mode in which the level of abstraction in some explicit knowledge is increased or explicit knowledge is combined with another explicit knowledge to create new explicit knowledge. The typical examples of this mode are when translating the concept of a new product into abstract and context-insensitive product specifications, and when trying to edit multiple articles so as to synthesize an overarching message throughout an entire magazine. In addition, the realization of information sharing that transcends time and space by using a computer network and such can also be seen as instances of this combination mode. It is a mode which is easily supportable from management information systems.

Internalization is a mode that transforms explicit knowledge into tacit knowledge through practice and introspection. To convert explicit knowledge into tacit knowledge, one must not only understand it with the mind, but also internalize it with the body. To maintain a strong belief and to be able to demonstrate the necessary skills at any time, re-experience by practice and repetitive exercise are required.

The dynamic process of the SECI model, as we have seen above, occurs in different layers of ontology. Knowledge transformation between tacit knowledge and explicit knowledge through the above four modes can be regarded as a dynamic process in the dimension of epistemology. This dynamic process takes place in the different ontological layers of individuals, groups, organizations, and societies.

The process by which the knowledge of individuals and organizations is amplified is referred to as the "knowledge spiral". The starting point of organizational knowledge creation is the tacit knowledge of an individual. The tacit knowledge of an individual ("personal tacit knowledge") is shared with others by socialization. Although tacit knowledge can be externalized into explicit knowledge by an individual alone, it is more effective and efficient to perform this in a group that shares tacit knowledge. This is because having diverse viewpoints and dialogues accelerates externalization. Combination, which is to combine explicit knowledge, can be performed at the organizational level. This is because explicit knowledge, which is less context-dependent, does not easily change or wear out with the passage of time or separation of space, so it is easy to expand the scope of acquisition of explicit knowledge. Internalization, which transforms explicit knowledge into tacit knowledge, takes place at the individual, group, and organizational levels. Explicit knowledge is embodied in individuals through actual practice and at the same time it is absorbed as tacit knowledge in groups or organizations. Nonaka et al. describe the process of amplifying both individual knowledge and organizational knowledge in this way as a "knowledge spiral". This expression evokes an image of how knowledge spreads as it rises like a spiral.

However, the process of knowledge creation in an actual organization follows a complicated path, unlike the smooth and simple pathway described above. Activities that connect different layers (booming-up and slipping-down) take place as well as those within each layer of individuals, groups, organizations, and societies (Wu et al., 2010).

Effects of Creating "Ba"

Nonaka argues that dialogue between actors with different contexts is necessary for the formation of new meanings, and regards the "Ba", which is a context-sharing relationship, as the main element of an organization. "Ba" appears not only within a company but also beyond the boundaries of a company with customers, suppliers, local communities, and so on. It is expected that each department and each individual of an organization will find and

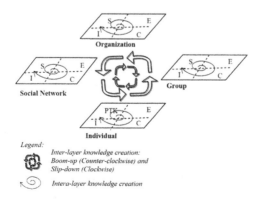

Figure 16.1   Four Layers Model

solve problems through team work that goes beyond corporate boundaries, and will discover new problems when a series of work is completed.

Unlike information-processing organizations, it is said that creating a Ba is more important than monitoring employees in a knowledge-creating organization. Knowledge creation is extremely accidental and cannot be managed or monitored. It does not always happen during work hours in the company, and it is not something that always happens with training or education. The leaders of knowledge-creating organizations are required to go beyond merely managing their subordinates, but also to create new meeting places and opportunities to encourage knowledge-creating activities.

Why is it necessary to create a Ba when attempting to encourage the knowledge creation process? We will look into the effect of creating a Ba. First, it seems that creating a Ba will help to create a greater consensus in terms of an organization's activity goals (knowledge vision). Each actor participating in an organization's activities has its own context and different desires to meet. Some people consider getting paid as their main objectives, others want to satisfy their needs for a sense of belonging, while others participate for self-fulfillment. The experience they have accumulated and their areas of expertise are also different. It is difficult to agree on a common objective if such diverse contexts are left as they are. Understanding each other's context through the creation of a Ba will facilitate the process of setting goals for an organization's activities. Second, it seems that creating a Ba will strengthen the members' willingness to collaborate. This is because sharing each other's context makes it easier to create cognitive empathy and increases friendship and psychological safety. Third, it seems that creating a Ba will make communication substantial and speed up the knowledge creation process. This is because the shared contexts make it easier to understand the true meaning of the conversation and reduces time wastage due to miscommunication and misunderstandings.

Analysis and Discussion

Revisiting the Question "How to Expand the Knowledge Creation Workplace?"

As mentioned in "The Question of This Chapter", the question for this chapter is "How to Expand the Knowledge Creation Workplace?" A more detailed way to express this question would be, "In what direction should we expand the working space so as to effectively enable the creation and activation of the Ba (relationships) that encourages knowledge creation?" In addressing this question, the authors regard the utilization of the current continuously evolving ICT as a premise.

Framework for Analysis

This section presents the analytical framework of this chapter. The four main concepts used are "space", "field", "knowledge creation activity", and "knowledge creation outcomes". Figure 16.2 shows these four concepts as an analytical framework. Figure 16.2 shows the influence of space on knowledge creation activities through two paths. The indirect influence of the upper part is through the Ba and is the main subject of analysis in this chapter. There is certainly a direct influence at the lower part. For example, introducing a desk with a large top plate, or introducing electronic sticky notes, may streamline individual editing activities. However, such direct effects are not the main subject of analysis in this chapter.

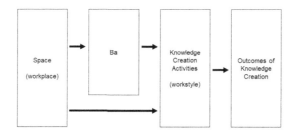

Figure 16.2 Framework for Analysis

Division of the Question by the Concept of "Ba"

A "Ba" is defined as a context-sharing relationship for the emergence of knowledge, also expressed as "shared context in motion" (Nonaka and Toyama, 2015). From the perspective of the three elements of "sharing", "in motion", and "context" contained in this expression, we will look at each element individually in order to approach the question of this chapter: "How to expand the knowledge creation workplace?"

In response to this question, we first approach it from the perspective of the element "in motion". The focal question is: "What does it mean to share context in motion (rather than statically)?"

Let us explore the analytical method for each generation of systems theory. Here, an actor is represented by a node and communication is represented by a link. In (static) "general systems", which are regarded as the first generation systems in systems theory, nodes and links are already fixed, and context sharing is expressed when a link in activated (i.e., inactive state becomes active state). In the "self-organizing systems", which are considered to be the second-generation systems, the nodes are fixed, but the links are unfixed. There is a possibility that a new link will be created even where a link is not established. In the "autopoietic systems", which are considered to be the third generation systems, both nodes and links are unfixed. The system grows when the first node creates the next node. The fact that context is shared "in motion" indicates that context sharing must be understood in a way which assumes second-generation and third generation systems that are highly system-extensible. When designing an expansion of the knowledge creation workplace, you need to keep in mind that relationships can develop in both nodes and links.

Next, we approach from the perspective of the element "shared". Here, the focal question is: "Who are the actors between which contexts are shared in the knowledge creation workplace?" In 'Technologies in Work Space', the authors proposed the use of the framework of actor network theory, which treats and analyzes artifacts in the same way as humans. However, in order not to make the discussion too divergent, we will deliberately limit the discussion here to humans.

The first humans to think of are the individual members of an organization. Specifically, they are the employees who belong to a company that owns a knowledge creation workplace. At the core of the knowledge creation workplace is context sharing among such employees. However, this is not sufficient. Given the potential for relationships to develop on both nodes and links, as discussed in the approach from the perspective of the "in motion" element, we should look not only within the system boundaries at some point, but also outside. When designing an expansion of knowledge creation workplace, it is necessary to consider the actor network that shares their contexts as an open system rather than a closed system.

Lastly, we approach the discussion from the perspective of the element "context". The focal question is: "What exactly should be considered as the contexts to be shared in a knowledge creation workplace?" If the exchange of words in communication between actors is a "figure", the meta information that defines from the upper level the premise that each actor has and the communication itself is the "ground". This context of "ground" has a decisive influence on the sense making. For example, it depends on the context whether the word "goodbye" means "see you tomorrow" or "we will never see each other again". To give a more extreme example, the word "thank you" can mean "Thank you" or "No, thank you", and it depends on the context. When designing an expansion of knowledge creation workplace, it is necessary to look not only at the language exchange, but also at the non-verbal context behind it, and consider it in a social constructionist manner. Non-verbal contexts include body language such as facial expressions and gestures, standing position and posture, loudness and tone of voice, intervals between utterances, timing, and premises, assumptions, beliefs, and tendencies of each actor.

Specific Considerations of Expansion of Knowledge Creation Workplace

From the theoretical discussions in "Division of the Question by the Concept of 'Ba'", we obtained some insights such as "sharing in an open system" and "non-verbal context". In this section, we will use these two concepts to consider measures that can be applied to actual sites of corporate management.

When we talk about an "open system", we often think about the trend of "open innovation". In the past, innovation focused on activities that can be completed within an organization. However, with advances in information technology, it has become possible to easily and inexpensively access external resources, and it is uneconomical to innovate with internal resources alone.

The situation of workplaces in Japan, which the authors have observed over the years, has changed significantly over the past 15 years or so. In addition to employee satisfaction, work productivity, turnover rate, number of new graduate applicants, etc., "number of customers coming to the place" has become an important indicator as a KPI (Key Performance Indicator) when improving a workplace as a result of relocation or renovation. Companies that used to only focus on making sales outside the workplace are adopting a strategy to increase the number of visitors to the workplace by changing their workplace to an original and attractive design. By changing to a sales model that attracts customers to the company, you can have them see products and services other than those they were looking for at the same time, or you can let the person in charge of another department of the company take over the conversation depending on the content of the talk. In addition to "explicit knowledge" that customers are already aware of, they will be able to create new knowledge by utilizing "tacit knowledge" that customers themselves cannot yet put into words.

"Design thinking" can be regarded as a trend similar to open innovation. Unlike the conventional tendency of "you can sell when you make good products" or "launching a flagship product that has been thoroughly refined by the company through many years", it is a work movement which takes as its starting point "insights on what customers want" and "how to change the customer's experience". Instead of the conventional posture of "please buy this product from us", we are switching to a posture of collaborative creation, that is, "would you like to create a job together?" In addition to inviting existing customers as visitors, more and more companies have set up co-working spaces near their offices to encourage interactions between other companies' employees (potential customers or potential partners) and their own employees. It can be said that the creation of a knowledge creation community that goes beyond boundaries is accelerating.

When expanding the knowledge creation workplace, it is effective to adopt a policy of expanding it geographically by opening it to the outside of its boundary and of utilizing external knowledge. The number of relationships, which previously had an upper limit in a closed environment, increases exponentially by creating a more open environment.

What comes to mind in connection with the other concept, "non-verbal", is the increase in the area and variety of shared spaces. This has also changed significantly over the past 15 years or so. In the previous era when the focus was on individual work, the emphasis was on creating an environment where people could "work comfortably", and workers longed for a personal space that will allow them to concentrate on their own individual work. However, nowadays, the emphasis is on team work, and the area of personal space has decreased due to the introduction of the free address (non-territorial) system, etc., and the area of shared space has increased instead. The types of shared spaces used to be disproportionally made up of smoking areas and conference rooms, but have now diversified into eating and drinking spaces, kitchens, entertainment and game corners, meditation rooms, and booths for short meetings and intensive work. In diversified spaces, special non-verbal contexts can be exchanged intensely in each space.

The activities carried out in the workplace are also diversifying. In the past, work was defined by place and time, such as "activities occurring in the office from 9am to 5pm". Now, workplaces can be at satellite offices and at home, while working time has also become flexible, and it is on longer possible to define work using time and place. The future is going to be one where individuals work autonomously. The increase in "slash careers" and side businesses is a sign of this trend. This diversification of activities increases the relative value of activities that have yet to be verbalized or documented. In other words, rather than performing "uniform and steady activities that are likely to create existing value" which have already been verbalized and documented, it is expected that we will instead focus on "diverse and uncertain activities that are likely to create new value" and observing people performing such activities and discovering potential value in the process. As a reaction, the phenomenon where activities that currently seem to be only hobbies or entertainment may generate great value in the future, the notion of "art thinking" has garnered attention in the study of business administration, and an increasing number of companies are inviting artists and activists to live on their premises.

When expanding knowledge creation workplace, from the perspective of time, it will be effective to adopt a policy of expansion which incorporates the changing environment of the present and future as a resource instead of being restricted by plans from the past, and to respond to these changes in an improvisational manner. This will prevent isomorphism that happens in the process of planning and institutionalization, and prevent stagnation due to the loss of creative conflicts.

Summary of This Section

In response to the question which this chapter sets out to answer, which is "In what direction should we expand the working space so as to effectively enable the creation and activation of the Ba (relationship) that encourages knowledge creation?", we would like to present a tentative hypothetical answer from the above discussion.

Hypothesis 1: In order to create a Ba for sharing in an open system, an effective way is to expand the working space geographically in the direction of "utilization of external knowledge".

Hypothesis 2: In order to create a Ba for the sharing of non-verbal contexts, an effective way is to expand the working space temporally in the direction of "improvisational response".

Case Study

This section introduces case studies of companies that skillfully utilize ICT to encourage knowledge creation. There are two successful cases related to the geographical expansion of Hypothesis 1 shown in the previous section, and two successful cases related to the temporal expansion of Hypothesis 2, with a total of four cases.

Cases of Successful Geographical Expansion

LEGO (platform using Internet, proposals of new product from the user community)

LEGO is a toy maker founded in Denmark in 1932, and its main product is assembly blocks. Until the 1980s, they were steadily increasing their sales by selling a wide variety of products. However, in addition to the rise of video games, many cheap imitation products have become available in the market due to the expiration of patents, and sales have fallen since the 1990s.

Therefore, LEGO reviewed its corporate culture through interviews with other companies and analysis of its own business. They found that customers have many creative ideas that lead to innovation, and that customers value not only the process of purchasing products but also the process of creating products together. This led LEGO to launch a website called LEGO IDEAS to commercialize customer ideas. After that, LEGO recovered its sales and has become the world's number one toy maker in 2014, surpassing Google in the brand ranking to become the number one in the world.

LEGO was able to recover its business performance because it utilized ICT to incorporate external knowledge and realized the geographical expansion of knowledge creation. They humbly learned from other companies and built a platform to actively incorporate customer knowledge by reviewing its corporate culture. As a result, the product-oriented values transformed to emphasize the process instead. Innovation cannot be realized from geographical expansion just by introducing the latest ICT. It is also important to foster a corporate culture that actively utilizes external knowledge.

avatarin (Virtual Space, Making Artifacts as Actors)

avatarin is a startup company launched by the airline ANA in 2020, aiming to make avatars a social infrastructure by providing popular-type communication avatars. Customers can go anywhere in the world by logging in to their alter ego, avatar, from a website or app. Development has been underway since around 2016 with the aim of teleporting consciousness so that anyone can do whatever they want when they want. It seems ironic that an airline company whose mission is to transport people starts a new business that requires people to move less, but the outbreak of the new coronavirus from 2020 has expanded its demand. This is a case where technological development and changes in social environment are well matched.

For example, by placing an avatar in a retail store, customers can walk around the store real-time with a clerk to find products that meet their needs. As a result, even rural stores that do not have an EC site have become able to expand their sales. It has also begun to be used for remote working. Conversations through avatars convey more information to the other party than online meetings using Zoom, etc., and serendipity is more likely to occur.

avatarin sees its business as a social infrastructure business rather than an avatar sales business. By placing avatars throughout the world as social infrastructure, customers can access various regions and explore new knowledge. In addition, avatars are fusing real and virtual knowledge creation spaces. Cameras on avatars show not only the dialogue partner but also the background environment in which the partner's avatar is. The interposition of avatars creates authentic physical sensations that are not limited to digital information, and it is likely to bring diversity and spontaneity that are effective for knowledge creation.

Cases of Successful Temporal Expansion

KOMTRAX (Global Positioning System, from Theft Prevention to Maintenance Services)

KOMTRAX is a machine operation management system that was installed on construction machinery as standard equipment by KOMATSU, in 2001. Originally, it started with attaching GPS devices on large machines to prevent theft. At that time, there were many cases of bank ATMs being destroyed using hydraulic excavators. The idea arose that a feature to verify the location of the excavator can prevent such cases from happening, and such devices began to be installed as standard equipment. As a result, theft cases were drastically reduced by the tracking system and the remote engine stop function.

By being able to remotely verify not only information about the location but also the engine operating status and power mode usage status, it has become possible to provide new customer services such as offering consultation and guidance to the operator, and suggesting when to replace parts, which greatly contributed to differentiation from other companies. In many other parts of the world, irregular events that rarely occur in Japan sometimes occur frequently, and this system can contribute to the prevention of such events. For example, it is possible to prevent fuel theft by tracking information about the level of remaining fuel, and to remotely lock a machine when the buyer continues to delay its installment payments.

By monitoring the status of public works projects using data collected from construction machinery around the world, KOMATSU managers can also accurately estimate future economic trends. This is an example of a pioneer in the big data business in the sense that they turned non-verbal information that had not been put to use until then into information that can be utilized by collecting and aggregating remote data from sensors. Similar trends have been observed in many other businesses in the world that combine mobile phone movement data and automobile driving data with various services.

ClipLine (Short Video Technology, Started Off as a Method of New Employee Education for Chain Stores before Moving to Other Businesses)

ClipLine is a Japanese start-up company founded in 2013, and its core resource is a system for creating and distributing short videos. Since its establishment, it has provided value by reducing educational costs and maximizing educational effects with a system that uses short videos (clips) of about 20 seconds for companies that develop multi-store businesses such as restaurant chains.

The founder was inspired by how athletes improve their skills by recording their own movements and comparing them with demonstration videos. This training method was found to be effective, and he adapted it to employee training such as how employees are expected to provide customer service. Employees can check the demonstration videos on a tablet, record their own physical movements (such as how they greet customers, bow, and cook food products), and play the self-video and the model video side by side for objective comparison. Since it is a cloud-based service, you can verify the usage status while looking at data such as the number of button clicks, the number of recordings taken, and the number of views. This technology is patented as an "autonomous learning system".

This system is now used by client companies in unique ways which were unexpected. Not only is it used as a support tool for new employee training, it is also used like a social media platform for communication between multi-site employees using videos (stress relief at one-man operation sites), used for monitoring by taking videos and checking store cleanliness, and used for personnel management, such as measuring the retention rate of part-timers at each store and how good their team work is. By referring to the innovations which are demanded by the customers, ClipLine is going ahead with the creation of additional system functions and new business development. This is an example of turning non-verbal contexts such as various know-hows generated in workplaces into explicit knowledge as video clips, distributing and accumulating them within customer organizations and also within the ClipLine organization, and continuing to develop its business model while responding improvisationally to changes.

Conclusion

This chapter considers the expansion of working space to promote knowledge creation. The question for this chapter is "How can we expand the knowledge creation workplace?" A more detailed way to express this question would be "In what direction should we expand the working space so as to effectively enable the creation and activation of the Ba (relationships) that encourages knowledge creation?"

In addressing this question, we used the concept of "Ba" in knowledge creation theory. We approached the question from the perspective of three elements, i.e., "sharing", "in motion", and "context" included in the definition of the Ba, and obtained the insights of "sharing in an open system" and "non-verbal context". After further specific consideration, we extracted "external knowledge utilization" from "open system sharing" and "improvisational response" from "non-verbal context" as policies for expansion of space, and proposed two hypotheses. We also introduced four successful case studies of excellent utilization of ICT. Although there is a need for further study, the tentative conclusions as of 2021 are as follows:

Conclusion 1: There can be greater use of ICT while considering how to geographically expand space to utilize external knowledge.

Conclusion 2: There can be greater use of ICT while considering how to temporally expand space to allow for improvisational responses.

References

Nonaka, I. and Toyama, R. (2015). The knowledge-creating theory revisited: Knowledge creation as a synthesizing process. In *The essentials of knowledge management* (pp. 95–110). Palgrave Macmillan, London.

Wu, Y., Senoo, D. and Magnier-Watanabe, R. (2010). Diagnosis for organizational knowledge creation: An ontological shift SECI model. *Journal of Knowledge Management*, Vol. 14, No. 6, pp. 791–810.

17

THREE GENERATIONS OF KNOWLEDGE MANAGEMENT PRACTICE MODE AND COMMON PITFALLS IN CHINESE ENTERPRISES

Qinghai Wu

Introduction

As more and more Chinese enterprises begin to compete globally, knowledge collection, knowledge transferring and knowledge creating (Jin Chen and Gang Zheng, 2016) become more and more important, which makes more and more enterprises begin to implement knowledge management (Jin Chen, 2017). When we review the important knowledge management events in China in the past 20 years, we will find that knowledge management has gradually moved from the ivory tower of academic research to the front line of enterprise practice (Qinghai Wu, 2016a). The practice of knowledge management of Chinese enterprises will show different characteristics at intervals. To sum up, it can be roughly divided into the ramp-up stage, KM1.0, KM2.0 and KM3.0 (Qinghai Wu, 2016b).

Three Generations of Practice Mode of KM in Chinese Enterprises

Ramp-up Stage

On May 4, 1998, Jiang Zemin, then general secretary of the Central Committee of the Communist Party of China and President of the People's Republic of China, delivered a speech at the celebration of the centenary of the founding of Peking University, saying that "the whole Party and the whole society should attach great importance to the important role of knowledge innovation and talent development in economic development and social progress, so as to make rejuvenating the country through science and education a broad consensus and practical action of the whole nation" (Jiang Zemin, 1998). Since then, the term "knowledge economy" (OECD, 1996) has appeared in China's public media. Many university scholars began to study knowledge management, and China's knowledge management has entered the ramp-up stage.

Some international well-known IT companies (such as IBM and Microsoft) and management consulting companies (such as McKinsey, Bain and Accenture) have come from

DOI: 10.4324/9781003112150-20

their own knowledge-based service cognition and practice, and have insight into the future development trend of knowledge management. As preachers, they begin to vigorously advocate knowledge management in China. HP has set up its first CKO position in China. Some leading enterprises in China, such as Lenovo, Haier, TCL, Neusoft and so on, began to practice knowledge management one after another at this time.

Local knowledge management service providers also began to set up, such as Great-wall Strategic Research Institute, AMT, Landray, CNKI, China Knowledge Management Center and CKO website. They began to provide knowledge management related education and training, consulting, software implementation, content resources and other services in China. China's knowledge management theory and practice expert seminar was held in Beijing in 2003. People are very interested in how to introduce knowledge management theory into enterprise practice.

KM1.0 – Capitalization Practice Mode

Since 2005, more and more enterprises (such as China Mobile, Livzon Pharmaceutical, Gemdale, China Merchants Securities, TsingTao Beer, Beijing Capital International Airport and Siemens China) have begun to further explore knowledge management. Various forums and salons of knowledge management have been held all over the country. The development of knowledge management in China has entered the "exploration stage" of KM1.0, and the upsurge of knowledge management has become popular.

Chinese enterprises have established document management software system, enterprise knowledge portal, enterprise wiki system, and physical entity archives and libraries. The guiding ideology is committed to maximize the collection of individual employees' knowledge and make it precipitate into valuable knowledge assets of the organization. We can call it "**Capitalization**" practice mode.

This model is content-oriented, emphasizes the explicit knowledge of management organization, and the main strategy is accumulation. After combining and standardizing many work results, we can improve the consistency of work, reduce the duplication of labor, save operating costs and reduce management risks, and the benefits are obvious.

With the practice of knowledge management in different enterprises, many knowledge management practitioners hope that the industry has a common knowledge management terminology, framework and model for reference. The first national knowledge management standard GB/T 23703.1 was officially issued in 2009 under the promotion of China Institute of Standardization. Since then, other knowledge management standards have been developed. So far, 10 knowledge management standards have been issued at the national level in China.

KM2.0 – Contextualization Practice Mode

Under the impact and influence of Internet Web2.0, platforms and applications based on social networks have emerged in China, such as renren.com, Sina Weibo and Wechat. Mobile Internet is in the ascendant, comprehensively and deeply affecting society and enterprises. After 2010, Huawei (Nick Milton, Patrick Lambe, 2018), COFCO Research Institute, New Oriental Education, China Aerospace, Baosteel, Tencent, Alibaba, Baidu and other companies began to introduce new ways such as knowledge community, employee network, expert yellow pages and team online space, and Chinese enterprise knowledge management practice entered the "upgrading stage" of KM2.0.

People oriented, emphasizing the connection between people, people and knowledge, people and business, emphasizing participation and interaction, paying attention to experience management, and driving the generation and application of content based on work scenarios, has become a new path choice for the implementation of knowledge management. This kind of knowledge management mode, which pays attention to tacit knowledge, combines with context and aims at specific business scenarios, can be called "**Contextualization**" practice mode.

In this practice mode, CoP (community of practice) plays a great role (Jin Chen, 2021). Connect people from all over the world with the same interests, hobbies and topics, form social networks and exchange knowledge quickly through communication, discussion, dialogue and activities. Questioning & Answering enables users to stimulate and promote others to interact and answer questions in the context of problems in work. Expert network is to identify those professionals with practical experience, create and share high-quality tacit knowledge.

Effective knowledge operation is also particularly critical. Through user operation, content operation, activity operation, data operation and other means, the right person, at the right time and in the right place can obtain the right knowledge. At the same time, knowledge extraction is carried out according to the business scenario (Qinghai Wu, 2020). Through the configuration or development of different knowledge maps, the knowledge in the business context is clustered and displayed, which ultimately promotes the application of knowledge and produces business value.

At this time, many knowledge management practitioners in China hope to further share and learn from each other's practice. Since 2014, some knowledge management practitioners' forums have been held spontaneously in COFCO, Tencent, Chinese Academy of Sciences and other places. In February 2015, the National Knowledge Management Standardization Technical Committee was formally established and held its first meeting. In October 2015, China Knowledge Management Alliance was established in Beijing. In March 2018, Innovation and Knowledge Management Alliance was established in Beijing.

During the same period, the book named **The secrets of knowledge+ practice**, the best practice cases of China, was systematically planned, crowdsourced, reviewed and revised, and the first and second series were published in 2015 (Qinghai Wu et al., 2015) and 2017 (Qinghai Wu et al., 2017) respectively. Among them, excellent knowledge management cases in China, such as the first Chinese Academy of aerospace, COFCO Research Institute, Huawei, New Oriental Education, China Merchants Securities, Alibaba, Yuexiu group, Neusoft, Arup, Baidu, Baosteel, CCDI international, Far East Holdings, Siemens China and UFIDA University, have been presented to readers after sorting out.

KM3.0 – Intellectualization Practice Mode

After 2018, after years of accumulation, many Chinese enterprises have begun to emerge from good to excellence. In the process of continuously advancing to the high-end value of the industry, many enterprises begin to walk into the "no man's land", and the demand for knowledge originality ability is also increasing. With the in-depth development of the Internet, Web3.0, big data, cloud computing, artificial intelligence and industrial Internet begin to affect enterprises.

In order to better represent knowledge, acquire knowledge and use knowledge, text mining, natural language processing, ontology, semantic network, knowledge graph, user portrait, intelligent recommendation and intelligent search begin to appear on the stage of enterprise application. It has become a general trend to let machines replace people's work as many, fast, good and economical as possible. The practice of knowledge management in Chinese enterprises has entered the "deepening stage" of KM 3.0, which can be called "**Intellectualization**" practice mode.

When more repetitive work is replaced by machines, people will have more time to meditate. This kind of activity with continuity, happiness and pleasure, and self-sufficiency, can really make the "spirit of all things" of human beings happy without external demand, surpass themselves and constantly inspire and awaken the inner wisdom, and return to the pursuit of the ultimate truth such as "truth, goodness and beauty" (Ikujiro Nonaka, Hirotaka Takeuchi, 2019).

The main strategy of this mode is to co-create, with intelligence as the appeal point, and at the same time, it emphasizes to stimulate more individual creativity. Through the construction and guidance of environmental atmosphere, the field that can make individual wisdom emerge dynamically is formed (Ikujiro Nonaka, Hirotaka Takeuchi, 2020). In the aspect of knowledge diversity, we also need to build an ecosystem to cultivate knowledge transaction, and form many knowledge alliances based on business value chain. Through crowdfunding, co-creating, subcontracting, knowledge web celebrity, livestream, tips and gifts, etc., flexible resource allocation and collaborative cooperation can be realized.

During this period, some more representative local knowledge service companies have begun to appear, such as DeDao APP, HunDun academy and SunXZ network. As new knowledge brokers, they began to try new business models such as reward of article content, paid subscription of columns and reward of online experts. Among them, Practitioner Alliance Technology Co. Ltd adheres to the concept of "unity of knowing and action", committed to "managing of knowledge, stimulating of innovation and awakening of wisdom", providing professional knowledge management services, such as training, certification, consulting and knowledge-broking related. Together, they support Chinese enterprises to face the development situation of knowledge economy and realize their dream of knowledge transformation and upgrading.

Comparison of Three Generations of Knowledge Management

The three generations of knowledge management are analyzed and summarized in Table 17.1 on the basis of their feature description, key elements, implementation strategy, functional points, and major problems.

A Case Study of Chinese Enterprise

Background

COFCO, full name China National Cereals, Oils and Foodstuffs Corporation, is the largest supplier of diversified products and services in the agricultural products and food industry in China. Founded in 1949, there are more than 148,000 employees all over the world. It has been one of the global top 500 enterprises chosen by Fortune Magazine in the most recent 20 years, with 71.8 billion USD revenue in 2015.

In order to enhance the whole company's competitive advantage and core competency, COFCO creatively put forward the strategy of establishing a "from-farm-to-table" company with fully integrated Agri-food industry chain to provide nutritious and healthy food for

Table 17.1 Comparison of three generations of knowledge management

	KM1.0	KM2.0	KM3.0
Practice Mode	*Capitalization*	*Contextualization*	*Intellectualization*
Feature Description	• focus on explicit knowledge • invest in the construction of content • strive to collect knowledge to make it become valuable intellectual assets of the organization	• focus on tacit knowledge • people oriented • emphasize the connection between people, content and business context	• build an intelligent ecosystem of knowledge • form knowledge diversity • stimulate more individuals' creativity and awaken their inner wisdom
KeyElements	Content	Context	Intelligence
Implementation Strategy	Accumulating	Connecting	Co-creating
Function Focused	Document management, knowledge classification, access rights management, knowledge search, knowledge wiki, knowledge statistics, etc.	Community of practice, Questioning & Answering, knowledge extraction, expert network, knowledge map, knowledge integral, etc.	Knowledge field, ecological alliance, intelligent recommendation, knowledge graph, wisdom awakening, knowledge transaction, etc.
MajorProblems	• How to construct organizational knowledge management software system scientifically and systematically? • How to balance the contradiction between knowledge sharing and information confidentiality? • How to find the knowledge quickly and conveniently? • How to motivate employees to submit knowledge spontaneously and actively?	• How to mine and extract tacit knowledge effectively? • How to integrate knowledge with business scenarios? • How to connect people with other people, people with content and content with other content? • How to establish knowledge network and knowledge service?	• How to stimulate knowledge creation by creating field environment? • How to push artificial intelligence technology into knowledge management software system? • How to effectively awaken the individual's self-sufficient wisdom? • How to realize value through knowledge management?

human beings. Thus, life science, health, and nutrition were hoisted to the strategic level of the Group's development.

In such an expectation, COFCO Nutrition and Health Research Institute (NHRI) emerged as the times require. Founded in 2011, NHRI has 8 R&D centers, including KM center, with more than 200 employees. As a central R&D and innovation institution of COFCO, NHRI is a typical knowledge technology intensive organization, with the creation of new knowledge as the main body and the gathering of knowledge talents. Since the establishment of the Research Institute, knowledge management has been accompanied and given high expectations. After that, it went through the "construction stage" (2011–2013) and began to move toward the "expansion stage" (2014–2016), with many twists and turns.

Challenge

NHRI has launched two different knowledge management software systems in 2010 and 2012, respectively. The first system is KM and the second system is newKM. The first KM system was established temporarily during the preparatory period of the Institute, and a ready-made knowledge management software product was purchased directly from the market for deployment and use. As a temporary transition, the KM system accumulated more than 3,300 knowledge systems or modules before and after, and was finally abandoned.

The second newKM system planned three modules, namely knowledge base, expert database and community. Under the guidance of a knowledge management service provider, the project has experienced the work of planning knowledge type, organizing file upload activities, perfecting platform integration and formulating knowledge management white paper. However, due to the replacement of project manager, lack of professional ability, unstable system performance and lack of interface friendliness, the new KM system only went online with a module of knowledge base, and finally became a pure document management system.

After experiencing the first two systems, NHRI is also reflecting on "what kind of knowledge management system needed". Is knowledge management software a system that allows people to upload documents mechanically and in accordance with fixed classification?

Approach of KM Practice

Therefore, the C3 platform strategy with the core concepts of "connect", "communicate" and "collaborate" has been formally put forward. Web2.0 elements such as social network, community of practice, comment & interaction, micro-blogging and mobile Internet were introduced (Qinghai Wu, 2016a).

Since late November 2013, C3 has been launched in succession, including portal, community, experts, blog, microblog, wiki, task, meeting, calendar, activity, news and other modules which are closely related to the work of employees.

At the same time, corresponding publicity and promotion, mechanism construction and cultural activities are coordinated. As soon as the new C3 platform was launched, it immediately won everyone's unanimous favor and numerous praise. Adhering to the spiral rising principle of fast running and agile iteration, C3 overall planning continuously absorbs the first-line needs of users for upgrading and optimization, and decomposes them into modules for short-term development, release and optimization.

Combined with the work scene, some knowledge topics were introduced, such as standard system, common templates, science and technology conference, introduction of Research Institute, new employee induction, etc.

In addition, C3 mobile app was officially launched in June 2014, which is convenient to view the personnel, news, announcements, blogs and other developments of the Research Institute through smart phones anytime and anywhere, greatly improving the efficiency of work.

According to statistics, the page view (PV) of C3 on weekdays is 18 times per person on average, and the unique visitor (UV) is 55% of the total number of people in the organization. At the end of 2014, according to the internal satisfaction survey, C3 became everyone's favorite application system, with a penetration rate as high as 98%, and 89% people said they liked to use it. According to the survey at the end of 2015, the satisfaction of C3 has improved to a certain extent, and 91% of the people said they like to use it.

In practice, NHRI tends to connect knowledge with business scenarios. Adhering to the core work guiding principle of "service innovation, support R&D", based on the analysis of research and development core business process, NHRI knowledge management chooses to focus on the following aspects to make key breakthroughs.

1) **Academic resources**: build a one-stop academic resources integration platform to integrate academic journals, conference papers, dissertations, standard patents, e-books, foreign literature and other resources.

2) **Innovative intelligence**: combined with the existing intelligence needs of the Research Institute, the feasibility study of the intelligence management system is carried out, the demand scheme is completed, the intelligence management system is established and the work of industry intelligence push is strengthened.

3) **Practice community**: improve and optimize different columns of C3 platform, consider thematic operation promotion mode in community operation and closely integrate with the culture and development stage of the Research Institute.

4) **Idea management**: creative work should be institutionalized and processed. It is stipulated that the source of all projects should come from the creative system. The collection of ideas from the outside should be paid attention.

5) **Project management**: improve the R&D process and PLM system construction, continue to optimize and expand PLM phase II, and explore the mode of promotion and expansion to other institutions outside the Research Institute.

6) **Drawing and file management**: build a book and file management system, cooperate with the project department to complete the infrastructure file sorting and shelving work. Based on the technology and product projects, the document management mechanism is established, and the knowledge harvesting link is embedded in the milestone node and project closing stage.

7) **Patent management**: patent mining work continues to improve the quality of patents on the basis of reaching a certain number, and try to study the feasibility of establishing intellectual property trading center.

8) **Internal journals**: try to sort out the R&D achievements, establish internal journals and enhance the industry influence of the Institute.

Result

After years of hard work, NHRI accumulated a lot of knowledge. In 2014 and 2015, it had some achievements and gradually been recognized by insiders. In 2014, NHRI won the most admired knowledge enterprise (MAKE) Award in China. In 2015, after winning the 2015 China MAKE award and the 2015 Asian MAKE award, NHRI achieved triple jump and won the 2015 global IOU (independent operating unit) MAKE award! This is the only enterprise from mainland China to enter the global MAKE award in 2015, and is also the second mainland Chinese enterprise to win the award!

As a foundation and backbone of the Institute, the benefits can be obtained from the following three levels through knowledge management:

1) **Leave behind traces of work.** For example, after C3 went online, it effectively precipitated the knowledge assets of the organization, and various types of knowledge increased year by year through continuous accumulation. By the end of 2015, the Institute had jointly

established 46 practical communities, including 442 experts, accumulated more than 10,000 documents, more than 13,000 comments, 16,000 micro blogs, more than 600 posts, 1,250 news announcements, more than 850 posts, 135 activities and 2,200 encyclopedia wikis. These knowledge resources provide a solid foundation for the subsequent staff to browse, search, process and so on.

2) **Process and reuse existing knowledge.** For example, the academic resources system has been put into trial operation since April 8, 2015, and has been widely praised by R&D personnel. By the end of 2015, there were 230,000 documents downloaded, more than 100 sci-tech novelty search needs, more than 350 agency search needs and nearly 10,000 documents delivered. For example, since the trial operation of the library management system on May 20, 2015, 3,563 paper books and 16,138 e-books have been put on shelves; by the end of 2015, more than 1,200 paper books had been borrowed.

3) **Improve and create new knowledge**. For example, in terms of patents, the Institute had achieved a significant breakthrough in the number of patent applications in 2014, and 102 new applications had been filed (222% growth over 2013), including 86 invention patents, 12 utility models and 4 designs patents. The Research Institute has won the most awesome award of the patent management of COFCO. In 2015, the patent work continued to make great achievements, with 108 new patents applied, including 87 invention patents, 9 utility model patents and 12 design patents. For example, in the aspect of creative idea collection, the Institute launched the "2015 COFCO nutrition and health research university enterprise joint creative idea competition", jointly with China Agricultural University, Jiangnan University, Hebei University of technology and other universities. A total of 55 outstanding food innovations related to the group's business were collected, and finally 13 outstanding ideas were successfully incubated.

Common Pitfalls in the Implementation of Enterprise Knowledge Management

Of course, many enterprises are promoting the implementation of knowledge management, not plain sailing. When enterprises implement knowledge management, we find some common pitfalls which need special attention and avoidance.

Pitfall 1: Focus Only on Software System, Not on Operation Planning

In many people's minds, knowledge management is often equivalent to knowledge base, the implementation of knowledge management is to develop a set of knowledge management software system platform. In fact, this is a very dangerous cognition. Many enterprises adhere to this kind of habitual thinking, so they have fallen too far in this aspect.

Knowledge management is an interdisciplinary field, which involves everyone and every department. In the practice cases of well-done enterprise knowledge management, we find that they tend to balance "strategy, process, technology, personnel, culture" and other elements, and attach importance to "planning + development + operation", rather than just one aspect.

Pitfall 2: Only Want Short-Term Harvest, Not Long-Term Persistence

The wine of knowledge needs time to polish and brew. The bench will be cold for ten years! If you can't bear it, you can't make achievements in your own field. The field of knowledge management is in line with the same law, with a small achievement in three years and a big achievement in ten years. Many enterprises expect knowledge management to achieve results and show its value in a short time, which often brings greater disappointment.

The logic of knowledge management often follows "thinking by reason". Just like physical fitness, we need to persist for a long time, and we can't relax. If it takes 30 days for the lotus to bloom all over the pond, half of the time is actually the day before the countdown. Experts also need to deliberately practice for 10,000 hours to make achievements in a certain field. In the end, it's not luck and intelligence, but perseverance.

Pitfall 3: Only Build System Framework, Not Bind Business

Knowledge management should not be separated from business. One is that knowledge comes from business and serves business at the same time. The second is to integrate the idea of knowledge management into business: knowledge management is business. Learning in advance, learning in practice and learning after the event run through the business, making the closed loop of learning, reflection and practice an inherent habit of everyone.

If you want to deeply bind business, you need to mine those typical knowledge scenarios that can produce business value, that is, to find business motivation. In addition, it is necessary to build knowledge management capability at the organizational level. For example, KMBP mechanism can be established to bridge the distance from the front line of business. At the same time, we need to establish a knowledge management seed team in the business department, and empower them through training, certification, exercise and other ways, so that they can become the engine of the business end.

Pitfall 4: Only When Tactical Movement, Not Strategic Change

For enterprises that do well in knowledge management, we also observe a common phenomenon: knowledge management is often a top-notch project, which will get the continuous attention and support of the company's senior leaders. The biggest twists and turns of knowledge management in many companies, one of the key factors is the change of leaders in charge and their strategic concerns. Therefore, knowledge management needs to be seen not only as a tactical movement, but also as an organizational strategic change.

To raise knowledge to the strategic level of the company, it is necessary to formulate knowledge management objectives, development plans, development paths, strategic grasp and action outlines at the organizational level, and form annual work priorities and action plans at the departmental level. Senior managers should set an example, actively advocate knowledge management and provide resource guarantee. Managers at all levels of the department can give specific support to knowledge management and participate in it personally. Employees should believe that knowledge can change their destiny and turn continuous learning, innovation, transformation and evolution into their lifelong belief.

Pitfall 5: Only in the Matter of External Demand, Not by Inner Driving Force

Of course, if we want to enable every employee to carry out "self-operation" knowledge management for a long time, the most difficult thing is how to stimulate their inner driving force. Enterprises can constantly require employees from the "thing" level, for example, to leave records in their work, to reflect and summarize best practices, to create and extract knowledge, to actively submit shared knowledge and finally to flexibly use knowledge in practice.

However, if we do not solve the problem from the "heart" of employees and let them realize that the first benefit of doing knowledge management is themselves, it is difficult to really let employees recognize knowledge management in their heart and then change their behavior. Therefore, the change of cognition needs to be from the beginning to the end. First, add points for personal learning and growth, and then enlarge the value through organization level knowledge management.

Summary

With the rapid development of technology, management ideas emerge one after another, and innovation and breakthrough are accelerating. The past is important, but the future is more important. Three generations of knowledge management: let's see clearly the development and iteration of knowledge management practice in Chinese enterprises over the past 20 years. Facing the future, the development path of knowledge management is not clear, and needs further practice and observation. The best way to subvert yourself is to give up the success of the past, enter the picture of the future and define the future with the future. The same is true of knowledge management practice, which needs more leaders to practice and explore.

References

Chen, J., (2017). *Management*. Beijing, China: Renmin University of China Press.
Chen J., (2021). *Holistic Innovation: Exploring an Emerging Innovation Paradigm of the New Era*. Beijing, China: Science Press.
Chen, J., Zheng G., (2016). *Innovative Management to Win Sustainable Competitive Advantage*. Beijing, China: Peking University Press.
Jiang, Zemin (1998). "Inheriting and Carrying Forward the Glorious Tradition of the May 4th Movement, Speech at the Centennial Celebration of Peking University", *People's Daily*, May 4.
Milton, N., Lambe, P., (2018). *The Knowledge Manager's Handbook: A Step-by-Step Guide to Embedding Effective Knowledge Management in your Organization*. Beijing: Posts and Telecommunications Press.
Nonaka, I., Takeuchi, H., (2019). *The Knowledge-Creating Company*. Beijing: Posts and Telecommunications Press.
Nonaka, I., Takeuchi, H., (2020). *The Wise Company: How Companies Create Continuous Innovation*. Beijing: Posts and Telecommunications Press.
Organization for Economic Cooperation and Development (OECD) (1996). "The Knowledge-Based Economy", Paris. Available online: https://basicknowledge101.com/pdf/KNOWLEDGE-BASED%20ECONOMY.pdf (accessed on 8 November 2021).
Wu, Q., (2016a). "Study on the Concept and Strategies of Organizational 'Knowledge Plus' in the Internet Era", *Knowledge Management Forum*, 2016(1): 17–24.
Wu, Q., (2016b). "Three Iterations of Knowledge Management Practice", *Enterprise Management*, 2016(11): 20–23.
Wu, Q., (2020). "Knowledge Extraction: Amplifying the Value of Knowledge Management", *Knowledge Management Forum*, 2020(4): 227–233, doi: 10.13266/j.issn.2095–5472.2020.021.
Wu, Q., Wang, M., Xia, J.-H., (2015). *The Secret of Knowledge + Practice*. Beijing: World Knowledge Press.
Wu, Q., Wang, B.-M., Gong, Y.-N., (2017). *The Secret of Knowledge+ Practice II*. Beijing: World Knowledge Press.

18

COLLECTIVE KNOWLEDGE AND SOCIAL INNOVATION IN COMMUNITIES OF PRACTICE

The Case of the Slow Food Movement in Italy

Luca Cacciolatti and Soo Hee Lee

Introduction

The purpose of this chapter is to present a novel knowledge management model for communities of practice (CoPs) to foster social innovation by leveraging collective knowledge. We use the case of the Slow Food Movement (SFM) in Italy to analyse how collective knowledge in a local population can be used by CoPs to enhance social innovation. The SFM is an organisation born in Italy in 1986 with the aim of promoting local food and traditional cooking as an alternative to fast food. As part of its remit, the SFM features the promotion of traditional and regional cuisine, small businesses operating in short food chains, sustainable farming of plants, seeds, and the rearing of livestock that are typical of a regional ecosystem.

In 1986, Mr Carlo Petrini started 'Arci Gola', a cultural association with the aim of spreading a new philosophy of appreciation of local culinary heritage that focused on the hedonistic pleasure deriving from the consumption of high-quality food and wine while having an eye of regard for that specialist knowledge that only food connoisseurs have, as reported in *Vent'anni a ritmo Slow da Arcigola a Terra Madre* (2006), published in the Italian national quality paper *La Stampa*.

In this chapter, we propose that collective knowledge gathered through market intelligence activity is a necessary social resource and input to the formation and development the CoP. We argue that collective knowledge contributes to the formation of a social structure and then leads to social innovation via mechanisms of joint enterprise, mutual engagement, and shared repertoire. More specifically, CoPs can leverage market intelligence as a social resource through customers' engagement and tacit knowledge embedded in the local culture of a geographical area can be captured by the CoP and made explicit so as to fuel participation and the reification process, typical of CoPs.

When looking at the case of the SFM, we see how the preservation of tacit knowledge (Von Krogh et al., 2012) enshrined in the local territory of the Piedmont region in Italy fuelled an anti-globalisation discourse that managed to spread like wildfire worldwide. The original trigger for the creation of the movement was the plan for the opening of a branch of MacDonald's in Rome's Spanish Steps in 1986. Although that specific attempt to prevent a MacDonald's branch opening failed, at a later stage the founding members of the SFM

DOI: 10.4324/9781003112150-21

started working collaboratively with whoever was concerned about how fast food negatively affected their lives. The discourse on fast-food restaurants is centred around the idea of modernity and a fast-paced lifestyle. On the contrary, the SFM symbolises the fight against the speed and efficiency promoted by corporate rationality, which purports to maximise value for shareholders of large corporations while eroding value for citizens who find their local food heritage threatened by mass production and consumption of food (Bessière, 1998).

In this chapter, we posit that the SFM contributed to a form of social innovation in its own right and it is relevant to an enhanced understanding of knowledge management (KM) because of a particular characteristic of the SFM, that is, a CoP where the consumer is also the producer. We already know that the

> engagement in social contexts involves a dual process of meaning making. On the one hand, we engage directly in activities, conversations, reflections, and other forms of personal participation in social life. On the other hand, we produce physical and conceptual artifacts—words, tools, concepts, methods, stories, documents, links to resources, and other forms of reification—that reflect our shared experience and around which we organize our participation.
>
> *(Wenger, 2010: 180)*

In this regard, the innovativeness of the SFM goes beyond antagonising fast food restaurants where mass producers quickly feed the masses. It proposes an alternative discourse by which the local culture of the Piedmontese region allows for the producer-consumer duality typical of a healthier, slower-pace lifestyle. Furthermore, it also extends this discourse into a system of collective knowledge that acts as a catalyst for change to the benefit of societal advancement.

The negative effects of rationalisation can be seen in the emergence of undisputable leadership (Weber, 2002) and in the suppression of traditional values and emotions for the sake of efficiency, calculability, predictability, and control (Ritzer, 1992). The SFM mitigated the effects of such a wave of rationalisation in the food industry by means of the founders' knowledge of the territory and the local culture. In this regard, their success is largely due to their ability in creating and manage knowledge effectively, proving that KM is functional to social prosperity. KM is useful for CoPs' understanding of the role that data and information play in generating knowledge that can contribute to the enhancement of social welfare and innovation.

While the SFM is a CoP with strong leadership, whether knowledge has to be managed by adopting a top-down rather than a bottom-up approach is a matter of debate (Fromhold-Eisebith and Eisebith, 2005). The issue of governance in the creation of knowledge is important because private and public actors have different agendas, with a predominant focus on social innovation issues in public sector organisations (Mulgan et al., 2007). Thus, it becomes paramount for countries to foster social innovation within the private and public sectors in order not to polarise power in either of the sectors, but should governments lead on social innovation?

Various forms of co-creation seem to be a successful model for innovation in many different parts of the world (Seltzer and Mahmoudi, 2013). Citizens can gather in association and find common solutions to common problems by trial and error (Lee et al., 2012) and they can become innovators under the condition of association into CoPs. CoPs set the ground for the cross-fertilisation of ideas, the creation of knowledge, and the pursuit of social innovation.

Thus, in this chapter, the SFM is explored in light of the dynamics typical of CoPs. We explain the mechanisms underlying the creation, consolidation, and dissemination of knowledge via CoPs in a social innovation context.

The SFM is an iconic case where a bottom-up approach to social innovation bore tremendous success. Our novel KM framework adopts Wenger's (1998a) CoP framework to analyse how the SFM leveraged on tacit collective knowledge embedded in the local population, collected it through market intelligence (information deriving from the local heritage and from customers' engagement) and then used it to establish a specific common knowledge domain. The creation of such a domain allowed the build-up of the social fabric of the Slow Food community that enabled participatory behaviour and reification. In what follows, we introduce the theoretical background for our novel KM model for CoPs fostering social innovation.

Theoretical Framework

The Community of Practice as an Enabler of Social Innovation

Social innovation and social mission. Social innovation is defined as 'innovative activities and services that are motivated by the goal of meeting a social need and that are predominantly diffused through organizations whose primary purposes are social' (Mulgan, 2006: 146). It is innovation for 'social needs of, or delivering social benefits to, communities – the creation of new products, services, organizational structures or activities that are better or more effective than traditional public sector [...] approaches in responding to social exclusion' (Moulaert, 2013: 1).

The boundaries of social innovation are defined by the motivation and diffusion of innovation. For instance, business innovation is 'motivated by profit maximization and diffused through organizations that are primarily motivated by profit maximization' (Mulgan, 2006: 146). Mulgan (2006) also acknowledges that there are several borderline cases to the definition of social innovation, e.g., products or services developed for a social purpose and then adopted by businesses or other for-profit organisations with a social mission.

To address these blurred definition boundaries, Cacciolatti, Rosli, Ruiz-Alba, and Chang (2020) point out that the social purpose is indeed important in determining the business motives of an organisation engaging with social innovation but not only social enterprises engage with social innovation. Therefore, they proposed that social mission should be incorporated in the definitions of social innovation and social enterprise as 'a lot of for-profit organisations engage in social innovation' (Altuna et al., 2015) as they could also have a social purpose without necessarily being classified as social enterprises.

As identified by Moulaert et al. (2005), three dimensions of social innovation are the satisfaction of unmet needs, changes in social relations, and an empowerment dimension that increases socio-political capabilities and access to resources. Although many definitions of social innovation have been developed over time (see Van der Have and Rubalcaba, 2016), for the purpose of this chapter, we define social innovation as '*innovative activities that provide a solution to societal problems and that are underpinned by the pursuit of a social mission*'. At the basis of social innovation, there is a need to promote a social mission and often this is made possible because of knowledge sharing among users, be it individuals or groups of users. CoPs offer a fertile ground for the accumulation, utilisation, and diffusion of collective knowledge.

Communities of Practice: domain and community. CoP as a concept originated from the situated learning theory (Lave, 1988). The constituting elements of CoPs are the participation of the members in the practices of a community and the identification of the members with that community, which gives them a sense of belonging (Lave, 1991). CoPs are 'are groups of people who share a concern, a set of problems, or a passion about a topic, and who deepen their knowledge and expertise in this area by interacting on an ongoing basis' (Wenger et al., 2002: 4). When looking at the boundaries of CoP, they differ from a club of friends or from a network because communities of practice need to satisfy the existence of a common *domain* of interest that justifies the members to get together and to engage with each other (Wenger, 2010). Examples of CoP are

> artists [that] congregate in cafés and studios to debate the merits of a new style or technique. Gang members learn to survive on the street and deal with an unfriendly world. Frontline managers running manufacturing operations get a chance to commiserate, to learn about upcoming technologies, and to foresee shifts in the winds of power.
>
> *(Wenger et al., 2002: 4)*

One of the fundamental processes observed in CoPs is related to CoP members finding

> their own ways of creating new work patterns, which are often different from those formally prescribed. [...] three central processes of CoPs emerged: social construction, collaboration and shared language. By adapting to these three processes, participants were engaging in joint problem solving. Thus, the focus in CoPs is not the individual or his or her cognition, but rather the interaction among participants.
>
> *(Lundkvist, 2004: 97)*

The sense of *community* in the CoP differs from other forms of social aggregation. The members of a CoP have mutually defining identities even though they contribute to the community with different skills and knowledge (Wenger, 1998b). Cox (2005) points out that Wenger's use of the term community in a CoP context implies tight-knit relationships amongst members, generally of a small scale, not clearly bounded, often presenting conflictual relationships, yet purposive and creative. In this sense, CoPs leverage a common language rooted in the members' collective knowledge to produce a social structure and then lead on social innovation via a mechanism of *joint enterprise, mutual engagement,* and *shared repertoire* (Wenger, 1998b). These are the elements that constitute the community.

They form the basis for the existence of the CoP in the concept of community *per se*. More specifically, joint enterprise refers to the partnering characteristics of a CoP. The members of the CoP comprise individual members and organisations that build a social relationship based on co-production and deliver shared value to different entities. 'Communities of practice connect people from different organizations as well as across independent business units. In the process, they knit the whole system together around core knowledge requirements' (Wenger et al., 2002: 6). Joint enterprise is binding all the members of the CoP around the understanding that their practice and the knowledge shared around that practice identifies them as part of the CoP (Roberts, 2006). An example of a joint enterprise is given by Wenger (Wenger et al., 2002) when looking at how Chrysler Corporation tried to shorten the product development life cycle to increase the company's competitiveness: the employees of different functional areas started meetings informally to share their knowledge and the managers, after seeing that informal sharing of knowledge leads to improvements in the way different functional areas were working, encouraged the creation of technology groups, i.e. informal knowledge-based groups.

While joint enterprise and the common area of interest around which practice is centred contribute to the identity of the community, members' engagement is key to the cohesion of the community. Mutual engagement consists of the established norms and interaction routines that regulate the relationships amongst members (Roberts, 2006). The relationships to guarantee mutual engagement need to be sustained over time, irrespective of whether the nature of the relationship is conflictual or harmonious (Wenger, 1998b) and 'the presence of a relationship of trust between individuals indicates an ability to share a high degree of mutual understanding, built upon a common appreciation of a shared social and cultural context' (Roberts, 2006: 628). Mutual engagement, to be effective, requires members to adopt a psychosocial filter that enables thoughtful and deliberate knowledge sharing among the CoP members. This is possible if CoP members trust each other and perceive other members as being approachable, credible and trustworthy of the knowledge they want to share (Andrews and Delahaye, 2000).

Finally, a shared repertoire refers to the production of knowledge that derives from practice and knowledge sharing, and such knowledge is embodied in some resources that are communal to the member of the CoP: a specific language or jargon, routines and scripts of behaviour, stories and narratives, and artefacts (Wenger, 1998b). As highlighted by Roberts (2006), the production of artefacts within a CoP, the 'doing things together' (p. 625) and talking about the artefacts produced creates mutual engagement. The same author also indicates that CoPs are spontaneously formed because of members' interest in a domain of knowledge which stimulates mutual engagement, thus a shared repertoire strengthens and amplifies the sense of community built around the practice by reinforcing the interest in the knowledge domain.

The element of knowledge creation and diffusion via communal resources in a shared repertoire raises some important questions about the role of practice in CoPs and the role that collective knowledge plays in the formation of CoPs. For instance, if CoPs are domain-centric and practice-focused and such a practice is exercised by means of members' participation and their creation of a shared repertoire, i.e. reification (Wenger, 1998b), what mechanism underpins CoPs' ability to capture tacit knowledge and unarticulated know-how and translate them into explicit knowledge? Also, if tacit knowledge and unarticulated know-how are held by a collective, what mechanism underpins the harvesting of such knowledge and its utilisation in building a discourse that fosters participation and reification? The theoretical foundations to these questions are explored in the next section.

Collective Knowledge as an Input for the Development of Cops

Collective knowledge is discussed in an organisational context and identified with a form of knowledge within a specific culture that is shared within an organisation (Penrose, 1959). This implies that the existence of collective knowledge necessitates an organisational structure (e.g., a collective) and agency (e.g., actions or practice).

Collective knowledge also comprises the collective understanding of social definitions, which are dependent upon human judgement (Toulmin, 1999). It builds on the personal knowledge of individuals belonging to the social group (Polanyi, 2015). Most importantly, collective knowledge found in an organisation informs collective practice (Spender, 1994). In this regard, as we have explained in the previous section, CoPs centre on a domain of knowledge whose definitions are shared by their members. CoPs' members are united in a community by means of joint enterprise, mutual engagement, and a shared repertoire. Thus, along with domain and community, the third constituting element of CoPs is practice.

Practice: participation and reification. Through practice, CoPs translate tacit knowledge into explicit knowledge through processes of participation and reification (Wenger, 1998b), which determine the negotiation of the meaning within CoPs (Roberts, 2006). It is a way of 'coupling action and connection. [...] An employee carries out tasks, belongs to a work-group, has a sense of identity through his or her skills and derives meaning through his or her experiences' (Baxter and Hirschhauser, 2004: 210). Participation implies a certain level of activity and proactivity in the community, and it contributes to learning, the creation of meaning, and the strengthening of the CoPs' identity.

Participation is intimately linked to the idea of reification. In defining reification, Wenger (1998:58) maintains that 'any community of practice produces abstractions, tools, symbols, stories, terms, and concepts that reify something of that practice in a congealed form'. An example from a quality management context is the following: reification can

> be applied to teaming as a process, statistical process control charts, the labels applied to the process, the corporate mission statements, the procedures in ISO 9000 documents, the specification of critical success factors. Improvement initiatives usually entail modifications to the way individuals participate and a new array of reification possibilities.
>
> *(Baxter and Hirschhauser, 2004: 210)*

Therefore, reification refers to the creation of tangible output or the embodiment of an abstraction into an object, or as reported by Wenger (Wenger, 1998: 58), 'we project our meanings onto the world and then we perceive them as existing in our world, as having a reality on their own'.

In summary, provided that the meanings, symbols, stories, concepts, tools, and artefacts make tacit knowledge explicit, it is not unlikely that once the reification process reaches critical mass in production and participation increases and creates some traction, then a spill-over effect may take place to enable the CoP to generate impactful social innovation. This could provide a plausible explanation for the mechanism underlying the generation of social innovation by a CoP, although the process of translation of tacit knowledge into explicit knowledge within a CoP context is unclear in the current literature. This process takes place in organisations as Nonaka et al. (1996) shows how speed and flexibility are key factors in a firm's development process and adaptation to a changing external environment. The iteration between participation and reification supposedly also requires speed and flexibility. However, these do not provide a sufficient account of KM in CoPs. We posit that social resources provide intelligence on the collective knowledge that fuels the knowledge domain of a CoP, playing a critical role in the development of the CoP and consequently in its ability to innovate. In what follows, we discuss the role of social resources.

Social resources and collective knowledge. There is an overall agreement in the KM literature that tacit knowledge is actionable and partially or fully based on personal experience (Leonard and Sensiper, 1998). Tacit knowledge comprises different types of automatic skills (e.g., use of tools, the instinctive reaction to an event) and, although not being yet explicated, can be codified (Spender, 1993). Tacit knowledge sometimes is 'semiconscious [...] while the tacit elements are subjective, experiential, and created in the "here and now"' (Polanyi, 2009, cited in Spender, 1993: 58).

Given the sense of the above definitions, tacit knowledge is a constituting element of collective knowledge as the latter is embedded in organisations or social groups (Holzmann, 2013) and allows organisations to share and recombine the individuals' tacit knowledge and to coordinate its diffusion (Zhao and Anand, 2009). Collective knowledge can fulfil the gaps of individual knowledge and reconfigure it in an instrumental way so to create value for the collective (Kogut and Zander, 1992).

The members of a collective represent a social resource (Lin et al., 1981) that CoPs can capitalise on to fuel their knowledge domain. In this regard, CoPs can leverage market intelligence to access collective knowledge through their social resources. Since CoPs are collectives in their own right, part of their knowledge may be harvested amongst like-minded adjacent collectives, and this creates a dyadic relationship between the knowledge seeker and the contributor of knowledge (Beck et al., 2014). However, the proximity of the two collectives blurs the boundaries of knowledge production. Both knowledge seekers and contributors are producers and consumers of knowledge at the same time (Jasanoff, 2004): their interactions co-produces the tacit knowledge that fuels the domain of the CoP. An example of collective knowledge is the tacit knowledge (Von Krogh et al., 2000) in the local territory (Shaw and McGregor, 2010) and

> to build a rich view of a community, a group of community members might collaborate to fully uncover heritage knowledge through conversation of joint story-telling – especially when individual knowledge might be insufficient, and requires a collective knowledge input to triangulate for accuracy and crude validation (p. 123).

CoPs can fuel their knowledge domain and feed their practice (participation and reification) by gathering intelligence on the knowledge embedded in a collective, thanks to a proactive engagement of customers (i.e., customers' engagement) and to the absorption of collective knowledge from the local culture. While this can help explain the acquisition of tacit knowledge that ignites CoPs and feeds their development, on its own, it is a necessary but insufficient condition for CoPs contribution to social innovation. In the next section, we discuss the contribution of the process of externalisation (Nonaka et al., 2000) to CoPs' innovation activity.

Thus, the ability to learn as an organisation (which fuels the CoP's knowledge domain) and a governance structure that allows for an involved and supportive leadership that facilitates community members' coordination and collaboration, set the basis for the CoP's innovation enabling role (Figure 18.1).

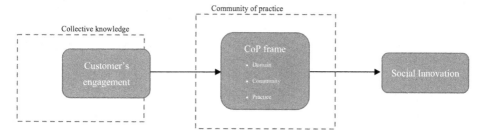

Figure 18.1 A conceptual model for collective knowledge and social innovation within communities of practice

Source: *CoP frame is adapted from Wenger (1998).

Case Analysis

Following the launch of the SFM in 1986 by Carlo Petrini, the official manifesto of the movement was published in 1987 in the supplement of the national quality paper Il Manifesto, and signed by Mr Petrini along with prominent Italian intellectuals, artists, and public personalities of the likes of Nobel Prize recipient Dario Fo. Notwithstanding the social purpose of SFM's mission, a wide network of privately run activities sprang up from this movement and their ability to externalise knowledge contributed to its expansion to over 100,000 affiliated members, over 1m supporters, 2,400 food communities, and 1,500 branches or chapters (aka *convivium, -a*) in 160 countries worldwide as reported by Dumitru, Lema-Blanco, Kunze, and García-Mira (2016).

The analysis of the SFM case study focuses on how CoPs can foster social innovation by leveraging collective knowledge acquired via market intelligence. To demonstrate the mechanisms underlying this process of tacit knowledge acquisition and transformation into explicit knowledge and its use to develop the CoP and lead to social innovation, we need to divide the case analysis into three main thematic areas: the community of practice as an enabler of social innovation, the social resources and the collective knowledge gathered through intelligence in the innovation activity of CoPs. We apply Wenger's (1998b) CoP frame throughout the thematic analysis and what follows presents our findings.

The Community of Practice as an Enabler of Social Innovation

Domain. The SFM presents a very well-defined domain of knowledge that builds an anti-rationalistic and anti-globalisation discourse. The basic starting assumption that justifies the existence of the SFM lies in the idea of *us*, i.e. the SFM, whose members appreciate the slowness of the pure enjoyment of food, along with an aesthetic and ecologic awareness of the role that the local food plays in people's lives. This idea follows a *us vs them* logic (with *them* intended as fast food), as fast food is the emblematic example of what society started accepting as the sole rational solution to the fast pace of modern life since the wave of globalisation 2.0 started.

> *Without such a thing as fast food, there would be no need for slow food*
>
> *(Pollan, 2006: 380)*

Thus, the starting assumption of the SFM lies in the fact that there is an antagonistic position between the SFM (in this case the hero) and fast food (in this case the anti-hero). This is a particularly important point as this antagonistic position to the Macdonaldisation process brought about by globalisation fosters an anti-rationalism discourse rooted in an anti-globalisation perspective. Therefore, the rationalistic values of efficiency, speed, and the search for competitiveness through a race to the lowest price have to be fought against because they are damaging to the rural communities.

> The critics to the process of Macdonaldization brought to our eyes *'an account of the purely profit-driven processes by which most people's regular food and all fast food are produced, and the dismal, often stomach-churning manufacture of meat'*
>
> *(Fox, 2008: 114)*

On the other hand, the SFM *'represents an act of rebellion against a civilisation based on the sterile concepts of productivity, quantity and mass consumption, destroying habits, traditions and ways of life, and ultimately the environment'*

(Petrini in Hodgson and Toyka, 2007: 138)

In light of this, the SFM picks the fight against that civilisation that destroys rather than nurture, that spoils peoples' lives and the environment by not respecting what centuries of local traditions taught people about the appreciation of food, the natural environment, and life itself on our planet.

Thus, the code domain of knowledge of the SMF as a CoP is *'based on the intrinsic cultural value of local production that critiques the globalized and delocalized food production system'*

(Dumitru et al., 2016: 4)

In this regard, the collective knowledge that fuels the SFM knowledge domain is embedded in the rural communities, where consumers are themselves producers of food but also have a life rooted in traditional values. The collective knowledge held in these communities is about the slow timings of mother nature, its seasons, the quality of food that is produced without putting the unnatural pressure of maximised yields in food production systems. This type of knowledge gives the identity to the SFM and allows them to distinguish between the SFM and *them* (i.e., fast-food whose production is all about efficiency and resources exploitation and consumption is focused on the delivery of convenience, fast service, and lower prices to urban citizens). Such collective knowledge contributes to the SFM's identity and puts the basis for its CoP development.

Community and practice. The level of enterprise, engagement, and the shared repertoire that define CoPs contribute to fostering social innovation, given the increase of political relevance and the ability to make changes in social dynamics. Thus, the community acts as an enabler of social innovation. The impact of the SFM on the global political scenario is undeniable and it created a novel organisational structure that brings social benefits to communities worldwide.

The Slow Food ideology *'is taken literally as to 'put perspective on the Fast Life' (De Grazia, 2005: 458 ff.) and its foundation is mentioned – together with the fall of the Berlin wall – as one of the most significant events of the last decades to mark a shift in the dynamics of Americanization. Small and slow are placed as opposed to big and fast, but – thus claims De Grazia – this happens within the market rather than against it'*

(Sassatelli and Davolio, 2010: 206)

In this regard, SFM's joint enterprise is evidenced by the initial engagement they started having back in 1983 when Petrini started the not-for-profit food and wine Arcigola association. Petrini leveraged his wide personal network as a former activist of the communist movement Partito di Unità Proletaria and as a former local political candidate for Marxist-inspired party Democrazia Proletaria in 1976 (Anon, 1976). The SFM engaged a wide number of followers through

The transnational network is present in 160 countries throughout the world with 1.500 convivia (local manifestations) formed by 100.000 affiliates and 1.000.000 of supporters. Slow Food also

counts with several national associations (Italy, Germany, Switzerland, USA, Japan, Netherlands, Brazil, Kenya and South Korea); two Slow Food International Foundations: The Slow Food Foundation for Biodiversity and the Terra Madre Foundation; and one University of Gastronomic Sciences (Bra, Italy)

(Dumitru et al., 2016: 5).

The process of co-creation through joint enterprise is evident by the large involvement of a very diverse audience ranging from the director of the National State Television (RAI), entrepreneurs and discographic directors, poets, theatrical writers and actors, editors of the specialised food-related press like Gambero Rosso, which is known nationwide, and famous singers and other intellectuals and artists.

At the time, they'd meet in a tavern called Unione in Treiso, in the Langhe region: what with tajarin and some good Barolo, Folco Portinari, who was then a director at Rai, a critic and a refined poet, got the right idea. Portinari wrote the text, Petrini collected the signatures and on the 3rd November 1987 the manifesto was published in Gambero Rosso with a snail designed by Gianni Sassi. The signatures of Portinari, Petrini, Bonilli, Parlato, were followed by those of famous intellectuals and artists such as Dario Fo, Francesco Guccini, Gina Lagorio, Enrico Menduni, Antonio Porta, Ermete Realacci, Sergio Staino and more

(Padovani, 2017)

Such a networked start of the movement allowed them to gain traction in the local area but the SFM spread nationally quite fast, thanks to all the people involved at the initial stages of development, as all of them had their own followers in their own enterprises, be it music or theatre, cuisine, or journalism. In this regard, Petrini himself had his own influence on the local community as a writer on leftist quality papers such as Il Manifesto and l'Unità, and the national La Stampa (Menétrey and Szerman, 2016). This initial group of like-minded people who were collaborating and sharing ideas in a friendly manner, e.g. over a meal at a tavern as indicated in Padovani's (2017) article, contributed to a strong mutual engagement and their ideals of democracy coming from their militancy in the communist party started being shared in the idea of democratisation of high-quality food and in the preservation of the local heritage of the peasants' world that characterises the Langhe region in Piedmont, where the SFM started.

Slow Food proposes a consumption model where people are no longer consumers, but co-producers in a democratic society [...] Slow Food has been able to introduce new ways of knowing, doing and relating in (mainly local) food systems, based on trust relations between food producers and consumers.

(Dumitru et al., 2016: 8)

The SFM contributed to the creation of *"food communities" worldwide that "break the cycle of wholesale, do not competing with the big brands but generate consumer demand of good local products, creating short marketing circuits that enhance different and direct relationships between consumer and producer. It also involves innovation in product selling...".*

(Slow Food activist, in Demetriu et al., 2016: 7)

Petrini at the incipit of the SFM was already influent in the local area and had a good knowledge of local food production and consumption routines and scripts. However, the leverage the SFM got from their engagement with local and national media and with specialised press (e.g., Gambero Rosso) that sets the standards for food and drink culture in Italy was not indifferent, and this facilitated the creation of a shared repertoire via the intense reification process that leads to the production of artefacts (e.g., creation of membership cards, intervention projects that comprise the creation of news items, publications, and events), and the creation of meaning through a narrative (e.g., the creation of a SFM manifesto and the organisation of *presidia*, participation to left wing political mass gatherings such as the Unità festival, the engagement of small food and drink producers and enabling them to be in the spotlight).

> *The movement enhances the sustainable development of local and rural communities as well as the preservation of the local cultures and biodiversity through intervention projects -"Ark of Taste", "Presidia", "Earth markets".*
>
> (Dumitru et al., 2016: 7)

> *"'Carlin" harangues the crowds at the Unity festivals: "Enough, friends and companions, with the ribs and the wine in bulk... It's a shame, so much ignorance and sloppiness! A well-finished dish, a bottle of good wine are not bourgeois luxuries, they are honest pleasures of life". A speech welcomed at the beginning with some scepticism or even somewhat of a scandalous but prophetic statement. This is true particularly today that both L'Unità and Il Manifesto publish food and wine supplements and that 15,000 Italians (3,000 as privileged "connoisseurs" members) have the Arci Gola membership card in their pocket. The association is now also known abroad, especially after the recent publication of a wine guidebook (11,000 copies sold in a few weeks) which was sensational due to the proposal to have small producers till now unknown alongside big names in national oenology, and for the revaluation of the "austere reds" for aging, at the peak of the fashion for young and light wines.*
>
> (Novellini, 1988)

The SFM managed to build a strong community around their practice. However, that practice would not have been possible without the SFM's ability to gather intelligence from their social resources and harvest the collective knowledge present on the territory. The following section presents more in detail the relationship between social resources and collective knowledge in a SFM context.

Social Resources and Collective Knowledge

The SFM, founded and lead by Carlo Petrini, gathered collective knowledge on food and drink quality directly from those social resources that held knowledge about the local traditions and history. The market intelligence collection effort the SFM that has been operating since its incipit taps into the local collective knowledge deriving from an active engagement with the SFM's stakeholders. In a rural world where producers and consumers overlap in a co-creation effort, customers' engagement becomes an essential source of information. The main sources of intelligence the SFM engaged with are:

Food experts. These experts are very specialised producers, e.g. wine producers, sommeliers, chefs, and restaurant owners. Food experts contributed with their knowledge of culinary trends to setting the direction of the objectives that the SFM embraced at its incipit and would have subsequently developed later on.

> When referring to sommeliers, *'Carlo Petrini, national manager of the Arci and president of the Free and Meritorious Association 'Amici del Barolo', a club of enthusiasts who selected Langa*

wines and delicacies and published a mail order catalogue, had summoned them from all over Italy. That experience of tastings and promotions suggested to Carlin Petrini (and to the others in the historical clique: Gigi Piumatti, Alfredo Bernoco, Silvio Barbero and Piero Sardo, all from Braida) the setting and objectives of what in a few years would become the most important Italian food and wine association and the international Slow Food movement. And that is to spread beyond the restricted sphere of specialists and gourmets the word of quality, territoriality, honest prices, the defence of the right to pleasure as one of the foundations of coexistence. «Wine - says Carlo Petrini (in the photo) - was immediately at the centre of Arcigola's interests'.

(Anon, 1996)

Farmers and producers, food processors, and artisans. Amongst the holders of collective knowledge, we find a plethora of actors in the food and drink supply chain, which in a local geographical area combined together in what we could interpret as the supply-side of the market (as opposed to consumers, i.e. the demand-side of the market). These supply-side actors engage proactively with each other and they immediately see opportunities in adhering to the SFM cause (be it for commercial reasons or for ideology, or both). The participation that derived from their engagement and their joint enterprise fuelled further the knowledge domain that strengthened the SFM identity.

The SFM Carlo Petrini reports: 'I think that, in order to get out of a strictly "missionary" perspective in dealing with the problems of the most difficult areas, it is now absolutely necessary to carry out these exchanges, bringing farmers, artisans and producers to know other realities, to allow them to find simple solutions to problems that seem insurmountable or simply to find encouragement to continue and improve their humble but precious "gastronomic" work'.

(Petrini, 2004)

A journalist of La Stampa, in an article that reports Petrini's words in double inverted commas, narrates that In Italy, the success and attention to food and wine issues have also created distortions and cunning acts ("how much Colonnata lard is available in the market today?"). This gave birth to the new rich ("in my Langhe region, the hills are covered with vines with Nebbiolo to make Barolo, the sons of wine producers drive Porsche»). And "fusion" cuisine appears in restaurants with "celebrity chefs, no longer with memories of the tradition, and thirst for success on TV programmes". Carlin looks at the heroic farmers who have not given up: "And I would like our president Ciampi, when he chooses the appointments to Knighthood for Labour, on the 2nd of June, to provide in this sector not only the biographies of the owner of MacDonald's in Italy and of that Francesco Amadori, who produces industrial chicken, but also the biographies of some real farmers"

(Miravalle, 2002)

Petrini recognised that there cannot be a culture of good food, of good taste, without an agriculture that produces that quality. The defence of farmers and biodiversity is an important part of the transition of the food system from the culture of fast food, of toxic food, to what the Slow Food movement seeks to spread, that is, a culture of eating well'.

(Shiva, 2005)

Category associations. The SFM also built strong ties with category associations and in some cases it enables their creation, channelling their knowledge in different areas of the food and drink industry and enabling the creation of initiatives focused on specific products and produce, nationally and internationally, e.g. Piedmontese meat, cheese, wine, and Indian

Basmati rice to mention just a few examples. Category associations, with their collective knowledge, inform the creation of the different *convivia* and fuel the SFM's discourse while enhancing their practices' legitimacy.

> *Special attention will be paid to Piedmontese meat, of which Fossano is considered the cradle. Proof of this is the fact that the first concrete Slow Food initiative on meat was born in the Fossano area: the "La Granda" association, which brings together about fifteen small Piedmontese cattle breeders, who adhere to very strict breeding regulations'.*
>
> (Anon, 2000)

> *Navdanya, the movement for biodiversity that I, Vandane have set up in India, has created two Presidia with Slow Food, one for Basmati rice and the other for mustard oil. It was necessary to protect Basmati - an aromatic rice that grows in my land, the Doon Valley - because a Texan company, RiceTec, had secured a patent claiming to have "invented" our rice, its aroma, its unique grain and even the cooking methods.*
>
> (Shiva, 2005)

Consumers. In a local geographical area, these actors combine together in what we could interpret as the demand-side of the market (as opposed to farmers, etc., i.e. the demand-side of the market, as seen in the previous few paragraphs). Customers include the end-user, i.e. households, and down-steam intermediaries such as wholesalers and retailers. Their collective knowledge is essential to stir the direction of the interventions of the different *presidia* and *convivia* and provide an audience, or some addressees, for the social innovation that is generated. The anti-globalisation discourse is also present in the engagement of the demand-side of the market, with the promotion of 'groups of purchase' as a practice to contrast supermarkets by influencing what the large distribution should offer to consumers. Ultimately, consumers hold some important collective knowledge but are also the recipients of the social innovation promoted by the SFM and their power is recognised as the power of collective action.

> *The next appointment will be characterized throughout Italy by consumers' purchasing groups - says the owner of the show [Petrini], overwhelmed by applause, in a room full of cameras and authorities – direct shopping centres that will calm the excessive power of large-scale distribution.*
>
> (Minucci, 2004)

The SFM over time inspired consumers in different parts of the world, for instance, the Indian *presidium* of the SFM influenced Indian consumers and *'in 1998, after the banning of mustard seed oil, women from Delhi's slums refused to eat food cooked with soybean oil. Even the poor choose quality and diversity in food, unless a food dictatorship denies them the fundamental right to their own culture and freedoms.*

> (Shiva, 2005)

In light of these findings, the knowledge harvested by the SFM from different social resources via different forms of market intelligence contributed to the strengthening and development of the movement over time, allowing it to expand globally. Notwithstanding the importance of the domain, community, and practice, the success of the SFM might not have had the same magnitude without strong externalisation abilities (Nonaka and Takeuchi, 2007) to support their organisation. Next section discusses how the SFM's KM fostered their innovation activity.

Discussion and Conclusion

The idea of the bottom-up generation of social innovation is deeply rooted in the current literature on innovation. What is less known is the exact mechanism that enables social innovation, as most studies on social innovation address the role of the public and private sectors in fostering social innovation (Nicholls and Murdock, 2012), the link between social innovation and social entrepreneurship (Nicholls, 2008), and open source innovation, collaboration, and social innovation diffusion (Phills et al., 2008). Currently, three main mechanisms have been associated with the production of social innovation (Vasin et al., 2017): the exchange of ideas and values, the shift in roles and relationships, and the integration of private capital and public philanthropy. Notwithstanding the importance of these aspects, we acknowledge that social innovation is associated with the emergence of new routines and practices (Di Domenico et al., 2010). By this rationale, we consider essential the role of CoPs in fostering social innovation, given the striking similarities between CoPs and some elements associated with social innovation, i.e. the exchange of ideas and the creation of relationships amongst people with shared values.

This study focused on explaining the mechanisms underlying the creation, consolidation, and dissemination of knowledge by exploring the KM dimension of CoPs. By adopting Wenger's (Wenger, 1998a) CoP frame for the analysis of the SFM, we uncovered how CoPs acquire collective knowledge to be used in their reification process. We then explained two fundamental mechanisms that lead to social innovation: the acquisition of tacit collective knowledge from existing social resources (Zhao et al., 2004) and the utilisation of such knowledge within the CoP to increase the production of artefacts and participation, which makes implicit knowledge become explicit (Huang and Chin, 2018) and consequently leads to social innovation.

First of all, the SFM case study provides a new insight on understanding how a bottom-up approach to KM results in social innovation with a large impact. Such an impact perhaps would not have been possible without a clear anti-globalisation discourse that determined the boundaries of the SFM's social definition (Toulmin, 1999) and allowed to build on the personal knowledge of the SFM members (Polanyi, 2015). Collective knowledge that fed the SFM community also informed the SFM practice (Spender, 1994) while the local knowledge of the founder, i.e., a knowledge activist (Von Krogh, Nonaka, and Ichijo, 1997), was also extended to the overall organisation. Petrini's mindset, shaped by his Catholic upbringing and his subsequent affinity with the socialist ideology, and his collectivist approach to leadership allowed the SFM to build a learning organisation (Probst and Borzillo, 2008). Much of the adaptation of the SFM's practice is due to the flexible mindset of the founder, his collaboration abilities (e.g., involvement of media, journalists, TV and music celebrities, and food experts), and his coordination abilities (e.g., creation of events and interventions, establishment of *convivia* and *presidia* worldwide), coupled with learning capabilities that pushed for an organic adaptation to changing times through social action (Cajaiba-Santana, 2014).

Second, this case study also shows how the SFM developed the community and the practice elements of the CoP by fuelling its identity and knowledge domain with the elaboration of tacit collective knowledge embedded within the local community and gathered from the SFM's social resources (e.g., farmers, food and drink producers and processors, category associations, consumers, and artisans).

With this study, we contribute to KM theories by advancing our understanding of the role of tacit collective knowledge in social innovation and its utilisation as part of a CoP's practice of making it explicit by means of the reification process. We demonstrate how participation and reification in the practice of a CoP generates some shared repertoire used by the CoP to strengthen and expand the boundaries of their joint enterprise and mutual engagement through the transfer of tacit collective knowledge into its knowledge domain.

The implications of our study are to be found in (i) the efficiency of knowledge transfer and knowledge scalability within a CoP, (ii) the effectiveness of CoPs' governance, and (iii) the design of formal decentralised structures for knowledge sharing.

First, the collective knowledge generated in a CoP is deemed to be greater than the individual knowledge of their members (Johnson, 2001) within the context of the SFM. However, the unique phenomenon observed from the SFM case study is that the domain knowledge generated in the SFM scaled up quickly due to the processes of participation and reification. In this sense, the production of artefacts and interventions in the SFM has occurred at a very fast pace, compared with other common CoPs. This suggests the relative efficiency of CoPs that exist independently from a dominant business organisation, in terms of transferring knowledge (Roberts, 2006).

The transfer of knowledge takes place via the addition of each individual's knowledge to the community, which increases rapidly in the process of production as individual members' knowledge also bears partial collective knowledge from the social resources. For instance, a farmer who collaborates with the SFM brings to the movement not only his/her own individual knowledge but also the overall baggage of collective knowledge derived from the local territory, i.e., tacit knowledge that is traditionally shared amongst farmers.

Second, although the current literature recognises that 'authoritarian management is replaced by self-management and ownership of work'(Collier and Esteban, 1999), in the case of the SFM, self-management and ownership of work are backed up by a very charismatic leader with solid values matured in the course of his life (i.e., specific mindset) and strong collaboration and coordination capabilities. Thus, self-management and ownership of work may not be a sufficient condition to explain the governance effectiveness of a CoP. As demonstrated by our case study, leadership undoubtedly plays a crucial role.

Third, the CoP and KM literature show that CoPs emerge from 'an evolutionary process of learning in groups, [...] ubiquitous, [... and] form out of necessity to accomplish tasks and provide learning avenues' (Wenger, 1998a: 2). Thus, 'communities of practice evolve, they are not created. As such, they resist management as we generally think of it' (Liedtka, 1999: 7). However, the SFM did not evolve just by limiting itself to encouraging learning. Along with creating a great deal of knowledge, it also managed to design and deploy a formal decentralised structure of *predisia* and *convivia,* and even a university to facilitate knowledge sharing within a global network. This peculiar finding can enable other CoPs to design and deploy a knowledge-sharing structure that can be decentralised and yet connected to a network, like in the case of the *presidia* and *convivia* that are spread worldwide.

Fourth, during the severe lockdowns experienced during the COVID-19 pandemic, while some consumers improved the quality of their diets, a lot of others experienced food insecurity due to the disruptions to large-scale food production (Lasko-Skinner and Sweetland, 2021). Furthermore, inequality was exacerbated even amongst farmers and food producers around the world due to restrictions on open food markets (Slow Food, 2020). CoPs can provide policymakers a means to access local tacit knowledge quickly and build communities that are resilient to crises.

Our study is not without limitations that can be addressed by future research. CoPs can gather collective knowledge from social resources that are accessible to them. Such knowledge can fuel the CoP's knowledge domain, enhance its identity, and transform tacit knowledge into explicit knowledge via a process of participation and reiteration. Our proposed framework explains how such a mechanism can be conducive to social innovation. However, other significant factors such as local heritage or environmental regulation could impinge upon CoPs' KM for social innovation. Future research could investigate how these factors influence participation and reiteration in more depth. The findings of this single case cannot be generalised to a wider population, future research could develop testable hypotheses out of the proposed model and test them in a variety of CoP settings.

References

Altuna, N., Contri, A. M., Dell'Era, C., Frattini, F., and Maccarrone, P. 2015. Managing Social Innovation in For-Profit Organizations: The Case of Intesa Sanpaolo. *European Journal of Innovation Management* 18(2):258–280.

Andrews, Kate M., and Brian L. Delahaye. 2000. 'Influences on Knowledge Processes in Organizational Learning: The Psychosocial Filter'. *Journal of Management Studies* 37(6):797–810.

Anon. 1976. 'Petrini in Corsa'. *La Stampa*, May 15, 113.

Anon. 1996. 'Slow Food Compie Dieci Anni'. *La Stampa*, November 26, Special issue.

Anon. 2000. 'Slow Food Anche a Fossano: Tenuta a Battesimo Da Petrini, Punterà Sulla Carne Piemontese'. *La Stampa*, June 1, Cultura e Spettacolo.

Baxter, Lynne F., and Constanze Hirschhauser. 2004. 'Reification and Representation in the Implementation of Quality Improvement Programmes'. *International Journal of Operations & Production Management* 24(2):207–224.

Beck, Roman, Immanuel Pahlke, and Christoph Seebach. 2014. 'Knowledge Exchange and Symbolic Action in Social Media-Enabled Electronic Networks of Practice'. *MIS Quarterly* 38(4):1245–1270.

Bessière, Jacinthe. 1998. 'Local Development and Heritage: Traditional Food and Cuisine as Tourist Attractions in Rural Areas'. *Sociologia Ruralis* 38(1):21–34.

Cacciolatti, Luca, Ainurul Rosli, José L. Ruiz-Alba, and Jane Chang. 2020. 'Strategic Alliances and Firm Performance in Startups with a Social Mission'. *Journal of Business Research* 106:106–117.

Cajaiba-Santana, Giovany. 2014. 'Social Innovation: Moving the Field Forward. A Conceptual Framework'. *Technological Forecasting and Social Change* 82:42–51.

Collier, Jane, and Rafael Esteban. 1999. 'Governance in the Participative Organisation: Freedom, Creativity and Ethics'. *Journal of Business Ethics* 21(2):173–188.

Cox, Andrew. 2005. 'What Are Communities of Practice? A Comparative Review of Four Seminal Works'. *Journal of Information Science* 31(6):527–540.

Di Domenico, MariaLaura, Helen Haugh, and Paul Tracey. 2010. 'Social Bricolage: Theorizing Social Value Creation in Social Enterprises'. *Entrepreneurship Theory and Practice* 34(4):681–703.

Dumitru, A., I. Lema-Blanco, I. Kunze, and R. García-Mira. 2016. *Transformative Social Innovation: Slow Food Movement. A Summary of the Case Study Report on the Slow Food Movement*. TRANSIT: EU SSH.2013.3.2-1.

Fox, Michael Allen. 2008. 'The Omnivore's Dilemma: The Search for a Perfect Meal in a Fast-Food World'. *Environmental Values* 17(1):113–116.

Fromhold-Eisebith, Martina, and Günter Eisebith. 2005. 'How to Institutionalize Innovative Clusters? Comparing Explicit Top-down and Implicit Bottom-up Approaches'. *Research Policy* 34(8):1250–1268.

Hodgson, Petra Hagen, and Rolf Toyka. 2007. *The Architect, the Cook and Good Taste*. Berlin, Germany: Walter de Gruyter.

Holzmann, Vered. 2013. 'A Meta-Analysis of Brokering Knowledge in Project Management'. *International Journal of Project Management* 31(1):2–13.

Huang, Yen-Chih, and Yang-Chieh Chin. 2018. 'Transforming Collective Knowledge into Team Intelligence: The Role of Collective Teaching'. *Journal of Knowledge Management* 22(6):1243–1263.

Jasanoff, Sheila. 2004. *States of Knowledge: The Co-Production of Science and the Social Order*. London: Routledge.

Johnson, Christopher M. 2001. 'A Survey of Current Research on Online Communities of Practice'. *The Internet and Higher Education* 4(1):45–60.

Kogut, Bruce, and Udo Zander. 1992. 'Knowledge of the Firm, Combinative Capabilities, and the Replication of Technology'. *Organization Science* 3(3):383–397.

Lasko-Skinner, Rose, and James Sweetland. 2021. *Food in a Pandemic. From Renew Normal: The People's Commission on Life after Covid-19*. London: Food Standard Agency.

Lave, Jean. 1988. *Cognition in Practice: Mind, Mathematics and Culture in Everyday Life*. Cambridge: Cambridge University Press.

Lave, Jean. 1991. 'Situating Learning in Communities of Practice'. Pp. 63–82 in *Perspectives on socially shared cognition*. Washington, DC: American Psychological Association.

Lee, Sang M., Taewon Hwang, and Donghyun Choi. 2012. 'Open Innovation in the Public Sector of Leading Countries'. *Management Decision* 50(1):147–162.

Leonard, Dorothy, and Sylvia Sensiper. 1998. 'The Role of Tacit Knowledge in Group Innovation'. *California Management Review* 40(3):112–32.

Liedtka, Jeanne. 1999. 'Linking Competitive Advantage with Communities of Practice'. *Journal of Management Inquiry* 8(1):5–16.

Lin, Nan, Walter M. Ensel, and John C. Vaughn. 1981. 'Social Resources and Strength of Ties: Structural Factors in Occupational Status Attainment'. *American Sociological Review*, 46(4):393–405.

Lundkvist, Anders. 2004. 'User Networks as Sources of Innovation'. Pp. 96–105 in *Knowledge Networks: Innovation through Communities of Practice*. Hershey, PA: IGI Global.

Menétrey, Sylvain, and Stéphane Szerman. 2016. *Slow: Rallentare per Vivere Meglio*. Evanston, IL: EGEA Spa.

Minucci, Emanuela. 2004. 'Gruppi d'acquisto Contro La Grande Distribuzione'. *La Stampa*, October 22.

Miravalle, Sergio. 2002. 'Un Partito Mondiale Chiamato Slow Food'. *La Stampa*, June 9.

Moulaert, Frank. 2013. *The International Handbook on Social Innovation: Collective Action, Social Learning and Transdisciplinary Research*. London: Edward Elgar Publishing.

Moulaert, Frank, Flavia Martinelli, Erik Swyngedouw, and Sara Gonzalez. 2005. 'Towards Alternative Model (s) of Local Innovation'. *Urban Studies* 42(11):1969–1990.

Mulgan, Geoff. 2006. 'The Process of Social Innovation'. *Innovations: Technology, Governance, Globalization* 1(2):145–162.

Mulgan, Geoff, Simon Tucker, Rushanara Ali, and Ben Sanders. 2007. 'Social Innovation: What It Is, Why It Matters, How It Can Be Accelerated', London: University of Oxford, Young Foundation. Retrieved October 20, 2020 from https://youngfoundation.org/wp-content/uploads/2012/10/Social-Innovation-what-it-is-why-it-matters-how-it-can-be-accelerated-March-2007.pdf.

Nicholls, Alex. 2008. *Social Entrepreneurship: New Models of Sustainable Social Change*. Oxford: Oxford University Press.

Nicholls, Alex, and Alex Murdock. 2012. 'The Nature of Social Innovation'. Pp. 1–30 in *Social Innovation*. London: Springer.

Nonaka, Ikujirō, and Hirotaka Takeuchi. 2007. 'The Knowledge-Creating Company'. *Harvard Business Review* 85(7/8):162.

Nonaka, lkujiro, Hirotaka Takeuchi, and Katsuhiro Umemoto. 1996. 'A Theory of Organizational Knowledge Creation'. *International Journal of Technology Management* 11(7–8):833–845.

Nonaka, Ikujiro, Ryoko Toyama, and Noboru Konno. 2000. 'SECI, Ba and Leadership: A Unified Model of Dynamic Knowledge Creation'. *Long Range Planning* 33(1):5–34.

Novellini, Grazia. 1988. 'Dalla Langa Nasce Il Manifesto Dello "Slow Food"'. *La Stampa*, April 16, Year 122-Issue 81.

Padovani, Gigi. 2017. '30 Years of Slow Food, a Nice Italian Story'. *Identità Golose*, November 14.

Penrose, Edith. 1959. *The Theory of the Growth of the Firm*. New York: Wiley.

Petrini, Carlo. 2004. 'Se Il Pastore Viaggia Slow'. *La Stampa*, May 8, tuttoLibri.

Phills, James A., Kriss Deiglmeier, and Dale T. Miller. 2008. 'Rediscovering Social Innovation'. *Stanford Social Innovation Review* 6(4):34–43.

Polanyi, Michael. 2009. *The Tacit Dimension*. Chicago, IL: University of Chicago Press.

Polanyi, Michael. 2015. *Personal Knowledge: Towards a Post-Critical Philosophy*. Chicago, IL: University of Chicago Press.

Pollan, Michael. 2006. *The Omnivore's Dilemma: A Natural History of Four Meals*. London: Penguin Books Limited.

Probst, Gilbert, and Borzillo, Stefano. 2008. 'Why Communities of Practice Succeed and Why They Fail'. *European Management Journal* 26(5):335–347.

Ritzer, George. 1992. *The McDonaldization of Society*. Thousand Oaks, CA: Pine Forge Press.

Roberts, Joanne. 2006. 'Limits to Communities of Practice'. *Journal of Management Studies* 43(3):623–639.

Sassatelli, Roberta, and Federica Davolio. 2010. 'Consumption, Pleasure and Politics: Slow Food and the Politico-Aesthetic Problematization of Food'. *Journal of Consumer Culture* 10(2):202–232.

Seltzer, Ethan, and Dillon Mahmoudi. 2013. 'Citizen Participation, Open Innovation, and Crowdsourcing: Challenges and Opportunities for Planning'. *Journal of Planning Literature* 28(1):3–18.

Shaw, Duncan, and Graham McGregor. 2010. 'Making Memories Available: A Framework for Preserving Rural Heritage through Community Knowledge Management (CKM)'. *Knowledge Management Research & Practice* 8(2):121–134.

Shiva, Vandana. 2005. 'SLOW FOOD Chi Mangia Piano va Lontano'. *La Stampa*, May 26, Cultura e Spettacolo.

Slow Food. 2020. 'COVID-19 Pandemic Highlights the Need to Fix the Flaws of Our Food Systems'. Retrieved https://www.slowfood.com/covid-19-pandemic-highlights-the-need-to-fix-the-flaws-of-our-food-systems/.

Spender, J. C. 1993. 'Competitive Advantage from Tacit Knowledge? Unpacking the Concept and Its Strategic Implications'. Pp. 37–41 in *Academy of Management Proceedings*. Vol. 1993. New York: Academy of Management Briarcliff Manor.

Spender, J. C. 1994. 'Organizational Knowledge, Collective Practice and Penrose Rents'. *International Business Review* 3(4):353–367.

Toulmin, Stephen. 1999. 'Knowledge as Shared Procedures'. Pp. 53–64 in *Perspectives on Activity Theory*. Cambridge: Cambridge University Press.

Van der Have, Robert P., and Luis Rubalcaba. 2016. 'Social Innovation Research: An Emerging Area of Innovation Studies?' *Research Policy* 45(9):1923–1935.

Vasin, Sergey Mikhailovich, Leyla Ayvarovna Gamidullaeva, and Tamara Kerimovna Rostovskaya. 2017. 'The Challenge of Social Innovation: Approaches and Key Mechanisms of Development', *European Research Studies Journal*, 20(2B): 25–45.

Von Krogh, Georg, Kazuo Ichijo, and Ikujiro Nonaka. 2000. *Enabling Knowledge Creation: How to Unlock the Mystery of Tacit Knowledge and Release the Power of Innovation*. Oxford: Oxford University Press on Demand.

Von Krogh, Georg, Ikujiro Nonaka, and Kazuo Ichijo. 1997. 'Develop Knowledge Activists!' *European Management Journal* 15(5):475–483.

Von Krogh, Georg, Ikujiro Nonaka, and Lise Rechsteiner. 2012. 'Leadership in Organizational Knowledge Creation: A Review and Framework'. *Journal of Management Studies* 49(1):240–277.

Weber, Max. 2002. *The Protestant Ethic and the" Spirit" of Capitalism and Other Writings*. London: Penguin.

Wenger, Etienne. 1998a. 'Communities of Practice: Learning as a Social System'. *Systems Thinker* 9(5):2–3.

Wenger, Etienne. 1998b. *Communities of Practice: Learning, Meaning, and Identity*. Cambridge: Cambridge University Press.

Wenger, Etienne. 2010. 'Communities of Practice and Social Learning Systems: The Career of a Concept'. Pp. 179–198 in *Social Learning Systems and Communities of Practice*. London: Springer.

Wenger, Etienne, Richard Arnold McDermott, and William Snyder. 2002. *Cultivating Communities of Practice: A Guide to Managing Knowledge*. Brighton, MA: Harvard Business Press.

Zhao, Jaideep Anand. 2009. 'A Multilevel Perspective on Knowledge Transfer: Evidence from the Chinese Automotive Industry'. *Strategic Management Journal* 30(9):959–983.

Zhao, Jaideep Anand, and Will Mitchell. 2004. 'Transferring Collective Knowledge: Teaching and Learning in the Chinese Auto Industry'. *Strategic Organization* 2(2):133–167.

19

IS THERE EMPIRICAL KNOWLEDGE? AN OBSERVATION BASED ON CLINICAL MEDICINE

Jin Chen, Juxiang Zhou and Yang Yang

Definition and Characteristics

Definition of Knowledge

Knowledge is a broad and abstract concept, which was first defined in philosophy. Plato, the Ancient Greek philosopher, first defined "knowledge" in *Meno* and analyzed the difference between correct opinions and knowledge in *Theaetetus*. Plato argued that knowledge was composed of three necessary conditions, i.e., belief, truth, and justification, namely justified true belief. Although this concept has triggered considerable controversy for its logical flaws, it still occupies a dominant position in Western philosophy (Nonaka and Takeuchi, 1995). Then, Locke proposed that knowledge was rooted in experience, and all knowledge comes from experience. However, with the publication of *Is Justified True Belief Knowledge* by Edmund L. Gettier (1963), the traditional view that "knowledge comes from experience" was fundamentally challenged, and the rationality of empirical knowledge arising from the unique or non-reproducible experience was questioned. With the advance of the times, the traditional view on knowledge has gradually evolved to hold renewed definitions and connotations. For instance, Piaget, a constructivism master, reckoned that knowledge was a subjective existence, which was proactively built by the subject based on his or her own experience and the social/cultural/historical context to mingle with the subject world. Postmodernists then pointed out that knowledge was a mathematical symbol system of experience, information, tools, logic, and ideas that were conducive to the survival and development of mankind as generated in activities. There is no such thing as truth or universality with uncertainty (Lu and Chen, 2008). Due to the multi-faceted nature and uncertainty of knowledge, scholars at home and abroad have not yet reached a unified definition. No matter how it changes, the definition invariably centers on the processes of learning, perception, and sublimation. For example, in *Webster's Dictionary*, knowledge is the cognition of facts or states obtained through practice, research, connection or investigation, and the understanding of science, art, or technology, incorporating the sum of perception of truths and principles acquired by human beings.

The definition of knowledge makes sense only in a specific era. In today's era of the knowledge economy, Peter Drucker's definition is more widely accepted. Drucker argued

DOI: 10.4324/9781003112150-22

that knowledge was the information capable of changing certain people or things – this includes basic methods to transfer information into action and ones that enable individuals or institutions to improve or enhance efficiency by using information.

Characteristics of Knowledge

The characteristics of knowledge refer to the ordinary things shared by different types of knowledge. In traditional theories, knowledge is considered to be homogeneous. All knowledge can be transferred, communicated, and shared (Guo, 2010). However, with the deepened knowledge research, its transferable, highly contextualized, and path-oriented nature has been proposed and received significant attention. The characteristics of knowledge directly determine the effects of technological innovation and production & operation, serving as one of the essential bases for classifying the knowledge types. The views of some scholars at home and abroad on the characteristics of knowledge are summarized in Table 19.1.

Based on the above analysis, entity knowledge and process knowledge are referenced. Basic understanding of knowledge in management science, especially dynamics and validity of knowledge in the modern view, is absorbed to define it as elements conducive to completing various activities obtained through thinking, including concepts, meanings, principles, know-hows, beliefs, insights, and practical understanding. As fruits of human cognition and all perception and experience acquired during people's understanding and changing of the world, it incorporates knowledge owned in the sense of stock and knowing of practical actions.

Table 19.1 Literature on characteristics of knowledge

Study investigator	*Characteristics of knowledge and description*
Zander and Kogut (1995)	Five characteristics: codifiability, teachability, complexity, system dependence, and observability
Teece (1996)	Seven characteristics: uncertainty, path dependency, cumulativeness, irreversibilities, technical inter-relatedness, tacitness, and inappropriability
Sveiby (1997)	Tacit, action-oriented, rules-based, individual, and constantly changing
OECD's Annual Report in 1996 The Knowledge-based Economy	Five characteristics: practicality, implicitness, sharing, irreversible reusability, and metabolism
He, Xiong, and Liu (2005)	Seven characteristics: originality, stability, genetic variability, dominance, hermeticity, compatibility, and environmental adaptability
Zhang and Ni (2005)	Three characteristics: conscientiousness or implicity, context-dependence, and comprehensiveness
Zhang (2008)	Three characteristics: continuous accumulation, qualitative change and its irreversibility, and increasing returns to scale

Source: Based on articles by Guo Aifang (2010) with reference to other relevant literature

Classification of Knowledge

Overview on Knowledge Classification

The rapid development of modern science is closely related to the maturity of taxonomy. Knowledge is an essential part of human culture, and its detailed classification is the basis for further in-depth study of its essence, connotation, and management. Knowledge classification is a system that divides all human knowledge into different categories by specific needs and standards through comparison according to attributes such as correlation, difference, and sameness, to show its proper position and interaction in the overall knowledge. However, knowledge classification is a very complex cognitive activity. Due to the difference in individual cognition, goals, and perspectives, multiple classification theories, and classification methods have emerged in the history of knowledge classification, thus forming various knowledge classification methods.

In the traditional theory-oriented research of knowledge classification, the most influential is the method of Polanyi, a British philosopher's research, that is dividing it into explicit knowledge and implicit knowledge (Polanyi, 1958) based on knowledge coding and transferable perspective as first proposed in his *Knowledge*. With far-reaching impact, this classification method is widely used in subsequent research on knowledge management and technology integration and innovation (Guo, 2010). Based on Polanyi's method, the United Nations' Organisation for Economic Co-operation and Development (OECD) divides human knowledge into four categories according to the content of knowledge: know-what, know-why, know-how, and know-who (OECD, 1996). Under the practice-oriented research tradition, Holsapple and Joshi (2001) proposed a dichotomy between schematic knowledge and content knowledge, the former consisting of purpose knowledge, strategic knowledge, cultural knowledge, and basic knowledge, while the latter enveloping the participant's knowledge and knowledge artifacts. However, neither of the above two classification methods takes into account both theoretical basis and the actuality. Thus, some scholars innovatively merge the two and try to construct a multi-dimensional knowledge classification framework. Zhang and Ni (2005) proposed the octave method to highlight three dimensions: connotation, contextualization, and comprehensiveness. Since there are so many ways of knowledge classification, we don't enumerate them here. Only Table 19.2 shows the knowledge classification methods the author has sorted out based on existing literature for further discussion.

It is not difficult to find that knowledge-related issues have attracted the attention of the academic community for a long time. With the advent of the era of the knowledge economy, knowledge has gradually become the core competitiveness of various industries, which objectively promotes the development of knowledge-related research. As shown in the table above, scholars have also put forward numerous methods for knowledge classification based on different perspectives. However, the existing researches on knowledge classification are still insufficient, and the traditional dualistic thinking pattern on knowledge classification has caused insufficient understanding of the connotation of knowledge. Many scholars are trapped by the precise definition and limitation between "explicit knowledge" and "implicit knowledge", thus losing imagination of the broader connotation of knowledge and neglecting specific knowledge that features explicit and implicit factors. Most of the existing research focuses on explicit knowledge and implicit knowledge. Many of them apply knowledge as a broad concept in the research process, but only refer to the explicit part.

Table 19.2 Literature on knowledge classification

Classification basis	Knowledge classification	Source or author
Purpose of knowledge	Theoretical knowledge, practical knowledge, and creative knowledge	Aristotle
Degree of coding	• explicit knowledge and implicit knowledge	Polanyi (1958); Nelson and Winter (1982); Nonaka and Takeuchi (1995); Grant (1996); Rodgers and Clarkson (1998)Hall and Andriani (2002); Zander and Kogut (1995)
	• Non-coded/coded knowledge, and standardized knowledge/non-standardized knowledge	OECD (1997)
	• know-what, know-why, know-how, know-who	
Knowledge content	Employee knowledge, process knowledge, corporate memory, customer knowledge, product and service knowledge, relationship knowledge, knowledge assets, etc.	Feng (2006)
Perspective of knowledge management	• Management skills, technical know-how, marketing know-how, manufacturing and production process knowledge, and product development knowledge	Lane et al. (2001)
	• Data layer knowledge, program layer knowledge, function layer knowledge, management layer knowledge, integration layer knowledge, update layer knowledge, and joint layer knowledge	Allee (1997)
Knowledge transfer method	Conceptual knowledge, systematic knowledge, common sense knowledge, and operation knowledge	Nonaka (2000)
Source of knowledge	Empirical knowledge and academic knowledge	Chen and Yang (2012)
Practice type	Scientific knowledge, technological knowledge, engineering knowledge	Deng and He (2007); He (2007)
Knowledge creates entity	• Individual knowledge, group knowledge, organizational knowledge, and cross-organizational knowledge	Nonaka (1994)
	• Individual knowledge, group knowledge, organizational knowledge, inter-organizational knowledge, and social knowledge	Zhou (2006)
Epistemological perspective	• Rational knowledge, perceptual knowledge	Qian (2004); Qian and Qian (2007); Yang (2003)
	• Perceptual knowledge, rational knowledge, and active knowledge	
Applicability	General knowledge and special knowledge	Breschi et al. (2000), Court et al. (1997)
Leading level of knowledge	Basic knowledge and professional knowledge	Lane and Lubatkin (1998)
Knowledge mobility	Static knowledge, reasoning knowledge, and dynamic knowledge	Rodgers and Clarkson (1998)
Knowledge structure	Constructional knowledge and irrelevant knowledge	Henderson and Clark (1990)
Knowledge relevance	Relevant knowledge and irrelevant knowledge	Miron-Spektor and Argote (2011)
Popularity	Local knowledge and global knowledge	Alcorta, Tomlinson and Liang (2009)
Knowledge complexity	• Deep knowledge, and shallow knowledge	Rodgers and Clarkson (1998)
	• Simple knowledge and complex knowledge	Garud and Nayyar (1994), Bhagat et al. (2002)
Abstraction degree of knowledge	Operational knowledge and principle knowledge	Rodgers and Clarkson (1998)
	Descriptive knowledge, procedural knowledge, and causal knowledge	Anderson (1995)
Inner connection of knowledge	Natural science, technology and engineering science, social and humanities	Lu Yongxiang (1998)

Source: compiled by this research.

Although the "explicit-implicit" classification method has laid the foundation for knowledge researches, it is not the only way to accurately grasp the knowledge issues in the complex management context. To break the limitation of this method at the cognitive level, it is vital to search for a knowledge concept with broader semantics and deeper extension and construct a more systematic and comprehensive thinking framework (Tu, Yang, and Yang, 2015). In recent years, some scholars (such as Spender, 1994; Zhang and Ni, 2005; Gao and Tang, 2008; Yang and Shan, 2017) have made tremendous efforts to break through the limitations of binary knowledge classification but unfortunately failed to get rid of the path dependence on binary classification.

As an essential way to acquire, accumulate, and apply knowledge, learning is closely related to knowledge. Therefore, the classification method of learning also has an important influence on the result of knowledge classification. In recent years, the basis for representative learning taxonomy can be summarized as the learning strategy and learning stage in the value chain. The latter is simply the STI/DUI learning proposed by Jensen and Johnson et al. (2004, 2007) and Lundvall et al. (2004). Because STI/DUI has built the basis for the follow-up knowledge classification method in this research, the author here makes a simple analysis of the two kinds of learning and the types of knowledge generated. Scholars have widely used the STI/DUI-related concept for a long time. In the 18th century, Adam Smith, the father of economics, pointed out two links between progress and innovation in the division of labor. One innovation is based on experience, and the other on science. The two are, respectively, connected with DUI and STI. In the late 1990s, the sixth-generation innovation model emerged that centers on knowledge and learning. Now let's straighten out the knowledge forms corresponding to STI/DUI learning proposed by Professors Jensen and Lundvall as follows (see Table 19.3).

As shown from Table 19.3, Jensen's views on the definition of the two learning modes and the types of knowledge generated are better than Lundvall, because Jenson further divides the coded knowledge into scientific knowledge and technological knowledge. However, due to the impact of the traditional dualistic thinking model, Jensen did not conduct a subdivision study of STI based on this and still combined scientific knowledge and technological knowledge into one, failing to refine the connotation of knowledge fundamentally.

Table 19.3 Knowledge types related to the STI/DUI model and the production & use

Study investigator	STI mode	DUI mode
Jensen et al. (2004)	Rooted in scientific knowledge, the main goal is to produce explicit coded knowledge	Learning that leads to the improvement of implicit abilities and the accumulation of implicit experiential knowledge
Jensen et al. (2007)	Produce and use coded scientific and technological knowledge	Experience-based learning mode in "action, use and interaction"
Lundvall et al. (2004)	Science-related learning, using the knowledge and technology of applied science as the main source of innovation	Related to experience-based "learning in action/use/interaction", and use this learning as the main source of innovation

Source: compiled by this research

A New Classification of Knowledge

Classification Basis

To improve understanding the connotation of knowledge, this chapter attempts to break the "binary" knowledge classification mindset. We take Polanyi's (1958), Nonaka and Takeuchi's (1995)'s knowledge dichotomy as the basis, and incorporate the findings of Jensen and Lundvall's research on learning and knowledge forms (Marsili, 2001; Meyer, 2002; Zheng, 2007; Chen, 2013; Chen, Zhao, and Liang, 2013). Furthermore, we draw from Zhang and Ni's (2005) multi-dimensional view on knowledge classification to combine theoretical and practical aspects. Finally, we integrate the three very similar approaches: "the stage of the value chain", "the formality or informality of the knowledge-generating activities", and "the sources of knowledge generation". Based on the learning perspective and the one-dimensional entry point of the "stage of the value chain", we classify knowledge into that generated by "pre-doing learning" (formal learning) before value creation activities and "learning by doing" (informal learning) during value creation activities based on task situations. The latter is empirical knowledge. Using "knowledge content" as the second-dimensional criterion, the knowledge generated by "pre-doing learning" (formal learning) is subdivided into scientific and technological knowledge. In the end, the "scientific knowledge-technological knowledge-experience knowledge" trichotomy is formed to grasp the connotation of knowledge more entirely and systematically and overcome the problems of existing knowledge classification methods such as dualistic thinking patterns and confusion of knowledge subdivision concepts.

Concept Definition

Out-sorting of Existing Concepts

Scientific knowledge, technological knowledge, and empirical knowledge are not newly proposed concepts. Scholars have long studied their definitions and relationships, but there has been no clear standard to integrate them. Here, the author first briefly reviews the scientific, technological, and empirical knowledge in existing materials.

From the literature on scientific knowledge, it can be found that scientific knowledge is defined in the broad sense and narrow sense. The difference between the two lies in the scope of the object described. The broad sense of scientific knowledge is oriented to the intellective system about nature, society, and thinking, reflecting objective facts and laws. In a narrow sense, scientific knowledge only refers to natural phenomena and laws, namely knowledge on natural science. Although scientific knowledge can be seen in broad and narrow senses, scholars have reached a consensus on its nature and characteristics. Specifically, they argue that it is a systematic cognitive system about natural (and social) phenomena obtained through scientific research methods, marking the reflection, explanation, and description of objective objects' attributes, laws, structures, phenomena, and essences. Technological knowledge was first attached to the scientific knowledge system. Since Layton (1974) put forward his milestone claim in the article *Technology as Knowledge* that technology is autonomous, which raised technology to a symbiotic, equal, and interactive level with science, technological knowledge has become a system independent of scientific knowledge. Now that technology is defined in broad and narrow senses, technological knowledge can also be understood in both ways. But be it broad or narrow sense, scholars generally believe that technological knowledge is about how to act, and it is the comprehensive, procedural, normative, and guiding knowledge about "what to do", "what to do with", and "how to do". It is neither a reflection of existing objective things nor inherent in the human mind. Against the premise and foundation of cognition to objective things, it transforms from the reflection of objective things to the cognition of guiding practice. Compared with scientific knowledge and technological knowledge, scholars at home and abroad have done less empirical knowledge. Based on the existing literature, it can be concluded that the complexity of experience itself not only directly leads to the relative dispersion of related research content but also makes it difficult to unify the concept of empirical knowledge. The existing definition of empirical knowledge is mainly made from the perspective of knowledge acquisition and epistemology. For example, Miron-Spektor and Argote (2011) proposed acquiring experience when the organization performs tasks from the source of acquisition. The interaction between experience and the environment ultimately creates empirical knowledge; according to Ni and Wu (2012), the empirical knowledge defined in the epistemological perspective depends on people's active participation and rational thinking. It is an individual's transformation and arrangement of experience and a blend of perceptual experience and rational knowledge.

Concept Definition under the "Scientific Knowledge-Technological Knowledge-Empirical Knowledge" Trichotomy

* Scientific knowledge

Scientific knowledge is a systematic cognition system about natural and human phenomena obtained through scientific methods. Composed of concepts, laws, theorems, formulas, and principles, it describes and understands the world. The descriptive knowledge with clear conclusions and reasons features the truth, objectivity, rationality, and universality. Concepts, judgments, and reasoning are the ways of thinking that form scientific knowledge.

* Technological knowledge

Technological knowledge is a kind embedded in a specific technical product or process, oriented to solve particular problems and achieve specific purposes. Not raised to the theoretical level, it features the procedural, normative, and instructive characteristics. It usually appears as a company of technological inventions rather than some inherent skills or inertia and manifests in operation manuals, guides, and other materialized products.

* Empirical knowledge

Empirical knowledge refers to the knowledge that is generated in a personalized concrete reality. It is organically integrated with scientific knowledge, technological knowledge, and existing relevant experience. It is processed through one's perception and understanding, feedback, and memory to fit the current situation but cannot be extrapolated to other levels yet.

The difference between scientific knowledge, technological knowledge, and empirical knowledge is shown in Table 19.4.

Table 19.4 Difference among scientific knowledge, technological knowledge, and empirical knowledge

Features	Scientific knowledge	Technical knowledge	Empirical knowledge
Essence	A guess or explanation of the cause of a natural phenomenon	It is developed by humans through planned and directed research to improve the effectiveness of practical activities.	It is the memory or reproduction of existing observations or experiences by humans, and a direct transformation of objective phenomena in the human mind
Main targets	Know and understand the world	Control and transform the world	Adapt and respond to the world
Object and its characteristics	The objective things existing in nature, which are not shifted by human will. It exists objectively before the subject gains scientific knowledge. Its existence precedes scientific knowledge	Artificial material things or man-made material things, namely artificial nature. Technological knowledge first, then technical practice. It can be accumulated and transferred	Personal encounters, experience, or things gone through that are created by the subject based on experience or observation, closely integrated with the specific individual, and affected by their personality
Knowledge forms	Generally appear in the form of scientific laws and propositions	Generally appear in the form of rules and instructions	Generally there is no specific form of externalization
Knowledge types	It is knowledge "we know why is so"; it is rational knowledge that can be obtained through thinking; it is universal and public knowledge	It is knowledge that solves operational problems such as "what to do" and "how to do" in the process of practice; its application is subject to time and space conditions	It is knowledge that "we know why is so", perceptual knowledge that can be obtained by the senses, and individual knowledge that is difficult to promote

The Relationship between the Three

Although the above analysis shows the differences in the essential characteristics of scientific knowledge, technological knowledge, and empirical knowledge, the three are not entirely isolated. Instead, they are independent of but interwoven with one another. Scientific knowledge and technological knowledge are like "mirror twins". Scientific knowledge guides the exploration of technological knowledge, while technological knowledge also promotes scientific knowledge (He, 2007). Scientific knowledge and empirical knowledge are inseparable. Generally speaking, scientific knowledge uses empirical knowledge as the basis and testing standards. A good deal of scientific knowledge is obtained through the processing and sublimation of the scientific spirit based on empirical knowledge. The empirical knowledge is abstracted into public and universal scientific knowledge through analysis, deduction, generalization, and other rational thinking processes. Unlike empirical knowledge to scientific knowledge, there is only one step between empirical knowledge and technology. As Aristotle said, when mankind sums up the general judgment of a class of things based on experience, technology comes into being. The evolution from technology experience is a summarizing and extrapolating process. Often without relying on any intermediary, it dramatically shortens the distance between empirical knowledge and technological knowledge. The difference between the two is that those possessing technological knowledge can easily teach others, while those with experience have difficulty imparting empirical knowledge to others. In a nutshell, each type features different connotations and attributes, but in many cases, the three can evolve to form a complete knowledge system.

Case Study

The medical industry is driven by both knowledge and information resources. Knowledge is the foundation of work and the basis for technological innovation and the formation of core competitiveness. Without sufficient knowledge as a guarantee, there is high-quality development and innovation. Integrating theories and application, clinical medicine pursues basic cognition and highlights actual application and practice. Clinicians in the front line of clinical decision-making and medical innovation are typical knowledge employees. In this part, we attempt to delve into the connotation of three types of knowledge: scientific knowledge, technological knowledge, and empirical knowledge.

Defining Basic Concepts in the Clinical Context

Since in the medical industry, the clinical context serves as the soil for the cultivation and reconstruction of heterogeneous knowledge and capabilities, and scientific knowledge and technological knowledge have significantly different roles, learning channels, and learning mechanisms. Thus, before conducting the case studies, the author gives more specific definitions of the three types of knowledge at the premise of clinical medicine.

* **Scientific knowledge** refers to the descriptive "what" and "why" knowledge about the etiology, pathology, diagnosis and treatment mechanism used by clinicians in clinical practice, scientific research, and teaching activities, consisting of concepts, laws, theorems, formulas, and principles. Specifically, it includes medical natural science knowledge, natural science knowledge closely related to medicine, and humanities and social science knowledge.

- **Technological knowledge** refers to the comprehensive, procedural, normative, and instructive knowledge of products and processes such as medical-specific artifacts and medical-specific diagnosis and treatment technologies. It is a unique knowledge system about "what to do", "what to do with", and "how to do". Specifically, it incorporates (1) User's instructions or guidelines contained in medical artifacts (such as medicines, medical equipment, and medical consumables); (2) operation instructions, procedures, rules, and guidelines contained in medical diagnosis and treatment techniques (such as physical examination techniques and auxiliary examination techniques). However, the empirical knowledge that has not been raised to a theoretical level and cannot be applied to a broader (quasi) clinical practice is excluded.

- **Empirical knowledge** refers to the strong individual and contextual knowledge about disease prevention and treatment consistent with the current clinical situation. However, it cannot be promoted yet, formed by the clinician in the (quasi) clinical practice activities by synthesizing the specific, realistic situation brought by the uniqueness and individuality of the current clinical practice itself, organically integrating scientific knowledge, technological knowledge, and existing relevant empirical knowledge and through the perception and understanding of their senses, feedback, and memory. The empirical knowledge referred to in this research is "knowledge obtained from clinical practices" by clinicians. It is a narrow concept of empirical knowledge.

Introduction to Doctor X

Basic information of Doctor X is shown in Table 19.5. Before analyzing the three types of knowledge of Doctor X, some basic information is provided. As shown in the picture above, Dr. X is 54 years old, a master's tutor, heir to the national academic experience of traditional Chinese medicine (TCM) experts, a national outstanding TCM clinical talent trainee, and a famous TCM doctor in Hangzhou. She is currently the subject leader of the national general hospital TCM work demonstration unit, the leader of the Zhejiang TCM famous department construction project, and the Hangzhou TCM-Western Medicine Integrated Oncology Division II Key Specialist, and leader of the Hangzhou General Hospital Pilot TCM Department Construction Project. She also serves as the deputy director of the Research Branch of Classical Chinese Medicine and Inheritance of Zhejiang Association of Chinese Medicine, standing member of the TCM Tumor Committee of Zhejiang Anti-Cancer Association, member of the Bone and Soft Tissue Tumor Committee of Zhejiang Anti-Cancer Association, member of the Tumor Committee of Zhejiang Association of Integrative Medicine, member of the Tumor Branch of Zhejiang Association of Traditional Chinese Medicine, member of the Department of Oncology of Anhui Medical University, a young member of the Internal Medicine Branch of Zhejiang Association of Traditional Chinese Medicine, deputy director of the Oncology Branch of Hangzhou Medical Association and the Oncology Committee of Hangzhou Society of Integrative Medicine. Dr. X has been engaged in this specialty for 23 years. She is well-trained in treating malignant tumors such as breast cancer, lung cancer, and gastric cancer with integrated Chinese and Western medicine. In particular, she has rich clinical experience in the resistance against recurrence and metastasis of malignant tumors and unique insights in treating spleen and stomach diseases such as chronic atrophic gastritis and chronic colitis.

Table 19.5 Basic information of Doctor X

	Gender	Date of birth	Technical title	Profession	Educational background
Oncologist X	Female	1967.10 October 1967	Chief TCM Physician	Tumor, spleen and stomach related diseases	Doctoral candidate

Analysis of Doctor X's Knowledge Level

Selection of Indicators

Based on the review of the existing literature, this research chooses to draw on the studies of DeCarolis and Deeds (1999), Argote and Ingram (2000), Meyer (2002), Zhang et al. (2005), and Zhao (2013) to evaluate the scientific knowledge through six indicators of "level of medical education", "scientific knowledge acquisition network", "number of relevant papers", "quality of relevant papers", "lab configuration required by basic research", and "basic research data recording"; draw on the studies of Díaz-Díaz et al. (2006), Xu and Lu (2007), Moorthy and Polley (2010), and Shawky et al. (2012) to measure the technological knowledge through eight indicators of "professional and technical titles", "technological knowledge acquisition network", "number and quality of relevant papers", "number and quality of patents", "laboratory equipment required for clinical application studies", "applied research data records"; draw on the studies of Hennart (1991), Luo and Peng (1999), Delos and Henisz (2000), and Herschel et al. (2001) to evaluate the empirical knowledge through three indicators of "years of professional work", "medical records", and "empirical knowledge acquisition network".

Knowledge Assessment

Level of Scientific Knowledge

Oncologist X graduated from Zhejiang Chinese Medical University (formerly Zhejiang University of Traditional Chinese Medicine) in July 1991, with a doctoral degree in Chinese medicine. Since 2012, she has served as a master's tutor of Chinese-Western Integrated Medicine major in the Second Clinical School of Zhejiang Chinese Medical University. Meanwhile, Dr. X also serves as the deputy director of the Research Branch of Classical Chinese Medicine and Inheritance of Zhejiang Association of Chinese Medicine and many other provincial and municipal social, academic positions. In possession of multiple academic titles, Dr. X has a relatively rich network for acquiring scientific knowledge, and the laboratory equipment required for basic research is also above average. Dr. X has always valued basic research, focusing on research design methods and research records. Since being appointed as head of the department in 2012, she devoted most of her time to department management and team building and had no time for academic papers or monographs based on preliminary research results. Only two academic papers on the fundamental research of the etiology and pathology of diseases and the diagnosis and treatment mechanisms have been published in the past five years.

Level of Technological Knowledge

In November 2007, Dr. X was promoted to the Chief TCM Physician. In addition to fundamental researches, Dr. X also pays more attention to the clinical application of diagnosis and treatment techniques and drugs. She has published 11 academic papers on clinical diagnosis and treatment techniques, drugs, and other clinical applications in the past five years, including six first-class papers. Among them, "Clinical and experimental research on Yiqi tonifying kidney oral liquid against postoperative metastasis of gastrointestinal cancer" won the third prize of Zhejiang Province Traditional Chinese Medicine Science and Technology Innovation. "Effect of Yiqi tonifying kidney formula on the invasive metastatic ability of gastric cancer cells SGD-7901" won the third prize of Zhejiang Province Traditional Chinese Medicine Science and Technology Innovation and the second prize of Hangzhou Medical and Health Science and Technology Progress Award. In 2011, the oncology department led by Dr. X has selected the second-class critical medical specialty of medical oncology in Hangzhou. With more hardware and software invested by the government and hospitals for this specialty, the current laboratory equipment can meet the demands of the application study of Dr. X.

Empirical Knowledge

Dr. X has been engaged in medicine for 23 years and has accumulated remarkable clinical experience and a personal network. In daily work, Dr. X values the quality of patients' medical records and keeps medical records in a scientific, standardized, and detailed manner. To identify new clinical issues from the clinical work, Dr. X currently attends expert oncology specialists for 1.5 days a week, and general outpatient clinics for 1.5 days, totaling more than 9,600 outpatient visits per year and 981 inpatient visits per year. Meanwhile, she participates in in-hospital consultations, the rescue of patients with intractable and critical illnesses, and various case seminars. In the past five years, she has hosted or attended an average of 323 in-hospital consultations, 12 rescues of complex and critical patients, and 16 seminars on clinical cases such as adverse events. Compared with clinical practices, Dr. X pays no attention to and rarely participates in quasi-clinical practices. However, she cares to participate in experience exchange meetings in order to gain clinical experience from peers. She attends an average of eight in-industry experience exchanges per year. Doctor X's Knowledge Level is shown in Table 19.6.

Table 19.6 Doctor X's knowledge level

Scientific knowledge	Technical knowledge	Empirical knowledge
PHD, master's tutor, extensive scientific knowledge acquisition network, medium level of laboratory equipment required for research, standardized research records, and medium to low quantity and quality of papers and monographs	Chief TCM physician, paying great attention to clinical application research, medium level quantity and quality of related papers and monographs, and the hardware and software of the laboratory basically meeting the demands of clinical application research	She has been in the medical profession for 23 years, and accumulated abundant clinical experience and personal network, with special attention paid to the quality of medical records. She undertakes more general outpatient workload and management of inpatients, mostly clinic consultation, treatment of difficult and critically ill patients, and in-hospital exchange of clinical experience. She rarely participates in quasi-clinical practice activities

Conclusion

In the era of the knowledge economy, knowledge marks the core production factor and the most precious asset. It plays a self-evident role in management. In recent years, knowledge management has become an important research field and produced many theoretical results. However, most of them have not been able to guide the development of knowledge management practice. Therefore, exploring influential knowledge management theories that integrate theory and practice is both an inevitable trend of academic research and primary demand of the development of the times. From the learning perspective, this section proposes a trichotomous knowledge classification framework of "scientific knowledge-technological knowledge-empirical knowledge". It explains it with specific cases of clinicians, hoping to improve the understanding of knowledge connotations and enhance the effectiveness of knowledge management. Knowledge classification is the foundation of knowledge management. This chapter intends to encourage more insights on this field of study, which are worthy of a more in-depth discussion in the future.

References

Alcorta, L., Tomlinson, M., and Liang, A.T. "Knowledge Generation and Innovation in Manufacturing Firms in China", *Industry Innovation*, Vol.16, No.3, p.435–461 (2009)

Allee, V., *The Knowledge Evolution*, Elsevier Inc. (1997)

Anderson, J., *The Architecture of Cognition*, London: Psychology Press (1995).

Argote, L., and Ingram, P., "Knowledge Transfer: a Basis for Competitive Advantage of Firms", *Organizational Behavior and Human Decision Processes*, Vol.82, No.1, p.150–169 (2000)

Bhagat, R. S., Kedia, B. L., Harveston, P. D., and Triandis, H. C., "Cultural Variations in the Cross-Border Transfer of Organizational Knowledge: An Integrative Framework", *Academy of Management Review*, Vol.27, No.3, p.204–225 (2002)

Breschi, S., Malerba, F., and Orsenigo, L., "Technological Regimes and Schumpeterian Patterns of Innovation". *The Economic Journal*, Vol.110, No.463, p.388–410 (2000)

Chen, J., The Rise of the Third Generation of Management, *Caijinjie (Guanlixuejia)*, Vol.7, p.104–105 (2013)

Chen, J., and Yang, Y. J., "The Essence of Management and the Evaluation of Management Research", *Chinese Journal of Management*, Vol.9, No.2, p.172–178 (2012)

Chen, J., Zhao, X. T., and Liang, L., "Science-based Innovation", *Science of Science and Management of S.&T.*, No.6, p.3–7 (2013)

Court, A. W., Culley, S. J., and McMahon, C. A., "The Influence of Information Technology in New Product Development: Observations of an Empirical Study of the Access of Engineering Design Information", *International Journal of Information Management*, Vol.17, No.5, p.359–375 (1997)

Decarolis, D. M., and Deeds, D. L., "The Impact of Stocks and Flows of Organizational Knowledge on Firm Performance: An Empirical Investigation of the Biotechnology Industry", *Strategic Management Journal*, Vol.20, No.10, p.953–968 (1999)

Delos, A., and Henisz, W. J., "Japanese Firm's Investment Strategies in Emerging Economics", *Academy of Management Journal*, Vol.43, No.3, p.305–323 (2000)

Deng, B., and He K., "On Scientific Knowledge, Technological Knowledge and Engineering Knowledge", *Studies in Dialectics of Nature*, No.10, p.41–46 (2007)

Díaz-Díaz, N. L., Aguiar-Díaz, I., Saá-Pérez, P. D., "Technological Knowledge Assets in Industrial Firms", *R&D Management*, Vol.36, No.2, p.189–203 (2006)

Feng, J.C., *The Theory, Technology and Application of Knowledge Management*, Beijing: Economic Press China (2006)

Gao, Z. C., and Tang, S. K., "The Analysis of Mechanism of Enterprise Knowledge-Creating Based on Cognitive Psychology", *Journal of Information*, Vol.27, No.8, p.87–91 (2008)

Garud, R., and Nayyar, P. R., "Transformative Capacity: Continual Structuring by Intertemporal Technology Transfer", *Strategic Management Journal*, Vol.15, No.5, p.365–385 (1994)

Gettier, E. L., "Is Justified True Belief Knowledge?", *Analysis*, Vol.23, No.6, p.121–123 (1963)

Grant, R. M., "Prospering in Dynamically Competitive Environments Organizational Capability as Knowledge Integration", *Organization Science*, Vol.7, No.4, p.375–387 (1996b)

Guo, A. F., Study on the Relationship Between Enterprise's STI/DUI Learning and Technological Innovation Performance, Zhejiang, Zhejiang University (2010)

Hall, R., and Andriani, P., "Managing Knowledge for Innovation", *Long Range Planning*, Vol.35, No.1, p.29–48 (2002)

He, J. S., Xiong, D. Y., and Liu H.W., "Knowledge Innovation Based on Knowledge Fermenting", *Science of Science and Management of S.&.T.*, Vol.26, No.2, p.54–57 (2005)

He, K., The Comparing Research on the Scientific Knowledge, the Technical Knowledge and the Engineering Knowledge, Xi'an University of Architecture and Technology (2007)

Henderson, R. M., and Clark, K. B., "Architectural Innovation: The Reconfiguration of Existing Product Technologies and the Failure of Established firms", *Administrative Science Quarterly*, Vol.35, No.1, p.9–30 (1990)

Hennart, J. F., "The Transaction Costs Theory of Joint Ventures: An Empirical Study of Japanese Subsidiaries in the United States", *Management Science*, Vol.37, No.4, p.483–497 (1991)

Herschel, R.T., Nemati, H., and Steiger, D., "Tacit to Explicit Knowledge Conversion: Knowledge Exchange Protocols "*Journal of Knowledge Management*, Vol.5, No.1,107–116 (2001)

Holsapple, C. W., and Joshi, K. D., "Organizational Knowledge Resources", *Decision Support Systems*, Vol.31, p.39–54 (2001)

Jensen, M. B., Johnson, B., Lorenz, N., et al., "Codification and Modes of Innovation", Elsinore: DRUID Summer Conference (2004).

Jensen, M. B., Johnson, B., Lorenz, N., et al., "Absorptive Capacity, Forms of Knowledge and Economic Development", *Paper Presented at the Second Globelics Conference in Beijing, 2004*, October 16–20.

Jensen, M. B., Johnson, B., Lorenz, E., et al., "Forms of Knowledge and Modes of Innovation", *Research Policy*, Vol.36, No.5, p.680–693 (2007)

Lane, P. J., and Lubatkin, M., "Relative Absorptive Capacity and Inter-Organizational Learning", *Strategic Management Journal*, Vol.19, No.5, p.461–477 (1998)

Lane, P. J., Salk, J. E., and Lyles, M. A., "Absorptive Capacity, Learning, and Performance in International Joint Ventures", *Strategic Management Journal*, Vol.22, No.12, p.1139–1161 (2001)

Layton, E. T., Jr., "Technology as Knowledge", *Technology and Culture*, Vol.15, No.1, p.31–41 (1974)

Lu, X. C., and Chen, F., "Industrial Technology in the Perspective of Knowledge Theory", *Journal of Northeastern University (Social Science)*, Vol.10, No.6, p.480–483 (2008)

Lu, Y. X., "Historical Experience and Future of Science", *Studies in the History of Natural Sciences*, Vol.17, No.3, p.197–206 (1998)

Lundvall, B. Å., Lorenz E., and Drejer, I. "How Europe's Economies Learn," *Report for the Loc Nis Policy Workshop* (2004)

Luo, Y. D., and Peng, M. W., "Learning to Compete in a Transition Economy: Experience, Environment, and Performance", *Journal of International Business Studies*, Vol.30, No.2, p.269–296 (1999)

Marsili, O., *The Anatomy and Evolution of Industries: Technological Change and Industrial Dynamics*, Cheltenham, UK, Northampton, E. Elgar (2001)

Meyer, M., "Tracing Knowledge Flows in Innovation Systems", *Scientometrics*, Vol.54, p.193–212 (2002)

Miron-Spektor, E., Argote L., "Organizational Learning: From Experience to Knowledge", *Organization Science*, Vol.22, No.5, p.1123–1137 (2011)

Moorthy, S., Polley, D. E., "Technological Knowledge Breadth and Depth: Performance Impacts", *Journal of Knowledge Management*, Vol.14, No.3, p.359–377 (2010)

Nelson, R. R., Winter, S. G., *An Evolutionary Theory of Economic Change*, Cambridge, MA: Belknap Press (1982).

Ni, Q.Y., and Wu, Q. J., "Case-based Knowledge Management and Its Strategy", *Modern Educational Technology*, Vol.22, No.6, p.20–23 (2012)

Nonaka, I., "A Dynamic Theory of Organizational Knowledge Creation", *Organization Science*, Vol.5, No.1, p.14–37 (1994)

Nonaka, I. A., and Takeuchi, H. A., *The Knowledge-Creating Company: How Japanese Companies Create Dynamics of Innovation*, Oxford: Oxford University Press (1995).

OECD. The Knowledge-Based Economy. http://www.oecd.org/dataoecd/51/8,1913021

Polanyi, M., *Personal Knowledge*, London: Routledge & Kegan Paul Ltd (1958)

Qian, Z. H., "Why Are the Experimental Method and Logical Method Unusual Important to Science?", *Science Technology and Dialectics*, Vol.21, No.2, p.20–22 (2004)

Qian, Z. H., and Qian, M., "Two Sources of Technology and their Enlightenment", *Science Technology and Dialectics*, No.2, p.68–71 (2007)

Rodgers, P. A., and Clarkson, P. J., "Knowledge usage in New Product Development (NPD)," Paper Presented at IDATER 1998 Conference, Loughborough, Loughborough University (1998)

Shawky, H., Siegel, D.S., Wright, M. "Editorial — Financial and Real Effects of Alternative Investments", *Journal of Corporate Finance*, Vol.18, No.1, p.105–107 (2012)

Spender, J.-C., "Organizational Knowledge, Collective Practice and Penrose Rents," *International Business Review*, Vol.3, No.4, p.353–367 (1994)

Sveiby, K, E., *The New Organizational Wealth: Managing Measuring Knowledge-Based Assets*, San Francisco: Berrett-Koehler (1997)

Teece, D. J., "Firm organization, Industrial Structure, and Technological Innovation", *Journal of Economic Behavior Organization*, Vol.31, No.2, p.193–224 (1996)

Tu, X. Y., Yang, B. Y., and Yang, J. L., "'Ternary' Knowledge in the Complex Management Context: Problems, Epistemology and Legitimacy", *Journal of Tsinghua University (Philosophy and Social Sciences)*, Vol.30, No.1, p.166–175 (2015)

Xu, D, and Lu, J. W., "Technological Knowledge, Product Relatedness, and Parent Control: The Effect on IJV Survival", *Journal of Business Research*, Vol.60, No.11, p.1166–1176 (2007)

Yang, B.Y. and Shan, X.C., "Active Knowledge: The Activator for the Rising of Enterprises in China", *Tsinghua Business Review*, No.Z1, p.105–112 (2017)

Zander, U., and Kogut, B., "Knowledge and the Speed of the Transfer and Imitation of Organizational Capabilities: An Empirical Test", *Organization Science*, Vol.6, No.1, p.76–92 (1995)

Zhang, G., and Ni, X. D., "From Knowledge Classification to Knowledge Map: An Analysis of Organizational Reality", *Journal of Dialectics of Nature*, No.1, p.59–68 (2005)

Zhang, G. W., "Study on Innovative Classification and Characteristics of Enterprise Knowledge", *Journal of Tianjin University of Commerce*, Vol.28, No.1, p.62–67 (2008)

Zhang, S. H., and Fang, H., "A Study of the Relationship Between Organizational Climate and Tacit Knowledge Sharing in Industry Enterprises", *Psychological Science*, Vol.28, No.2, p.383–387 (2005)

Zhao, X. T., *Impact of Scientific Knowledge Resources on Innovation Performance*, Zhejiang University (2013)

Zheng, Y. Y., *Impact of Firm Science Capability*, Zhejiang University (2007)

Zhou, Y., The Innovative Mechanism and Innovative Model of Enterprises' Organization Innovation from the Angle of Knowledge, Xiangtuan University (2006)

20

TOWARD A KNOWLEDGE-BASED VIEW OF A BUSINESS MODEL

A Multi-Level Framework and Dynamic Perspective

Guannan Qu, Luyao Wang and Jin Chen

Introduction

As a firm's strategy means emphasizing value creation and conversion, business models (BMs) have gained widespread attention both in academia and practice in recent years (Chesbrough & Rosenbloom, 2002; Morris et al., 2005; Johnson et al., 2008; Björkdahl, 2009; Demil & Lecocq, 2010; Teece, 2010; Zott et al., 2011; Casadesus-Masanell & Zhu, 2013; Wirtz et al., 2016).

In 1957, the term *"business model"* was first introduced to academia by Bellman et al. (1957) to describe a firm's business behaviors including *"multi-stage and multi-person."* Since then, the concept of a BM began to be used in the field of administrative science as a management tool to analyze business operations and competition (Konczal, 1975). The academic interpretation of the concept of a BM has also evolved over time. In the early literature, a BM was generally described as a mode of a firm's operative activities. In recent years, with the development of information technology and the advent of the *"digital era,"* e-business has begun to rise, and the research on BMs has ushered in new situations, showing a more vigorous trend. However, although BMs have been studied for several decades, there are still great discrepancies in scholars' interpretations of the nature, structure, and dynamics of BMs (Chen et al., 2021). Neither have an underlying logic and an integrated framework based on the BM been well established (Zott et al., 2011). This is primarily due to the lack of clear ontological comprehension of this concept (Wirtz et al., 2016).

To fill up this gap, Chen et al. (2021) introduced a knowledge-based view (KBV) to re-explore the nature and structure of a BM and linked them to a firm's competitive advantages. In this part, we follow this stream to propose a multi-level framework of a BM and discuss its design and diffusion from the perspective of knowledge management (KM).

Definitions: BM as a Structured Knowledge Cluster

Why from KBV

Knowledge is often considered to be a significant asset, even more important than other resources (Quinn, 1992; Druker, 1993; Grant, 1996), for a firm to achieve managerial success

DOI: 10.4324/9781003112150-23

and gain competitive advantages through organizational learning (Lam, 2000), innovation (Lam, 2000), and product development (Kreiner, 2002), and so forth. However, when it comes to the research of business-related activities in the design, imitation, and reconfiguration of a BM, fewer perspectives have been taken from KM or KBV. In other words, existing researches have taken BM and knowledge as two separate parts and concern mainly about the role of knowledge in realizing the value creation function of the BM (Wu et al., 2013). Few studies have focused on the knowledge properties of the BM itself and discussed in depth the underlying implications of its properties (Chen et al., 2021).

In fact, a BM itself could be taken as an aggregation of knowledge. The notion of BM was first brought into the administrative science by Bellman et al. (1957) and was defined by Konczal (1975) as a "management tool" containing management-related guidance and knowledge. Then, the rising focus of e-business is helping drive a boom in BM research from different angles (see Table 20.1). Afuah and Tucci (2001) and Chesbrough and Rosenbloom (2002) see it as a "method" of doing business. Magretta (2002) regarded it as the "stories that explain how enterprises work." Morris et al. (2005) viewed it as the "representation of how an interrelated set of decision variables…are addressed to create sustainable competitive advantage[s]." Casadesus-Masanell and Ricart (2010) defined it as "a reflection of the firm's realized strategy" and (Teece, 2010) proposed that a BM is "the logic, the data, and other evidence that support a value proposition for the customer." Although difference remains in the above definitions of the BM, it is not difficult to discover that the above interpretations (such as "story," "reflection," "representation," and "logic") have become commonplace that a BM could be understood, in nature, as a kind of knowledge in conducting firm's value creation process.

What Is BM from KBV?

By introducing a KBV, we would like to propose a nature-oriented BM definition. As shown in Table 20.1, scholars have tried to interpret a BM and explore its connotation and nature from different aspects. Representative definitions such as a logic (Chesbrough & Rosenbloom, 2002; Magretta, 2002; Teece, 2010), a statement (Stewart & Zhao, 2000), a method (Afuah & Tucci, 2001), a conceptual tool (Osterwalder, 2004; Osterwalder et al., 2005), a hypothesis (Teece, 2007), an abstraction (Seddon et al., 2004), or a representation (Morris et al., 2005) show that all these understandings of the nature of a BM, in some ways, are related and converge toward the notion of knowledge. Moreover, definitions such as "an architecture" (Chesbrough & Rosenbloom, 2002; Teece, 2010), "a framework" (Afuah, 2004), "a structural template" (Amit & Zott, 2001), "a pattern" (Brousseau & Penard, 2007), or "a system" (Zott & Amit, 2010; Wirtz et al., 2016) imply that BM is the aggregation of knowledge in a specific structure.

From the perspective of KBV, the BM could be conceptualized as:

> a structured knowledge cluster of how a firm conducts business, it depicts how a firm combines business-related components (factors, resources, institutional conditions, etc.) to form business themes, and how it coordinated these themes (core strategy, sense-making processes, representative sub-models, etc.) to create and deliver value.
>
> *(Chen et al., 2021, p. 28)*

Properties of BM from KBV

In the previous section, we proposed that a BM could be understood as a cluster of knowledge. Based on this view, it is necessary to discuss further the composition and characteristics

Table 20.1 Representative definitions of business model (from Chen et al. 2021)

Author(s)	Keywords	Year	Definition
Konczal	A management tool	1957	BM is a management tool for conducting business, and "managerial guidance and knowledge is important throughout model construction and implementation" (p. 12).
Stewart & Zhao	Statement	2000	BM is "a statement of how a firm will make money and sustain its profit stream over time" (p. 290).
Afuah & Tucci	Method	2001	BM is "the method by which a firm builds and uses its resources to offer its customers better value than its competitors and to make money doing so" (Ch. 1, p. 4).
Chesbrough & Rosenbloom	Logic	2002	BM is "the heuristic logic that connects technical potential with the realization of economic value" (p. 529).
Osterwalder	Logic	2004	BM "contains a set of elements and their relationships and allows expressing a company's logic of earning money" (p.15).
Morris et al.	Representation	2005	BM is "a concise representation of how an interrelated set of decision variables in the areas of venture strategy, architecture, and economics are addressed to create sustainable competitive advantage in defined markets" (p. 727).
Casadesus-Masanell & Zhu	A set of choices	2010	"The business model is a set of committed choices that lays the groundwork for the competitive interactions that will occur between the incumbent and the ad sponsored entrant down the line" (p. 3); "a reflection of its [firm's] realized strategy" (p. 205).
Demil & Lecocq	Articulation	2010	"The concept refers to the description of the articulation between different business model components or 'building blocks' to produce a proposition that can generate value for consumers and thus for the organization" (p. 227).
Teece	Logic	2010	"A business model articulates the logic, the data and other evidence that support a value proposition for the customer, and a viable structure of revenues and costs for the enterprise delivering that value" (p. 179).
Johnson, et al	Integration of elements	2008	BM is an integration of business-related elements that "taken together, create and deliver value" (p. 52).
Zott & Amit	Activity system	2010	BM is "a system of interdependent activities" (p. 216). "An activity system is thus a set of interdependent organizational activities centered on a focal firm, including those conducted by the focal firm, its partners, vendors or customers, etc..." (p. 217).
Doz & Kosonen	Representation	2010	"…for the firm's management, business models also function as a subjective representation of these mechanisms."
Martins et al.	Activity system	2015	"The designed system of activities through which a firm creates and captures value" (p. 99).
Wirtz et al.	Representation of activity	2016	"A business model is a simplified and aggregated representation of the relevant activities of a company. It describes how marketable information, products and/or services are generated by means of a company's value-added component" (p. 41).

of the knowledge cluster. First, as one of the influential discussions from KBV, the classical division of explicit knowledge and implicit knowledge is a helpful way to understand the BM's composition and properties. From this point of view, we see the BM as a structured knowledge cluster that contains not only explicit parts such as organizational activity patterns (Brousseau & Penard, 2007), customer value propositions (Afuah & Tucci, 2001; Weill & Vitale, 2001; Chesbrough & Rosenbloom, 2002), a revenue model (Cantrell & Linder, 2000; Petrovic et al., 2001), and key resources and processes (Johnson et al., 2008), but also implicit parts such as practical skills (Hau & Evangelista, 2007), mental maps and schemas (Leonard & Sensiper, 1998), emerging meanings (Strombach, 1986), and sense-making processes (Malhotra, 2000). And the construction of a BM can be measured by the proportion of the implicit (or explicit) component.

Besides, despite the coexistence of both explicit and implicit parts in a BM, we propose that BM researchers and practitioners pay more attention to the implicit parts since it could help us better understand the essence of the BM. Unlike the explicit parts such as the formed operating systems and models in a BM that can be recorded and transferred with ease, the un-verbalized (un-coded) or even non-verbalizable (uncodified) implicit part of the BM constitutes a more secure portion of knowledge.

Implicit parts are hard to be immediately disseminated and imitated, and cause difficulty (Hall & Andriani, 2003) for competitors to copy the BM that is beginning to bear fruit. Thus, the implicit parts of the BM are essential in terms of creating the incumbent's competitive advantage.

The properties of ambiguity and high contextualization of implicit components of a BM not only act in a natural "imitation defense" to help firms gain competitive advantage, but also play a critical role in our understanding of the dynamic development of a BM. The BM was not built in a day. It is a long journey with a constant struggle, learn, and trial and error that facilitate to the emergence, formation, and development of a BM. "It is often the case that the right business model may not be apparent up front, and learning and adjustments will be necessary" (Teece, 2010, p. 187). And the implicit parts are practically useful to promote the dynamic learning and adjustment process for the implicit knowledge is often born and embedded in a social context and is conducive for individuals or teams to comprehend, adapt, and cope with the concrete situations (Collins, 2001) and rapid changes in the development of a BM.

The KBV tells us that a BM is more than just a "formula" consisting of interdependent components; it also contains the tacit, underlying logic, and wisdom of implementing and realizing the value capture and creation and putting the designed "scheme" into effect. From this perspective, the implicit part is not only the "soil" produced by a BM from practice, but also a bridge to link it with practice. A firm's core competency relies on the implicit "know-how" to put "know-what" into practice (Brockmann & Anthony, 1998; Brown & Duguid, 1998) and a BM cannot survive without using it. We believe the adoption of a KBV is conducive to a better understanding of the BM's nature, a balanced perspective on its explicit and implicit parts, a holistic view on its structure, and a more comprehensive analysis of its dynamics. In the next section, we systematically discuss the architecture of the knowledge cluster by proposing a three-level model which includes its basic components, sub-cluster themes, and the integrated cluster.

Architecture: A Multi-Level Framework of BM

Based on the previous discussion on the definition and properties of the BM, a multi-level framework is proposed (in this section) to explore its architecture. In essence, a BM is about

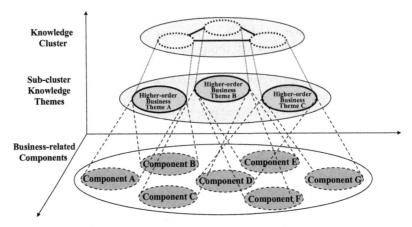

Figure 20.1   The Architecture of a Business Model

how firms do business (Johnson & Lafley, 2010; Zott & Amit, 2010; DaSilva & Trkman, 2014). To be regarded as a system (Zott & Amit, 2010; Zott et al., 2011; Wirtz et al., 2016), a BM may contain numerous components with linkages between them (Afuah & Tucci, 2001). From a KBV, this system can be theorized as a hierarchical framework. Like the structure of a firm's ***capabilities*** (Collis, 1994; Schilke, 2014), business-related knowledge can also exist on various levels. Therefore, the proposed framework here includes three sets of parameters that describe a BM's architecture: components, linkages, and hierarchies. These three parameter sets are discussed in a three-level model (see Figure 20.1).

Level 1: Basic Business-Related Components

The basic components refer to the knowledge components about fundamental (material/immaterial and internal/external) ***resources*** (Hedman & Kalling, 2003; Afuah, 2004; Demil & Lecocq, 2010), ***core assets*** (Wirtz et al., 2016), (tangible/intangible) ***input factors*** (Petrovic et al., 2001; Currie, 2004), ***value propositions*** (Chesbrough & Rosenbloom, 2002; Morris et al., 2005; Johnson et al., 2008; Teece, 2010), ***market opportunities*** (Applegate & Collura, 2000; Johnson et al., 2008), ***institutional conditions*** (Meyer & Rowan, 1977; DiMaggio & Powell, 1983; Scott, 2005), ***partners*** (Applegate & Collura, 2000; Osterwalder, 2004), ***competitors*** (Hedman & Kalling, 2003; Afuah, 2004; Kallio et al., 2006), ***customers*** (Hamel, 2000; Stewart & Zhao, 2000; Wirtz et al., 2016), ***products, and services*** (Applegate & Collura, 2000), among others. Together, these basic components—acting as "bricks" of higher-order knowledge clusters and sub-clusters—form the first level of our analytical framework as the foundation of a BM (see also Table 20.2).

Level 2: Higher-Order Business Themes

In a complex external environment, the designers of a BM are faced with a large number of decision variables (components). Some of these bring advantages to the enterprise, some might act as constraints, and some (e.g., institution conditions and networks) do both. The complex interdependence between components prevents designers from arriving at an optimal BM through exhausting the possible combinations. In this regard, the design of a BM is an innovation process that enables a valuable combination of existing components in a

Table 20.2 The hierarchical framework of business model

Level 3	Level 2	Level 1
Business model (*knowledge cluster*)	**Business themes** (*sub-cluster knowledge*)	**Basic (business-related) knowledge components**

Business model	• Core strategy
	• Key capabilities
	• Value creation processes
	• Representative sub-models:
	  • Customer model
	  • Market model
	  • Profit model
	  • Financial model
	  • Supply chain model
	• ...
		• Knowledge about resources
		• Knowledge about (tangible/intangible) input factors
		• Knowledge about value propositions
		• Knowledge about market opportunities
		• Knowledge about institutional conditions
		• Knowledge about partners
		• Knowledge about competitors
		• Knowledge about customers
		• Knowledge about products and services
		• ...

complex adaptive system (CAS). According to the NK model (Kauffman, 1993; Fleming, 2001), the usefulness of a combination is affected by its architecture. In order to efficiently search for valuable combinations in the "landscape" of numerous interdependent components, designers must "modularize" their models (Baldwin & Clark, 2000). Designers tend to nearly "de-composite" a BM into a series of business themes and then search for the components and structure to support them (Yayavaram & Ahuja, 2008). That is to say, the BM needs a second level to involve some "sub-clusters" of knowledge which represent some higher-order business themes.

These themes cover a series of sub-clusters of knowledge such as ***core strategy*** (Hamel, 2000), ***core competencies*** (Wirtz et al., 2016), ***value-related meanings*** (Strombach, 1986), ***sense-making processes*** (Malhotra, 2000), and ***representative sub-models***, which include: ***customer model*** (Wirtz, 2001; Magretta, 2002), ***market model*** (Petrovic et al., 2001), ***product and service (provision) model*** (Wirtz et al., 2016), ***profit model*** (Osterwalder et al., 2005; Johnson et al., 2008; Osterwalder & Pigneur, 2010), ***capital/financial model*** (Afuah, 2004; Demil & Lecocq, 2010), and ***supply chain model***. Each of these knowledge-based themes may involve some or all of these components above (see Table 20.2). From our point of view, these business-related knowledge themes can be specified as core strategy, key capabilities, value creation processes, and some representative sub-models.

The first sub-cluster knowledge theme is ***"core strategy."*** Core strategy describes the logic of how resources, capabilities, institution conditions, and other internal/external factors are integrated to gain competitive advantages. The relationship between strategy and BMs has long been discussed. Although there are still disagreements on some specific issues, mainstream scholars agree that strategy has an essential impact on the development of a firm's BM (Afuah & Tucci, 2001; Afuah, 2004; Teece, 2010; Wirtz et al., 2016). For some scholars, "core strategy" may even be considered the main BM component (Hamel, 2000; Seddon et al., 2004; Casadesus-Masanell & Ricart, 2010).

"Key capabilities" constitute another theme that cannot be ignored, for it portrays the design of processes and routines to realize the core strategy by configuring and reconfiguring an enterprise's overall resources. In this regard, not only are the components of core re-sources involved but the related organizational capabilities, routines, managerial experience, and practical skills are required to exploit and coordinate these resources. These capabilities could be used to form a firm's core competencies and help improve and revise an established BM to adapt to the rapidly changing environment. Key capabilities are used in the design, promotion, adjustment, and remodeling processes of a BM. It is an important parameter set in the whole life cycle of the BM and is a concentrated reflection of the merging and co-evolution of explicit and implicit knowledge.

"Value creation processes" describe the logic of the value discovery and transformation processes of a BM. As Nonaka and Takeuchi (1995) argue, the traditional information processing paradigm (Neisser, 1976) largely ignores the implicit part of knowledge creation based on value or meaning. From a KBV, we argue that the value creation process originates from the "problem setting" part, which is deeply rooted in the designer's experience, emotions, ideas, behaviors, and interactions. It integrates the processes of sense-making and information processing (Malhotra, 2000, 2005). The value created through the BM has both "semantic" and "syntactic" aspects (Nonaka, 1994): the former represents the knowledge of "problem setting" developed from subjectivity (Nonaka & Peltokorpi, 2006) and intersubjectivity (Nonaka et al., 2016), while the latter conveys the information of "problem-solving" that transforms these discovered "valuable" problems into realized value.

In addition, some *"representative sub-models,"* such as customer model, market model, product and service model, profit model, financial model, and supply chain model together form the major explicit part of a BM knowledge cluster which constitute the higher-order business themes of it.

- *Customer Model* describes the logic of how a firm's business-related offers (products and services) can meet customers' demand in a better way and create more value for them. "The special importance of customer is frequently referred to in the literature" (Wirtz et al., 2016, p. 41). The customer model represents the BM designer's understanding of customers' existing demands and the prediction of their potential demands. For some e-commerce enterprises or platform enterprises (e.g., Facebook, WeChat, Alibaba, etc.), a "customer portrait model" has become the cornerstone of their BM and is responsible for their primary business income.

- *Market Model* depicts the BM designer's understanding of competitors and the competitive environment, the decision-making of market positioning, and the awareness of *an* entry opportunity. Specifically, enterprises need to consider the competitors in the same market position while meeting customer demand. In most cases, a change in the competitive environment will moderate the relationship be-tween the supply of products and services and the performance of a focal BM (Hed-man & Kalling, 2003; Afuah, 2004). From Porter's point of view, the enterprise's market positioning is the core of its competitive strategy and the most important factor affecting its performance (Porter, 1980, 1985, 1996).

- *Product and Service Model* portrays the design of a firm's internal/external process of transforming practical skills, managerial capabilities, means of production, and labor force into valuable output. This model describes the intermediate part of a BM, and essentially concerns the implementation of a value proposition. In the lit-erature, researches on this part have mainly focused on BM-related "activities" and "processes" (Afuah, 2004; Johnson & Lafley, 2010; Zott & Amit, 2010). It should be noted that the traditional view holds that the above process is internal to the enterprise (Wirtz et al., 2016). However, we believe that the process may also be external. For the BMs of some platform enterprises, the provision process of products and services is not necessarily undertaken by the enterprise itself but can also be outsourced to partners.

- **Profit Model** portrays the design of a firm's "profit-making" logic under a specific BM. In short, it is a "formula" that portrays how a firm makes money while delivering the value proposition. As discussed by Johnson et al. (2008), a profit model could be divided into four basic parts (revenue model, cost structure, margin model, and resource velocity). From our point of view, a simplified and representative profit model of a BM should at least contain the following: revenue stream, revenue structure, cost structure, and margin condition. The model's revenue and cost could be transaction-dependent or independent, and direct or indirect (Wirtz et al., 2016).

- **Financial Model** describes the logic of a firm's financial plan concerning its BM. The financial model involves a series of sub-issues, for example, debt and equity structure (Petrovic et al., 2001; Wirtz, 2001), as well as indicators such as asset-liability ratio, equity ratio, current ratio, quick ratio, current asset turnover, and total asset turnover, etc. A sophisticated financial model provides substantial and sufficient resources to support the implementation of a focal BM and build a "buffer area" for possible shocks. It is important to note that while the financial model is a supporting element of the overall BM, it is often a matter of success or failure in practice. The financial model is a dynamic plan which requires higher-order knowledge to guide and adjust. Designers need to keep track of the firm's operation state and, if necessary, modify the financial model in a timely manner.

- **Supply Chain Model** depicts a firm's procurement structure which is subject to its BM. Although this part of BM is rarely mentioned in the existing literature, it is necessary to consider the supply chain since "neglecting this aspect may have far-reaching consequences for other components" (Wirtz et al., 2016, p. 42). This model is at the "upstream" of the product and service model, which is the basis of ensuring the stability, efficiency, and high quality of a firm's products and services. It helps the understanding of a BM from an "input-based" view (Hedman & Kalling, 2003; Yip, 2004).

Level 3: Integrated Business Model

At the highest level (3rd-level) of our framework, the aforementioned sub-cluster knowledge themes are integrated into a complete knowledge cluster as the ontology of a BM. The integrated BM is a higher-order knowledge; it refers to the knowledge about how to use, coordinate, and configurate diverse factors (resources, institutions, technologies, customers, partners, and markets) to achieve value capture, creation, and delivery. It could be viewed as a reflection of a firm's core strategy (Seddon et al., 2004) and an abstraction of its business-related activities.

In order to design a satisfactory BM, designers must have a holistic vision and integration ability. In addition, any change in the external environment or the development of the enterprise itself will put the original BM under the pressure of transformation. Therefore, it is necessary to explore the dynamic evolution of BM from a KBV.

Dynamics: Design, Imitation, and Diffusion of BM

Previous studies take BM dynamics as a systematic co-evolution of business-related activities (Wirtz et al., 2016), a series of interactions between and within core components (Afuah & Tucci, 2001; Casadesus-Masanell & Ricart, 2010; Demil & Lecocq, 2010), or a type-changing process (Cavalcante et al., 2011), etc. These studies generally lack the underpinning logic deeply rooted in the knowledge nature of a BM and the integrated framework based on it.

From the KBV, we argue that the dynamics of BMs could be regarded as evolutionary processes of a new knowledge cluster's creation, renewal, and diffusion beyond a firm's boundaries. To be considered as a new analysis unit, the processes of the design and reconfiguration of a new BM and an established BM's diffusion and imitation are discussed.

The Design of New Business Models

As a structured knowledge cluster, a BM is "designed" through a dynamic organizational knowledge creation process. As Nonaka (1994) remarked, it could be understood as "a process that 'organizationally' amplifies the knowledge created by individuals, and crystallizes it as a part of the knowledge network of organization" (1994: 17). We further theorized this process as a sequential cycle of interaction, transformation, and merging of explicit and implicit knowledge components. Drawing on the framework proposed above, we discuss new business designs in three levels.

At the first level, knowledge components, such as value propositions, practical skills, and managerial experience, emerge from the interaction between individuals. Unlike other corporate entity resources and factors, BM-related knowledge components arise from an "informal community" or a "Ba" of social interaction within a certain organizational context (Nonaka & Takeuchi, 1995; Nonaka & Konno, 1998; Nonaka et al., 2000). Implicit knowledge is first generated from individual practice and then acquired by others through "shared experience" (observation, imitation, practice) but not through codified information (Nonaka, 1994). In this way, an individual's implicit knowledge becomes "socialized," which includes both "mental models" (Johnson-Laird, 1983) such as values, beliefs, and schemata, and technical "know-how," like crafts and skills. Some of these knowledge components remain implicit, while others are converted into explicit components through the process of "externalization" (Nonaka, 1994; Nonaka & Takeuchi, 1995; Nonaka & Toyama, 2003; Nonaka & Peltokorpi, 2006). Through this process, each knowledge component's nature (explicit or implicit) is relatively fixed, and designers can use these "bricks" to compose knowledge sub-clusters for higher-order themes.

At the sub-cluster level, the explicit components (e.g., value proposition, product ingredient) interact with the implicit components (e.g., practical skills, managerial experience) to form higher-order business themes such as core competencies, key capabilities, value creation processes, etc. It should be noted that even at this stage, the higher-order knowledge regarding the composition and architecture of business themes can still be generated from "informal communities" (and some "informal communities" naturally span firm boundaries). For instance, a "potential" BM designer may summarize collaboration or service practices into a new business model during long-term interactions with suppliers and customers.

At the cluster level, a unique and novel architecture and accompanying implementation guidelines (Morris et al., 2005) are established. The architectural part is explicit. Although the architecture of some BMs is very complicated, as an open and codified knowledge, it is relatively easy to replicate. In contrast, implementation guidelines contain many implicit components (e.g., strategic insights, managerial experience), which are highly situational. The replication of this element of a BM would be relatively difficult.

In summary, the design of a BM is a dynamic process of knowledge creation. It is important to note that at each analysis level, the "fixity" of a component or architecture is relative, which means any single change to them (e.g., codification of a former implicit component, optimization, or outsourcing of a process) might potentially lead to a disruption of a focal BM "archetype"(Morris et al., 2005; Zott et al., 2011).

The Imitation and Diffusion of Existing Business Models

Once a business model is created and proven to create value in a focal niche, the next important issue will be "***whether, when***, and ***how***" it is imitated. A successful BM will create value for not only focal firms, but also their partners, customers, and other stakeholders (Massa et al., 2017). However, if a BM is easily imitated, the value it created to the above actors will be unsustainable. As Teece (2010) argued, a BM could bring competitive advantage unless it is not easily imitated. Thus, the "imitation" of BM could be a valuable issue to be investigated and the introduction of KM may bring new implications (Chen et al., 2021).

From the perspective of KM, BM's imitation can be discussed at two levels. First, at the firm level, the new entrants' imitation of a focal BM can be regarded as a process of organizational learning and knowledge absorption, in which the knowledge cluster of a BM (previously belonging to the incumbent) is acquired by the new entrants. Second, at the industry (or niche) level, the imitation process of a BM can be seen as the diffusion of a focal knowledge cluster, which includes both explicit and implicit components. Due to the different nature and diffusion modes of diversified types of knowledge components, the "***imitability***" and "***imitation process***" of BMs with different "***architecture***" may also be different. Therefore, although any BM can be imitated eventually (Teece, 2010; Casadesus-Masanell & Zhu, 2013), the difficulty and process of imitation are still very worthy of discussion.

As Chen et al. (2021) argue, the degree of a BM's "imitability" depends on the proportion of its implicit knowledge component, the more implicit knowledge components a BM contains, the more obstacles it will face during imitation. Specifically, the explicit BM components such as a firm's activity patterns (Brousseau & Penard, 2007), customer value propositions (Afuah & Tucci, 2001; Weill & Vitale, 2001; Chesbrough & Rosenbloom, 2002), and the revenue model (Cantrell & Linder , 2000; Petrovic et al., 2001) often exist in the form of "public information," so it is easily observed, analyzed, and learned by new entrants or other competitors. For implicit components such as mental maps and schemas (Leonard & Sensiper, 1998), emerging meanings (Strombach, 1986), and sense-making processes (Malhotra, 2000), it is not so easy to "learn" by the imitators. As mentioned above, the "transfer" of implicit knowledge requires actual interaction between individuals in a specific "community," because these implicit components are often contained in individuals, teams, or even the whole department. To replicate an entire BM, imitators would need not only to observe, analyze, and learn the "***public parts***" but also engage in long-term communication/ interaction with or simply hire those (employees, managers, or teams) who are carrying core resources (knowledge, skills, or experience). Hence, the imitation of a focal BM could be regarded as a "double channel" process as shown in Figure 20.2.

In the first channel, the explicit component of a BM can be transferred as "public information." According to our analysis above, the transfer of this part of knowledge components is relatively easy. The "owner" of a BM cannot set up barriers based on its knowledge

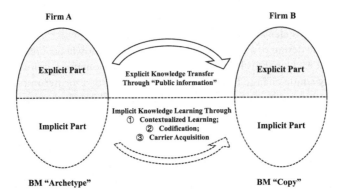

Figure 20.2   The Imitation Process of a Business Model

attributes, and it is also challenging to set legal protections similar to the "intellectual property protection (IPP)" (Teece, 2010).

In the second channel, we link the processes of implicit components of diffusion to the "SECI Model," and identify three main paths.

Path One: Contextualized Learning. Since the diffusion of implicit knowledge needs to rely on the communication "Ba" (Nonaka & Takeuchi, 1995; Nonaka & Konno, 1998), the diffusion of the implicit part of a BM often depends on the long-term cooperation of partners and/or colleagues. Thus, path one can be named as "*contextualized learning*." Furthermore, the "contextualized learning" path of BM can be regarded as a special type of the "*socialization*" process of the SECI model (Nonaka, 1994; Nonaka & Takeuchi, 1995; Nonaka & Konno, 1998; Nonaka et al., 2000; Nonaka & Toyama, 2003). On the one hand, for the incumbent firm (BM owner), this part of knowledge has completed the "socialization" and formed internal shared knowledge. On the other hand, the new entrants (firm) may learn this part of implicit knowledge by participating in the above interaction. Therefore, we often see the replication of a BM as a result of the outflow of employees from the "archetype" firm or based on the division of an original company. In the broader field, BMs rely on the diffusion of such paths to expand the shared scope of the previously socialized implicit components (in a small scope) and form a wider range of "socialization."

Path Two: Codification. The reason some implicit knowledge remains "un-coded" may not be because it is "uncodified," but because it is artificially chosen to keep "*tacit*" for the considerations of business interests. In some cases, this knowledge can be encoded for the strategic development of the enterprise or other purposes. For example, in some Chinese restaurants, the cooking skills of chefs are an essential part of a firm's core competencies. In order to maintain this advantage in the long term, some restaurants encourage a form of "mentoring" to transfer this implicit knowledge. This choice not only helps maintain the competitive advantage, but also limits the expansion of enterprise scale. In order to obtain scale advantage, some enterprises code it into a "standardized process" to create new BMs, thus forming a Chinese restaurant chain.

From the perspective of KM and the **SECI** model, Path Two could be viewed as a dynamic process of "*externalization* and *combination*." In this process, implicit knowledge is conversed to explicit through the mechanisms of "*articulation* and *translation*" and then aggregated into a knowledge cluster by means of "*integrating, transferring, diffusion* and *editing*" (Nonaka & Toyama, 2015).

Path Three: Carrier Acquisition. From the KM perspective, the "*carrier*" of implicit knowledge is either the individual or the organization. So one of the most effective ways for imitators to gain access to the implicit part of another BM could be named "*carrier acquisition*." According to the main level (see the framework proposed in 'Architecture: A Multi-level Framework of BM') which the implicit knowledge exist for different BMs, new entrants may need to "buy" the incumbent firm's employees, teams, or even a whole department to "learn" the implicit part of a focal BM.

The "*carrier acquisition*" path is actually a "quasi-learning" process of the implicit knowledge components of a BM. In this path, new entrants may "directly acquire" the individuals, teams, and even a whole department who share the focal implicit knowledge from the incumbent enterprises. From the individual level, the focal implicit knowledge components are not "*really learned*" by the new firm synchronously when the employees move, but flow "*with*" the acquired individuals or teams. They (the implicit knowledge components) are still kept in the original "*carrier*." That is the reason why it is called "*Quasi*" learning. Of course, new entrants can try to "*absorb*" these implicit knowledge components by incorporating the merged team into their organization, thus truly learning these components through "*contextual learning*" or "*codification*."

Discussions and Conclusions

The findings of this chapter may help broaden the research boundary of KM by conceptualizing the definition, architecture, and dynamics of a BM from a KBV. This chapter took off by systematically reviewing the dominant conceptualization literature on BM and pointing out the limitation of existing research on BM's ontology. Then, the chapter reconceptualized BM from KBV and proposed a hierarchical framework to depict its architecture and dynamics (design, imitation, and diffusion).

The BM was conventionally defined from an explicit and activity-based perspective, which ignored its implicit part and led to the misunderstanding of its ontology in academia. There is no doubt that the manifestation of a BM is a series of firm activities. However, the ontology of a BM should be the designer's understanding of how a firm conducts business. Thus, it could be seen as an abstraction of a pile of "know-how" and "know-why." In this chapter, BM is defined as a structured knowledge cluster of how a firm conducts business; it depicts how a firm combines business-related components to form business themes and how it coordinates these themes to create and deliver value.

Based on KBV, the architecture of a BM is proposed as a three-level hierarchical framework. Level 1 includes the basic business-related components such as internal/external resources, core assets, input factors, value propositions, market opportunities, institutional conditions, partners, competitors, customers, products, and services, etc. Level 2 represents some business themes, including core strategy, core competencies, value-related meanings, sense-making processes, and representative sub-models. From KBV, these business themes can be viewed as sub-cluster knowledge. At Level 3, the sub-cluster knowledge (business themes) is integrated into a complete knowledge cluster as a BM.

Using the proposed framework, the dynamics (design, imitation, and diffusion) of BM are explored. As a structured knowledge cluster, a BM is "designed" through a dynamic organizational knowledge creation process. In this process, the explicit and implicit parts of knowledge interact with each other at the three levels to realize the evolution of the whole knowledge cluster (BM). Moreover, the imitation of BM is regarded as a "double channel" process, in which a focal BM can be imitated through three paths: ***contextualized learning, codification***, and ***carrier acquisition***.

Theoretical Contributions

This chapter broadens the research boundary of KM by redefining the BM concept and exploring its architecture and dynamics. The introduction of the KBV brings new insights into the BM research and helps us focus on the importance of the implicit part of the BM. The theoretical contributions are as follows:

All in all, it reveals the underpinning nature of a BM. The definition based on the "knowledge ontology" facilitates the convergence of existing diversified concepts to a simple core scope. It has the potential to help scholars develop a deeper consensus on the definition of BMs.

Besides, with the proposed framework, a three-level BM architecture is established, which implies a third analysis dimension — "hierarchy" — while the conventional structure of a BM contains mainly two dimensions: the components and their linkages. Different levels of knowledge in BMs can be located, and the nature of components and higher-order knowledge can be analyzed using this framework.

Finally, the "cross-border" dynamics of a BM can be preliminarily analyzed. Though the "boundary-spanning" nature of the BM has been acknowledged (Amit & Zott, 2001; Zott & Amit, 2010), current researches are still "firm-centric" (Zott et al., 2011). From a KBV, the "informal community" in which a new BM is cultivated, and the diffusion of a focal BM are naturally "boundary-spanning." Hence, research on BM dynamics (design and diffusion) can be conducted with a "business model-centric" paradigm, and it is expected to "truly" realize the research paradigm shifts (Malhotra, 2000) with the BM as the new analysis unit.

Limitations and Future Research

In this chapter, we theorized a BM from a KBV and proposed a three-level hierarchical framework to explore the architecture and dynamics of the BM. Although the pioneering research of Chen et al. (2021) has proved that the structure (the ratio of explicit knowledge to tacit knowledge) of a business model can affect the sustainability of enterprises' competitive advantage, the more detailed BM framework and mechanisms proposed in this chapter and the propositions derived from the analytical framework are not supported by empirical evidence. This will limit the reliability of the conclusions in this study. In the future, both quantitative and qualitative method may need to be used to support the new findings. Among them, the design of BM can be explored by case study, while the imitation and diffusion of the BM can be analyzed through quantitative data.

References

Afuah, A. (2004). *Business models: A strategic management approach.* Boston, MA: McGraw-Hill/Irwin.

Afuah, A., & Tucci, C. L. (2001). *Internet business models and strategies: Text and cases.* New York: McGraw-Hill Irwin.

Amit, R., & Zott, C. (2001). Value creation in e-business. *Strategic Management Journal, 22*(6–7), 493–520.

Applegate, L. M., & Collura, M. (2000). *Emerging E business models: Lessons from the field.* Brighton, MA: Harvard Business School Press.

Baldwin, C. Y., & Clark, K. B. (2000). *Design rules: The power of modularity* (Vol. 1): Cambridge, MA: MIT Press.

Bellman, R., Clark, C. E., Malcolm, D. G., Craft, C. J., & Ricciardi, F. M. (1957). On the construction of a multi-stage, multi-person business game. *Operations Research, 5*(4), 469–503.

Björkdahl, J. (2009). Technology cross-fertilization and the business model: The case of integrating ICTs in mechanical engineering products. *Research Policy, 38*(9), 1468–1477.

Brockmann, E. N., & Anthony, W. P. (1998). The influence of tacit knowledge and collective mind on strategic planning. *Journal of Managerial Issues, 10*(2), 204–222.

Brousseau, E., & Penard, T. (2007). The economics of digital business models: A framework for analyzing the economics of platforms. *Review of Network Economics, 6*(2), 81–110.

Brown, J. S., & Duguid, P. (1998). Organizing knowledge. *California Management Review, 40*(3), 90–111.

Cantrell, L. J., & Linder, J. (2000). Changing business models: Surveying the landscape. *Accenture Institute for Strategic Change, 15*(1), 142–149.

Casadesus-Masanell, R., & Ricart, J. E. (2010). From strategy to business models and onto tactics. *Long Range Planning, 43*(2–3), 195–215.

Casadesus-Masanell, R., & Zhu, F. (2013). Business model innovation and competitive imitation: The case of sponsor-based business models. *Strategic Management Journal, 34*(4), 464–482.

Cavalcante, S., Kesting, P., & Ulhøi, J. (2011). Business model dynamics and innovation:(re) establishing the missing linkages. *Management Decision, 49*(8), 1327–1342.

Chen, J., Wang, L., & Qu, G. (2021). Explicating the business model from a knowledge-based view: Nature, structure, imitability and competitive advantage erosion. *Journal of Knowledge Management, 25*(1), 23–47. doi:10.1108/JKM-02-2020–0159

Chesbrough, H., & Rosenbloom, R. S. (2002). The role of the business model in capturing value from innovation: Evidence from Xerox Corporation's technology spin-off companies. *Industrial and Corporate Change, 11*(3), 529–555.

Collins, H. M. (2001). What is tacit knowledge? In T. R. Schatzki, K. Knorr Cetina, & E. von Savigny (Eds.), *The practice turn in contemporary theory* (pp. 115–128). London: Routledge.

Collis, D. J. (1994). Research note: How valuable are organizational capabilities? *Strategic Management Journal, 15*(S1), 143–152.

Currie, W. (2004). *Value creation from e-business models*. Amsterdam: Elsevier.

DaSilva, C. M., & Trkman, P. (2014). Business model: What it is and what it is not. *Long Range Planning, 47*(6), 379–389.

Demil, B., & Lecocq, X. (2010). Business model evolution: In search of dynamic consistency. *Long Range Planning, 43*(2–3), 227–246.

DiMaggio, P. J., & Powell, W. W. (1983). The iron cage revisited: Institutional isomorphism and collective rationality in organizational fields. *American Sociological Review, 48*(2), 147–160.

Druker, P. F. (1993). *Post-capitalist society*. New York: HarperCollins.

Fleming, L. (2001). Recombinant uncertainty in technological search. *Management Science, 47*(1), 117–132.

Grant, R. M. (1996). Toward a knowledge-based theory of the firm. *Strategic Management Journal, 17*(S2), 109–122.

Hall, R., & Andriani, P. (2003). Managing knowledge associated with innovation. *Journal of Business Research, 56*(2), 145–152.

Hamel, G. (2000). *Leading the revolution*. Boston: Harvard Business School Press.

Hau, L. N., & Evangelista, F. (2007). Acquiring tacit and explicit marketing knowledge from foreign partners in IJVs. *Journal of Business Research, 60*(11), 1152–1165.

Hedman, J., & Kalling, T. (2003). The business model concept: Theoretical underpinnings and empirical illustrations. *European Journal of Information Systems, 12*(1), 49–59. doi:10.1057/palgrave.ejis.3000446

Johnson, M. W., Christensen, C. M., & Kagermann, H. (2008). Reinventing Your business model. *Harvard Business Review, 86*(12), 50–59.

Johnson, M. W., & Lafley, A. G. (2010). *Seizing the white space: Business model innovation for growth and renewal*. Brighton, MA: Harvard Business Press.

Johnson-Laird, P. N. (1983). *Mental models: Towards a cognitive science of language, inference, and consciousness*. Cambridge, MA: Harvard University Press.

Kallio, J., Tinnilä, M., & Tseng, A. (2006). An international comparison of operator-driven business models. *Business Process Management Journal, 12*(3), 281–298.

Kauffman, S. A. (1993). *The origins of order: Self-organization and selection in evolution.* OUP USA.

Konczal, E. F. (1975). Models are for managers, not mathematicians. *Journal of Systems Management, 26*(165), 12–15.

Kreiner, K. (2002). Tacit knowledge management: The role of artifacts. *Journal of Knowledge Management. 6*(2), 112–123.

Lam, A. (2000). Tacit knowledge, organizational learning and societal institutions: An integrated framework. *Organization Studies, 21*(3), 487–513.

Leonard, D., & Sensiper, S. (1998). The role of tacit knowledge in group innovation. *California Management Review, 40*(3), 112–132.

Magretta, J. (2002). Why business models matter. *Harvard Business Review, 80*(5), 86–92.

Malhotra, Y. (2000). Knowledge management and new organization forms: A framework for business model innovation. *Information Resources Management Journal 13*(1), 5–14.

Malhotra, Y. (2005). Integrating knowledge management technologies in organizational business processes: Getting real time enterprises to deliver real business performance. *Journal of Knowledge Management, 9*(1), 7–28. doi:10.1108/13673270510582938

Massa, L., Tucci, C. L., & Afuah, A. (2017). A critical assessment of business model research. *Academy of Management Annals, 11*(1), 73–104.

Meyer, J. W., & Rowan, B. (1977). Institutionalized organizations: Formal structure as myth and ceremony. *American Journal of Sociology, 83*(2), 340–363.

Morris, M., Schindehutte, M., & Allen, J. (2005). The entrepreneur's business model: Toward a unified perspective. *Journal of Business Research, 58*(6), 726–735.

Neisser, U. (1976). *Cognition and reality: Principles and implications of cognitive psychology.* New York, NY: W H Freeman.

Nonaka, I. (1994). A dynamic theory of organizational knowledge creation. *Organization Science, 5*(1), 14–37.

Nonaka, I., Hirose, A., & Takeda, Y. (2016). 'Meso'-foundations of dynamic capabilities: Team-level synthesis and distributed leadership as the source of dynamic creativity. *Global Strategy Journal, 6*(3), 168–182.

Nonaka, I., & Konno, N. (1998). The concept of "Ba": Building a foundation for knowledge creation. *California Management Review, 40*(3), 40–54.

Nonaka, I., & Peltokorpi, V. (2006). Objectivity and subjectivity in knowledge management: A review of 20 top articles. *Knowledge and Process Management, 13*(2), 73–82. doi:10.1002/kpm.251

Nonaka, I., & Takeuchi, H. (1995). *The knowledge-creating company: How Japanese companies create the dynamics of innovation.* Oxford: Oxford University Press.

Nonaka, I., & Toyama, R. (2003). The knowledge-creating theory revisited: Knowledge creation as a synthesizing process. *Knowledge Management Research & Practice, 1*(1), 2–10. doi:10.1057/palgrave. kmrp.8500001

Nonaka, I., & Toyama, R. (2015). The knowledge-creating theory revisited: Knowledge creation as a synthesizing process. In *The essentials of knowledge management* (pp. 95–110): Heidelberg: Springer.

Nonaka, I., Toyama, R., & Konno, N. (2000). SECI, Ba and leadership: A unified model of dynamic knowledge creation. *Long Range Planning, 33*(1), 5–34.

Osterwalder, A. (2004). *The business model ontology a proposition in a design science approach.* University of Lausanne, Switzerland. (Dissertation 173)

Osterwalder, A., & Pigneur, Y. (2010). *Business model generation: A handbook for visionaries, game changers, and challengers.* Hoboken, NJ: John Wiley & Sons.

Osterwalder, A., Pigneur, Y., & Tucci, C. L. (2005). Clarifying business models: Origins, present, and future of the concept. *Communications of the Association for Information Systems, 16*(1), 1–25.

Petrovic, O., Kittl, C., & Teksten, R. D. (2001). Developing business models for ebusiness. *Available at SSRN 1658505.*

Porter, M. E. (1980). *Competitive strategy.* New York: The Free Press.

Porter, M. E. (1985). *Competitive advantage.* New York: Free Press.

Porter, M. E. (1996). What is strategy? *Harvard Business Review, 74*(6), 61–78.

Quinn, J. B. (1992). *Intelligent enterprise: A Knowledge and service based paradigm for industry.* New York: The Free Press.

Schilke, O. (2014). Second-order dynamic capabilities: How do they matter? *Academy of Management Perspectives, 28*(4), 368–380.

Scott, W. R. (2005). Institutional theory: Contributing to a theoretical research program. In K. G. Smith & M. A. Hitt (Eds.), *Great minds in management: The process of theory development* (Vol. 37, pp. 460–484). Oxford: Oxford University Press.

Seddon, P. B., Lewis, G. P., Freeman, P., & Shanks, G. (2004). The case for viewing business models as abstractions of strategy. *Communications of the Association for Information Systems, 13*(1), 25.

Stewart, D. W., & Zhao, Q. (2000). Internet marketing, business models, and public policy. *Journal of Public Policy & Marketing, 19*(2), 287–296.

Strombach, W. (1986). "Information" in epistemological and ontological perspective. In *Philosophy and technology II* (pp. 75–81). Springer.

Teece, D. J. (2007). Explicating dynamic capabilities: The nature and microfoundations of (sustainable) enterprise performance. *Strategic Management Journal, 28*(13), 1319–1350.

Teece, D. J. (2010). Business models, business strategy and innovation. *Long Range Planning, 43*(2), 172–194.

Weill, P., & Vitale, M. (2001). *Place to space: Migrating to ebusiness models.* Boston: Harvard Business Press.

Wirtz, B. W. (2001). *Electronic business.* Gabler: Wiesbaden.

Wirtz, B. W., Pistoia, A., Ullrich, S., & Göttel, V. (2016). Business models: Origin, development and future research perspectives. *Long Range Planning, 49*(1), 36–54.

Wu, J., Guo, B., & Shi, Y. (2013). Customer knowledge management and IT-enabled business model innovation: A conceptual framework and a case study from China. *European Management Journal, 31*(4), 359–372.

Yayavaram, S., & Ahuja, G. (2008). Decomposability in knowledge structures and its impact on the usefulness of inventions and knowledge-base malleability. *Administrative Science Quarterly, 53*(2), 333–362.

Yip, G. S. (2004). Using strategy to change your business model. *Business Strategy Review, 15*(2), 17–24.

Zott, C., & Amit, R. (2010). Business model design: An activity system perspective. *Long Range Planning, 43*(2–3), 216–226.

Zott, C., Amit, R., & Massa, L. (2011). The business model: Recent developments and future research. *Journal of Management, 37.* doi:10.2139/ssrn.1674384

INDEX

Note: **Bold** page numbers refer to tables; *italic* page numbers refer to figures and page numbers followed by "n" denote endnotes.

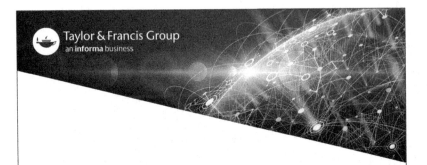